Washington, D.C., Williamsburg,

Busch Gardens,® Richmond, and Other Area Attractions

ECONOGUIDE.COM | 2001

Corey Sandler

CONTEMPORARY BOOKS

To Janice, my fellow traveler

Econoguide is a registered trademark of Word Association, Inc.

Cover photograph copyright © Doug Armand/Stone

Published by Contemporary Books
A division of NTC/Contemporary Publishing Group, Inc.
4255 West Touhy Avenue, Lincolnwood (Chicago), Illinois 60712-1975 U.S.A.
Manufactured in the United States of America
International Standard Book Number: 0-8092-2636-7
International Standard Serial Number: 1099-2111

01 02 03 04 05 06 LB 18 17 16 15 14 13 12 11 10 9 8 7 6 5 4 3 2 1

Contents

Acknowledgments

Dozens of hard-working and creative people helped move my words from the keyboard to the place where you read this book now.

Among the many to thank are Editor Adam Miller of Contemporary Books for working with me as we expand the Econoguide series, and Julia Anderson of Contemporary Books who managed the editorial and production processes.

Our appreciation extends to the attractions and museums and the Washington, D.C., Convention and Visitors Association for their assistance. Thanks to the hotels, restaurants, and attractions that offered discount coupons to our readers.

Here at Word Association, I want to thank Val Elmore, who edited and fact-checked the book with professionalism. As always, thanks to Janice Keefe for running the office and the author so well.

And finally, thanks to you for buying this book. We all hope you find it of value; please let us know how we can improve the book in future editions. (Please enclose a stamped envelope if you'd like a reply; no phone calls, please.)

Corey Sandler
Econoguide Travel Books
P.O. Box 2779
Nantucket, MA 02584

To send electronic mail, use the following address:
info@econoguide.com.
You can also consult our Web page at:
www.econoguide.com.

Introduction to the 2001 Edition

Washington, Williamsburg, and northern Virginia are America's theme park, a world of wonder, where the history and the discoveries are real.

It is a theme park where you can walk into the theater in which Abraham Lincoln was shot and then cross the street to stand in the room where he died.

You can listen to the echoes of history within the **White House**, stroll the halls of **Congress**, and salute the flag that flew by the dawn's early light.

In the nation's attic—the **Smithsonian**—you can get up close and personal with dinosaurs, massive steam engines from the nineteenth century, modern spacecraft, and pieces of the moon brought back to Washington. Dozens of museums celebrate the arts and sciences.

Across the river is George Washington's **Mount Vernon** and Thomas Jefferson's **Monticello**. A few hours south—passing through some of the sites of important Civil War battles—is **Richmond**, where you can visit the spot where Patrick Henry demanded liberty or death.

Farther on is **Colonial Williamsburg**. Here you can visit the re-created palace of the King's colonial governor, stand in the place where the Revolution was born, and visit the church where Washington, Jefferson, and James Monroe worshiped.

Nearby are two more important places in American history: **Jamestown** settlement, the English colony that dates back to 1607, fourteen years before the Pilgrims landed in Plymouth; and **Yorktown**, site of the climactic battle of the American Revolution.

And then there are the very real thrills of the make-believe world of **Busch Gardens Williamsburg**.

There are few other places in the United States with such a sense of history. And I know of few other places that offer so much to do.

A Declaration of Independence

The *Econoguide* book series was born out of a recognition that there has to be a way to take a fulfilling and entertaining vacation without throwing away money and time.

This is *not* a guide for the cheapskate interested in sleeping in bus terminals (or motels that look like bus terminals) and eating exclusively at restaurants that use plastic forks. What we mean by "Econoguide" is this: helpful information so you can get the most out of your trip. I'll show you how to save time and money on travel, hotels, restaurants, and entertainment. I'll show you how to pay the best price for shows and theme parks. Even if you choose to go for first-class airfare, luxury hotels, and the most expensive restaurants in town, I'll help you spend your money wisely.

And we include a selection of money-saving coupons from hotels and attractions. Pardon me for saying so, but buying this book is a no-brainer: you'll save many times the cover price by using just a few of the coupons.

And finally, it is important to emphasize that with the *Econoguide* you'll get an independent, insider's guide to all of the major attractions of Washington, Williamsburg, and surrounding areas. The author and publisher of this book have no connection with any of the attractions written about here. Similarly, there is no financial interest in any of the discount coupons published within the book.

Our profit comes from you, the readers of this book, and it is you we hope to serve as best we can.

About the Author

Corey Sandler is a former newsman and editor for the Associated Press, Gannett Newspapers, IDG, and Ziff-Davis. He has written more than 150 books on travel, video games, and computer topics; his titles have been translated into French, Spanish, German, Italian, Bulgarian, Portuguese, Polish, and Chinese.

When he's not traveling, he lives with his wife and two children on Nantucket island, thirty miles off the coast of Massachusetts.

Look for these other Econoguide titles by Corey Sandler. All are published by Contemporary Books:

- *Econoguide 2001 Las Vegas: Also Includes Reno, Lake Tahoe, and Laughlin*
- *Econoguide 2001 Walt Disney World, Universal Orlando: Also Includes SeaWorld and Central Florida*
- *Econoguide 2001 Disneyland Resort, Universal Studios Hollywood, and Other Major Southern California Attractions*
- *Econoguide 2001 London: with Day Trips to Bath, Brighton, Cambridge, Oxford, Windsor, and Other Popular Destinations*
- *Econoguide 2001 Canada: Coast to Coast in Canada's Great Cities, Mountains, Parks, and Attractions*
- *Econoguide 2000–01 Cruises: Cruising the Caribbean, Mexico, Hawaii, New England, and Alaska*
- *Econoguide 2000–01 Pacific Northwest: Seattle, Portland, Victoria, Vancouver, and Other Area Destinations*

Part I
Washington Bound

Chapter 1
How to Buy the Lowest-Cost Airline Tickets and Protect Yourself from the Uncertainties of Modern Travel

Let's get real: do you really prefer one airline over another because it offers a better quality sandwich-in-a-plastic-bag, plumper pillows, or three whole inches of extra legroom?

The way I figure it, one major airline is pretty much like any other. Sure, one company may offer a larger plastic bag of peanuts while the other promises its flight attendants have more accommodating smiles. Me, I'm much more interested in other things:

1. Safety
2. The most convenient schedule
3. The lowest price

Sometimes I'm willing to trade price for convenience, but I'll never risk my neck for a few dollars.

That doesn't mean I don't try my darnedest to get the very best price on airline tickets. I read newspapers for seasonal sales and price wars, clip coupons from the usual and not-so-usual sources, consult the burgeoning world of Internet travel agencies, and happily play one airline against the other.

We'll explore some of these strategies in this chapter.

Alice in Airlineland

There are three golden rules to saving hundreds of dollars on travel: be flexible, be flexible, and be flexible.

• Be flexible about when you choose to travel. Go during off-season or low-season when airfares, hotels, and other attractions offer substantial discounts.

• Be flexible about the day of the week you travel. In many cases, you can save hundreds of dollars by changing your departure date one or two days in either direction. Ask your travel agent or airline reservationist for current fare rules and restrictions.

The lightest air travel days are generally midweek, Saturday afternoons, and Sunday mornings. The busiest days are Sunday evenings, Monday mornings, and Friday afternoons and evenings.

1

In general, you will receive the lowest possible fare if you include a Saturday in your trip, buying what is known as an *excursion fare*. Airlines use this as a way to exclude business travelers from the cheapest fares, assuming that businesspeople will want to be home by Friday night.

• Be flexible on the hour of your departure. There is generally lower demand—and, therefore, lower prices—for flights that leave in the middle of the day or very late at night.

• Be flexible on the route you will take, or your willingness to put up with a change of plane or stopover. Once again, you are putting the law of supply and demand in your favor. A direct flight from California to Washington for a family of four may cost hundreds more than a flight from California that includes a change of planes in Dallas (an American Airlines hub) or Minneapolis (a Northwest hub) before proceeding to Washington.

Don't overlook the possibility of flying out of a different airport, either. For example, metropolitan New Yorkers can find domestic flights from La Guardia, Newark, or White Plains. Suburbanites of Boston might want to consider flights from Worcester or Providence as possibly cheaper alternatives to Logan Airport. In the Los Angeles area, there are planes going in and out of LAX, Orange County, Burbank, and Palm Springs, to name a few airports. Look for airports where there is greater competition: try Birmingham instead of Atlanta, or Louisville instead of Cincinnati, for example.

You may even be able to save money, time, or both by flying into a Washington-area airport other than National; consider Dulles, Baltimore, or Richmond—they're each a bit of a drive from D.C., but if they save you a few hundred dollars, it may be worthwhile to use them.

• Plan way ahead of time and purchase the most deeply discounted advance tickets, which usually are noncancelable. Most carriers limit the number of discount tickets on any particular flight; although there may be plenty of seats left on the day you want to travel, they may be offered at higher rates.

In a significant change during the past few years, most airlines have modified "nonrefundable" fares to become "noncancelable." What this means is that if your plans change or you are forced to cancel your trip, your tickets retain their value and can be applied against another trip, usually for a fee of about $50 per ticket.

• Conversely, you can take a big chance and wait for the last possible moment, keeping in contact with charter tour operators and accepting a bargain price on a "leftover seat" and hotel reservation. You *may* also find that some airlines will reduce the prices on leftover seats within a few weeks of departure date; don't be afraid to check regularly with the airline, or ask your travel agent to do it for you. In fact, some travel agencies have automated computer programs that keep a constant electronic eagle eye on available seats and fares.

• Take advantage of special discount programs such as senior citizens' clubs, military discounts, or offerings from organizations to which you may belong. If you are in the over-60 category, you may not even have to belong to a group such as AARP; simply ask the airline reservationist if there is a discount available. You may have to prove your age when you pick up your ticket or boarding pass.

- It may even make a difference what day of the week you buy your tickets. In recent years, airlines have tested out higher fares over the relatively quiet weekends. They're looking to see if their competitors will match their higher rates; if the other carriers don't bite, the fares often float back down by Monday morning. Shop during the week.

Other Money-Saving Strategies

Airlines are forever weeping and gnashing their teeth about huge losses due to cutthroat competition. And then they regularly turn around and drop their prices radically through major sales.

I don't waste time worrying about the bottom line of the airlines; it's my own wallet I want to keep full. The savvy traveler keeps an eye out for airline fare wars all the time. Read the ads in daily newspapers and keep an ear open to news broadcasts that cover the outbreak of price drops. If you have a good relationship with a travel agent, you can ask to be notified of any airline fare sales.

The most common times for airfare wars are in the weeks leading up to the quietest seasons for carriers, including the periods from mid-May to mid-June (except the Memorial Day weekend), between Labor Day and Thanksgiving, and winter, with the exception of Christmas, New Year's, and Presidents' Day holiday periods.

Don't be afraid to ask for a refund on previously purchased tickets if fares drop for the period of your travel. The airline may refund the difference, or you may be able to reticket your itinerary at the new fare, paying a $50 penalty for cashing in the old tickets. Be persistent—if the difference in fare is significant, it may be worthwhile making a visit to the airport to meet with a supervisor at the ticket counter.

Study the fine print on discount coupons distributed directly by the airlines, or through third parties such as supermarkets, catalog companies, and direct marketers. A typical coupon offers $50 to $100 off full fare or certain types of discount fares. It has been my experience that these coupons are often less valuable than they seem. Read the fine print carefully, and be sure to ask the reservationist if the price quoted with the coupon is higher than another fare for which you qualify.

If you are traveling to a convention, you may be able to get in on a discount negotiated by the group with a particular airline.

In fact, you may not need any affiliation at all with a convention group to take advantage of special rates, if offered. All the airline will ask is the name or number of the discount plan for the convention; the reservationist is almost certainly not going to ask to see your union card or funny hat.

Consider doing business with discounters, known in the industry as consolidators or, less flatteringly, as "bucket shops." Look for their ads in the classified sections of many Sunday newspaper travel sections. These companies buy the airlines' slow-to-sell tickets in volume and resell them to consumers at rock-bottom prices.

Some travel agencies can also offer you consolidator tickets. Just be sure to weigh the savings on the ticket price against any restrictions attached to the tickets; for example, they may not be changeable, and they usually do not accrue frequent flyer mileage.

Beating the Airlines at Their Own Game

As far as I am concerned, airlines deserve all the headaches travelers can give them because of the illogical and costly pricing schemes they throw at us—things such as a fare of $350 to fly ninety miles between two cities where they hold a monopoly, and $198 bargain fares to travel 3,000 miles across the nation. Or round-trip fares of $300 if you leave on a Thursday and return on a Monday versus $1,200 if you leave on a Monday and return the next Thursday.

A creative traveler can find ways to work around most of these roadblocks. Nothing I'm going to suggest here is against the law; some of the tips, though, are against the rules of some airlines. Here are a couple of strategies:

- *Nested tickets.* This scheme generally works in either of two situations—where regular fares are more than twice as high as excursion fares that include a Saturday night stay over, or in situations where you plan to fly between two locations twice in less than a year.

  Let's say you want to fly from Boston to Washington. Buy two sets of tickets in your name, one from Boston to Washington and back to Boston with the return date for when you want to come back from your second trip. The other ticket would be from Washington to Boston and back to Washington, this time making the first leg of the ticket for the date you want to come back from the first trip, and the second leg of the trip the date you want to depart for the second trip.

  If this sounds complicated, that's because it is. It will be your responsibility to keep your tickets straight when traveling.

  In recent years, several major airlines announced they would crack down on such practices by searching their computer databases for multiple reservations. And travel agencies have been threatened with loss of ticketing privileges for assisting their clients in this way.

  But that doesn't mean you can't buy such tickets. Check with a travel agent for advice. One solution: buy one set of tickets on one airline and the other set on another carrier.

- *Split tickets.* Fare wars sometimes result in supercheap fares through a connecting city. For example, an airline seeking to boost traffic through a hub in Dallas might set up a situation in which it is less expensive to get from Chicago to Las Vegas by buying a round-trip ticket from Chicago to Dallas, and then a separate round-trip ticket from Dallas to Las Vegas.

Be sure to book a schedule that allows enough time between flights; if you miss your connection you could end up losing time and money.

Standing Up for Standing By

One of the little-known secrets of air travel on most airlines and most types of tickets is the fact that travelers who have valid tickets are allowed to stand by for flights other than the ones for which they have reservations on the same day of travel; if there are empty seats on the flight, standby ticket holders are permitted to board.

Here's what I do know: if I cannot get the exact flight I want for a trip, I make the closest acceptable reservations available and then show up early at the airport and head for the check-in counter for the flight I really want to take. Unless you are seeking to travel during an impossibly overbooked holiday period or arrive on a bad weather day when flights have been canceled, your chances of successfully standing by for a flight are usually pretty good.

Call the airline the day before the flight and check on the availability of seats for the flight you want to try for.

About Travel Agencies

Here's my advice about travel agents in a nutshell: get a good one, or go it alone.

Good travel agents remember who they work for: you. There is, though, a built-in conflict of interest here, because the agent is in most cases paid by someone else. Agents receive a commission on airline tickets, hotel reservations, car rentals, and many other services they sell you. The more they sell (or the higher the price), the more they earn.

I recommend you start the planning for any trip by calling the airlines and a few hotels directly and finding the best package you can put together for yourself. *Then* call your travel agency and ask them to do better.

If your agent contributes knowledge or experience, comes up with dollar-saving alternatives to your own package, or offers some other kind of convenience, then go ahead and book through the agency.

If, as I often find, you know a lot more about your destination and are willing to spend a lot more time to save money than will the agent, do it yourself.

There is one special type of travel agency worth considering. A number of large agencies offer rebates on part of their commissions to travelers. Some of these companies cater only to frequent flyers who will bring in a lot of business; other rebate agencies offer only limited services to clients.

I often use an agency that sends me a 5 percent rebate on all reservations booked through them. I have never set foot in their offices, and I conduct all of my business over the phone; tickets arrive by mail or by overnight courier when necessary.

You can find discount travel agencies through many major credit card companies (Citibank and American Express among them) or through associations and clubs. Some warehouse shopping clubs have rebate travel agencies.

And if you establish a relationship with your local travel agency and bring them enough business to make them glad to see you walk through their door, don't be afraid to ask them for a discount equal to a few percentage points.

Another important new tool for travelers is the Internet. Here you'll find computerized travel agencies that offer airline, hotel, car, cruise, and package reservations. You won't receive personalized assistance, but you will be able to make as many price checks and itinerary routings as you'd like without apology. Several of the services feature special deals, including companion fares and rebates you won't find elsewhere.

Some of the best Internet agencies include:

Atevo	www.atevo.com/
Flifo	www.flifo.com
Microsoft Expedia	expedia.msn.com
Travelocity	www.travelocity.com

Overbooking

Overbooking is a polite industry term that refers to the legal business practice of selling more than an airline can deliver. It all stems, alas, from the unfortunate habit of many travelers who neglect to cancel flight reservations that will not be used. Airlines study the patterns on various flights and city pairs and apply a formula that allows them to sell more tickets than there are seats on the plane, in the expectation that a certain percentage will not show up at the airport.

But what happens if all passengers holding a reservation do show up? Obviously, the result will be more passengers than seats, and some will have to be left behind.

The involuntary bump list will begin with the names of passengers who are late to check in. Airlines must ask for volunteers before bumping any passengers who have followed the rules on check-in.

Now, assuming that no one is willing to give up their seat just for the fun of it, the airline will offer some sort of compensation—either a free ticket or cash, or both. It is up to the passenger and the airline to negotiate an acceptable deal.

The U.S. Department of Transportation's consumer protection regulations set some minimum levels of compensation for passengers who are bumped from a flight as a result of overbooking.

It is not considered "bumping" if a flight is canceled because of weather, equipment problems, or the lack of a flight crew. You are also not eligible for compensation if the airline substitutes a smaller aircraft for operational or safety reasons, or if the flight involves an aircraft that has sixty seats or less.

How to Get Bumped

Why in the world would you *want* to be bumped? Well, perhaps you'd like to look at missing your plane as an opportunity to earn a little money for your time, instead of as an annoyance. Is a two-hour delay worth $100 an hour to you? How about $800 for a family of four to wait a few hours on the way home—that could pay for a week's stay at a motel plus a meal at the airport.

If you're not in a tremendous rush to get to your destination—or to get back home—you might want to volunteer to be bumped. I wouldn't recommend doing this on the busiest travel days of the year, or if you are booked on the last flight of the day, unless you are also looking forward to a free night in an airport motel.

My very best haul: on a flight home from London, my family of four received a free night's stay in a luxury hotel, $1,000 each in tickets, and an upgrade on our flight home the next day.

Bad Weather, Bad Planes, Strikes, and Other Headaches

You don't want your pilot to fly into unsafe weather, of course. You also wouldn't want your pilot to take up a plane that has a mechanical problem. No matter how you feel about unions, you probably don't want to cross a picket line to board a plane that's piloted by strikebreakers. And so, you should accept an airline's cancellation of a flight for one of these legitimate reasons.

Here's the bad news, though: if a flight is canceled for an "Act of God" or a labor dispute, the airline is not required to do anything for you except give you your money back. In practice, carriers will usually make a good effort to find another way to get you to your destination more or less on time. This could mean rebooking on another flight on the same airline, or on a different carrier. It could mean a delay of a day or more in the worst situations, such as a major snowstorm.

Here is a summary of your rather limited rights as an air passenger:

- An airline is required to compensate you above the cost of your ticket only if you are bumped from an oversold flight against your will.
- If you volunteer to be bumped, you can negotiate for the best deal with the ticket agent or a supervisor; generally, you can expect to be offered a free round-trip ticket on the airline for your inconvenience.
- If your scheduled flight is unable to deliver you directly to the destination on your ticket, and alternate transportation such as a bus or limousine is provided, the airline is required to pay you twice the amount of your one-way fare if your arrival will be more than two hours later than the original ticket promised.
- If you purchase your ticket with a credit card—strongly recommended in any case—the airline must credit your account within seven days of receiving an application for a refund.

All that said, in many cases you will be able to convince an agent or a supervisor to go beyond the letter of the law. I've found that the very best strategy is to politely but firmly stand your ground. Ask the ticket clerk to put you on another flight, or for a free night in a hotel and a flight in the morning, or for any reasonable accommodation. Don't take no for an answer, but stay polite and don't move. Ask for a supervisor; stay polite and start over again. Sooner or later, they'll do something to get you out of the way.

And then there are labor problems like those that faced American Airlines in 1997 and again in 1999. Your best defense against a strike is to anticipate it before it happens; keep your ears open for labor problems when you make a reservation. Then keep in touch with your travel agent or the airline itself in the days leading up to any strike deadline. It is often easier to make alternate plans or seek a refund in the days immediately before a strike; wait until the last minute and you're going to be joining a very long and upset line.

In the face of a strike, a major airline is likely to attempt to reroute you onto another airline if possible; if you buy your own ticket on another carrier, you are unlikely to be reimbursed. If your flight is canceled, you will certainly be able to claim a full refund of your fare or obtain a voucher in its value without paying any penalties.

Airline Safety

There are no guarantees in life, but in general, flying on an airplane is considerably safer than driving to the airport. All of the major air carriers have very good safety records; some are better than others. I pay attention to news reports about FAA inspections and rulings and make adjustments as necessary. And though I love to squeeze George Washington until he yelps, I avoid start-up and super cut-rate airlines because I have my doubts about how much money they can afford to devote to maintenance.

Among major airlines, the fatal accident rate during the last twenty-five years stands somewhere between .3 and .7 incidents per million flights.

The very low numbers, experts say, make them poor predictors of future incidents. Instead, you should pay more attention to FAA or NTSB rulings on maintenance and training problems.

Not included in these listings are small commuter airlines (except for those that are affiliated with major carriers).

Tour Packages and Charter Flights

Tour packages and flights sold by tour operators or travel agents may look similar, but the consumer may end up with significantly different rights.

It all depends whether the flight is a scheduled or nonscheduled flight. A scheduled flight is one that is listed in the *Official Airline Guide* and available to the general public through a travel agent or from the airline. This doesn't mean that a scheduled flight will necessarily be on a major carrier or that you will be flying on a 747 jumbo jet; it could just as easily be the propeller-driven pride of Hayseed Airlines. In any case, though, a scheduled flight does have to meet stringent federal government certification requirements.

In the event of delays, cancellations, or other problems with a scheduled flight, your recourse is with the airline.

A nonscheduled flight is also known as a charter flight. The term *charter* is sometimes also applied to a complete package that includes a nonscheduled flight, hotel accommodations, ground transportation, and other elements.

Charter flights are generally a creation of a tour operator who will purchase all of the seats on a specific flight to a specific destination or who will rent an airplane and crew from an air carrier.

Charter flights and charter tours are regulated by the federal government, but your rights as a consumer are much more limited than those afforded to scheduled flight customers.

Written Contracts

You wouldn't buy a hamburger without knowing the price and specifications (two all-beef patties on a sesame seed bun, etc.). Why, then, would you spend hundreds or even thousands of dollars on a tour and not understand the contract that underlies the transaction?

When you purchase a charter flight or a tour package, you should review and sign a contract that spells out your rights. This contract is sometimes referred to as the "Operator Participant Contract" or the "Terms and Conditions." Look for this contract in the booklet or brochure that describes the packages; ask for it if one is not offered. The proper procedure for a travel agent or tour operator requires they wait until the customer has read and signed the contract before any money is accepted.

Remember that the contract is designed mostly to benefit the tour operator, and each contract may be different from others you may have agreed to in the past. The basic rule here is: **if you don't understand it, don't sign it.**

Drive?, He Said

Everyone's concept of the perfect vacation is different, but for me, I draw a distinction between *getting there* and *being there*. I want the getting there part

The Roman Rapids raft ride at Busch Gardens Williamsburg
Photo by Lawrence Jackson. ©2000 Busch Entertainment Corp.

to be as quick and simple as possible, and the being there part to be as long as I can manage and afford. Therefore, I fly to most any destination that is more than a few hundred miles from my home. The cost of driving, hotels, meals en route, and general physical and mental wear and tear rarely equals a deeply discounted excursion fare.

If you do drive, though, you can save a few dollars by using the services of the AAA or another major automobile club. Spend a bit of time and money before you head out to make certain your vehicle is in traveling shape: a tune-up and fully inflated, fully inspected tires will save gas, money, and headaches.

If you plan to travel by bus or train, be aware that the national carriers generally have the same sort of peak and off-peak pricing as the airlines. The cheapest time to buy tickets is when the fewest people want them.

Renting a Car for a Washington Trip

Washington, D.C., like most other major cities, is not a particularly friendly place for cars. You'll probably find it a lot easier to use taxis, buses, or the Metro subway system. I'd recommend you consider renting a car for excursions out of the city to Williamsburg, Mount Vernon, Baltimore, and other places.

The Washington-area airports have a good selection of national car rental agencies, but rates are not as competitive as you might find in tourist destinations such as Orlando or Las Vegas. Expect to pay $40 to $50 per day for a small car. Be sure to seek discounts from auto clubs, airline frequent flyer clubs, and other sources.

Car rental companies will try—with varying levels of pressure—to convince you to purchase special insurance coverage. They'll tell you it's "only" $7 or $9 per day. What a deal! That works out to about $2,500 or $3,330 per year for a set of rental wheels. The coverage is intended primarily to protect the rental company, not you.

Check with your insurance agent before you travel to determine how well your personal automobile policy will cover a rental car and its contents. I strongly recommend you use a credit card that offers rental car insurance; such insurance usually covers the deductible below your personal policy. The extra auto insurance by itself is usually worth an upgrade to a "gold card" or other extra-service credit card.

The only sticky area comes for those visitors who have a driver's license but no car, and therefore no insurance. Again, consult your credit card company and your insurance agent to see what kind of coverage you have, or need.

Be sure you understand the rental car company's policies on minimum age for drivers (generally 25), and whether a second driver can take the wheel.

Your travel agent may be of assistance in finding the best rates; you can make a few phone calls by yourself, too. Rental rates generally follow the same low-season–high-season structure. I have obtained rates as low as $145 a week for a tiny subcompact in low-season.

Although it is theoretically possible to rent a car without a credit card, you will find it to be a rather inconvenient process. If they cannot hold your credit card account hostage, most agencies will require a large cash deposit—perhaps as much as several thousand dollars—before they will give you the keys.

Be aware that the least expensive car rental agencies usually do not have their stations at the airport itself. You will have to wait for a shuttle bus to take you from the terminal to their lot, and you must return the car to the outlying area at the end of your trip. This may add about twenty to thirty minutes to your arrival and departure schedule.

Pay attention, too, when the rental agent explains the gas tank policy. The most common plan requires you to return the car with a full tank; if the agency must refill the tank, you will be billed a service charge plus what is usually a very high per-gallon rate.

Other optional plans include one in which the rental agency sells you a full tank when you first drive away and takes no note of how much gas remains when you return the car. Unless you somehow manage to return the car with the engine running on fumes, you are in effect making a gift to the agency with every gallon you bring back.

I prefer the first option, making a point to refill the tank on the way to the airport on getaway day.

Accident and Sickness Insurance

The idea of falling ill or suffering an injury while hundreds or thousands of miles away from home and your family doctor can be a terrifying thought.

But before you sign on the bottom line for an accident and sickness insurance policy, be sure to consult with your own insurance agent or your company's personnel office to see how far your personal medical insurance policy will reach. Does the policy cover vacation trips and exclude business travel? Are all international locations excluded? Can you purchase a "rider," or extension, to your personal policy to cover travel?

The only reason to purchase an Accident and Sickness policy is to fill in any gaps in the coverage you already have. If you don't have health insurance of any kind, a travel policy is certainly valuable, but you might want to consider whether you should spend the money on a year-round policy instead of taking a vacation in the first place.

Also be aware that nearly every kind of health insurance has an exclusionary period for preexisting conditions. If you are sick before you set out on a trip, you may find that the policy will not pay for treating the problem.

WASHINGTON TO WILLIAMSBURG CORRIDOR

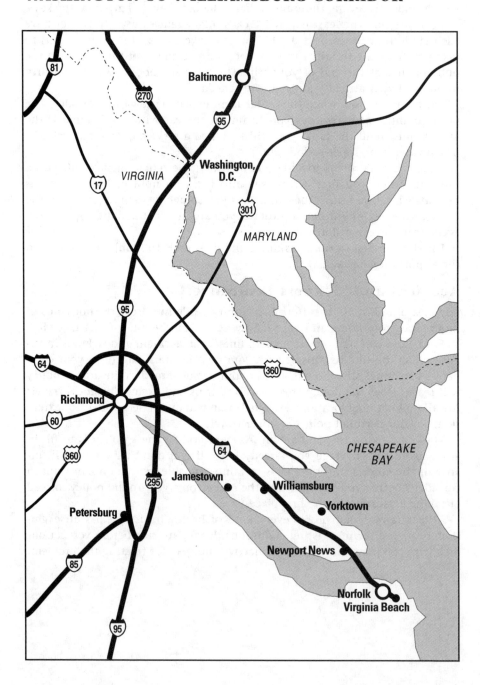

Chapter 2
Washington, D.C.: A Capital City

The Story of Washington, D.C.

In 1790, the nation's first president lived at his estate in Mount Vernon and traveled when necessary to Pennsylvania and New York, where many of the various official elements of government were first located.

The site for the nation's capital had already been much debated by Congress. Northerners led by Alexander Hamilton of New York wanted a capital in the North, while Southerners led by Thomas Jefferson of Virginia wanted it in the South.

In true federal government fashion, it all came down to politics and money. John Adams, presiding officer of the Senate in the First Congress, cast the deciding vote in 1789 to establish the nation's capital in Germantown, Pennsylvania. A year later, Congress moved the capital to Philadelphia where it remained for ten years.

Southern forces, lead by the powerful Virginia delegation, wanted to put the permanent federal capital on the eastern bank of the Potomac but were blocked by Northerners. While all this went on, the Congress was debating Alexander Hamilton's Assumption Bill, which would have the nation take over the Revolutionary War debts of the thirteen original states.

Finally, a compromise was reached: the Southern contingents voted for the Assumption Bill and the Northerners accepted the Potomac location for the capital.

Washington chose a site in 1790 that was not coincidentally only eighteen miles up the Potomac River from Mount Vernon, between the thriving ports of Alexandria, Virginia, and Georgetown, Maryland.

The Grand Design

Washington hired Andrew Ellicott, a respected Maryland surveyor, and Benjamin Banneker, a self-taught African American, to survey the land at the confluence of the East and West Potomac rivers. The parameters of the new city were set as a 100-square-mile site, ten miles on each side. Maryland donated

MUST-SEES

69.75 square miles and Virginia 30.25 miles. (In 1846, Virginia's donation was returned; it is now Arlington County.)

Major Pierre Charles L'Enfant, a former member of Washington's Continental Army Staff, first saw the boggy lowlands south of Georgetown in March of 1791.

The Frenchman fashioned a design based on the grand schemes of Paris and Versailles. His plan called for 160-foot-wide avenues radiating from scenic squares and circles, each adorned with monumental sculptures and fountains. When the design was completed, L'Enfant called it, "a pedestal waiting for a monument." The monument was to be the U.S. Capitol building.

Despite Washington's endorsement of the plan and its architect, L'Enfant ran into trouble because of the way he went about realizing his project. When a wealthy landowner refused L'Enfant's demand that he remove his new manor house because it obstructed a vista, the architect went ahead and demolished it anyway; President Washington was forced to step in and dismiss the architect in 1792.

L'Enfant refused a $2,500 payment for his work and sued Congress for $95,500; he eventually died a pauper in 1825. In 1909, as a belated token of appreciation, L'Enfant's remains were moved from an obscure grave in the city to Arlington National Cemetery. And a major commercial plaza today bears his name.

After L'Enfant left, taking his plans with him, Benjamin Banneker was called upon to reconstruct the design from memory. In 1792, amateur architect James Hoban's design for the President's Mansion won a competition, and work on what was to become the White House was begun. In 1793, President George Washington laid the cornerstone for the U.S. Capitol.

It was in 1800 that President John

Adams and the Congress finally moved to Washington, occupying unfinished buildings.

The concept for the federal city was that it would be a separate entity, not part of any individual state. The District of Columbia was originally governed by the Congress. (In recent times, the District was given limited "home rule" under supervision of a congressional committee. Residents can cast votes for President and Vice President, but have only a nonvoting delegate in the House of Representatives.)

Washington did not sleep there. George Washington was the only president not to live in the executive mansion that became known as the White House; he died in 1799 and was buried at his home in Mount Vernon.

In 1803, President Thomas Jefferson appointed Benjamin Latrobe as surveyor of public buildings. Latrobe's "Classic Revival" architecture was first used for the design of the Capitol.

The War of 1812 Intervenes

The expansion of the capital city was interrupted by the War of 1812. The next year, British Rear Admiral Sir George Cockburn boasted that he would "make his bow" in President James Madison's drawing room. In August 1814, the British did succeed in invading Washington and burning the White House, the Capitol, and the Library of Congress. Dolley Madison rescued Gilbert Stuart's famous painting of George Washington—the only object in today's East Room dating to 1800—taking it with her when she fled from the advancing British army to the farmlands of northern Virginia.

The District was spared total destruction only because a thunderstorm quelled the flames.

In 1815, Washington began the slow process of rebuilding. Congress met in a hastily built brick structure, Thomas Jefferson sold his personal collection to replace the destroyed contents of the Library of Congress, and Charles Bulfinch succeeded Latrobe as architect of the Capitol.

The Madisons lived temporarily at the Octagon House, a local mansion, while the President's Mansion was repaired; it was there that the Treaty of Ghent, which ended the war with Great Britain, was signed. The rebuilt mansion's charred foundation and wooden planks were painted white, and thereafter it was known as the "White House."

Between the end of the War of 1812 and the outbreak of the Civil War, Washington grew slowly. In 1842, visiting English author Charles Dickens described the city as "spacious avenues that begin in nothing and lead nowhere; streets miles long that only want houses, roads and inhabitants; public buildings that need but a public to be complete. . . ."

The capital city was also swampy and bug-infested, thanks in part to the canal that ran from the East Potomac through the heart of the city, past the Capitol and the White House to the Potomac. The canal was continually flooding, and streets were often muddy.

Washington During the Civil War

The Civil War spurred the rapid expansion of Washington. President Lincoln's call to arms in 1861 brought thousands of Union soldiers to Washington, boosting its population from 61,000 to 109,000; many never left.

Lincoln was determined to continue construction in the capital city, despite fear of attack by Southern forces only a few dozen miles outside the city. Several of the war's bloodiest and most decisive battles were waged within ninety miles of the city, including Gettysburg, Antietam, Winchester, and Bull Run.

While construction on the Washington Monument was suspended during the war, the present-day tiered dome of the Capitol was completed in 1863. The 7½-ton bronze "Statue of Freedom" was bolted into place later that year. Said Lincoln, "If the people see the Capitol going on, it's a sign we intend the Union shall go on."

Five days after General Lee surrendered at Appomattox, President Lincoln was shot by John Wilkes Booth while attending a play at Ford's Theatre, a few blocks from the White House. Lincoln died the next day at the Petersen House, across the street from Ford's.

The end of the war brought an era of tremendous growth. Former slaves from the South and war-weary soldiers settled in the area. The fetid canal running through the city was filled and named Constitution Avenue; an original lockhouse can still be seen at the intersection with Seventeenth Street.

Postwar Expansion

In 1867, under President Ulysses S. Grant's administration, Congress granted the District of Columbia territorial status, consisting of a governor appointed by the president, a council, and boards of public works and health. Between 1871 and 1874, the Board of Public Works built sewers and sidewalks, condemned 400 unsanitary buildings, paved streets, and planted 60,000 trees.

By 1874, Frederick Law Olmsted, designer of New York's Central Park and other great urban preserves, began filling the Capitol grounds with rare trees.

The ornate Smithsonian Arts and Industries Building was completed in 1881 to become the home of six cartloads of exhibits from the 1876 Philadelphia Centennial; much of that exhibit is still on display. The building complemented the existing 1855 Norman-Gothic Smithsonian Castle, which was the first building constructed with the funds donated to America by British scientist James Smithson.

After considerable deliberation, including controversy over its "modernistic design," the crown of the Washington Monument was set in place in 1884, ending the 36-year construction project. A steam-driven elevator, taking twenty minutes, carried men to its top; women and children were forced to climb the 897 steps because the elevator was considered too dangerous. (The current ride takes about seventy seconds.)

By the start of the twentieth century, Washington included such showplaces as the Library of Congress, Union Station, the Corcoran and Renwick Galleries of Art, the Bureau of Engraving and Printing, the Treasury Building, and the National Portrait Gallery.

Twentieth-Century Washington

In 1901, a committee of experts was assembled to make plans for the development and improvement of Washington's park system. Those appointed to the commission included famous landscape and architectural designers of the area. Most of the commission's plans—many based on L'Enfant's original design—were adopted and lead to the construction of the National Mall and memorials.

The famous Japanese cherry blossom trees, whose blossoming heralds the city's annual Cherry Blossom Festival each spring, became a part of the Washington scene in 1912. A gift of 3,000 trees was sent that year as a token of friendship between the people of Japan and the United States.

Other architectural and cultural additions to the nation's capital during the first quarter of the twentieth century include the United States Botanic Garden, the Museum of Natural History, the Lincoln Memorial, and the Freer Gallery of Art.

Although much of the nation's economy ground to a halt during the Great Depression of the 1930s, construction of federal buildings continued unabated in Washington. President Franklin Roosevelt's WPA program put thousands of jobless men to work building the Federal Triangle. Also built during that time was the Supreme Court and the Federal Reserve.

In 1941, the National Gallery of Art opened its doors, a gift from Pittsburgh millionaire Andrew Mellon. Two other grand structures were completed during World War II in 1943—the pantheon-styled Jefferson Memorial and the Pentagon, still the world's largest office building with seventeen miles of corridors.

Modern Washington

During the 1950s, Washington grew rapidly again as the federal government expanded. Accompanying the growth of the business of government was a boom in the residential suburbs of Virginia and Maryland.

After the assassination of John F. Kennedy, contributions from private citizens and foreign governments helped finance the creation of the John F. Kennedy Center for the Performing Arts, which opened in 1971.

Also in 1971, ground was broken for Washington's Metrorail subway system; the first trains ran in 1976. Today, the system covers most of downtown Washington and reaches into the Maryland and Virginia suburbs.

The nation's Bicentennial celebration in 1976 saw the opening of the spectacular Smithsonian National Air and Space Museum, today the world's most popular museum.

Other cultural additions to the National Mall—all part of the Smithsonian—were the Hirshhorn Museum and Sculpture Garden in 1974, the East Building of the National Gallery of Art in 1978, and the Arthur M. Sackler Gallery, the Enid A. Haupt Gardens, and the National Museum of African Art.

Washington, D.C., Weather

Washington has a somewhat moderate winter climate; the coldest month is January, followed closely by February. Significant snowfall in the District is rare, although suburban areas can sometimes receive a few inches in a storm.

The summer months, from June through early September, are hot and humid. The *average* maximum temperature in July is 88 degrees, which means that many days will see thermometers reaching into the 90s and occasionally into triple digits. And just to make things interesting, the summer months usually drip with humidity, and rain is fairly common.

Historical Averages

	Minimum Temperatures (˚F)	Maximum Temperatures (˚F)	Precipitation (inches)
January	26.8	42.3	2.72
February	29.1	45.9	2.71
March	37.4	56.4	3.17
April	46.0	66.5	2.71
May	56.2	76.0	3.66
June	65.5	84.3	3.38
July	70.4	88.1	3.80
August	69.1	86.5	3.90
September	62.3	80.1	3.31
October	50.0	69.1	3.02
November	40.8	58.3	3.12
December	31.7	47.0	3.12

Visitor Service Phone Numbers

Alexandria Convention & Visitors Association. 221 King Street, Alexandria, VA 22314. (703) 838-4200 or (800) 388-9119. http://ci.alexandria.va.us\alexandria.html.

Arlington Convention & Visitors Service. 735 South Eighteenth Street, Arlington, VA 22202. (703) 228-5720 or (800) 677-6267. www.co.arlington.va.us.

D.C. Chamber of Commerce. 1301 Pennsylvania Avenue NW, #309, Washington, DC 20004. (202) 347-7201. www.dcchamber.org/.

D.C. Committee to Promote Washington. 1212 New York Avenue NW, #200, Washington, DC 20005. (800) 422-8644. www.washington.org.

D.C. Office of Tourism & Promotion. 1212 New York Avenue NW, #200, Washington, DC 20005. (202) 724-5644. www.dchomepage.net/.

Fredericksburg Tourism. 706 Caroline Street, Fredericksburg, VA 22401. (540) 373-1776 or (800) 678-4748. www.fredericksburgva.com.

Gettysburg Travel Council. 35 Carlisle Street, Gettysburg, PA 17325. (717) 334-6274. www.gettysburg.com.

Prince George's County Conference & Visitors Bureau. 9200 Basil Court, Suite 101, Largo, MD 20774. (301) 925-8300.

Prince William County Tourism Office. 14420 Bristow Road, Manassas, VA 20112. (703) 792-4254 or (800) 432-1792. www.visitpwc.com.

Virginia Division of Tourism. 901 East Byrd Street, Richmond, VA 23219. (804) 786-2051 or (800) 932-5827. www.virginia.org.

Chapter 3
Planes, Trains, and Automobiles

Mileage to Washington, D.C.

From	Mileage
Alexandria, VA	12
Atlanta, GA	641
Baltimore, MD	40
Boston, MA	461
Chicago, IL	732
Dallas, TX	1,323
Denver, CO	1,641
Fredericksburg, VA	56
Gettysburg, PA	82
Harpers Ferry, WV	63
Los Angeles, CA	2,645
Miami, FL	1,066
Minneapolis, MN	1,149
New York, NY	238
Richmond, VA	109
Salt Lake City, UT	2,085
San Francisco, CA	2,815
Williamsburg, VA	159

Washington, D.C.–Area Airports
Ronald Reagan Washington National Airport

Ronald Reagan Washington National is one of the closest major airports to a metropolitan area in the country, about a ten-minute cab or twenty-minute Metro ride from downtown.

National is Washington's short-haul airport, serving mostly East Coast destinations. Located in Crystal City, Virginia, about five miles from downtown Washington, it is served by Metrorail's Blue and Yellow lines.

In recent years, National opened its new state-of-the-art main terminal with thirty-five gates, linked to a 4,300-space parking garage. The $1 billion project includes a moving sidewalk to deliver visitors from the new terminal to the Metro or parking lot. More than thirty artists were involved in creating

Ronald Reagan National Airport Gates
New Terminal (Concourses B and C)
Gates 15–22	America West
	Delta
	Delta Connection
	Delta Shuttle
Gates 23–34	Air Canada
	American
	American Eagle
	Midwest Express
	United
	US Airways
Gates 35–44	US Airways
	US Airways Express
	US Airways Shuttle

Old Terminal (Concourse A)
Gates 1–9	Midway
	Northwest
Gates T1-T2	TWA
	TW Express

sculptures, murals, and other decorations for the airport.

Note that the Metro operates from 5:30 A.M. until midnight on weekdays and 8 A.M. until midnight on weekends. *For more details on the Metro, see Chapter 4.*

Taxis to and from Ronald Reagan Washington National Airport

Using a Washington taxi sometimes seems like negotiating for the price of a camel in a Middle Eastern bazaar. Some taxis use meters, some work off the odometer, and others have preset prices for travel between zones. Some taxi rides have special surcharges added. Here's a buyer's guide:

- Virginia- and Maryland-licensed taxicabs use a meter. Make sure the meter is turned on after you enter the cab, not before.
- Washington, D.C.–licensed taxis determine fares by use of their automobile odometers.
- All taxis add an airport fee of $1.25 for trips to a single destination. Individuals traveling separately in the same taxicab do not pay the surcharge.
- There are no rush-hour surcharges.

Airport authorities suggest that passengers ask the driver for an approximate fare before departure; if you have any questions about the range of fares, ask one of the dispatchers at the airport before you board.

Here are some typical fares from National Airport, including the $1.25 airport fee:

Ronald Reagan Washington National to:
Alexandria	4.5 miles	$8.00
Smithsonian and Mall	4.0 miles	$9.00
U.S. Capitol	4.5 miles	$9.25
National Zoo	7.5 miles	$14.25
Pentagon	3.0 miles	$7.75
Dulles International	28.5 miles	$45.25

Shuttle Bus Service

If you have a bit of time and don't mind sharing the ride, you can travel to and from the airport on one of two minibus services.

The **Washington Flyer Express Bus** is operated by the Metropolitan Wash-

REAGAN WASHINGTON NATIONAL AIRPORT

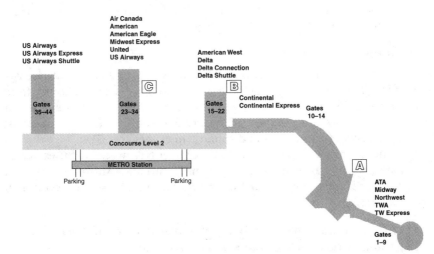

ington Airports Authority, offering frequent service from National Airport to downtown's Washington Convention Center at 900 Ninth Street NW; from there you can pick up courtesy buses to many popular hotels and to Union Station for train services. The Washington Flyer also connects National to Washington Dulles International Airport.

Tickets for the bus are sold at the Washington Flyer Desks in Terminal A near the Northwest Airlines counter, and in Terminals B and C at the Ground Transporation Information Counters on the baggage claims level. For additional information, call (703) 685-1400, or (888) 927-4359. You can also visit the Internet to consult a chart of schedules and rates at www.metwashair ports.com/dulles/washflyer.htm.

Another service, **SuperShuttle**, provides door-to-door shared ride service from the District of Columbia and nearby Maryland and Virginia to National and Dulles airports. A fleet of 117 seven-passenger vans are available; 24-hour advanced reservations are recommended.

For information on SuperShuttle services, call (800) 258-3826.

Rental Car Agencies
Alamo, Avis, Budget, Hertz, and National are located within the main parking garage at the airport; take the Airport Shuttle to their offices to pick up cars. Other rental car companies run shuttle buses to more-distant facilities.

Note that parking is extremely limited in the District. Metered street parking is hard to find and is generally unavailable during rush hours of 8–9:30 A.M. and 4–6:30 P.M. Parking lots and garages typically charge $10 to $20 for the day.

The D.C. Department of Public Works, (202) 541-6060, warns that offending cars will be towed; and those taken after 7 P.M. on Friday and all day on weekends and holidays will not be available for return until Monday morning.

I recommend you use the Metro and taxis for transport within the District; rent a car to explore Virginia and Maryland.

Nonstop Buses to Downtown

Weekday buses depart every half hour from 6:25 A.M. to 9:25 P.M. at twenty-five and fifty-five minutes past the hour. On weekends, buses run hourly from 6:25 A.M. to 12:25 P.M. at twenty-five minutes past the hour, and every half hour from 12:55 P.M. to 9:25 P.M. at twenty-five and fifty-five minutes past the hour. One-way fares are $8 and round-trip tickets cost $14.

From the Downtown Terminal at 1517 K Street NW, weekday buses depart for Ronald Reagan National every half hour from 6:05 A.M. to 9:05 P.M.; on weekends, buses leave every hour from 6:05 A.M. to 1:05 P.M., and every half hour from 1:35 P.M. to 9:05 P.M.

Driving from Ronald Reagan Washington National Airport

To Smithsonian Institutions and the National Mall

Exit airport onto Route 395 North toward Washington. Stay to the right lane for about one-fourth of a mile and bear right to go over the Fourteenth Street Bridge.

On the bridge, get into the left lanes marked for Route 1; the lanes will bring you to Fourteenth Street. Go six blocks on Fourteenth Street and turn right onto Constitution Avenue to the Mall.

To Georgetown

Exit the airport to Route 66 West. Drive for about half a mile to the Rosslyn-Key Bridge; turn right and cross the bridge. Turn right onto M Street.

The center of Georgetown is at M Street and Wisconsin Avenue, about five blocks away.

To Baltimore

Exit the airport to Route 1 South toward Alexandria. Proceed about four miles on Route 1 South to the Washington Beltway. Exit onto Route 95 North, toward Baltimore. Continue on Route 95 about thirty-five miles.

Use Exit 53 to Route 395 to downtown Baltimore. Follow signs to the Inner Harbor on Pratt Street.

Total distance is about forty-one miles.

Dulles International Airport

Dulles Airport is primarily used for international flights, although a number of airlines use it for domestic flights because they are unable to squeeze more planes into the more-

Terminal velocity. Saarinen's unusual design for the roof of the terminal at Dulles presented a difficult engineering task in the 1960s, and the doubling of the terminal in the new project was no easier.

The curving wing-like roof has an asymmetrical shape and is constructed somewhat like a suspension bridge. Lightweight precast panels were supported on each pair of cables and they were then encased in poured-in-place concrete to form stiffening ribs.

convenient but cramped space of Ronald Reagan Washington National Airport. Dulles is located in Loudon County, Virginia, about twenty-six miles from downtown Washington.

The original plan for Dulles Airport and its terminal, by famed architect Eero Saarinen, used "mobile lounges"—oversized buses that took passengers from the terminal directly to their planes.

Dulles, opened in 1962, is now overwhelmed by today's level of air travel, and is in the midst of a major overhaul of its facilities. Saarinen's terminal, looking as if it is poised to take off all by itself, is to be doubled in length to 1,240 feet. Three midfield concourses are scheduled to be connected to the main terminal, with walkways replacing the mobile lounges. The goal is to position Dulles to go well beyond its current load of twelve million passengers toward future capacities of several times that amount.

Taxi fares to Dulles from downtown Washington are about $40.

Breaking the code. When you fly from New York's La Guardia Airport to Dulles International you are making a trip from LGA to IAD. The aviation industry uses three-letter codes to indicate the name of nearly every airport in the world; you'll see the codes on airline tickets and in some airline schedules. If you want to head for the nearby Ronald Reagan Washington National Airport be sure your ticket is sending you to DCA. The code for Baltimore-Washington Airport is BWI.

There is no direct Metrorail service to Dulles. The nearest stop is the West Falls Church station about twenty minutes away; you'll need to take a taxi or bus from there to the airport.

Dulles Airport to West Falls Church Metrorail Station

Buses connect Dulles to the Metrorail service for about $9 one-way. On weekdays, buses leave Dulles every half hour from 6 A.M. to 10 A.M., every twenty minutes from 10:20 A.M. to 6 P.M., and every half hour from 6:30 P.M. until 10:30 P.M. From the Metro station, weekday buses leave every half hour from 6:30 A.M. to 10:30 A.M., every twenty minutes from 10:50 A.M. to 6:10 P.M., and every half hour from 6:30 P.M. to 11 P.M. On weekends, buses run every half hour from 7:30 A.M. to 10:30 P.M. from Dulles, and every half hour from 8 A.M. to 11 P.M. from the Metro station.

Dulles Nonstops to Downtown

Buses depart from Dulles weekdays from 5:20 A.M. to 10:20 P.M. at 20 and 50 minutes past the hour; on weekends, the buses run every hour from 5:20 A.M. to 11:20 A.M. at twenty minutes past the hour, and from 12:20 P.M. to 10:20 P.M. at twenty and fifty minutes past the hour. The one-way fare is $16, and round-trip is $26.

From the Downtown Terminal at 1517 K Street NW, weekday buses depart for Dulles every half hour from 6:15 A.M. to 9:15 P.M.; on weekends, buses leave every hour from 6:15 A.M. to 1:15 P.M., and every half hour from 1:45 P.M. to 9:15 P.M.

The trip should take about forty-five minutes; allow extra time during rush hours.

Baltimore-Washington International Airport

Located twenty-eight miles north of Washington, just south of Baltimore, Maryland. Amtrak or MARC (Maryland Rail Commuter) trains run from Washington's Union Station. Tickets are priced at about $9 one-way; shuttle service costs about $18 from downtown hotels.

Chapter 4
Getting Around Within the District of Columbia

Washington is one of the easier American cities to navigate. It is relatively small, with a good mass transit system, and it more-or-less retains the logic of L'Enfant's original design.

Tourists generally spend nearly all their time in the downtown government sector, and that is where most of the District's services are concentrated.

Understanding the Logic of Washington's Streets

As cities go, Washington has one of the most logical street grids.

To begin with, all addresses include a quadrant indicator: NW, NE, SW, or SE. The White House and most of downtown is in NW. Pay attention to the quadrant: there can be identical addresses miles apart in different sectors.

Most of the streets in the District are laid out in a grid. In general:

North-south streets are numbered. First Street NW and First Street SW lie west of Capitol Street. First Street NE and First Street SE lie east of Capitol Street.

East-west streets are named and are in alphabetical order split at the Mall. (There are no streets beginning with J, X, Y, or Z.) After W, the alphabet begins again with two-syllable names, and then three-syllable names. Farthest away from downtown, east-west streets use the names of flowers or trees.

Avenues, an important element of L'Enfant's original design, run diagonally and are named for states.

Circles and squares are located at the intersection of diagonal avenues and numbered and lettered streets.

All this said, there are some inconsistencies. Consult a map before heading out to any out-of-the-way location.

Cars, Trains, and Taxis

Let's start with the worst way to get around in Washington: by private car. Actually, the District's traffic is no worse than the downtown of most major cities. However, parking is very scarce and expensive anywhere near the muse-

Metro phones.
Metro Information
Center: (202) 637-7000.
www.wmata.com.
Events Hotline:
(202) 783-1070

ums, government buildings, and theaters, which are the goals of most visitors.

On the weekends and on federal holidays, though, downtown Washington becomes a much smaller town. Traffic is very light, and parking is available on most side streets.

In general, the best way to get around town is by clean, inexpensive Metro or taxi.

Taxis within the District are reasonably priced, and for a group of three or four, a taxi can actually be less expensive than taking the Metro. The cabs work on a zone pricing scheme. Transit within any one zone is about $4, between two zones $5.50, and across to a third zone $7. A three-zone fare should cover anywhere in the District.

A few more details: drivers add a $1 per trip surcharge during the afternoon rush hour from 4–6:30 P.M.; trunks or other large items placed in the trunk of the cab are levied a charge of $1.25 each. And telephone dispatch adds $1.50 to the fare. There are also surcharges during snow emergencies. Waiting time is billed at $1.50 per five minutes.

Using Metrorail

Washington's Metrorail is one of the few government successes most Washingtonians can agree upon. The trains are fast and clean, the stations are attractive and generally safe, and fares are very reasonable.

With slightly more than 103 miles of track and eighty-three stations, the Metro has five lines, identified by color and the two ends of the track. There are eight transfer points where two or more of the lines come together for free interchange. The Metro has done an excellent job of providing route maps in stations, on platforms, and on the trains themselves.

The Metro routes are:

Red Line (Wheaton/Shady Grove). Includes stops at the National Zoo, Dupont Circle, Metro Center, and suburban Maryland.

Blue Line (Addison Road/Van Dorn Street). Includes stops at National Airport, the Pentagon, Arlington Cemetery, Foggy Bottom, several downtown stops, including Metro Center and the Smithsonian, and eastern suburbs.

Orange Line (New Carrollton/Vienna). From Vienna, Virginia, to eastern suburbs with stops including Metro Center, Smithsonian, and other downtown stations.

Yellow Line (Mount Vernon Square–UDC/Huntington). A quick shot from National Airport and points south to L'Enfant Plaza and Gallery Square/Chinatown.

Green Line (U Street–Cardozo/Anacostia). A mostly north-south connector, with stops in Anacostia and Gallery Square/Chinatown.

See the section in this chapter that tells you important tourist attractions at major Metrorail stations.

The Metrorail operates on weekdays from 5:30 A.M. until midnight, and weekends from 8 A.M. until midnight. Last trains leave some stations before midnight; last-trains schedule times are posted in stations. Weekend schedules are in effect on certain holidays, including New Year's Day, Memorial Day, July 4th, Labor Day, Thanksgiving Day, and Christmas Day.

METRORAIL SYSTEM MAP

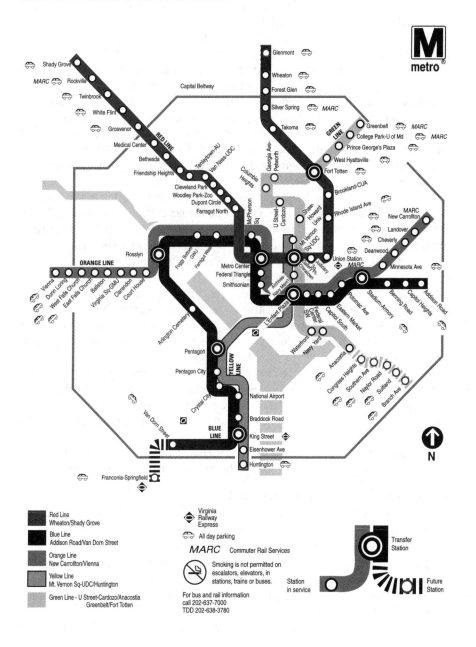

M metro®

Red Line
Wheaton/Shady Grove

Blue Line
Addison Road/Van Dorn Street

Orange Line
New Carrollton/Vienna

Yellow Line
Mt. Vernon Sq-UDC/Huntington

Green Line - U Street-Cardozo/Anacostia
Greenbelt/Fort Totten

◆ Virginia Railway Express

🚗 All day parking

MARC Commuter Rail Services

🚭 Smoking is not permitted on escalators, elevators, in stations, trains or buses.

For bus and rail information
call 202-637-7000
TDD 202-638-3780

Station in service

Transfer Station

Future Station

Peak fares are charged for trips that *begin* weekdays between 5:30 and 9:30 A.M. or from 3 to 8 P.M. Off-peak fares are in effect at all other times.

Fares are calculated on distance traveled. The maximum peak fare is $3.25, and highest off-peak fare is $2.10.

One of the best deals in town for tourists is the Metrorail One Day Pass. For $5, the card allows unlimited travel on weekdays after 9:30 A.M., and all day on weekends and holidays. You can also purchase a 7-Day Fast Pass, valid for seven consecutive days of unlimited Metrorail use, for $25.

Farecards can be purchased at any station for the minimum fare of $1.10, up to a maximum of $45. If you're going to be using the Metro heavily during your visit or if you expect to make a return visit, consider buying $20 worth of travel; you will automatically be given a bonus of 10 percent for a high-ticket purchase. The value of the card is recorded on the magnetic stripe on its back.

Every passenger must have their own ticket. When you enter the station, you must feed the ticket into the electronic reader at the turnstile; the device records your point of entry and time on the magnetic stripe. When you arrive at your destination, you must feed the ticket into the exit turnstile where a computer will deduct your fare from the card. (It also prints the value on the card so you'll know its current worth.)

If you don't have enough credit on the card, each station has a terminal within the turnstiles where you can add value and escape the Metro. You cannot sell back a Metro pass for cash, but you can trade in a damaged card at the Metro Center ticket office; you can also buy special passes there and browse through a rack of bus schedules.

In addition to the paper electronic passes, the reusable SmarTrip pass was added to the mix in 1999. The credit card-like pass is embedded with a special computer chip that keeps track of the card's value. The card can hold as much as $180, and can be recharged at any time. Any fare purchase over $20 earns a 10 percent bonus.

One advantage of the SmarTrip card is that it can be replaced if it is lost, for a $5 fee—if you have registered it beforehand with Metrorail, that is.

How to Buy and Use a Farecard

Buying a Metro Farecard seems a lot more complicated than it really is. Here's how it works:

The fare machines are located near the turnstiles at each station. The machines accept coins, and bills from $1 to $20. Put the money into the coin slot or bill carrier. The machines issue change in coins, up to a maximum of $4.95; in other words, if you put in a $20 bill, you're going to have to buy at least $15.05 in travel.

Use the +/– keys to select the value you want recorded on the farecard.

When the display indicates the amount you want to spend, press the white "Push for farecard" button.

To go through the turnstiles, find a gate that has a green arrow and insert your card face up into the slot. The card will come out on the top of the turnstile; take the card and keep it with you. (On some turnstiles the card comes back out from where you put it in, while on others, the card moves through the reader and exits on top.)

When you arrive at your destination, go to the exit turnstiles and put your card into the slot. Your fare will be automatically subtracted from the balance remaining, and your card will be returned to you.

Now, what happens if the fare for your trip is $2.00 and you have only $1.10 on your card? First of all, the turnstile will not open and your card will be rejected. Take the card and go to one of the "Exitfare" machines that can be found on the station side of the turnstiles; there you can add value to the card until there is enough for you to exit.

There are station managers on duty in the kiosks at turnstiles most of the time, and they can assist in emergencies.

Metrobus

In recent years, the fare structure was simplified from the hodgepodge of rates and zones. On the Metrobus, the fare was set at $1.10 on regular routes, $2 on express routes. Eliminated were peak and off-peak fares, transfer charges, and zone or state crossing charges.

Metrobus fares are at fifty cents for senior citizens and disabled riders who have a valid Metro ID or Medicare card (and an additional picture ID if requested). Up to two children, younger than five, may ride free with each paying customer.

Also available are Weekly Bus Passes, priced at $10, which permit unlimited bus rides on regular routes for a seven-day

Bikes by rail. You can purchase a special permit that permits you to take a bicycle aboard Metro trains after 7 P.M. on weekdays and all day on weekends and most holidays. (Commuters can also rent bicycle lockers at many stations.) Contact the transit authority at (202) 962-1116 for information.

How deep is deep? The Forest Glen station on the Red Line is the deepest hole in the ground in the Metro system, about 196 feet below the street—nearly twenty stories down. Six high-speed elevators carry passengers to and from the surface.

The longest and deepest single escalator in the system is at the Wheaton station, one stop farther along on the Red Line. The set of moving stairs at the station is nearly 230 feet long and rises nearly 115 feet.

The busy Dupont Circle's north entrance is the sixth-ranking escalator in the system, at nearly 189 feet long and rising about ninety-five feet.

Metrorail and Metrobus to
Museums, Memorials, and Agencies

Destination	Metro Line	Metro Station	Metrobus Lines
Arlington National Cemetery	Blue	Arlington Cemetery	13A, 13B
Bureau of Engraving and Printing	Orange/Blue	Smithsonian	13A, 13B, 52, V6
Capitol Building	Orange/Blue	Capitol South	32, 34, 36, 96
Capital Children's Museum	Red	Union Station	D2, D4, D6, D8, X2, X4
Chinatown	Green/Yellow/Red	Gallery Place–Chinatown	42, 62, 64, 70, 80, G6, P6, S2, S4, X2, X4
Convention Center	Orange/Blue/Red	Metro Center	62, 64, 80, G6, P6, S2, S4, X2, X4
Corcoran Gallery	Orange/Blue	Farragut West	32, 34, 36, 80
Federal Bureau of Investigation	Orange/Blue/Red	Metro Center	13A, 13B, 32, 34, 36, 42, 54, 62, D2, D4, D6, D8, G6, P2, P6, S2, S4
Ford's Theatre	Orange/Blue/Red	Metro Center	42, 62, 64, D2, D4, D6, G6, P6, S2, S4, X4
Freer Gallery	Orange/Blue	Smithsonian	13A, 13B, 52, V6
Georgetown	Orange/Blue	Foggy Bottom/GWU	32, 34, 36, 36B, D2, D4, D6, D8, G2
Hirshhorn Museum and Sculpture Garden	Green/Yellow/Orange/ Blue	L'Enfant Plaza *or* Smithsonian	13A, 13B, 32, 34, 36, 52, 70, V6
House Where Lincoln Died	Orange/Blue/Red	Metro Center	42, 62, 64, D2, D4, D6, D8, P6, S2, S4, X2, X4
Iwo Jima Memorial	Orange/Blue	Rosslyn	4B, 4H
Library of Congress	Orange/Blue	Capitol South	32, 34, 36, 96
National Air and Space Museum	Green/Yellow/Orange/ Blue	L'Enfant Plaza	13A, 13B, 32, 34, 36, 52, 70, P2, P6
National Aquarium	Orange/Blue	Federal Triangle	13A, 13B, 32, 34, 36, 52, 54
National Archives	Green/Yellow	Archives–Navy Memorial	13A, 13B, 32, 34, 36, 70, P2, P6
National Building Museum	Red	Judiciary Square	42, 70, 80, B6, D2, D4 , D6, D8, P6, X2, X4

Destination	Metro Line	Metro Station	Metrobus Lines
National Gallery of Art	Green/Yellow	Archives–Navy Memorial	13A, 13B, 32, 34, 36, 70, P2, P6
National Geographic Society	Red	Farragut North	
National Museum of African Art	Orange/Blue	Smithsonian	13A, 13B, 32, 34, 36, 52, 70, V6
National Museum of American Art	Green/Yellow/Red	Gallery Place–Chinatown	42, 62, 64, 70, 80, D2, D4, D6, D8, P6, S2, S4
National Museum of Women in Arts	Orange/Blue/Red	Metro Center	32, 34, 36, 42, 52, 54, 80, D2, D4, D6, D8, S2, X2, X4
National Portrait Gallery	Green/Yellow/Red	Gallery Place–Chinatown	42, 62, 64, 70, 80, D2, D4, D6, D8, P6, S2, S4, X2, X4
National Postal Museum	Red	Union Station	42, 80, 96, D2, D4, D6, D8, X2, X4, X8
National Zoo	Red	Woodley Park–Zoo *or* Cleveland Park	H2, H4, L2, L4
Old Town Alexandria	Blue/Yellow	King Street *or* Braddock Road	9A, 9B, 9C, 10A, 10B, 10C, 10D, 28A, 28B, 29K, 29N, DASH AT2, AT3, AT4, AT5, AT8, Fairfax Connector 110
Phillips Gallery	Red	Dupont Circle	42, D2, D4, D6, D8, G2, L2, N2, N4, X2, X4
Renwick Gallery	Orange/Blue	Farragut West	32, 34, 36, 38B, 42, 80, D2, D4, D6, D8, G4, L2, N2, N4, X2, X4
RFK Stadium	Orange/Blue	Stadium–Armory	42, 96, B2
Arthur M. Sackler Gallery	Orange/Blue	Smithsonian	13A, 13B, 32, 34, 36, 52, 70, V6
Smithsonian Castle	Orange/Blue	Smithsonian	13A, 13B, 32, 34, 36, 52, 70, V6
Starplex/D.C. Armory	Blue/Orange	Stadium–Armory	42, 96, B2
Supreme Court	Orange/Blue	Capitol South	32, 34, 36, 96
Textile Museum	Red	Dupont Circle	42, L4, N2, N4

Destination	Metro Line	Metro Station	Metrobus Lines
Torpedo Factory Art	None	None	9A, 9B, 9C, 10A, 10B, 10C, 10D, 28A, 28B, 29K, 29N, DASH AT2, AT3, AT4, AT5, Fairfax Connector 110
United States Botanic Garden	Orange/Blue	Federal Center SW	32, 34, 36, D12, P6
U.S. Holocaust Memorial Museum	Orange/Blue	Smithsonian	13A, 13B, 52, V6
U.S. Navy Memorial	Yellow/Green	Archives–Navy Memorial	13A, 13B, 32, 34, 36, 70, D2, D4, D6, D8, P2, P6
Vietnam Veterans Memorial	Orange/Blue	Foggy Bottom/GWU	13A, 13B, 80
Washington Monument	Orange/Blue	Smithsonian	13A, 13B, 52, V6
White House	Orange/Blue	McPherson Square	32, 34, 36, 36B, 42, 52, 54, 80, G4, N2, N4, S2, S4, X2, X4
Woodrow Wilson House	Red	Dupont Circle	42, D2, D4, D6, D8, G2, L2, N2, N4, X2, X4

Metrorail and Metrobus to Theaters and Libraries

Destination	Metro Line	Metro Station	Metrobus Lines
Arena Stage	Green	Waterfront	70, V6
Constitution Hall	Orange/Blue	Foggy Bottom/GWU	13A, 13B, 80
Folger Shakespeare Library	Orange/Blue	Capitol South	32, 34, 36, 96
Kennedy Center	Orange/Blue	Foggy Bottom/GWU	80, L4
Martin Luther King, Jr. Memorial Library	Blue/Red/Orange *or* Red/Green/Yellow	Metro Center *or* Gallery Place–Chinatown	42, 62, 64, 70, 80, G6, P6, S2, S4, X2, X4
Lisner Auditorium	Orange/Blue	Foggy Bottom/GWU	32, 34, 36, 38B, 80, D2, D4, D6, D8, L2
National Theatre	Orange/Blue/Red	Metro Center	32, 34, 36, 42, 70, D2, D4, D6, D8
Shakespeare Theatre	Green/Yellow	Archives–Navy Memorial	32, 34, 36, 42, 70, D2, D4, D6, D8
Wolf Trap Farm Park for the Performing Arts	Orange	West Falls Church	Transfer to Wolf Trap Metro Shuttle Express

Metrorail and Metrobus to Shopping Centers and Malls

Destination	Metro Line	Metro Station	Metrobus Lines
Ballston Common	Orange	Ballston	1C, 1B, 1F, 2A, 2B, 2C, 10B, 10C, 10D, 22B, 23A, 23B, 23T, 24M, 25A, 25B, 25J, 38B
Chevy Chase Pavilion	Red	Friendship Heights	32, 34, 36, E2, E3, E4, L8, N2, N4
Crystal City Underground	Blue/Yellow	Crystal City	9A, 9B, 9C, 10A, 23A, 23B, 23T
Fashion Centre	Blue/Yellow	Pentagon City	24M
L'Enfant Plaza	Blue/Green/Orange/ Yellow	L'Enfant Plaza	13A, 13B, 32, 34, 36, 52, 70, V6
Pavillion at the Old Post Office	Blue/Orange *or* Blue/Orange/Red	Federal Triangle *or* Metro Center	13A, 13B, 32, 34, 36, 42, 52, 54, 62, 64, D2, D4, D6, D8, G6, P2, P6, S2, S4
The Shops at National Place	Blue/Orange/Red *or* Blue/Orange	Metro Center *or* Federal Triangle	13A, 13B, 32, 34, 36, 42, 52, 54, 62, 64, 80, D2, D4, D6, D8, G6, P6, S2, S4, X2, X4
Union Station Shops	Red	Union Station	42, 80, 96, D2, D4, D6, D8, X8
Washington Square	Red	Farragut North	36B, 42, D2, D4, D6, D8, L2, N2, N4

period and cover $1.10 of the $2 fare on express routes. Passes are also available for longer periods.

A weekly bus/rail Short Trip Pass, priced at $20, permits unlimited Metrobus travel and covers the cost of Metrorail trips up to $1.75 during regular fare hours. At other times, it will cover the cost of any Metrorail trip.

Transfers from one bus to another cost 10 cents.

A Selection of Metrorail Stations

Following is a guide to the most-visited Metrorail stations. At each stop, we'll tell you which exit to use if there is more than one available, and point you in the proper direction to major tourist attractions.

Archives–Navy Memorial. The station exits within the Navy Memorial.
  Federal Bureau of Investigation. Continue walking west and cross Ninth Street.
  National Archives. Make a left turn from the exit and cross Pennsylvania Avenue.
  House Where Lincoln Died and Ford's Theatre. Continue west to Ninth Street and turn right; turn left on E Street and right on Tenth Street.
  National Museum of Natural History. Continue west to Ninth Street and turn left. Cross Pennsylvania Avenue and Constitution Avenue to entrance.

Capitol South.

Library of Congress. Turn right on C Street and left on First Street. The Library's Madison Building is located at First and C Streets; the Jefferson Building is a block farther north at First Street and Independence Avenue. The Adams Building is at Second Street and Independence Avenue.

U.S. Capitol. Hard to miss. Continue north on First Street to Independence Avenue and turn left.

Dupont Circle.

Phillips Collection. Use Q Street Exit from Metro.Turn left on Q Street and right on Twenty-first Street.

Farragut North.

National Geographic Society. Use L Street Exit from Metro. Turn left on L Street and left on Seventeenth Street.

Federal Triangle.

National Aquarium. Turn right on Thirteenth Street and left on Pennsylvania Avenue. Turn left on Fourteenth Street to Aquarium.

National Museum of American History. Turn left from exit to Constitution Avenue; the museum is across the street to your right between Twelfth and Fourteenth Streets.

National Museum of Natural History. Turn left from exit to Constitution Avenue; the museum is across the street to your left between Twelfth and Ninth Streets.

Foggy Bottom.

Watergate. Reverse your direction from the exit and walk west on I Street and turn left on New Hampshire Avenue. The Watergate is three long blocks ahead on your left.

Kennedy Center. Follow the instructions for the Watergate, and continue another two long blocks. Note that you may not want to make this walk late at night because of security concerns.

Gallery Place–Chinatown.

Chinatown. Use Seventh and H Streets exit. Chinatown is all around you.

Convention Center. Use Seventh and H Streets exit. Reverse your direction and walk west on H Street for three blocks toward Tenth Street.

Museum of American Art, Portrait Gallery. Use Ninth and G Streets exit to arrive directly at museum.

Federal Bureau of Investigation. Use Ninth and G Streets exit and continue walking south for two blocks to E and Ninth Streets.

National Building Museum. Use Seventh and G Streets exit. Reverse direction from exit and walk to G Street; turn right and walk on G Street to Fifth Street.

Judiciary Square.

National Building Museum. Use F Street exit. The museum is across F Street between Fourth and Fifth Streets.

National Law Enforcement Officers Memorial. Use F Street exit. Memorial is in plaza at exit.

L'Enfant Plaza.

National Air and Space Museum. Use Seventh Street/Maryland Avenue/Smithsonian Museums exit from Metro. Make a hard left from exit and walk north toward the mall on Seventh Street. Turn right on Independence Avenue.

Hirshhorn Museum. Use Seventh Street/Maryland Avenue/Smithsonian Museums exit from Metro. Make a hard left from exit and walk north toward the mall on Seventh Street. Turn left on Independence Avenue.

Smithsonian Arts and Industries Building and Smithsonian Castle. Follow instructions to Hirshhorn Museum and continue west.

McPherson Square.

White House. Use Vermont Avenue/White House exit. Continue walking from exit to H Street; cross Lafayette Square and Pennsylvania Avenue to the White House. The tour gate is on East Executive Avenue, to your left as you face the building.

Metro Center.

Federal Bureau of Investigation. Use Eleventh Street exit from the Metro. Continue walking south on 11th Street to E Street; turn left and walk two blocks to the FBI.

House Where Lincoln Died and Ford's Theatre. Use Eleventh Street exit from Metro. Continue walking south on Eleventh Street to F Street; turn left and walk one block to Tenth Street. Turn right on Tenth Street.

Smithsonian Station.

National Museum of American History/National Museum of Natural History. Use the Mall exit from the Metro. Turn left from the exit and cross the Mall. American History is ahead on your left side; Natural History is ahead on your right side.

Freer Gallery/Arthur M. Sackler Gallery. Use Independence Avenue exit. Reverse direction from exit and walk east on Independence Avenue to museums on your left.

Smithsonian Castle/Smithsonian Arts and Industries Building. Use Independence Avenue exit. Reverse direction from exit and walk east on Independence Avenue. Museums are on your left after Sackler Gallery.

Union Station.

National Postal Museum. Use Massachusetts Avenue exit. Turn left from exit and cross street to museum.

DOWNTOWN WASHINGTON

STANTON PARK · SEWARD SQUARE · MARION PARK · FOLGER PARK · GARFIELD PARK · ADAMS BUILDING · FOLGER SHAKESPEARE LIBRARY · SUPREME COURT · THE LIBRARY OF CONGRESS · U.S. CAPITOL · UNION STATION · NATIONAL POSTAL MUSEUM · CAPITAL CHILDREN'S MUSEUM · GEORGETOWN LAW SCHOOL · UNION STATION PLAZA · TAFT MEMORIAL CARILLON · PEACE MONUMENT · GRANT MONUMENT · GARFIELD MONUMENT · BOTANIC GARDEN · Capitol Reflecting Pool · DEPARTMENT OF LABOR · U.S. COURT HOUSE · JOHN MARSHALL PARK · DEPARTMENT OF HEALTH & HUMAN SERVICES · EAST WING NATIONAL GALLERY · NATIONAL GALLERY OF ART · NATIONAL AIR AND SPACE MUSEUM · THE MALL · DEPARTMENT OF EDUCATION · NASA · DEPARTMENT OF TRANSPORTATION · NATIONAL BUILDING MUSEUM · FEDERAL TRADE COMM. · THE NATIONAL ARCHIVES · ICE SKATING RINK · SCULPTURE GARDEN · HIRSHHORN MUSEUM · NATL. MUSEUM OF AFRICAN ART · HANCOCK PARK · BENJAMIN BANNEKER PARK · NATIONAL MUSEUM OF NATURAL HISTORY · SMITHSONIAN · NATIONAL MUSEUM OF AFRICAN ART · DEPT. OF ENERGY · FREER GALLERY · NATIONAL PORTRAIT GALLERY & MUSEUM OF AMERICAN ART · FORDS THEATRE NATIONAL HISTORIC SITE · THE PAVILION OLD POST OFFICE · MARTIN LUTHER KING JR. MEMORIAL LIBRARY · D.C. CONVENTION CENTER · NATIONAL MUSEUM OF WOMEN IN THE ARTS · CHINATOWN · MT. VERNON PLACE · NATIONAL THEATER · WARNER THEATRE · DEPT. OF JUSTICE · IRS · U.A.S. · NATIONAL MUSEUM OF AMERICAN HISTORY · THE MALL · INTERSTATE COMMERCE COMMISSION · DEPARTMENT OF COMMERCE · THE NATIONAL AQUARIUM · FREEDOM PLAZA · PERSHING SQUARE · FRANKLIN PARK · DEPARTMENT OF THE TREASURY · DEPARTMENT OF VETERANS AFFAIRS · McPHERSON SQUARE · FARRAGUT SQUARE · EDWARD R. MURROW PARK · LAFAYETTE SQUARE · THE WHITE HOUSE · CORCORAN GALLERY OF ART · RENWICK GALLERY · BLAIR HOUSE · EXECUTIVE OFFICE BUILDING · DECATUR HOUSE · WORLD BANK · DEPARTMENT OF THE INTERIOR · OCTAGON HOUSE · DAUGHTERS OF THE AMERICAN REVOLUTION · O.A.S. BUILDING · THE ELLIPSE · ZERO MILESTONE · SYLVAN THEATER · WASHINGTON MONUMENT · THOMAS JEFFERSON MEMORIAL · Tidal Basin · WEST POTOMAC PARK · DECLARATION MEMORIAL · DEPARTMENT OF STATE · U.S. NAVY BUREAU OF MEDICINE AND SURGERY · GEORGE WASHINGTON UNIVERSITY · FEDERAL RESERVE BUILDING · NATIONAL ACADEMY OF SCIENCES · CONSTITUTION GARDENS · Reflecting Pool · VIETNAM VETERANS MEMORIAL · LINCOLN MEMORIAL · FOGGY BOTTOM · WATERGATE COMPLEX · JOHN F. KENNEDY CENTER FOR THE PERFORMING ARTS · THEODORE ROOSEVELT ISLAND · COLUMBIA ISLAND · LADY BIRD JOHNSON PARK · ARLINGTON NATIONAL CEMETERY · Potomac River · Washington Channel · Rock Creek And Potomac Pkwy · Arlington Memorial Bridge · Washington Circle

Part II
The Jewels of the
District of Columbia

Chapter 5
The Smithsonian Institution

The Smithsonian Institution: The World at Our Feet

The Smithsonian Institution is truly one of the world's most precious treasures, a collection of the nation's and the planet's historical and artistic past. It has been called "the nation's attic," but it's a lot more than that. The Smithsonian is a celebration of life on this planet.

In This Chapter

Anacostia Museum and Center for African American History and Culture
(Reopens spring of 2001)

WOW Arts and Industries Building

Freer Gallery of Art

Hirshhorn Museum and Sculpture Garden

WOW National Air and Space Museum

WOW National Museum of African Art

National Museum of American Art
(Reopens in 2003 as the Smithsonian American Art Museum)

WOW National Museum of American History

WOW National Museum of Natural History

National Portrait Gallery
(Reopens in 2003)

WOW National Postal Museum

WOW National Zoological Park

WOW Renwick Gallery of the American Art Museum

Arthur M. Sackler Gallery

Smithsonian Castle (Smithsonian Institution Building)

National Museum of the American Indian

Econo-shopping. See
the coupons in this book
for special offers of 15
percent to 20 percent
discounts at ten
Smithsonian gift shops.

The public good.
Admission to all
Smithsonian Institution
buildings is free, and the
majority of buildings are
open from 10 A.M. to
5:30 P.M. every day of
the year except
December 25. Extended
spring and summer
hours are determined
annually. The
Smithsonian Information
Center (located in the
Castle) is open daily from
9 A.M.

Our English Benefactor

The story of the Smithsonian itself is one of history's wonderful quirks, a magnanimous gift with its roots shrouded in mystery.

The original benefactor was an English scientist, one James Smithson. Though he never visited the United States, he chose to leave nearly his entire sizable fortune to the young nation.

Smithson, born in 1765, was the illegitimate son of Hugh Smithson Perey, the Duke of Northumberland, and Elizabeth Hungerford Keate Macie of Bath, England. A well-educated member of the gentry, he traveled through Europe for most of his life, maintaining a residence in Paris where many of the most famous scientists of the time were his friends. He also engaged in some research of his own, and in 1802 a zinc ore he identified was named *smithsonite* in his honor.

He died in 1829 in Genoa, Italy, and was interred in a small cemetery at San Benigno. At his death he left his fortune to a nephew, Henry James Hungerford. Under the terms of his will, if Hungerford died without an heir, the estate would go to the "United States of America, to found at Washington, under the name of the Smithsonian Institution, an establishment for the increase and diffusion of knowledge among men." Hungerford died in 1835, without an heir, and the money crossed the ocean.

In 1904, when the Smithsonian Institution learned that authorities in Genoa intended to abolish the cemetery, Alexander Graham Bell—a regent of the institution—was sent to escort the tomb to the United States. Smithson's tomb was then installed alongside the north foyer in the Smithsonian Castle. While the tomb was in transit, Smithsonian scientists took the opportunity to find out this much about the great benefactor: he was 5'6" tall, smoked a pipe, had an extra vertebra, and died of natural causes. The development of his shoulders indicated he was probably a fencer.

Not much more is known about Smithson. Why did he leave his fortune to America? Was it a comment on his home country, or a vote of confidence in a new nation he had never visited?

The Establishment of the Institution

Congress was at first reluctant to accept the gift because of concerns of foreign entanglement and indecision on how to best use the money. It was 1846

MUSEUMS ON THE MALL

before the Smithsonian Institution was established. One of the champions was John Quincy Adams in the final years of his life. Said Adams in a report on the creation of the Smithsonian, "To furnish the means of acquiring knowledge is . . . the greatest benefit that can be conferred upon mankind. It prolongs life itself and enlarges the sphere of existence."

By the 1850s, the U.S. National Museum was housed in the Smithsonian Castle on the Mall. In 1876, most of the U.S. Centennial Exhibition at Philadelphia was moved to the castle temporarily while a new building was constructed to accommodate it. In 1881, the Centennial Exhibition moved to the Arts and Industries Building; the collection was restored in 1976.

Today, the Smithsonian Institution is an independent trust of the United States devoted to public education and national service in the arts, sciences, and history. Centered in Washington where it operates fourteen museums and galleries and the National Zoo, it also has the Cooper-Hewitt Museum and the National Museum of the American Indian in New York City. Financial support comes from federal appropriations and private funds.

Sometime in the early years of the twenty-first century, the new National Museum of the American Indian is expected to open on the Mall.

Of Special Interest to Children

Children of all ages will find something of interest at every Smithsonian Institution museum, but here are the best bets for youngsters: National Air and Space Museum, National Museum of American History, National Museum of Natural History, National Postal Museum, and National Zoological Park.

Smithsonian Museums

Anacostia Museum and Center for African American History and Culture *(Reopens in Spring of 2001)*

1901 Fort Place SE at Morris Road. Metro: Anacostia. Daily 10 A.M.–5 P.M. Free. (202) 287-3369 or (202) 357-2700. www.si.edu/organiza/museums/anacost/.

The Anacostia Museum is a national resource devoted to the African-American experience and culture, focusing on Washington, D.C., and the Upper South. The museum also examines contemporary urban issues, including housing, transportation, and health care, and their impact upon the African-American communities in the region.

The museum draws its roots from the Anacostia Neighborhood Museum, which opened in 1967 in a former theater to bring a bit of culture to an underserved community. During the years, it came to concentrate more on the nature and history of the community itself, and in 1987 moved into a new building in Fort Stanton Park.

The museum was closed for all of 2000 for a major renovation; it is expected to reopen in the Spring of 2001. Be sure to call to confirm the schedule.

WOW Arts and Industries Building

900 Jefferson Drive SW. Metro: Smithsonian. Daily 10 A.M.–5:30 P.M. Free. (202) 357-2700. www.si.edu/organiza/museums/artsind/artsind.htm.

For many of us, the Arts and Industries exhibit is as close to time travel as we expect to experience in our lives: when you step through the doors of the Arts and Industries Building, you arrive in a barely changed display of American arts and manufactured goods that were created for the 1876 Centennial Exposition in Philadelphia.

In fact, the building was completed in 1881 specifically for that purpose. Grand expositions in the parks of major cities were all the rage in the nineteenth century, including the one held in the famous Crystal Palace built in London's Hyde Park in 1851. Both the Washington pavilion and the building in Philadelphia that first housed its treasures were based on a structure at the Vienna Exposition of 1873.

The multicolored brick and sandstone design of Arts and Industries is a mixture of Victorian and Renaissance styles.

Over the Mall entrance is Columbia Protecting Science and Industry, a sculpture by Caspar Buberl, who also executed many other pieces of art for public buildings in Washington, including the Old Pension Building.

The original name for the structure was the United States National Museum; that title is still engraved over the doorway. The first use of the building in 1881 was as the site of the inaugural ball for President James A. Garfield.

The items on display were changed over the years to go beyond the Philadelphia exhibit; among items first shown there was Charles Lindbergh's *Spirit of St. Louis*. In 1976, in honor of the nation's bicentennial, the museum was restored to its original appearance and many of the centennial exhibits were returned.

The Philadelphia 1876 Centennial Exposition included more than 200 buildings with a total floor space of about seventy-five acres. Exhibits were divided into categories such as mining, manufacturing, art, and horticulture. There were also exhibits from many foreign nations. The symbol of the fair was the giant Corliss steam engine; a model of a similar engine is on display at the Arts and Industries Building.

Other elements from the centennial fair include the Nicholson File Company display, an exhibit by Otis Brothers and Company of Otis Patent Life and Labor Saving Hoisting Machinery, which we now know as the elevator.

The centerpiece of the East Hall is a Baldwin Locomotive; at the time the original exhibit was put together, Baldwin Locomotive was the oldest active manufacturer of locomotives in America. The Jupiter, a gorgeous conglomeration of brass, steel, and wood, is an eight-wheel, 36-inch-gauge, wood-burning passenger locomotive, that according to its specifications, was capable of hauling 670 tons on a level track at speeds of twenty-five to forty miles per hour.

There is a display of some frightening medical devices by the Codman and Shurtleff Surgical and Dental Instruments Co. of Boston, and a case full of hundreds of different types and styles of Rudolph Koenig tuning forks.

In the Illinois State Exhibit is the case of medical instruments used at the autopsy of Abraham Lincoln on April 15, 1865, just eleven years before the opening of the Philadelphia show. The Massachusetts exhibit includes the diplomatic uniform worn by Samuel F. B. Morse, inventor of the telegraph; you'll also find two chips off Plymouth Rock.

As new collections were moved to the expanding roster of Smithsonian institutions, including Natural History in 1910, American History in 1964, and Air and Space in 1976, the vacated exhibition space was converted to office space. At the same time new floors were created for offices, reducing exhibition space and natural light. Today, only the rotunda and four of the original seventeen exhibit halls remain.

Freer Gallery of Art

Jefferson Drive at Twelfth Street SW. Metro: Smithsonian. Daily 10 A.M.–5:30 P.M. Free. (202) 357-2700. www.si.edu/asia.

The Freer became the Smithsonian's first art museum when it opened in 1923. Its initial collection of Asian and American art was a gift from Detroit industrialist Charles Lang Freer. In 1993, the museum was reopened after a four-year renovation project. As part of the new work, the Freer was connected via an underground gallery to its neighbor, the Arthur M. Sackler Gallery.

Today, the Freer's collection of Asian art is considered among the best in the world, including some 28,000 pieces of Japanese, Chinese, Korean, South and Southeast Asian, and Near Eastern art, dating from the fourth millennium B.C. to the early twentieth century. The collection is so huge that only 2 percent to 3 percent of the holdings are on display at any time; selections are changed regularly.

Freer Gallery of Art, Smithsonian Institution
Photo by Freer Gallery of Art/John Tsantes

The American collection features paintings and other works by James McNeill Whistler, including *Harmony in Blue and Gold: The Peacock Room*, a dining room decorated by Whistler for a London patron—the room was dismantled and shipped to the museum in 1919.

There are also small holdings of ancient Egyptian and early Christian art.

The Freer's treasures include an extensive collection of Japanese folding screens; ancient Chinese jades and bronzes and more contemporary paintings, calligraphy, ceramics, and lacquer objects; Korean ceramics; Persian manuscripts and Islamic artwork; paintings from the Hindu, Jain, and Muslim religious traditions of India; and the Washington Manuscript of the Gospels, made in Egypt in the late fourth or fifth century.

Charles Freer began a collection of Asian art in 1895 and added works by American artists he felt complemented those pieces. His gift to the nation in 1905 included 9,000 pieces and funds to create a building to house them.

The Freer Gallery was designed by American architect and landscape planner Charles A. Platt with work completed in 1928. Constructed in the Italian Renaissance style with a central courtyard, it uses pink Massachusetts granite and Tennessee marble for much of its detail. The front of the museum facing the Mall is derived from the Palazzo del Te, built 1524–1534 in Mantua, Italy.

Hirshhorn Museum and Sculpture Garden

Independence Avenue at Seventh Street SW. Metro: L'Enfant Plaza or Smithsonian. Daily 10 A.M.–5:30 P.M.; sculpture garden open from 7:30 A.M. to dusk. Tours are offered at 10:30 A.M. and noon Monday through Friday, and at noon and 2 P.M. on weekends. Sculpture Garden tours are offered at 12:15 P.M. Monday through Saturday in May and October, weather permitting. Free. (202) 357-2700. Recorded information, (202) 357-2020. You can consult a web page at www.si.edu/organiza/museums/hirsch/start.htm.

There is nothing ordinary about this museum, from its in-your-face design (some call it the "Doughnut on the Mall") to the works of modern art on display.

Joseph H. Hirshhorn (1899–1981) was a self-made millionaire financier and uranium mining magnate. He built a private holding of more than 6,000 works of art in forty years of collecting. He gave his collection to the nation in 1966.

Opened in 1974, the museum and sculpture garden was designed by Gordon Bunshaft of the architectural firm of Skidmore, Owings and Merrill. Bunshaft was also responsible for the renowned Lever House in New York City, built in 1952.

The 232-foot, three-story hollow drum of a building rests on four massive piers rising above a central courtyard and walled plaza.

The building's textured exterior surface is composed of pulverized pink granite aggregate exposed by sandblasting; Bunshaft's original plan for pink travertine was unfulfilled because of budgetary constraints and federal laws limiting the import of materials for government buildings.

The collection contains some 12,000 pieces, including 5,000 paintings, 3,000 sculptures and mixed-media pieces, and 4,000 works on paper. About 600 objects are on display in the gallery, plaza, and garden at any one time.

Among artists represented in the collection are Constantin Brancusi, Alexander Calder, Edgar Degas, Alberto Giacometti, Henri Matisse, Henry Moore, and Auguste Rodin. Modern-day paintings held by the museum include Francis Bacon, Balthus, Willem de Kooning, Jean Dubuffet, Edward Hopper, and Piet Mondrian.

The sculpture garden features the largest American collection of Henry Moore sculptures and Rodin's *Monument to the Burghers of Calais.*

The museum is one of the most-popular art museums in North America, with an average of more than 900,000 visitors per year.

Full Circle, an outdoor café, is open for lunch in the summer.

WOW National Air and Space Museum

601 Independence Avenue at Seventh Street SW. Metro: L'Enfant Plaza or Smithsonian. Daily 10 A.M.–5:30 P.M. Tours depart daily at 10:15 A.M. and 1 P.M. from the desk in Gallery 108. Free. Tickets for Langley Theater IMAX films and Einstein Planetarium adult $5; child ages 2–21 and senior 55 and older $3.75. (202) 357-2700. www.nasm.si.edu/.

The history of flight is, literally, one of the most uplifting accomplishments of modern civilization, and one area in which America's successes have been mostly undiminished.

For that reason, and because of its own soaring design, the National Air and Space Museum zoomed from its opening in 1976 to become the most popular institution in Washington, drawing between eight million and nine million visitors a year. In fact, it's the most popular museum in the world.

There are twenty-three exhibition areas; eight are essentially unchanged from the 1976 opening of the museum. In a typical year, one or two galleries are changed.

The museum is in the midst of a massive project to replace every skylight and window; until sometime in 2001, two or three galleries will be closed at any one time while work is underway. Call the information number for specific closures at the time of your visit.

Nearly all of the aircraft and spacecraft on display in the museum are real—veterans of actual flights or vehicles used as backup. Aircraft at the Smithsonian are usually restored to exhibition quality but not to flying condition. If they were brought to original "specs," they would require new parts, which would violate the museum's charter to treat all parts as artifacts.

Treasures on display include the Wright brothers' 1903 *Flyer I*, Charles Lindbergh's *Spirit of St. Louis*, Amelia Earhart's Lockheed 5B Vega, the high-flying X-15 spy plane, and John Glenn's Mercury spacecraft. Suspended high above the lobby is *Voyager*, the lightweight aircraft that flew around the world in December of 1986 without stopping or refueling. Other galleries include the history of military aviation.

As you enter from the Mall you'll walk directly to the Apollo 11 command module *Columbia*, used on the first manned lunar landing mission. In July of 1969, the spacecraft carried Neil Armstrong, Edwin "Buzz" Aldrin, and Michael Collins to the moon. This is the same type of spacecraft used in the ill-fated Apollo 13 mission.

The lunar rock sample near the Mall entrance was cut from a rock picked up from the surface of the moon by the crew of Apollo 17 in December of 1972. The very hard, fine-grained basalt rock was produced by volcanic activity and is estimated to be nearly four billion years old. It has been touched by tens of millions of human hands since its installation at the museum.

From 1996 through the end of 1998, the museum displayed the *Enola Gay* B-29 bomber that dropped the world's first atomic bomb on Hiroshima, Japan.

The 99-foot-long plane, with a wingspan of 141 feet and a top speed of 375 miles per hour, was the largest plane ever restored by the Smithsonian.

The *Enola Gay* exhibit moved out in late 1998; it is scheduled to be reassembled—in a larger and more extensive display—at the museum's new facility at Dulles Airport when it opens sometime in late 2001. Also on display at the new facility will be a Space Shuttle and an SR–71 Blackbird spy plane.

Planners hope the new facility will draw as many as three million visitors per year.

Among recent acquisitions of the museum was the gondola capsule of the *Breitling Orbiter 3*, the craft that completed the first non-stop circumnavigation of the world by balloon. The *Breitling Orbiter 3*, piloted by Bertrand Piccard and Brian Jones, began its historic flight on March 1, 1999 from Château d'Oex in the Swiss Alps. The official completion of the trip around the world occurred March 20, 1999 over Mauritania, North Africa. The team landed the next day in Egypt.

Other favorite galleries include Air Transportation, which displays the early days of passenger and cargo service; shown are a Pitcairn Mailwing, Northrop Alpha, Ford Trimotor, Fairchild FC-2, Grumman G-21, Boeing 247-D, and Douglas DC-3.

In the Jet Aviation gallery are craft from the first forty years of jet aviation (1939–79), including the world's first operational jet fighter, the Messerschmitt Me 262, a Lockheed XP-80, and a McDonnell FH-1 Phantom.

Space Hall contains large rockets, guided missiles, and manned spacecraft, including the Skylab Orbital Workshop, the Apollo–Soyuz joint spacecraft, and a model of the Space Shuttle. The Lunar Exploration Vehicles include models of the Apollo Lunar Module, Lunar Orbiter, Surveyor, and Ranger.

The Apollo to the Moon gallery tells the story of U.S. manned space flight from Project Mercury through Apollo 17. Artifacts include the Mercury Freedom 7 and Gemini 7 spacecraft, the Skylab 4 command module, and the Lunar Roving Vehicle.

The Golden Age of Flight is one of the little secrets of the museum, packed with lots of very interesting artifacts from the early days of flight, including all sorts of trophies from races. There are some racing planes on display.

The Langley Theater shows a series of spectacular IMAX wide-screen movies including *To Fly!*, which takes viewers from an 1800s balloon ascension to a flight in space, along with a trip with the U.S. Navy's Blue Angels, a hitchhike on a hang glider off the coast of Hawaii, and more; *Mission to Mir* is an unusual view of life aboard Russia's giant 130-ton, six-module space station. Special offerings of classic IMAX and standard films are offered on many weekend evenings. For information on presentations, call (202) 357-1686.

My favorite film is *The Dream Is Alive*, which tells the story of one mission on the Space Shuttle. One incredible scene shows two American astronauts, one male and one female, knocking on the outside windows of the Space Shuttle.

A spectacular IMAX film, *Cosmic Voyage*, takes viewers on an exploration of

Air time. The Wright brothers' 1903 *Flyer I*, which is on display at the Air and Space Museum made the first powered, manned, controlled flight of a heavier-than-air craft near Kitty Hawk, North Carolina, on December 17, 1903.

Rocket science. For twenty-nine years, from 1916 to 1945, the Smithsonian was associated with Robert H. Goddard, considered the father of the liquid-fuel rocket. The Smithsonian provided funding for his early research and published his major articles.

*Astronauts set foot on the moon at the
National Air and Space Museum; this display
was a NASA prototype.*

Photo by Corey Sandler

time and space. The film includes a "cosmic zoom" that extends in an unbroken sequence from the surface of the Earth to the largest observable structure in the universe and then down to the subnuclear realm, a guided tour across forty-two orders of magnitude.

Narrated by actor Morgan Freeman, the thirty-five-minute film presents the latest scientific information on the formation and structure of our universe in a breathtaking blend of live-action footage and cutting-edge computer animation. At one end of the tour, you'll "observe" the Big Bang that is credited with the creation of our universe, and at the other, the incredible tiny universe that exists on the submicroscopic level.

The zoom portion of the universe begins appropriately in Venice, Italy, where Galileo Galilei developed the telescope more than 400 years ago. Then we all take a step out into space—a mere ten meters away—and then farther and farther; after twenty-six steps, we are at the outer edge of space some fifteen billion light years from Earth. Continuing the tour, we retrace our steps to touch down in the Dutch town of Delft, home of Antonie van Leeuwenhoek, who developed the microscope. There we go inward, into the living kingdom of a drop of water, and from there into the minuscule world of electrons, protons, and neutrons—the building blocks of all matter. Our tour ends with a computer's vision of a quark, the smallest known particle.

The best seats in the IMAX theater are in the middle of the steep rows of seats—rows J, K, and L—which places you more or less in the center of the huge screen.

The Einstein Planetarium presents three programs daily. The Stars Tonight is a free presentation each afternoon that shows highlights of the current night sky. The remainder of the day includes admission-charge presentations of Universe of Illusions, which explores some of the anomalies of space including black holes and wandering planets, and The New Solar System, a multimedia program that takes the audience on a tour of solar system neighbors as if they were carried on the nucleus of a comet.

The planetarium uses a Zeiss VI projector, a bicentennial gift to the people of the United States from the people of the Federal Republic of Germany. The device projects about 9,000 stars onto the planetarium's 70-foot dome, accurately simulating the apparent movements of the sun and the Earth's five closest planetary neighbors.

Other planetarium shows include New Solar System, a breathtaking trip from faraway Pluto to the blazing sun, and Sky Quest, a family-oriented voyage to the stars through the eyes of a young girl.

Part of the celebration of the museum's twentieth anniversary saw the opening of the How Things Fly gallery, an interactive introduction to the scientific principles of aviation and spaceflight. Among the displays is a Cessna 150 cockpit that visitors can enter, with controls they can use to move the elevators, ailerons, and rudder. Other highlights are a remote-control blimp and five wind tunnels, including a supersonic tunnel. As part of the gallery, the museum debuted its corps of "Explainers," college students who answer questions about the principles of flight, conduct demonstrations, and assist in operating interactive displays.

Another impressive exhibition is Space Race, which focuses on the half-century-long contest for supremacy in space that arose out of the Cold War between the United States and the Soviet Union. Among objects never before shown in a public museum is a formerly "top secret" camera from the world's first spy satellite and a collection of rarely seen American and Soviet space hardware, including the spacesuit built for the never-accomplished mission to land a Russian on the Moon.

Plan on spending several hours or more at the museum. The best time to visit is probably mid-January to mid-February. The busiest season runs from Easter and Spring Break to Labor Day, with typical crowds of 30,000 visitors and more on weekends. Any holiday period is sure to draw crowds, and the busiest single day of the year is typically Black Friday (the day after Thanksgiving), when as many as 70,000 visitors are usually welcomed. The museum's single-day attendance record was 118,437 on April 14, 1984.

Museum galleries open at 10 A.M., but visitors are permitted into the lobby area at 9:45 A.M.; enter at that time and buy IMAX tickets and pick up passes for any special exhibitions. The museum is almost the busiest place in town, but you'll find relative quiet in the period between Columbus Day and Thanksgiving.

The Museum Shop is an extraordinary collection of books and items related to aviation, space, and science. On the second floor is **Flight Line** cafeteria, a popular spot for a light lunch, and **The Wright Place**, a full-service restaurant.

Outside the museum are several interesting sculptures, including *Ad Astra* by Richard Lippold, symbolizing mankind's conquest of space; *Continuum* by Charles O. Perry; and *Delta Solar* by Alejandro Otero, a bicentennial gift from the government of Venezuela.

The museum itself was designed by Gyo Obata, who credited John Russell Pope's National Gallery of Art as an influence to his plan.

And finally, if you haven't seen enough, you might want to make a trip to the National Air and Space Museum's reserve collection of historically significant aircraft and spacecraft at the Paul E. Garber Preservation, Restoration, and Storage Facility in Suitland, Maryland. Visits are by appointment through the National Air and Space Museum. See the information about the Garber facility in the Maryland section of this book.

WOW National Museum of African Art

950 Independence Avenue, between Seventh and Twelfth Streets SW. Metro: Smithsonian. Open daily 10 A.M.–5:30 P.M. Free. (202) 357-4600. www.si.edu/organiza/museums/africart/nmafa.htm.

The only national art museum dedicated to the collection and exhibition of African art. Treasures include wood, metal, ivory, textile, and ceramic items. The Eliot Elisofon Photographic Archives has a collection of hundreds of thousands of prints and transparencies and miles of film and video on African art. The Warren M. Robbins Library, named for the museum's founder, has 20,000 volumes.

Founded in 1964 as a private institution, the museum became a bureau of the Smithsonian in 1979 and moved to its modernistic, mostly underground home on the National Mall, behind the main Smithsonian building, in 1987.

The entrance to the museum, located behind the Smithsonian Castle, is through a small pavilion somewhat like an African adobe in design; architect Carlhian, who also designed the Arthur M. Sackler Gallery and pavilion in the same compound, borrowed as well from the semicircular arches of the Freer Gallery in his design.

Among the items on display are traditional African masks. In many parts of West and Central Africa, masks are used in rituals of daily life and in supplication for harvests and fertility. Masked dancers are often intended to represent ancestral or natural spirits.

An important permanent exhibition at the museum is The Ancient West African City of Benin, A.D. 1300–1897, a replication of the items from the royal court of the capital of the Kingdom of Benin before British colonial rule. On display are images of kings and attendants in sculptures, figures, and plaques.

The ancient Nubian city of Kerma flourished from 2500 to 1500 B.C. in what is now Sudan. Objects in the exhibition were excavated between 1913 and 1916 by an expedition mounted by the Museum of Fine Arts in Boston.

According to the museum, the leader of the expedition, George A. Reisner, though famed for his technique and observations, completely misunderstood his finds in Kerma. The material wealth and evidence of an Egyptian presence convinced him that Kerma was the site of a remote Egyptian trading post and fort in Nubia. Modern researchers have concluded that Kerma was the center of a highly sophisticated Nubian civilization and the capital of the state ruled by a line of powerful kings heavily involved in trade with Egypt.

The city now known as Kerma—its original residents used no writing, and its ancient name is not known—was almost certainly the capital of the ancient Nubian kingdom known as Kush, which is mentioned frequently in ancient Egyptian texts. It was located about thirty to forty days travel by caravan to Aswan.

Kerma was the focal point of overland trade routes linking central Africa with Egypt, supplying the pharaohs with gold, exotic woods, ivory, animal products, precious stones, rare oils, aromatic resins, and more. Kerma itself grew wealthy, and its rulers acquired expensive tastes and imperial aspirations. About 1700 B.C., Kerma extended its political and military influence northward to the borders of Egypt, and by 1570 B.C. the Egyptian pharaohs made war against them. The Egyptians eventually conquered Kush and burned Kerma.

Other interesting exhibits include extraordinary personal utensils from African life, such as beer straws of the Ganda people from Uganda collected in 1882, hair ornaments, spoons carved out of bone fragments, and snuff spoons from the Zulu people of South Africa.

The museum's gift shop has some very unusual offerings, including jewelry, fabric, and artwork.

National Museum of American Art *(Reopens in 2003 as the Smithsonian American Art Museum)*
Eighth and G Streets NW. Metro: Gallery Place. Daily 10 A.M.–5:30 P.M. Guided tours 11 A.M. and noon weekdays, 2 P.M. weekends. Free. (202) 357-2700. www.nmaa.si.edu.

The oldest national art collection, the museum is located in the Old Patent Office Building, the fourth-oldest public building in Washington. The only older official buildings in the capital are the White House, the U.S. Capitol, and the Treasury Building.

The building, also home to the National Portrait Gallery, closed in 2000 for extensive renovations; it is scheduled to reopen in 2003 with a new name: the Smithsonian American Art Museum.

Nearly 500 of the treasures of the permanent collection, gathered in eight shows, will be on loan to more than seventy museums, including the Renwick Gallery in Washington.

The $60 million renovation will include restoration of the exterior masonry and interior, plus replacement of heating, air-conditioning, electrical and plumbing systems.

A new entrance and lobby at Eighth and F Streets will introduce visitors to the art and portrait gallery collections. Approximately 60,000 square feet will become available for new galleries and public areas when the library and the staff move permanently to the Victor Building, located at Ninth and H Streets N.W. That structure, acquired by the Smithsonian Institution, will also house a new American Art Center offering resources for educators, researchers and the general public.

The museum's building is among the most interesting in town. The Patent Office was completed in 1840, replacing the original structure, which had been destroyed by fire. The Greek Revival design included porticoes very closely based upon the Parthenon in Athens. Sandstone came from the Aquia Creek quarries in Virginia, once owned by George Washington. When three wings were added to the building in 1867, it was for a while the largest building in the country.

After several particularly bloody battles of the Civil War, including Antietam, Second Bull Run, and Fredericksburg, a makeshift hospital was set up and 2,000 beds were installed in and among the display cases of the Patent Office. Among those who came to minister to the wounded was Clara Barton, a Patent Office clerk and founder of the American Red Cross. The First Rhode Island Militia set up barracks in the north wing.

The eastern hall of the building—now known as the Lincoln Gallery—was used for President Lincoln's second inaugural ball on March 6, 1865.

In the 1950s, after the Patent Office and other government agencies that used the building had moved on to other sites in Washington, the building came close to being demolished. Instead, though, it was decided to restore the building, and it opened in 1968 as a Smithsonian museum.

The 264-foot-long Lincoln Gallery is one of the most spectacular museum rooms in America, with thirty-two marble pillars rising to a vaulted ceiling.

WOW National Museum of American History

Fourteenth Street and Constitution Avenue NW. Metro: Smithsonian or Federal Triangle. Daily 10 A.M.–5:30 P.M.; extended summer hours sometimes offered. Free. (202) 357-2700. www.si.edu/organiza/museums/nmah/nmah.htm.

The appropriately eclectic holdings include Thomas Edison's phonograph, Judy Garland's ruby slippers from *The Wizard of Oz*, a massive steam locomotive and the relatively tiny John Bull steam engine, a World War II "Enigma" cryptographic decoder, a collection of inaugural ball gowns, Native American artworks, and gallery after gallery of fascinating stuff. In all, the museum is responsible for the collection and preservation of more than sixteen million artifacts, including fourteen million stamps housed in the National Postal Museum near Union Station.

The Smithsonian's collection of historical items dates back to its founding, with early galleries in the Smithsonian Castle and the Arts and Industries building. The National Museum of History and Technology opened in 1964 as the fifth Smithsonian building on the National Mall; it was one of the last buildings designed by the renowned architectural firm of McKim, Mead, and White. In 1980, the museum's name was changed to the National Museum of American History. Today, nearly six million visitors enter its doors each year.

The conservative exterior of the building is considered a Beaux-Arts design, somewhat echoing the Lincoln Memorial. The simplicity of the outside is not repeated inside, though, and some visitors find the sprawling museum a jumble of galleries that have no obvious path through them.

You can enter the museum from the Mall on Madison Street at the second-floor level, or at the first-floor level from the Constitution Avenue side.

Near the Mall entrance is a stainless steel Mobius Strip sculpture *Infinity*, by Jose de Rivera. As you enter into the museum on this floor you are literally stopped by the Foucault pendulum, which moves in its slow arc all day. In 1851, French physicist J. B. Foucault used a pendulum to demonstrate the rotation of the earth around its axis. The museum's pendulum has a hollow 240-pound brass bob suspended from the ceiling of the fourth floor by a 54-foot steel cable. Because we are standing on the earth and moving with the planet beneath our feet, it seems as if the pendulum is moving and the earth is standing still.

During the eight hours of a business day, the bob passes through about seventy degrees of the compass rose mark on the floor. There is, of course, no such thing as a perpetual motion machine, and the swing of the pendulum is assisted slightly by a ring magnet at the top of the cable that pulses on and off as the cable swings to replace the energy lost because of air resistance and vibration.

The backdrop behind Foucault's pendulum is the original Star-Spangled Banner, the large American flag raised over Fort McHenry near Baltimore in the last hours of the nighttime attack by British Naval forces on September 13, 1814.

It was the sight of the flag by the dawn's early light on the morning of the fourteenth that led Francis Scott Key to write a stirring poem he titled "The Defense of Fort McHenry." It was later renamed "The Star-Spangled Banner" and set to music. It became the national anthem in 1931.

After the War of 1812, the flag was given to Colonel George Armistead, the commander of Fort McHenry; it was in the possession of his family until it was presented to the Smithsonian Institution in 1912.

The John Bull engine in the East Hall is the oldest locomotive in operating condition, and probably the oldest self-propelled vehicle of any type that can still run. It was built in 1831 in England for the Camden and Amboy Railroad of New Jersey. It pulled passengers and freight on the New York to Philadelphia run until 1865.

Preserved by the railroad, it was restored in 1876 so it could be displayed at the Centennial Exposition in Philadelphia. In 1885, it was given to the Smithsonian where it has been maintained. It last ran on its own power on September 15, 1981, on the Georgetown branch of the B & O Railroad to commemorate its 150th year.

Other displays at the museum include a Conestoga wagon from the early nineteenth century used to haul freight and products across southern Pennsylvania and Maryland. These wagons were being made as early as 1715 near Conestoga Creek in southeastern Pennsylvania; most required a team of four to six horses. The driver either walked, rode the left horse nearest the wagon, or sat on a "lazy board" that projected from the left side of the wagon.

A trip to this museum is not complete without standing in the shadow of the massive Pacific Locomotive in the ground-floor Railroad Hall. Built in 1926, it stands nearly fourteen feet tall; the driving wheels alone are more than six feet in diameter.

Moving experience. The Pacific Locomotive was moved from Alexandria, Virginia, by rail to tracks about ten blocks away from the museum at Sixth and C streets. Two wrecking cranes lowered it over an embankment onto a special tractor trailer, and it was moved by road during the night of November 25, 1961, to the museum grounds. The locomotive was lifted onto tracks installed outside the museum and then moved through an opening in the window. Once inside, the train was swung onto a temporary turntable and moved to its current position.

The 281-ton behemoth could haul 14-car passenger trains at about 80 miles per hour. It continued in service until 1951.

Also on display in the Railroad Hall is an 1888 cable car from the Yesler Way Line, part of the Seattle City Railway. The car is typical of cars used on cable railways in San Francisco, Cincinnati, Chicago, New York, and other cities.

Nearby is a gallery that showcases some of the great achievements in civil engineering, including the story of the great Hoosac Tunnel, blasted from 1854 to 1876 in western Massachusetts through five miles of solid rock in the Hoosac Mountains, at a cost of nearly 200 lives.

In a back hallway you can find the famed Enigma device that was used to secretly decode intercepted German and then Japanese secret messages during World War II.

Outside the Palm Court restaurant is a section of a Horn and Hardart Automat. These restaurants, common in New York and Philadelphia, featured coin-operated vending machines that offered hot and cold foods prepared in a kitchen behind the scenes. The first Automat, purchased in Germany for $30,000 by Joseph Horn and Frank Hardart, was installed in 1902 in Philadelphia.

The museum's Archives Center includes documents related to the life and career of American composer and jazz musician Duke Ellington. The History of American Entertainment Collection surveys popular entertainment in the United States. In addition to the aforementioned "Oz" slippers (and Ray Bolger's Scarecrow costume), the museum possesses armor from the 1926 version of *Ben Hur* and costumes from *Auntie Mame* and *Superman*.

You may also see the hat worn by Jimmy Durante during the last ten years of his life, Ted Knight's blue blazer from "The Mary Tyler Moore Show," Henry Winkler's "Fonz" leather jacket from "Happy Days," Bozo the Clown's costume, the ape masks used by comic Ernie Kovacs and his Nairobi Trio, a "phaser" from "Star Trek," and the chairs used by Archie and Edith Bunker on "All in the Family."

Items from popular performers include bow ties worn by Frank Sinatra, a baton used by composer and band leader John Philip Sousa and a uniform worn by a member of his band, backdrops and other 1920s–1940s memorabilia from the Palace Burlesque Theater of Buffalo, New York, and the baseball diamond backdrop used by Abbott and Costello in their "Who's on First?" routine. Animation holdings include six original pencil drawings made for Walt Disney's first Mickey Mouse cartoon, *Steamboat Willie*, in 1928.

The National Numismatic Collection, the official repository for the United States Mint, holds about a million objects, including U.S. and foreign coins, medals, paper money, and tokens, as well as coins from the Medieval, Byzantine, and Roman Republic eras. Unique objects in the collection include the large stone money of Yap, shell wampum, and beaver pelts used as currency in North America.

The Division of Agriculture and Natural Resources' vast collection of objects traces the growth and development of the nation's farming, fishing, forestry, and mining industries. Artifacts include a collection of nineteenth-century plows, featuring a John Deere plow from 1837, an 1886 Holt combine, steam traction engines, and an early twentieth-century cotton gin. You'll also find a collection of whaling harpoons and fleshing knives.

The Division of Armed Forces History's collections consist of more than 110,000 objects, including uniforms, firearms, ship models, and more.

The Division of Biological Sciences, one of the newer divisions of the museum, collects research instruments, laboratory and field apparatus, and educational materials of the biological sciences. Concentrations include genetics, molecular biology, reproductive physiology, and cell culture. Holdings include microscopes and corn samples from the cytogenetics laboratory of Barbara McClintock, who won the Nobel Prize in 1983; apparatus used by physiologists Gregory Pincus and Min Chu Chang in their research on the birth-control pill; early commercial versions of the ultracentrifuge and electrophoresis instruments; and prototypes of the gene gun and polymerase chain reaction thermal cyclers now widely used in DNA studies.

The Division of Computers, Information, and Society collects objects and documents relating to the history of computing, mathematics, and information technology. The collection includes devices from the abacus to the hand-held calculator, to computers and computer software.

The Division of Medical Sciences has a broad collection of objects that include drugs, laboratory equipment, medical and dental devices, and more from medicine, pharmacy, dentistry, and public health.

The Division of Physical Sciences holds items such as instruments used by Andrew Ellicott and Benjamin Banneker to lay out plans for the Federal City, the 13-inch refracting telescope used by Maria Mitchell and her students at Vassar College, America's first plastic object, and the machine that produced the world's first commercial nylon thread.

The Hall of American Maritime Enterprise depicts three centuries of ocean and river commerce with photographs, objects, material from shipwrecks, films, and models of sailing ships and steamships; and it features dioramas and period settings representing the whaling industry, a colonial warehouse, a ship's engine room of about 1930, a tattoo parlor, a maritime insurance office, and a modern river towboat pilothouse.

The Road Transportation Hall displays about forty important vehicles, including carriages, bicycles, automobiles, motorcycles, trucks, and buses. Vehicles in the collection include an 1866 Dudgeon, an 1893 Duryea, a 1903 curved-dash Oldsmobile, a 1913 Ford Model T, and a 1929 Miller Indianapolis racing car.

The Division of Ceramics and Glass has a collection of about 30,000 artifacts, including American red earthenware, common in seventeenth- to nineteenth-century kitchens and taverns; American stoneware; and European ceramics and Chinese porcelain of the type that was marketed in this country in its early years. The American glass collection includes Tiffany art glass from the late nineteenth and early twentieth centuries.

The Division of Community Life collects items that relate to popular and ethnic cultures in the United States. The largest segment in the ethnic collection covers the lives of Hispanic Americans as seen in Latin America and the U.S. Southwest. Other holdings include the African-American, German-American, Gypsy-American, Asian-American, and Arab-American traditions.

The popular collections include sports uniforms and equipment; motion picture, radio, television, theatrical, and circus posters; costumes and props; American puppets and puppetry items; phonograph records and sheet music; gambling devices such as pinball and slot machines; and much more. Holdings include an 1879 bandstand from Jacksonville, Illinois; an 1890 confectionery; and a 1930s beauty parlor.

The Division of Costume holds some 10,000 garments and 19,000 accessories and pieces of jewelry. In "The Ceremonial Court," some of the museum's collection of art deco jewelry is displayed.

The Division of Domestic Life collects wooden and metal furniture and household object and toys, from the seventeenth century to the present.

The Division of Graphic Arts, one of the oldest specialties at the museum, has more than 45,000 objects, including prints, drawings, and tools documenting the history and technology of printing and printmaking. The print collection dates from the fifteenth century, and significant holdings include some 150 wood engravings and woodcuts by Alexander Anderson and his school, and nearly fifty wood engravings by Timothy Cole. The division also possesses the early eighteenth-century Benjamin Franklin press, the first Harris offset press of 1906, and other important devices.

Drawings in the collection include some 13,000 pattern drawings for type matrices from the American Type Founders Company of New York, representing about 100 type families, and a collection of cartoon drawings by American artists such as Rube Goldberg and Walt Disney.

The Division of Musical History collects musical instruments and materials about the development of musical styles; the division also produces live concerts, radio broadcasts, and recordings, including some that use restored instruments from the collection. The collection began when a trainload of objects was presented to the Smithsonian Institution after the Philadelphia Centennial Exposition of 1876. In addition to a large group of old keyboards, the collection boasts a wide variety of stringed instruments (including violins, viola da gambas, cellos, guitars, and lutes), wind instruments, traditional American folk instruments (banjos, dulcimers, and other Appalachian instruments), and a growing collection of automatic, electronic, and electric instruments.

Some recently acquired treasures are a Steinway concert grand piano used by Paderewski on his American tour in 1892, a 1701 violoncello by Stradivari, a gold-and-platinum flute, and a theremin and a Rhythmicon from the beginnings of electronic music.

The Division of Photographic History studies the worldwide history of the technology and practice of photography from its invention in 1839 to the present. The museum holds some 150,000 photographic images, including many early tintypes and daguerreotypes, and 12,000 pieces of apparatus are stored elsewhere. Artists represented include Mathew Brady, Alfred Stieglitz, Ansel Adams, and Richard Avedon.

The Division of Political History maintains nearly 100,000 objects related to presidential and First Ladies history, political campaigning, the White House, civil rights, women's suffrage, and labor history. "We the People," which opened in 1987, commemorates the American Bicentennial of the U.S. Constitution with posters, cartoons, photographs, banners, and of course, buttons. The division collects and preserves inaugural gowns from First Ladies.

The showplace restaurant is the **Palm Court**, a re-creation of a nineteenth-century ice cream parlor. The restaurant offers a selection of moderately priced sandwiches and salads, as well as some spectacular ice cream sundaes and sodas.

【WOW】 National Museum of Natural History

Constitution Avenue at Tenth Street NW. Metro: Smithsonian. Daily 10 A.M.–5:30 P.M.; later hours in summer in some years. Free. (202) 357-1300. www.mnh.si.edu/.

From the Hope Diamond to a ninety-foot-long *Diplodocus* dinosaur skeleton to a creepy Insect Zoo, the Natural History Museum astounds at every turn. The new jewel of the museum is the Hall of Geology, Gems, and Minerals, which includes a walk-through re-creation of a mine.

Opened in 1910 and expanded in 1960 and again in 1976, the museum has more than twenty acres of exhibit halls. The permanent exhibits radiate out from the central rotunda—another spectacular Washington dome. The central hall is also the home of a preserved African bush elephant, the largest and most powerful land animal in today's world; this particular guy stands thirteen feet at the shoulders and weighed about eight tons in life.

Outside the building near the Mall are a pair of natural sculptures—a massive 2.5 billion-year-old boulder of banded iron ore from Michigan's Upper Peninsula and two large petrified logs from Arizona. *Uncle Beazley*, a life-sized replica of a *Triceratops*, stands sentry at the Mall entrance.

Inside the museum, the real dinosaur on display is *Diplodocus longus*, a 145 million-year-old skeleton from the late Jurassic period. The skeleton was collected in 1923 in Utah at what is now Dinosaur National Monument. It took a year to remove the dinosaur's skeleton from the rock, encase the bones in plaster, and haul them in wagons to the railroad. Then it took another seven years to prepare and mount the skeleton for exhibition.

The dinosaur display offers an unusual collection of baby dino skeletons. Another interesting display is a geologic map of the United States showing

Cold comfort. In the winter, the National Park Service erects the outdoor National Sculpture Garden Ice Rink between the Museum of Natural History and the National Gallery on the Mall.

the approximate ages of rocks found in the area and indicating which rocks are likely to contain dinosaur skeletons. You can look up your hometown and see whether you are in an area that is likely to have felt the rumble of the dinosaurs.

Other unusual creatures include a *glyptodont*, which became extinct relatively recently, just 23,000 or so years ago. It looks like an armadillo the size of a cow; in fact, the fortress-like animal is related to the modern armadillo.

An exhibit about the seas is lit from above by floodlights that shine through tanks of water, lending a shimmering glow to the flippers, fins, and skeletons that date back as much as sixty-five million years, including an early whale from the late Eocene period thirty-nine million to thirty-seven million years ago. Also on display is a life-sized model of a blue whale created in the 1950s, based on a 92-foot-long female taken by a whaling ship in Antarctic waters in 1926.

The museum's famous collection of mammals of all descriptions includes a number of extinct species and some specimens that have histories of their own. The orangutans above the primate display were put on display in 1882. Former president Theodore Roosevelt donated the rhinoceros and lion specimens in 1909. A large tiger, frozen forever in attack, was shot and given to the museum in 1967 after it killed several people in India.

Other treasures include 530 million-year-old fossils of the Burgess Shale; these were discovered by Smithsonian Secretary Charles D. Walcott in 1910. The Reptiles gallery includes skeletons of many of the great dinosaurs that lived on our planet for about 140 million years until their extinction sixty-five million years ago. Among those on display are *Camptosaurus*, *Stegosaurus*, and *Antrodemus*. Hanging over the gallery is a life-sized model of a *pterosaur*, a flying reptile that had a 40-foot wingspan.

Also shown are a stone head from Easter Island in the South Pacific, artifacts from American-Indian cultures, and a collection of birds from the common to the rare, including a few extinct species such as passenger pigeons and great auks.

Pardon the pun, but the new jewel of the museum is the Janet Annenberg Hooker Hall of Geology, Gems, and Minerals. The collection begins with the famed Hope Diamond, of course, but it goes beyond there, exhibiting more than 7,500 gemstones from half-carat sparklers to 23,000-carat eyepoppers.

The Hope Diamond, weighing in at a whopping 45.52 carats, is the world's largest deep blue diamond. Found in the 1600s in what is now India, scientists estimate the stone is more than a billion years old.

During the centuries, the diamond has crossed oceans and continents and passed from owner to owner, including Louis XIV of France, King George IV of England, and famed collector Henry Philip Hope. It has been stolen and recovered, cut and recut, increasing in real and mythological value. In

1958, jeweler Harry Winston donated the Hope Diamond to the Museum, and it now belongs to the people of the United States. It is displayed on a rotating platform within an armored glass case.

Among other treasures is a deep red diamond, believed to be the only known example of its type, and the 127-carat Portuguese Diamond, the largest cut diamond in the collection.

In addition to the stunning display of cut diamonds and gems of all types mounted in

Hooker Emerald
Photo courtesy of Smithsonian Institution's
National Museum of Natural History

fine jewelry, the exhibit includes a simulation of four important American mines, including a historic zinc mine from Sterling Hill, New Jersey, a semi-precious gem mine in Amelia County, Virginia, a lead mine from the Copper Queen Mine in Bisbee, Arizona, and the Fletcher Mine in Viburnum, Missouri. The goal, according to the museum, is to explain that diamonds don't come from Fifth Avenue.

Another section includes some interesting multimedia displays, including computer simulations that allow you to design your own volcano or earthquake.

The exhibit is one of the most popular in Washington, and lines can build to several hours in the middle of the day; come early or late for the most reasonable queues. You can expect a full tour to take two hours or more; there's a marked "fast track" down the center of the exhibit for visitors who want to hit the highlights.

The reconstruction of the hall was paid for with $13 million in private funds, including a major gift from the woman whose name now adorns the entryway.

Future development at the museum's West Court will include an IMAX theater and a Discovery Center for educational activities.

Hopeful. The Hope Diamond was given its name for Henry Philip Hope of England, a former owner. The stone was given to the Smithsonian in 1959; it was mailed to Washington— the container is on display at the National Postal Museum.

Getting stuffed. The museum has its own taxidermist, who spends a good deal of time restoring old or damaged animal mounts. The skins for the wildlife on display come from dead animals. Underneath are mannequins of papier mâché, wire, and burlap.

The museum mineral shop is nearby. One of the most unusual stores we know of, it has shelves packed with extraordinary geodes, crystals, and rock samples. Many are cut and polished for display or for use as bookends or coffee-table curiosities. I know this place well—my wallet is lighter and my suitcase is heavier each time I visit. (If you make a large purchase, ask to have the items shipped home.)

National Portrait Gallery *(Reopens in 2003)*

Eighth and F Streets NW. Metro: Gallery Place–Chinatown. Daily 10 A.M.–5:30 P.M. Tours are offered on the hour from opening until 3 P.M., and by request. Free. (202) 357-2700. www.npg.si.edu.

Home of some of the faces of American history, the museum (along with its cousin the National Museum of American Art) closed in 2000 for a major renovation. It is due to reopen in 2003.

Treasures include Gilbert Stuart's portraits of George Washington, Edgar Degas's portrait of Mary Cassatt, sculptures and paintings in the Hall of Presidents, a collection of early photographs by Mathew Brady, and the *Time* magazine cover collection.

While it is closed, some of the treasures will travel to museums around the country, plus Europe and Japan.

Other high points of the collection include a rare photograph by Mathew Brady from about 1865 of William Tecumseh Sherman and his six Civil War generals, and a collection of photographs covering the 50-year career of Pulitzer Prize–winning *New York Times* photographer George Tames (1919–1994).

Back to the future. Architect Pierre Charles L'Enfant had planned for a pantheon-like structure to honor the nation's immortals. This was adapted somewhat when the site was used for the Patent Office, although it was said at the time that the nation's genius was embodied in its inventions. The eventual use of the Old Patent Office for a National Portrait Gallery marks a return to a use closer to L'Enfant's original conception.

Among the more interesting paintings are portraits of Pocahontas; a self-portrait by Samuel F. B. Morse from 1812, before he turned from art to electrical inventions such as the telegraph; and nineteenth-century performers such as Edwin Booth (brother of John Wilkes Booth) and John Philip Sousa.

The federal government first began assembling portraits of important Americans in 1859, when Congress commissioned George Peter Alexander Healy to paint a series of the presidents to hang in the White House. It took another century for the establishment of a formal collection.

The collection today comprises more than 7,000 images. With the exception of portraits of the Presidents of the United States, images of other Americans are not made part of the permanent collection until ten years or more after the death of the subject.

The rich collection of the National Portrait Gallery includes Washington, Jefferson, and Lincoln, of course, but also displays photographs and paintings of all manner of people who were important in the lives of Americans.

The museum is in the Old Patent Office, sharing the building with the National Museum of American Art. The story of the Old Patent Office, the fourth-oldest public building in the nation's capital, is detailed in the earlier section about the National Museum of American Art.

The Great Hall of the Portrait Gallery, the largest room in America when it was built for the Patent Office, was originally conceived to display miniature models of patented devices.

It was here that the Declaration of Independence was publicly displayed between 1841 and 1871. The guests at Lincoln's second inaugural ball passed through this room to join the receiving line in what is now known as the Lincoln Gallery. A fire in 1877 damaged other portions of the third floor of the building, and the Great Hall was redone in the American Victorian-Renaissance style to which it has now been restored.

Last stand. On April 10, 1865, President Abraham Lincoln was photographed in the Washington studio of photographer Alexander Gardner. During the printing process, the glass plate cracked and Gardner threw it away after making only one print. The crack appears on the print, running from the top left corner through the president's head.

Lincoln never saw the portrait, and it was the last one he sat for; he was assassinated four days later.

In 1981 the National Portrait Gallery purchased the original "cracked plate" portrait of Lincoln, along with 5,400 other Civil War–era negatives and prints from the descendants of Frederick Hill Meserve, an amateur historian and authority on Lincoln.

The establishment of a national patent system in 1790 was one of the first acts of the new government. The system, largely based on English patent law, required drawings, a written description of the device, and wherever possible a model of the invention. Because of space limitations and the growing complexity of inventions, the requirement for submission of a model was ended after 1880. In 1926, the models were sold after the Smithsonian Institution was allowed to select the most important ones for its collection.

WOW National Postal Museum

2 Massachusetts Avenue NE. Daily 10 A.M.–5:30 P.M. One-hour highlight tours are offered weekdays at 11 A.M., 1 P.M., and 2 P.M., and weekends at 11 A.M. and 1 P.M. Closed Christmas. Free. (202) 357-2700. www.si.edu/organiza/museums/postal/start.htm.

The National Postal Museum's home is on the lower level of the historic City Post Office Building near Union Station.

The building, which served as the Washington Post Office from 1914 through 1986, was considered a marvel of its time and a prime example of Beaux-Arts architecture. It was designed by Daniel Burnham, also responsible for Union Station a few steps away. Together, the two massive buildings frame the U.S. Capitol to the south and form an architectural gateway to the city to the north—the direction official Washington was originally expected to develop.

The post office had an ornate lobby that stood in front of a skylit atrium used for sorting the mail. Modern visitors enter through the restored public hall with the fully opened atrium.

The Postal Museum is a good example of a hands-on gallery, with exhibits that appeal to visitors of all ages. One section is a re-creation of part of the early nineteenth-century Boston Post Road between New York and Boston, 268 miles through the woods following an Indian trail. There are no road signs along the path—look for the notches in the trees to find your way.

Postal oddities include the pneumatic tube mail-delivery service introduced in the 1890s in cities, including Philadelphia, Boston, Brooklyn, New York, Chicago, and St. Louis. Tubes carried packages of as many as 600 letters at thirty-five miles an hour beneath the streets. The system was problematic, though; when cylinders full of mail jammed in underground tubes, sometimes the only way to recover the mail was to dig up the street. The system continued in parts of New York and Boston until the 1950s, though.

The extension of Rural Free Delivery to all parts of the nation helped contribute to the development of the national road system. The first automobile to carry the mail was used in 1902 in Adrian, Michigan. By 1906, rural carriers were permitted to use automobiles and motorcycles, but horse- and mule-drawn wagons were the rule until the 1920s. On display is an unusual mail-delivery vehicle used in New England, a 1926 Ford Model T that has a steel track on the rear drive shaft and sled treads in the front.

You'll also learn that 100 years ago, people feared that the mail could spread germs from one community to another, causing epidemics of cholera, smallpox, and other diseases. When yellow fever broke out in Philadelphia in the summer of 1890, postal officials used a mail paddle to punch small holes in letters and packages, and the mail was then fumigated with heated sulfur vapors.

Also memorialized is Owney, a stray mutt who wandered into the Albany, New York, post office in 1888 and fell asleep on some mailbags. The clerks let him stay, and Owney was soon riding mailbags across the country with the railway mail service. In 1895, he traveled with the mail on steamships to Asia and across Europe. Railway mail clerks adopted Owney as their mascot and began to record the dog's travels with medals and tags attached to his collar; eventually he had so many tags that U.S. Postmaster General John Wanamaker gave him a jacket to display his trophies.

Moving to more modern times, the museum proudly displays the postal uniform worn by actor John Ratzenberger in his role as Cliff Claven in the television sitcom *Cheers*.

Beneath a 90-foot-high atrium three airmail planes are suspended, including a 1911 Wiseman-Cooke, a 1924 De Havilland mail plane, and a 1930s Stinson Reliant. The Reliant was used in 1939 to test a unique airmail service for communities that did not have a landing field. Mail was loaded into a container and then placed on top of a structure resembling a football goalpost. The pilot guided the airplane down over the mail container while the flight officer lowered a grappling hook to snag the container. Mail for the community was then dropped from the plane onto the airfield. The technique was modeled after the railway service's mail-on-the-fly pickups. The Stinson Reliant could operate at about 150 miles per hour with a two-person crew.

On the floor of the museum are artifacts that include a Concord-style mail stagecoach of the type that first appeared in the 1820s and remained in use in the United States well into the early 1900s.

Another exhibition gallery is devoted to the display of select portions of the world's largest and most comprehensive stamp collection. Among items on display are a letter carried by the Bristol Sailing Packet Ship from England to New York in May of 1711 and a "Rarities Vault" of valuable American and Hawaiian philatelic items.

The National Philatelic Collection was established at the Smithsonian in 1886 with the donation of a sheet of 10-cent Confederate postage stamps. Gifts from individuals and foreign governments, transfers from government agencies, and occasional purchases have increased the collection to today's total of more than sixteen million items. In addition to the stamp collection, the museum has postal stationery, postal history material that predates stamps, vehicles used to transport the mail, mailboxes, meters, greeting cards, covers, and letters.

The original stamp collection was located in the Smithsonian's Arts and Industries Building until 1964 when it moved across the Mall to the National Museum of American History and then to the new Postal Museum in 1993.

The museum's new Library Research Center is the world's largest philatelic and postal history research facility with more than 40,000 volumes and manuscripts. It is open to the public by appointment, weekdays 10 A.M.–4 P.M.

Among exhibits at the museum are interactive computer games that permit visitors to become involved in the subject of the postal service. In the Binding the Nation gallery, the "Create-a-Route" game explores the development of postal routes in the 1800s. The game offers four stories that encourage visitors to create an original mail route using topographical maps. In Taking to the Air, visitors discover some of the problems faced by early pilots of the airmail service. Rail, Sail, or Overland Mail asks the player to select a form of transportation and then overcome various obstacles to deliver the mail.

The museum has two shops, the Stamp Store and a Museum Shop.

🌟 National Zoological Park

3001 Connecticut Avenue NW. Metro: Cleveland Park or Woodley Park–National Zoo. L2 and L4 buses stop at the Connecticut Avenue entrance; H2 and H4 buses stop at Harvard Street. From mid-September through April 30, the zoo grounds are open 6 A.M.–6 P.M.; animal buildings are open 10 A.M.–4:30 P.M. From May 1 through September 15, grounds are open 6 A.M.–8 P.M.; animal buildings are open 10 A.M.–6 P.M. Free. Limited parking is available for an hourly fee. (202) 673-4717 or (202) 673-4800 for recorded information. You can also consult www.si.edu/organiza/museums/zoo/npzhome.htm.

Famed landscape architect Frederick Law Olmsted laid out the original design for the National Zoo along a valley cut by Rock Creek in the 1890s. Today, Olmsted Walk is the central pathway of the zoo, and all of the animal trails branch off from it.

The first collection of animals was a small menagerie behind the Smithsonian Institution Building; among its first residents were bison, which were fast disappearing from the American West.

The zoo draws three million visitors per year; it is one of only three major free zoos in the country. Today's stars include Hsing-Hsing, a giant Chinese panda, and Kraken, one of thirteen Komodo dragon lizards that were the first hatchlings ever produced outside their homeland in Indonesia. Hsing-Hsing, alas, has been ailing in recent years; the zoo has hopes of negotiating a lease with the Chinese government to obtain a new pair of pandas.

In the Great Flight Cage, visitors enter into the home of some thirty species of bird. Some other special areas at the zoo are the Great Ape House, Gibbon Ridge, and Amazonia, a large exhibit that permits visitors to enter into a re-creation of an Amazon rain forest.

Special exhibits at the zoo include the Pollinarium, dedicated to the complex interactions between animals and plants; golden lion tamarins, free-roaming in the valley during the summer; the Reptile Discovery Center; and the Orangutan Transportation System, where orangutans swing from building to building on overhead cables.

Animal park. Frederick Law Olmsted (1822–1903) is probably best known as the designer of New York City's huge Central Park. He also designed Prospect Park in Brooklyn, New York, and other parks in Chicago, Boston, Buffalo, and Montreal, as well as the grounds for the 1893 Columbian Exposition in Chicago. He first came to public attention in the 1850s for his travel books, which exposed slaveholding society in the South.

The tamarins are part of a species survival "boot camp" program at the park; they run wild in a protected valley during summer months and are then packed off to Brazil and freedom. At the Pollinarium, watch for hummingbirds (who dive-bomb your head) and butterflies in all of their glorious states. The apes cross over daily about 11 A.M.

In the Think Tank, keepers work with orangutans on a language project. Demonstrations are given as many as ten times a day, generally between 11 A.M. and 2 P.M. Stop by to check the schedule on the white board.

The zoo's lion and tiger areas have been

recently improved. And sometime in 2000, the zoo plans to open a new Grasslands exhibit that will feature American Bison, a prairie dog exhibit, and educational facilities.

Note that the zoo lies between two Metro stops. Going to the zoo, your best bet is to get off at the Cleveland Park station and walk downhill to the zoo entrance. Leaving the zoo, walk downhill to the Woodley Park–National Zoo station.

WOW! Renwick Gallery of the American Art Museum

Seventeenth Street and Pennsylvania Avenue NW. Metro: Farragut West. Daily 10 A.M.–5:30 P.M. Tours are available by appointment; (202) 357-2531. For general information, call (202) 357-2700. Free.

The elegant Renwick Gallery is a work of art by itself, a mid-nineteenth-century French Second Empire–style gallery with a spectacular collection of American craft artists' work.

The gallery was originally designed to house the collections of William Wilson Corcoran when work began in 1858. Construction was halted during the Civil War, and the building was taken over as the headquarters for Montgomery Meigs, the Union Army's quartermaster general. The Corcoran Gallery of Art moved into the completed building in 1874 and remained there until 1897, when it moved into a newer and larger space nearby. The next occupant was the United States Court of Claims, which took possession in 1899 and used the building for the next sxity-five years.

The structure was saved from the wrecking ball in 1965 when it was given to the Smithsonian and renovated; it was renamed at that time in honor of its architect, James Renwick, Jr. The gallery opened in 1972 as part of the National Museum of American Art. Two of the rooms in the present-day gallery have been restored to their former grandeur.

The Grand Salon is a Victorian room of the 1860s and 1870s and is appointed with paintings from the National Museum of American Art.

The Octagon Room was designed to be the showplace for the Corcoran's crown jewel sculpture, *The Greek Slave* by Hiram Powers.

Arthur M. Sackler Gallery

1050 Independence Aveue at Twelfth Street SW. Metro: Smithsonian. Daily 10 A.M.–5:30 P.M. Free. (202) 357-2700. www.si.edu/asia.

A national museum of Asian art, the Sackler Gallery opened in 1987 as the home of some 1,000 pieces of art given by Dr. Arthur M. Sackler, a New York research physician and medical publisher. The gallery is connected to the Freer Gallery of Art via an underground passageway.

Treasures include early Chinese bronzes and jades, Chinese paintings and lacquerware, ancient Near Eastern ceramics and metalware, and sculpture from South and Southeast Asia. Since its opening, the gallery's collections have expanded through purchases and donations and now include the Vever Collection, an assemblage of Islamic illustrated books dating to the eleventh

Arthur M. Sackler Gallery, Smithsonian Institution
Photo by Arthur M. Sackler Gallery/Neil Greentree

century; nineteenth-century Japanese prints; paintings from India, China, Japan, and Korea; arts of rural India; and contemporary Chinese ceramics.

The Sackler Gallery is entered through a small 4,130-square-foot granite pavilion in the Haupt Garden; the rest of the 115,000-square-foot museum is built on three skylit levels and extends fifty-seven feet below ground.

Architect Jean Paul Carlhian used the angles of the Arts and Industries building as his inspiration for the entry pavilion.

A public research library in the Sackler Gallery houses some 60,000 volumes, about half of them in Asian languages; the facility is open to the public. The library archives also preserve photograph and manuscript collections that contain more than 100,000 images.

Smithsonian Castle (Smithsonian Institution Building)

1000 Jefferson Drive at Tenth Street SW. Daily 9 A.M.–5:30 P.M. Free. (202) 357-2700. www.si.edu/organiza/museums/castle/start.htm.

The empire of the Smithsonian Institution is symbolically and actually centered in the landmark Castle on the Mall. Designed in 1855 by 29-year-old self-taught architect James Renwick Jr., the Norman-style structure of red sandstone echoes twelfth-century Romanesque and Gothic styles. Renwick had already proved himself as designer of Grace Church in New York and would later go on to plan St. Patrick's Cathedral in New York, as well as other notable buildings.

The building included a residence for Joseph Henry, the first secretary of the Smithsonian, as well as administrative offices and research facilities. It was used as exhibition space from 1858 until the 1960s. A bronze statue of Henry stands outside on the Mall.

The National Zoological Park had its start at the Smithsonian Institution building in 1889. A photo inside the exhibition area shows buffalo grazing on the grounds of the institution in that year.

Near the north entrance is the crypt of James Smithson, benefactor of the

Institution. Smithson died in Genoa, Italy, in 1829; his remains were brought to the United States in 1904 for reinterment. Among items on display are Smithson's calling card and a piece of smithsonite, a variety of zinc ore he identified in 1802 and that was named for him.

Today, the castle houses the Smithsonian Information Center, the institution's administrative offices, and the Woodrow Wilson International Center for Scholars.

A very useful exhibit within the castle is the large map of the District, with push buttons for most of the major tourist areas. Press a button and a light illuminates on the map showing you where you are and how to get to many important Washington destinations.

The Commons Restaurant in the Castle serves a luncheon buffet daily except Sunday, but is limited to contributing members of the Smithsonian and their guests.

On the Horizon: National Museum of the American Indian

The National Museum of the American Indian in Washington is a museum without walls to hang its art.

The museum's collection of nearly one million objects was assembled over a 54-year period by New York banker George Gustav Heye. The U.S. Congress established the museum in 1989 and decreed that the holdings were to be located in three facilities.

The Heye Center opened in 1994 in the historic Alexander Hamilton U.S. Custom House in New York City; a Cultural Resources Center opened in 1997 in Suitland, Maryland.

The museum hopes to open in 2002 on the last major space in the National Mall, between the Air & Space Museum and the Botanical Gardens below Capitol Hill. However, there have been many delays in funding the project.

Call (202) 357-2700 for additional information.

Chapter 6
Other Museums in Washington

An Excess of Riches

Perhaps the most amazing thing about the museum scene in Washington is this: if there were no such thing as the Smithsonian Institution, the District of Columbia would still be considered home to some of the greatest collections of art and artifacts in the world.

In this chapter, we'll look at thirty-four institutions worth visiting in Washington.

In This Chapter

Kreeger Museum

Martin Luther King, Jr., Memorial Library

Meridian International Center

National Aquarium

 National Building Museum

 National Gallery of Art

National Geographic Society

National Museum of American Jewish Military History

National Museum of Women in the Arts

Octagon Museum

Old Stone House

The Phillips Collection

The Society of the Cincinnati at Anderson House

The Textile Museum

United States Botanic Garden
(Reopens late 2000)

United States National Arboretum

United States Navy Memorial and Visitors Center

U.S. Chess Hall of Fame

Washington Navy Yard and Navy Museum

The Washington Post

Woodrow Wilson House

B'nai B'rith Klutznick National Jewish Museum

1640 Rhode Island Avenue NW. Metro: Farragut North. Sunday to Friday 10 A.M.–5 P.M. Closed Saturday, and Jewish and national holidays. Contributions accepted. (202) 857-6583.

One of the nation's leading collections of Judaica, including ritual and folk-art objects, archeological artifacts, and art.

Among items on display is the 1790 correspondence between George Washington and Moses Seixas, sexton of the Touro Synagogue in Newport, Rhode Island, about religious freedom in the new nation. The collection also includes the Torah binder created to mark the wedding in 1556 of the Finzi and Contini families; the binder holds a Torah scroll from the same century, possibly the oldest in North America. The museum mounts exhibits of art and historical items on Jewish themes and the Holocaust.

Corcoran Gallery of Art

500 Seventeenth Street at New York Avenue NW. Metro: Farragut North or Farragut West. Daily 10 A.M.–5 P.M. except Tuesday. Open Thursday except Thanksgiving until 9 P.M. Closed Christmas and New Year's. Donation: adult $3; student and senior $1; and family groups $5 requested. (202) 639-1700 for recorded information. www.corcoran.org.

The largest privately supported art museum in Washington, it was also the capital's first art museum in 1869 and ranks with Boston's Museum of Fine Arts and New York's Metropolitan Museum of Art as one of the three oldest museums in the United States.

The beauty of the 1897 Beaux-Arts building a block from the White House is surpassed only by the spectacular art within. The private collection was begun by banker William Wilson Corcoran in the 1850s and today includes works by European and American masters such as Degas, Hassam, Homer, Rembrandt, Renoir, and Rubens. The Corcoran's European holdings are based upon two individual collections. The Clark Collection, given to the museum in 1925 by U.S. Senator William A. Clark, includes extensive Dutch, Flemish, and French paintings, as well as the Salon Doré, a transplanted eighteenth-century French period room from the hôtel de Clermont in Paris. The Walker Collection, given by Edward and Mary Walker, includes examples of French art from the late nineteenth and early twentieth centuries. In May of 1996, the museum received a major donation of African-American art from the Evans-Tibbs collection.

The Corcoran's collection of Greek antiquities dates from the eighth to the first centuries B.C.

The Corcoran School of Art, founded in 1890, is one of the few art schools that is directly part of a major museum. The school offers a Bachelor of Fine Arts program, and about 300 full-time students are enrolled each year in fine arts, graphic design, and photography courses.

The **Café des Artistes** at the Corcoran is a favorite eatery for lunch, afternoon tea, and Thursday evening dinner. On Sunday from 11 A.M. to 2 P.M., the museum has a "Jazz Gospel Brunch" featuring local ensembles. Tickets, including admission to the museum and a Creole and traditional buffet, are adult $18.95; child 12 and younger $12.95. Call (202) 639-1786.

Daughters of the American Revolution Museum

1776 D Street at Seventeenth Street NW. Metro: Farragut West. Weekdays 8:30 A.M.–4 P.M.; Sunday 1–5 P.M. Docent-led tours are given between 10 A.M. and 2:30 P.M. Free. *Discount coupon in this book.* (202) 879-3241. www.dar.org.

Several dozen "period rooms" in the grand Beaux-Arts museum are decorated as tributes to the early American states. The Tennessee Room includes furnishings from James Monroe's presidency; the New Hampshire Attic is packed with antique toys and dolls. Artifacts from the Revolutionary War era include silver crafted by Paul Revere.

The museum's Continental Hall includes one of the most extensive genealogical libraries in the country; its resources are available to researchers for a small charge.

The building, with its historically significant address, is also the headquarters for the DAR itself; membership requirements include lineage that dates back to the Revolution.

Decatur House

748 Jackson Place at Connecticut Avenue NW. Metro: Farragut North or Farragut West. Tuesday to Friday 10 A.M.–3 P.M.; Saturday and Sunday noon–4 P.M. Adult $4 senior/student $2.50. (202) 842-0920. www.decaturhouse.org.

Commodore Stephen Decatur settled into a sumptuous new Washington residence across from the White House in 1819; some detractors claim his wealth came from some of the proceeds of freelancing during the Tripolitan War in 1804 (the origin of the line in the Marine Corps Hymn about the "shores of Tripoli"). In the War of 1812, Decatur earned fame for various bold and sometimes reckless feats, including capture of the British frigate *Macedonian*.

Decatur is also known for his famous toast given at Norfolk in 1816: "Our country! In her intercourse with foreign nations may she always be in the right; but our country, right or wrong."

He was mortally wounded in a duel with James Barron in 1820. After he died, his widow Susan Decatur rented the house to a series of distinguished tenants, including French, Russian, and English diplomats. From 1827 until 1835, Decatur House was the unofficial residence of the U.S. secretary of state, housing Henry Clay, Martin Van Buren, and Edward Livingston. The home was purchased by the Beale family in 1871. In 1902, the house was owned by Truxtun Beale, a diplomat; his wife Marie Oge Beale made the home the center of a very active social life.

The elegant Federal-style home was designed by Benjamin Henry Latrobe, an English émigré. He was superintendent for the completion of the U.S. Capitol in 1803 and also designed Saint John's Church in Washington.

Today, the ground-floor rooms of the house are decorated much as they were when it was built by Decatur in 1819; the formal parlors on the second floor are much as they were in the Victorian heyday of the Beales. The home is furnished with nineteenth-century decorative arts, Chinese porcelain, and naval mementos.

The Decatur House is a museum property of the National Trust for Historic Preservation. Jacqueline Kennedy Onassis was credited with helping to save Decatur House and a number of other nineteenth-century buildings around Lafayette Square from destruction to make way for government buildings.

Frederick Douglass National Historic Site

1411 W Street, near Martin Luther King Drive SE. Metro: Anacostia. Daily 9 A.M.–5 P.M. in spring and summer, and 9 A.M.–4 P.M. in fall and winter. Admission adult $3; senior 62 and older $1.50; child younger than 6 free. Call for reservations. (202) 426-5961. www.nps.gov.

The former home of the famed black abolitionist from 1877 until his death in 1895 now offers a visitor center with exhibits and films about his life.

Douglass was born in 1818 as Frederick Augustus Washington Bailey in Talbot County, Maryland. His mother was a slave and his father a white man, perhaps her owner. As a house servant in Baltimore, he secretly taught himself to read and write.

After escaping from slavery in 1838 and moving to New Bedford, Massachusetts, he took the name Douglass from Sir Walter Scott's novel *Lady of the Lake*. He wrote his life story, *Narrative of the Life of Frederick Douglass*, in 1845, and had to move to Europe to escape slave hunters who were alerted to his identity by the book.

Two years later supporters from England purchased his freedom; he moved to Rochester, New York, and founded the *North Star* newspaper, which became one of his platforms to argue for abolition. After President Lincoln's Emancipation Proclamation in 1863, he issued "Men of Color, to Arms!" urging free African Americans to join the Union Army. After the war, he held several government posts, including auditor of the U.S. Treasury.

In 1872, Frederick and Anna Douglass moved to Washington; in 1877, they broke a "whites only" covenant by purchasing "Cedar Hill." Douglass served as the U.S. Marshal of the District of Columbia from 1877 to 1881. In 1881, he published his third autobiography, *Life and Times of Frederick Douglass*. He continued throughout his life to advocate on behalf of blacks and women until his death in 1895.

At times, the National Portrait Gallery has displayed some of the nation's treasures related to Douglass, including the documents drawn up for the purchase of his freedom by his British admirers in the amount of $711.66.

Also shown was a copy of Douglass's weekly newspaper that recounts the arrival of Henry "Box" Brown at Philadelphia in the late 1840s. Brown escaped from slavery hunched up in a cargo box that was sent by commercial shipper from Virginia to Philadelphia. The escape was widely reported, and cartoons showing Frederick Douglass helping to remove the box's lid were widespread, despite the fact that Douglass was not present at Brown's arrival in Philadelphia. In fact, Douglass objected to the publicity, saying that without it there might have been a thousand "Box" Browns a year.

Cedar Hill includes Abraham Lincoln's cane, given to Douglass by Mrs. Lincoln after the assassination; a leather rocking chair from the people of Haiti; and his library. The visitors center includes exhibits and a film about Douglass, and tours of the first floor of Cedar Hill are offered.

Dumbarton Oaks

1703 Thirty-second Street, between Thirty-first and R Streets NW. Georgetown. Collections: Tuesday to Sunday 2–5 P.M.; donations of $1. Gardens: daily (weather permitting). Admission is free. (202) 339-6400, or (202) 339-6401 for recorded information. www.doaks.org.

The spectacular mansion and formal gardens are among the relative secrets of Washington. A nineteenth-century estate, part of the original Port of Georgetown land grant of 1702, had fallen into disrepair when it was purchased in the 1920s by former U.S. Ambassador to Argentina Robert Woods Bliss and his wife, Mildred. Both were independently wealthy. Mrs. Bliss was heir to the Fletcher's Castoria patent medicine fortune.

The estate draws its name from the great oaks that were once common on the property and the Rock of Dumbarton in western Scotland.

During the years Dumbarton Oaks was restored and decorated with fabulous European art and furnishings. The Music Room, added in 1929 and including a sixteenth-century stone chimney piece and an eighteenth-century parquet floor, was the location for many famous performances, and composer Igor Stravinsky wrote the Concerto in E Flat, the "Dumbarton Oaks Concerto," in honor of the Blisses' thirtieth anniversary.

The Blisses conveyed the house, gardens, and collections to Harvard University in 1940.

In 1944, two international meetings known as the Dumbarton Oaks Conferences were held in the Music Room; some of the principles agreed to at the meeting were incorporated in the charter of the United Nations after the end of World War II.

In 1963, architect Philip Johnson designed a museum to house a spectacular collection of Byzantine and pre-Columbian art. The Courtyard includes nomadic bronzes from Asia, Egyptian lamps, and large ancient sculptures. The Textile Gallery displays selections of Byzantine and Islamic fabrics.

Surrounding the house are sixteen acres of formal gardens, including the famous "Pebble Garden Fountain."

Twenty-seven acres of the original estate were given to the nation and now form Dumbarton Oaks Park, controlled by the National Park Service.

Folger Shakespeare Library

201 East Capitol Street, near Second Street SE. Metro: Capitol South. Open Monday to Saturday 10 A.M.–4 P.M. Tours are offered daily at 11 A.M. Free. (202) 544-7077. www.folger.edu.

One of the world's greatest collections of books and manuscripts by and about William Shakespeare, including a copy of the 1623 First Folio, the first collected edition of Shakespeare's plays.

The reading and research rooms are open only to scholars, but the Elizabethan-design Great Hall offers visitors closeup views of original manuscripts and books. The core of the library was endowed by Henry Clay Folger, an American industrialist who died in 1930.

The exterior of the building features nine bas reliefs depicting Shakespearean scenes.

Fondo del Sol Visual Arts Center

2112 R Street NW. Metro: Dupont Circle. Wednesday to Saturday 12:30–6 P.M. Suggested admission adult $3 to $5. (202) 483-2777.

A celebration of the cultural heritage and arts of the Americas, with exhibitions of the works of contemporary artists and a permanent collection of pre-Columbian, folk, and contemporary art. The annual Caribbeana Festival in late summer includes outdoor performances of salsa and reggae.

WOW Ford's Theatre National Historic Site

511 Tenth Street, between E and F Streets NW. Metro: Metro Center. Daily 9 A.M.–5 P.M.; the theater is closed during rehearsals and matinees, but the museum remains open. Free. (202) 426-6924. www.nps.gov/foth.

Few places have such a feeling of history frozen in time as Ford's Theatre, where assassin John Wilkes Booth took the life of President Abraham Lincoln.

John T. Ford was a successful theatrical promoter from Baltimore. In 1861, he expanded to Washington. After fire destroyed his first theater, he built his "New Theatre" in 1863. After the assassination, the theater was closed by the government during the investigation and trial; Ford attempted to reopen the building, but it was closed again because of arson threats. In 1866, the theater was purchased for $100,000 by the government and was used for office space. On June 9, 1893, all three of the interior floors collapsed, killing twenty-two workers. The shell was used for storage until 1932 when the Lincoln Museum opened. It took until 1968 for the building to be fully restored to its original appearance.

The theater has been restored to very much the way it was on April 14, 1865, at about 10:15 P.M., and visitors can view from a short distance the presidential box. Within the compartment is the original red sofa where Major Rathbone was seated and reproductions of the other furnishings. Exhibits include Booth's Derringer pistol and a knife, along with Lincoln's suit. The theater itself is still in use for legitimate theater, with Lincoln's box still overlooking stage left.

The Civil War had officially come to an end just five days before, on April 9, 1865, when General Robert E. Lee surrendered to Union General Ulysses S. Grant at Appomattox Court House, Virginia. As part of the general celebration of the end of the war, President and Mrs. Lincoln and their guests Major Henry Reed Rathbone and his fiancée Clara Harris, daughter of U.S. Senator Ira Harris, attended a performance

Family ties. John Wilkes Booth was an acclaimed Shakespearean actor. His father, Junius Brutus Booth, came to the United States from England in 1821 and was considered the leading tragic actor of his times. His brother, Edwin Booth, was a great success as an actor, surviving the scandal of his family and building Booth's Theatre in New York City, where he was the founder and first president of the Player's Club, an actors' society.

Take out. A few blocks away from Ford's Theatre in what is now Chinatown a plaque on the wall outside a restaurant at 604 H Street identifies the place where the conspirators were said to have plotted the abduction of President Lincoln in 1865.

of a play titled *Our American Cousin* at Ford's Theatre. They were seated in a formal box overlooking the stage.

At about 10:15 P.M., while actor Harry Hawk was alone on the stage, John Wilkes Booth entered the presidential box from the hallway behind. He shot Lincoln, and then stabbed Rathbone who attempted to defend the president.

Booth jumped from the box to the stage, breaking a small bone in his left leg as he landed; he somehow managed to hobble across the stage to an exit where his horse was waiting.

The mortally wounded president was carried across the street to a boarding house, the **Petersen House**, and placed in a back bedroom.

Booth and co-conspirator David Herold hoped to escape to the deep South where they expected a hero's welcome. They were found by Union troops twelve days later near Bowling Green, Virginia. Booth was shot by troops or perhaps by his own hand, and died there. Herold was captured; and he, along with three others, was hanged on July 7, 1865.

WOW House Where Lincoln Died

The Petersen House; 516 Tenth Street NW. Daily 9 A.M.–5 P.M. Free. (202) 426-6924.

One of the simplest and most moving exhibits in Washington is the ordinary guest house across the street from Ford's Theatre where the mortally wounded president was taken to spend his last hours.

The front parlor is known as "Mary's waiting room." Here Mrs. Lincoln spent the night, consoled by actress Laura Kane, star of *Our American Cousin*, and Clara Harris, the Lincolns' guest in the presidential box at the theater.

Through the night Mary Lincoln made regular visits to the small back bedroom where her husband lay dying. On one of her early morning visits, Mrs. Lincoln became hysterical and fell across the body of the dying president. After then she was barred from the room and was not with her husband when he died on April 15 at 7:22 A.M.

The back parlor served as a temporary White House, under the direction of Secretary of War Edwin M. Stanton. Witnesses were interviewed through the night.

The actual room where Lincoln died is a dark back bedroom, barely lit by the two side windows overlooking an alleyway. The room was rented by William T. Clark, a former soldier who was out celebrating the end of the war when Lincoln was brought to the house. Historians note that the bedroom is about the same size as the cabin in which Lincoln was born.

One last note: only in America would the Hard Rock Café be installed next to Ford's Theatre and across the street from where President Lincoln died.

Christian Heurich Mansion

1307 New Hampshire Avenue at Twentieth Street NW. Metro: Dupont Circle. Monday to Saturday 10 A.M.–4 P.M. Tours Wednesday to Saturday noon–3 P.M. on the hour. Adult $3; senior/student $1.50; child younger than 5 free. (202) 785-2068. www.hswdc.org.

The Victorian-Renaissance Dupont Circle mansion of brewer and businessman Christian Heurich is decorated with spectacular examples of Victorian furniture.

Christian and his wife Amelia lived in the 1894 home with their three children and a household staff of butler, cook, housekeeper, upstairs and downstairs maids, nanny, governess, chauffeur, laundress, and gardener. The main hall includes a marble mosaic floor, stucco walls, silver-painted plaster medallions, marble and onyx stairs, and a musicians' balcony. The formal parlor is decorated with French Rococo Revival objects and painted canvas ceilings; original light fixtures combine gas and electric lighting. The basement *bierstube*, or tavern room, includes a painted motto in German that means "Never let yourself be pained by thirst; there is many a keg left in the cellar."

Heurich and a partner purchased the run-down Schnell brewery on Twentieth Street NW, in Washington, in 1872. A year later Schnell died and Heurich married his widow. By 1881, Christian Heurich's Lager Beer Brewery occupied much of a city block. Famed brands produced by the brewery and later moved to Foggy Bottom included Senate and Old Georgetown beer. The brewery reached its peak in 1908, finally closing in 1956; it was demolished in 1961 to make room for the Theodore Roosevelt Bridge and the John F. Kennedy Center for the Performing Arts.

The mansion is now headquarters of the Historical Society of Washington; its library has an extensive collection of books and items related to the city.

Hillwood Museum *(Reopens in Fall of 2000)*

4155 Linnean Avenue, near Tilden Street NW. Metro: Van Ness. Tuesday to Saturday 9 A.M.–4:30 P.M. Tours are by reservation only. Donation requested $10. Children younger than 12 are not admitted. (202) 686-8500. The house and museum were closed in 1999 for a major renovation and will reopen in the fall of 2000 with a new visitors center.

With a fortune born of a cereal empire, Marjorie Merriweather Post invested a lot of money in eggs—Fabergé eggs, that is.

Post's forty-room Georgian mansion is maintained as a museum, showcasing eighteenth- and nineteenth-century French and Russian decorative art. There is also a collection of Native American art and some spectacular formal gardens in the French and Japanese style.

🌟 United States Holocaust Memorial Museum

100 Raoul Wallenberg Place SW. Metro: Smithsonian. Daily 10 A.M.–5:30 P.M., except Yom Kippur (usually in October) and Christmas. Free. (202) 488-0400. www.ushmm.org.

The most overwhelming sensation at the Holocaust museum is *silence*. The quiet weighs heavily, a testament to the emotion that wells up within every visitor. There are stunning videos of the cruelties of the concentration camps and incredible stories of heartbreak and heroism on display, but for many the most chilling exhibits are the mundane: a room full of shoes recovered from a storage area at a death camp and an actual rail car used to transport Jews

Never again. A quote on the wall of the permanent exhibit is attributed to Martin Niemöller (1892–1984), a German pastor who worked against the Nazis: "First they came for the socialists, and I did not speak out because I was not a socialist. Then they came for the trade unionists, but I did not speak out because I was not a trade unionist. Then they came for the Jews, and I did not speak out because I was not a Jew. Then they came for me and there was no one left to speak for me."

to the camps. The path through the museum leads through the wooden door of the rail car, a heart-fluttering experience.

You enter the museum through one of the only flashes of color, a hall of flags of the twenty Allied divisions active in liberating Nazi concentration camps.

The permanent exhibition finishes at the Hall of Remembrance, a circular shrine with an eternal flame; you can light a candle as a token of respect. Outside the hall is a quote from the Old Testament, Deut. 4:9. "Only guard yourself and guard your soul carefully lest you forget the things your eyes saw, and lest these things depart your heart all the days of your life. Then you shall make them known to your children and to your children's children."

A series of very well produced short videos tell the story of anti-Semitism during the centuries, the rise of Adolf Hitler, and eventually the story of Kristallnacht (the "Night of Broken Glass"), which gave rise to the Nazi era. The exhibit leads you to a display of the ark that held the Torah of the synagogue of Mentershausen on Kristallnacht. That night, Nazi sympathizers trashed the temple and defaced the inscription on the ark, "Know before whom you stand."

A section of the museum tells the almost-forgotten story of the voyage of the *St. Louis*. In May 1939, 936 passengers—all but six of whom were Jews seeking to escape the darkening clouds of Nazism—set sail from Hamburg for Cuba; they had Cuban landing certificates when they left, but when the ship reached Havana, Cuban authorities refused to let them disembark. American Jewish groups tried without success to negotiate with Cuban authorities. The *St. Louis* left Cuba and sailed close enough to America so that the passengers could see the lights of Miami, but the U.S. Coast Guard patrolled the waters to make certain no one jumped to freedom. Eventually, the *St. Louis* headed back to Europe, where Belgium, The Netherlands, Britain, and France each accepted some of the refugees; hundreds were later killed during the Holocaust.

Another chilling remembrance of the horrors of the Holocaust is a casting of the famous inscription over the entrance gate to the Auschwitz death camp: "Arbeit macht Frei" ("Work will make you free"). Visitors pass beneath the gates into a section of concentration camp barracks. Just beyond is a collection of Zylon B poison gas canisters; this common and highly poisonous fumigant was used to kill rats and insects until the German SS employed it for the extermination of human beings.

Tickets to the permanent exhibit are usually gone by mid-morning on the weekends and during holiday periods; call the museum to inquire about advance reservations available for a service charge. If you are shut out of the main exhibit, you can still visit the Hall of Remembrance and other changing galleries.

If the purpose of a museum is to move you, to make you understand and think about things you hadn't thought about before, then the Holocaust museum is almost without peer.

Some young visitors may find the displays disturbing. On the main floor of the museum is a display titled "Daniel's Story," which presents the story of the Holocaust through the eyes of a young boy—toned down a bit, it's still an upsetting story. It is certainly something you will want to discuss with your children before and after your visit.

Constructed entirely with private funds, the museum stands on land donated by the federal government; the museum was dedicated in 1993.

Down on the farm. The Holocaust Museum and the Bureau of Engraving and Printing are both within the shadows of the gigantic Department of Agriculture complex. If you ever had any questions about the size of the federal bureaucracy, here's your answer. Now, here's another question most Americans probably cannot answer: What exactly do all of those thousands of bureaucrats do within the Fortress of Agriculture? Hint: there's not a grain of wheat or stalk of corn within sight on Fourteenth Street.

John F. Kennedy Center for the Performing Arts

New Hampshire Avenue at Rock Creek Parkway NW. Metro: Foggy Bottom–GWU. Free tours daily 10 A.M.–1 P.M. by reservation. Box office open Monday to Saturday 10 A.M.–9 P.M.; Sunday noon–9 P.M. (202) 467-4600. www.kennedy-center.org.

A spectacular monument to a fallen president and to the arts in America. Washington's cultural center includes six stages for music, dance, and theater and is home to the National Symphony, the Washington Opera, and the American Film Institute.

The building on the banks of the Potomac was designed by Edward Durell Stone and includes terraces above the river. The design arose out of another Stone building, the smaller U.S. Embassy in New Delhi. The Concert Hall, largest of the six theaters, was completely renovated in 1997 to remove obstructed views, improve access, and fine-tune its acoustics.

The guided tours offer an interesting peek backstage at one of the nation's finest arts palaces.

Kreeger Museum

2401 Foxhall Road NW. Open Tuesday through Saturday by tour at 10:30 A.M. or 1:30 P.M. Suggested donation $5. Visitors must make an advance reservation by calling (202) 338-3552.

The former residence of insurance magnate David Lloyd Kreeger opened as a museum in 1994. The structure, designed by noted architect Philip Johnson, is nestled into more than five acres of land in northwest Washington. The collection includes paintings and sculptures of the nineteenth and twentieth centuries, including works by Renoir, Courbet, Monet, Degas, Cézanne, Chagall, and Munch, as well as African masks and figures.

Martin Luther King Jr. Memorial Library

901 G Street NW. Metro: Metro Center or Gallery Place. Open Monday, Wednesday, and Thursday 10 A.M.–7 P.M.; Tuesday 10 A.M.–9 P.M.; Friday and Saturday 10 A.M.–5:30 P.M.; and Sunday 1–5 P.M. (202) 727-1111.

The main branch of the D.C. public library system includes a collection about the civil rights activist as well as books, movies, and photographs on the history of Washington, D.C. The modern glass structure is the only building in Washington designed by architect Mies van der Rohe.

Meridian International Center

1624 and 1630 Crescent Place NW. Metro: Dupont Circle. Wednesday to Sunday 9 A.M.–5 P.M. Free. (202) 667-6800. www.meridian.org.

A nonprofit educational and cultural institution that presents a variety of exhibits, concerts, and lectures. The two mansions that make up the center were designed by John Russell Pope and overlook the city from Meridian Hill. Meridian House, designed in 1921, is in the eighteenth-century French style; the Georgian-style White-Meyer House was designed in 1911 and was later purchased by Eugene Meyer, owner of the *Washington Post*. The grounds include an unusual linden grove.

National Aquarium

Department of Commerce Building; Fourteenth Street and Constitution Avenue NW. Metro: Metro Center. Daily 9 A.M.–5 P.M. Closed Christmas. $2 adult; child 2–10, 75 cents. (202) 482-2826. *Discount coupon in this book.*

Founded in 1873, the National Aquarium is the oldest aquarium in the United States. At one time it was housed on the grounds of the Washington Monument; it moved to the Department of Commerce Building in 1932.

The small museum—not serious competition for newer, larger aquariums in Boston, New York, and other major cities—nevertheless includes 260 species from around the world in eighty tanks. Among creatures on display are electric eels, sea turtles, skates, rays, lungfish, and alligators. Kids might enjoy the Touch Tank, which has spider crabs, horseshoe crabs, and whelks. Highlights of the week are shark feedings Monday, Wednesday, and Saturday, and piranha feedings Tuesday, Thursday, and Sunday, both at 2 P.M.

WOW National Building Museum

Judiciary Square; F Street, between Fourth and Fifth Streets NW. Metro: Judiciary Square. Monday to Saturday 10 A.M.–4 P.M.; Sunday noon–4 P.M. Tours at 12:30 P.M. Monday through Wednesday; Thursday through Saturday at 11:30 A.M., 12:30 P.M., 1:30 P.M.; Sunday at 12:30 P.M. AND 1:30 P.M. Admission: $3 per person donation suggested. (202) 272-2448. www.nbm.org.

Washington is a place that has many grand buildings full of exhibits; the National Building Museum is a grand building exhibit all by itself. One of the relative secrets of the nation's capital, it is worth a trip by any visitor.

The museum is in the Old Pension Building, which dates back to 1881; for more than forty years, it was the home to more than a thousand clerks processing pension payments for Civil War and World War I veterans.

How important was the work of the Pension Bureau at the time of the construction of its headquarters? In 1883, the revenues of the U.S. government were $398,287,582; the expenditures for military and naval pensions were $88,460,000, or about one quarter of the total.

The building, which includes a spectacular interior central court, is a football-field long and sixteen stories tall.

The spectacular structure almost met the wrecking ball in the 1950s after it was deemed inadequate for modern government offices. Instead, it was restored. The Old Pension Building became the Building Museum in 1980, the home of permanent and changing exhibitions about the history of the capital and architecture.

The museum's gift shop is among the best in Washington; the bookstore has a rich collection on architecture, engineering, and building as well as sections on gardening and home improvement.

The interior space of the Pension Building is one of the two largest indoor spaces in Washington along with Union Station. Architect Montgomery Meigs graduated from West Point in 1836 and began a long career in the U.S. Army Corps of Engineers. One of his earliest accomplishments was the design and construction of the Cabin John Bridge in Maryland, at the time the longest masonry span in the world. Soon afterward, he collaborated with Thomas U. Walter as the supervising engineer on the design and construction of the Senate and House chambers and the cast-iron dome of the U.S. Capitol. During the Civil War, Meigs served as quartermaster in charge of provisions for the Union Army.

Meigs based his design for the Pension Building on an Italian Renaissance palace with a series of interconnecting rooms, each entered from an arcaded loggia, arranged around an open central space. The Italian origin for the building is also evident in the division of the exterior walls, where three stories are crowned by a heavily projected cornice, and the alternating rhythm

To the penny. The Pension Building had no formal cornerstone, but the builders held a brief ceremony in which a handful of coins— totaling 31 cents—was placed under the first pressed brick to be laid on the exterior.

Gateways. Each of the four entrances to the Old Pension Building has a theme. The east and west doorways have art symbolizing war, with a male mask of Neptune on the keystone and the figures of Minerva and Mars, the goddess and god of war, in the left and right spandrels (the ornamented space between the exterior curve of an arch and the enclosing right angle). The north and south entrances signify death, with depictions of the three Fates, who spin the thread of life; Clotho (on the left) holds the spindle, Atropos (on the right) has a scale to weigh life's balance and scissors to cut the thread, and Lachesis watches over the process.

Another brick in the wall. The Pension Building when completed was the largest brick structure in the world, containing 15.5 million bricks. The total cost of construction was $886,614.04.

of the windows. Meigs said he was inspired by the sixteenth-century Palazzo Farnese in Rome.

The authorization from Congress called for a fireproof structure, and Meigs constructed most of the huge building from brick. The only wood in the building was in the cornice at the roofline and in the office flooring.

The most distinct exterior element of the Pension Building is a dramatic frieze that encircles the entire structure. Created by Caspar Buberl, a well-known sculptor of the day, the terra-cotta frieze consists of twenty-eight different panels repeated to convey the feeling of an endless procession around the building. Six military units of the Civil War are featured: infantry, cavalry, artillery, quartermaster corps, medical corps, and navy.

Above the second-floor windows, crossed sabers alternate with cannon balls and chains and are accompanied by the wave motif of traditional Vitruvian scroll. Just below the cornice, another frieze combines upright cannons and bursting bombs.

The massive horizontal aspect of the exterior contrasts with the vertical interior of the Great Hall, 316 feet tall by 116 feet long. The soaring central space is tall enough to house a 15-story modern building and is separated from two lower side courts by eight colossal Corinthian columns that may be the world's tallest. The 75-foot-tall columns are made of 70,000 bricks each, covered with plaster and painted to resemble marble.

Meigs's design for the Great Hall was intended to provide an abundance of light and air for the clerks of the Pension Building, a counter to the traditionally dark and dank offices of the time. Fresh air entered the perimeter offices through the large windows and special vents beneath each sill (note the three missing bricks under each window on the exterior of the building). Air flowed out through open archways into the Great Hall—Meigs's design did not include doors on the offices—and up and out through the first row of clerestory windows at the top of the Great Hall. In his report of 1886, he claimed that time lost to sickness among bureau employees was reduced by 8,622 days in the first year of use of the new building.

The Great Hall was used for President Grover Cleveland's inaugural ball in 1885, two years before the building was completed; a temporary wooden roof was built over the open courtyard, and decorations masked the unfinished interior. Up to 1909, six more balls were held there, for Presidents Harrison, McKinley, Roosevelt, and Taft. When Woodrow Wilson chose not to have a ball, the parties at the Pension Building stopped. In the intervening years, the Great Hall was subdivided into temporary work cubicles for hundreds of additional clerks, and it was impossible to use it for ceremonies. In 1973, after the partitions had been removed, one of Richard Nixon's three inaugural balls was held at the Pension Building and the tradition was resumed.

Galleries today include changing exhibitions about architecture and the history of the nation's capital, and educational programs introduce students to the concepts of engineering, construction, and housing. There are lunchtime concerts on a regular schedule.

🌟 National Gallery of Art

600 Constitution Avenue at Sixth Street NW. Metro: Archives–Navy Memorial or Judiciary Square. Monday to Saturday 10 A.M.–5 P.M.; Sunday 11 A.M.–6 P.M. Free. (202) 737-4215. www.nga.gov.

The National Gallery of Art was a gift to the nation from the Mellon family, beginning with the original building and collection donated by financier Andrew W. Mellon in 1937. That museum, designed by John Russell Pope (also responsible for the Jefferson Memorial and the National Archives) and now called the West Building, opened in 1941. One of the largest marble structures in the world, it stretches 780 feet in length; its design is based on a sixteenth-century Renaissance temple. The National Gallery presents yet another spectacular Washington rotunda in its main entryway, this one distinguished from others by the black marble columns that form a complete circle around the core of the building.

In 1978, the East Building, a modern symphony of angles and skylights designed by I. M. Pei, opened; it's a trapezoid divided into a pair of triangular sections (an isosceles triangle for the museum, and a right triangle for the museum's research center). The same Tennessee quarry used for the pink marble of the West Building was reopened to provide stone for Pei's project. The East Building features twentieth-century art and special exhibitions.

The East and West buildings are connected by an underground passageway.

The West Building features European paintings and sculptures from the thirteenth through the nineteenth centuries and American art. This is the place of the Old Masters, displaying the only painting by Leonardo da Vinci outside of Europe, as well as examples by Raphael, Rembrandt, Titian, and Whistler.

The American pieces on display at the museum date from about 1790 to about 1911. Gilbert Stuart's famous painting of George Washington—check out the version on the dollar bill in your pocket if you need a reminder—is on display. But you'll first come to his less famous but highly acclaimed painting of a man skating on the Serpentine River in Hyde Park, London. It was unusual at the time because it was one of the first portraits to show someone in motion. *The Skater*, a portrait of William Grant, was painted in 1782.

Other areas of strength in the museum's collection are the artists of the Hudson River school and the Ashcan school. One room displays Thomas Cole's evocative collection of landscapes up and down the Hudson.

A favorite stop is *Morning in the Tropics* by Frederic Edwin Church. This 1877 painting is amazing in how it evokes the feeling of oppressive heat and humidity; a docent told us he doesn't spend a lot of time in front of this picture in August because what is in the picture is what is outside on the Mall. In the cool of autumn or winter, viewing it is a much more pleasant experience.

Restaurants at the National Gallery of Art include the **Garden Cafe**, the **Terrace Cafe**, and the **Cafe/Buffet**.

The newest addition to the gallery is an impressive website, which offers several thousand full-view digital images from its collection. The Gallery page can be seen at www.nga.gov.

National Geographic Society

1145 Seventeenth Street at M Street NW. Metro: Farragut North. Monday to Saturday 9 A.M.–5 P.M.; Sunday 10 A.M.–5 P.M. Free. (202) 857-7588.

This is the headquarters of the famous exploration and research society, publisher of the magazine of the same name, and home to a specialized museum and interactive exhibit on geography.

The centerpiece is Earth Station One, a 72-seat amphitheater that faces the society's 11-foot-diameter globe; in a simulated space flight, visitors view earth's geography from space. Other features include an interactive aquarium and a live satellite feed of meteorological information.

National Museum of American Jewish Military History

1811 R Street NW. Metro: Dupont Circle. Weekdays 9 A.M.–5 P.M.; Sunday 1–5 P.M. Closed Saturday, and Jewish and some national holidays. Free. (202) 265-6280. www.penfed.org/jwv/museum.htm.

Historical exhibits chronicle the sacrifices of Jewish men and women in the armed forces of the United States.

National Museum of Women in the Arts

1250 New York Avenue NW. Metro: Metro Center. Monday to Saturday 10 A.M.–5 P.M.; Sunday noon–5 P.M. Closed Thanksgiving, Christmas, and New Year's. Suggested donation $3 adults, $2 students and seniors. *Discount coupon in this book.* (202) 783-5000. www.nmwa.org.

More than 2,500 works by women around the world and across time are in the collection, which is based around objects donated by Wallace and Wilhelmina Holladay in 1982. Works include *Holy Family with St. John* by Renaissance artist Lavinia Fontana; prints by Mary Cassatt; and paintings by Georgia O'Keeffe and Helen Frankenthaler. The museum conducts an active education program and also houses what is probably the largest library about women's art, with more than 11,000 volumes.

The museum's elegant Renaissance Revival home was designed in 1907 and ironically once served as a bastion of male bonding, the Masonic Grand Lodge of the National Capital.

Octagon Museum

1799 New York Avenue at Eighteenth Street NW. Metro: Farragut West. Tuesday to Sunday 10 A.M.–4 P.M. $5 adults, $3 seniors/students. (202) 638-3221.

The building was constructed as a townhouse in 1798 in the Federal style. The unusual shape was conceived to deal with the radiating spokes of roads in the area. Somewhere in the mists of history in a town where reality does not always rule, the building was given a name that would imply it to be eight-sided, but it is actually a six-sided hexagon that has a semicircular tower at its entrance.

When the British burned the White House and surrounding area in 1814, the Octagon House was somehow spared, and it became the temporary home of President James Madison and his wife Dolley. It was in the Octagon House that Madison signed the Treaty of Ghent, which finally established peace between Great Britain and her former colony.

In 1899, the Octagon House was acquired by the American Institute of Architects, which still owns it. The structure underwent major restoration at the turn of the nineteenth century and again in the 1950s, but the basic structure is mostly original.

The AIA moved to new, larger headquarters on the same property but has maintained the Octagon House as a museum and as an example of American Federal-period architecture. The interior is decorated with original Chippendale and Federal-period furniture. The original Coade stone mantels in the dining and drawing rooms were made in England in 1799.

Old Stone House

3051 M Street, between Thirtieth and Thirty-first Streets NW. Daily 9 A.M.–5 P.M. Closed Monday and Tuesday in winter. Free. (202) 426-6851. www.nps.gov/rocr

The oldest house in Washington, built a decade before the Revolution, in 1765. The home and surrounding gardens have been restored to former style.

The Phillips Collection

1600 Twenty-first Street at Q Street NW. Metro: Dupont Circle. Tuesday to Saturday 10 A.M.–5 P.M.; Thursday 10 A.M.–8:30 P.M.; Sunday noon–7 P.M.; summer hours may differ. Adult $6.50; senior/college student $3.25; child free. (202) 387-2151.

Claiming the mantle as America's first modern art museum, the institution had its start in 1921 when Marjorie and Duncan Phillips opened their four-story brownstone to the public to view their fabulous personal collection, including works by Monet, van Gogh, Degas, Cézanne, Rothko, and O'Keeffe.

The Society of the Cincinnati at Anderson House

2118 Massachusetts Avenue NW. Metro: Dupont Circle. Tuesday to Saturday 1–4 P.M. Free. (202) 785-2040.

The national headquarters, museum, and library of the Society of the Cincinnati, a patriotic organization founded in 1783 by officers who served under George Washington in the Continental Army and Navy. Collections include objects related to the American Revolution and the society.

Membership has been passed down the generations to eldest male relatives of Revolutionary War veterans in the American and French armies.

The city of Cincinnati, Ohio, received its name from members of the society who settled there.

The Anderson House, built in the Beaux-Arts style from 1902 to 1905, is furnished with European and Asian art objects.

The Textile Museum

2320 S Street NW. Metro: Dupont Circle. Monday to Saturday 10 A.M.–5 P.M., Sunday 1–5 P.M. Highlight tours Wednesday, Saturday, and Sunday at 1:30 P.M. Suggested donation of $5. *Discount coupon in this book.* (202) 667-0441.

The extensive collection of more than 15,500 textiles and carpets dating from 3,000 B.C. to the present day had its genesis when George Hewitt Myers purchased an Oriental rug for his Yale dormitory room. In 1925, Myers founded the museum with his own collection as its base. Today one of the two buildings of the museum is in Myers's former home, designed in 1912 by John Russell Pope, architect of the Jefferson Memorial and the West Wing of the National Gallery.

The museum's collection of Oriental carpets is one of the greatest in the world, including Turkish, Caucasian, Chinese, Egyptian, Spanish, and Persian items. Other civilizations represented are Coptic, Islamic, pre-Columbian, Peruvian, Indian, and African. Only a small portion of the collection is on display at any one time.

The Arthur D. Jenkins Library includes more than 15,000 books and journals about the textile arts.

The museum shop is a one-of-a-kind collection of publications and items inspired by the collection, including T-shirts, ties, and tote bags.

United States Botanic Garden *(Reopens in Late 2000)*

100 Maryland Avenue, near First Street SW, at the east end of the National Mall. Metro: Federal Center Southwest. Gardens are open daily 9 A.M.–5 P.M.; in some years, the gardens have remained open later in the summer. Free. (202) 225-8333, or (202) 225-7099 for a recording of special events.

Many of the Founding Fathers of the nation were planters and scientists, and the idea of a botanic garden was an early goal of the United States. The national charter was passed by Congress in 1820, and its first greenhouse was constructed in 1842. As such, the U.S. Botanic Garden is the oldest such institution in North America and has been located at the eastern end of the Mall since 1849.

The U.S. Botanic Garden Conservatory closed its doors for a massive renovation at the end of 1997; when it reopens sometime about the end of 2000, the original 1933 structure will be completely restored. Alongside will be a spectacular new National Garden. Bartholdi Park remains open.

Perhaps the most visible element of the project is the reconstruction of the Palm House, the central structure that rose eighty feet to crown the Conservatory. The Palm House was dismantled in 1992 because of structural problems.

The National Garden, which will be privately funded, will be a showcase for unusual, useful, and ornamental plants, as well as a living laboratory.

United States National Arboretum

3501 New York Avenue NE. Metro: Stadium–Armory. Daily 8 A.M.–5 P.M. Closed Christmas Day. (202) 245-2726. www.ars-grin.gov/ars/Beltsville/na.

The nation's garden spot, 444 acres of trees, plants, and shrubs from around the world, including a spectacular Japanese bonsai garden (a Bicentennial gift). One of the largest arboretums in the nation, it is administered by the U.S. Department of Agriculture.

The National Arboretum was a dream that dates back to the turn of the nineteenth century; in 1927, Congress approved a charter to establish the collection, but the first major project—mass plantings of Glenn Dale azaleas on Mount Hamilton—began in 1946. Today there are spectacular collections, which include an Asian Collection, the Gotelli Dwarf Conifer Collection, Fern Valley, the Historic Rose Collection, and the National Herb Garden.

The Arboretum is out of the way in the northeast quadrant, but it is worth a trip anytime, especially in the spring when the azaleas are in bloom. To get there by public transportation, take Metrorail to the Stadium–Armory station and then change to bus B2, B4, or B5. Get off at Bladensburg Road and R Street and walk 300 yards east to the R Street gate.

United States Navy Memorial and Visitors Center

701 Pennsylvania Avenue, between Seventh and Eighth Streets NW. Metro: Archives–Navy Memorial. Visitors center open Monday to Saturday 9:30 A.M.–5 P.M.; Sunday noon–5 P.M. From November to March, hours are 10:30 A.M.–4 P.M. Tuesday to Saturday. Free. Movie tickets adult $3.75; senior and child younger than eighteen, $3. (202) 737-2300. http://lonesailor.org.

A tribute to the men and women who went to sea in the Navy. The Naval Heritage Center includes a widescreen theater and displays.

On the outdoor plaza—a favorite luncheon spot for workers in the area—the base of the monument has a huge granite map of the world; stand in the United States and look toward the British Isles on the map and you are looking in the direction of Britain. The scale of the map is comparable to the view of the earth from 800 miles above.

There are two sculpture walls with twenty-two bronze reliefs honoring famous naval events and accomplishments, including Naval Construction Battalions, Naval Aviation, Naval Airships (the blimp corps), Navy Astronauts, the U.S. Marine Corps, the U.S. Coast Guard, and heroes such as John Paul Jones, Commodore Perry, and Admiral Farragut.

Inside the Naval Heritage Center is a glass "Wave Wall," which displays etched profiles of thirty-two ships spanning more than two centuries of naval history.

The theater on the lower level of the heritage center shows the film *At Sea*, a thirty-five-minute, high-resolution 70mm film displayed every hour on a two-story-high, fifty-two-foot-wide screen.

An interesting exhibit at the heritage center is the Navy Memorial Log room, with computers that are connected to a log that contains the name, photo, and service information for veterans of the Navy, Marine Corps, Coast Guard, and Merchant Marine who have enrolled in the log.

From Memorial Day to Labor Day, free outdoor concerts are offered on Tuesdays.

U.S. Chess Hall of Fame

1501 M Street. Metro: Farragut North. Monday to Thursday evenings; Saturday noon–9 P.M.; Sunday noon–6 P.M. Abbreviated hours in winter. (202) 857-4922. Call for admission and other information.

A celebration of American chess competition located at the U.S. Chess Center. On display are chess artworks, rare photographs, trophies, books, and memorabilia.

Washington Navy Yard and Navy Museum

M Street between Sixth and Eleventh Streets SE. Metro: Navy Yard. www. history.navy.mil.

The Washington Navy Yard, established in 1799, is the U.S. Navy's oldest shore establishment. Burned by the Navy itself to prevent its falling into enemy hands, it was rebuilt after the War of 1812; by the 1850s its primary function had become ordnance production. In addition to producing weapons, the yard also developed the first marine railway in 1822, the first successful shipboard catapult in 1912, and a wind tunnel for testing in 1914. During World War I, the yard designed and manufactured the Navy's first 16-inch guns and the U.S. Navy Railway Batteries that were used in France.

Factory production ended in 1961, and the yard became a key supply and administrative center for the Navy.

The former United States Navy destroyer *Barry* (DD-933) is permanently moored at Pier #2. The *Barry* was commissioned in 1956 and served twenty-six years in the Atlantic and Pacific fleets.

Navy Museum. Washington Navy Yard; Ninth and M Streets SE. Building 76. Metro: Eastern Market. Weekdays 9 A.M.–5 P.M. Memorial Day to Labor Day, 9 A.M.–4 P.M. remainder of year. Weekends and holidays 10 A.M.–5 P.M. Free. (202) 433-4882.

A chronicle of the history of the U.S. Navy from Revolutionary times to the present day, with exhibits including a re-creation of the gun deck of the *Constitution;* a model of the *Turtle*, America's first military submarine, which was first used in 1776; a World War II 40-millimeter quadruple gunmount; and a full-sized model of the deep-sea submarine the *Alvin*.

The Navy Museum is located in the former Breech Mechanism Shop of the old Gun Factory of the Washington Navy Yard. Built before the turn of the nineteenth century, the 600-foot-long building was used to produce weapons and missile components until 1962. The museum is part of the Naval Historical Center, which includes a research library and archives.

Nearby is the Marine Corps Historical Center, which maintains the archival, research, library, and museum facilities of the United States Marine Corps. The Marine Corps Museum on the first floor presents the history of the Corps through a collection of historical objects and works of art.

Docked at the museum as a permanent "visit ship" is the USS *Barry*, a naval destroyer that served in the Cuban missile quarantine in 1962 and in the Vietnam War. The 424-foot-long ship was decommissioned in 1982 after twenty-six years of service.

The Washington Post

1150 Fifteenth Street NW. Metro: Farragut North. (202) 334-7969. Call for hours and reservations. Free. www.washingtonpost.com.

Here's your chance to walk through the hallways, newsroom, and presses of one of the nation's most famous newspapers. Although it is one of the most technologically advanced newspapers anywhere, the basic chaos and pressure of the journalism trade is unchanged. The tour takes about an hour.

Woodrow Wilson House

2340 S Street, near Massachusetts Avenue. Metro: Dupont Circle. Tuesday to Sunday 10 A.M.–4 P.M. Adult $5; senior $4; student $2.50; child younger than 7 free. (202) 387-4062. Special behind-the-scenes tours are also offered. *Discount coupon in this book.*

Woodrow Wilson was one of the most highly educated and accomplished of American presidents, the author of several books, president of Princeton University, and a major force behind the creation of the League of Nations. He was also the only president to live in Washington after the end of his term in office. His home includes political memorabilia and furnishings of the 1920s.

The house is the only presidential museum in the nation's capital. Items on display include objects from the White House and elaborate gifts of state from around the world, as well as family and personal objects. The house also presents a glimpse of "modern" American life in the 1920s, from early sound recordings and silent films to flapper dresses and zinc sinks.

Chapter 7
Government Institutions

Your Government in Action

Washington is, of course, corporate headquarters for the biggest business in America, and the city is filled with spectacular buildings to house the official and ceremonial functions of government. Many of the government offices and agencies include great works of art and architecture, and nearly all are important in our nation's history.

In This Chapter

Executive Office Building

Federal Bureau of Investigation

Bureau of Engraving and Printing

WOW National Archives

United States Department of State

WOW United States Capitol

WOW United States Supreme Court

WOW White House

WOW Library of Congress

Department of Defense (The Pentagon)

Department of the Interior

Department of Labor

Department of State

Department of the Treasury

Congressional Tours

Executive Office Building

Seventeenth Street and Pennsylvania Avenue NW. Reservations required for guided tours, given Saturday mornings only. Free. (202) 395-5895.

A Second-Empire bookend to the Treasury Building that flanks the other side of the White House on Pennsylvania Avenue. When completed in 1888, it brought together the State, War, and Navy departments under one mansard roof.

Federal Bureau of Investigation

Tenth Street and Pennsylvania Avenue NW. Metro: Gallery Place–Chinatown. One-hour tours given weekdays 8:45 A.M.–11:45 A.M. Free. (202) 324-3447. www.fbi.gov.

Cool it, it's the "Feds." The Federal Bureau of Investigation grew larger than life during the long stewardship of Director J. Edgar Hoover. Today, the FBI's headquarters is one of the biggest tourist draws in Washington, taken by nearly 500,000 people each year. On the one-hour tour you'll see a carefully drawn, celebratory version of the history of the bureau, from its early days of war against the gangsters to its modern-day pursuit of foreign and industrial spies, drug runners, and terrorists.

Actually, one of the things you will see very little of are the Feds. The tour concentrates on second-rate museum displays and a few peeks through glass windows at several FBI labs. The only place where you are guaranteed to meet a G-man is in the shooting gallery during the brief visit, at the end of the tour.

During the summer, the FBI tour is one of the more difficult tickets to obtain in Washington, and lines of more than an hour are commonplace; in the off-season, you can usually walk into a tour within twenty minutes of arrival. But the FBI, like many other federal agencies, knows on which side its budget is buttered: you can avoid waiting in line by obtaining an appointment for a tour through your congressional representative or another federal contact.

In these days of terrorist threat, the already-tight FBI building has become even more security conscious. Cars can no longer park near the building, guards watch comings-and-goings from booths, and visitors for the tour have to go through one of the most sensitive metal detectors you have ever experienced, capable of spotting items as small as a tiny piece of tin foil around an allergy pill in my pocket. In 1999, the tour itself was shut down for several months because of security concerns.

After a view of a video about the operations of the agency today, you'll move into a gallery that celebrates the FBI's Greatest Hits. Cardboard cutouts display the faces of gangsters John Dillinger, Charles Arthur "Pretty Boy" Floyd, and Lester J. "Baby Face Nelson" Gillis, all three killed by the FBI in 1934.

In recent years, the Ten-Most-Wanted wall included three Middle Eastern terrorists, two of them allegedly involved in the bombing of Pan Am Flight 103 over Lockerbie, Scotland, in 1988. During the years, there have been about 500 names on the list—including less than a dozen women—and the FBI claims that more than 411 were apprehended. In recent years, some of the captures have been credited to viewers of "America's Most Wanted" and "Unsolved Mysteries." Two more were captured as the result of tips by visitors on the FBI tour.

Nearby is a panel outlining modern organized-crime groups, including the Mafia, the Japanese Yakuza (with a display of some of the body tattoos worn by members), and the Russian crime families.

Today, the FBI is just as interested in white-collar crimes such as defense procurement fraud, mortgage fraud, health care provider fraud, public corruption, and environmental lawbreaking.

The first lab on the tour is the DNA Analysis Lab. From there it's on to the Firearms Evidence Collection, a glassed-in NRA fantasy that has more than 5,000 pistols, machine guns, and other weapons. All the devices are kept operational for research and test-firing.

The Materials Analysis unit maintains automotive paint files that have more than 100,000 samples of foreign and domestic paints to assist in solving crimes involving vehicles.

Knights of lore. The land now occupied by the J. Edgar Hoover Building is the site where the Knights of Pythias was founded on February 19, 1864, under a charter granted by President Lincoln.

Silver screen. The FBI has always been very conscious of its public image and actually has helped build its image during the years through books written by or for J. Edgar Hoover, movies, and television shows. Old movie posters in the exhibits on the FBI tour promote films such as *Down Three Dark Streets*, with Broderick Crawford and Ruth Roman; *G-Men Never Forget*, a Republic serial; and *Queen of the Mob*, based on J. Edgar Hoover's book, *Persons in Hiding*.

Bureau of Engraving and Printing

Fourteenth and C Streets SW. Metro: Smithsonian. Peak season April 3 to September 30, tours 9 A.M.–2 P.M. every twenty minutes. The ticket booth is located on Raoul Wallenberg Place (Fifteenth Street) and opens at 7:45 A.M. Evening tours, 4–7:30 P.M., are offered June 1 to August 31. In the off-season, no tickets are necessary for the tours 9 A.M.–2 P.M., with lines queuing on Fourteenth Street. Free. (202) 874-3019. www.bep.treas.gov.

The government's "money factory," where most of our paper currency is printed, is the best place in town to see your greenbacks in action. It's an interesting, twenty-minute guided tour that gives you a view of the process from behind glass windows. Security, of course, is very tight, and there are restrictions against photography. There are no free samples, although the gift shop at the bureau has some interesting souvenirs for sale, including uncut sheets of bills.

Production of paper money involves more than sixty-five steps, beginning with a hand-engraved piece of soft steel, known as a master die. The original etching is used to make printing plates; the Lincoln portrait on the five-dollar bill was first engraved in 1869 but can still be used to make a modern note.

No peeking. OK, class, here's a quiz. Name the portraits on the $1, $5, $10, $20, $50, and $100 bills.

For extra credit, who is pictured on the $2 bill?

Ready? Washington, Lincoln, Hamilton, Jackson, Grant, and Franklin. The $2 bonus: Jefferson.

Just be thankful we didn't ask for a description of what's on the back of the bills: the Great Seal ($1), the signing of the Declaration of Independence ($2), the Lincoln Memorial ($5), the U.S. Treasury Building ($10), the White House ($20), the U.S. Capitol ($50), and Independence Hall ($100).

By the way, although the Bureau of Engraving and Printing is authorized to produce $500, $1,000, and $5,000 bills, these denominations have not been printed since 1969 because of lack of use. The unappreciated $2 bill has also been dropped from production.

The die is heated and subjected to tremendous pressure to make an "intaglio" printing plate that holds ink in its recesses; paper is pressed to the plate under twenty tons of pressure to create the slightly raised surface on the front of the currency.

The Bureau's rotary presses run twenty-four hours a day for much of the year, producing more than 8,000 sheets of thirty-two bills per hour. After inspection, the sheets of bills are cut into smaller and smaller stacks until they consist of 100-bill units; a "brick" of forty units, or 4,000 bills, is wrapped and shipped to one of the twelve Federal Reserve Districts around the nation for distribution to local banks.

The BEP was established in 1862 and was first quartered in the basement of the Main Treasury building; it moved to its present site in 1914 and expanded across Fourteenth Street in 1938. The actual printing of currency began in 1863; before then notes had been issued by private companies and banks. By 1877, all United States currency was coming out of the Washington facility.

A new facility in Fort Worth, Texas, went on line in 1991 and today annually produces about a quarter of the nation's crop of paper money. Bills produced there bear a small "FW" near the front's bottom right corner.

🆆🅾🆆 National Archives

Constitution Avenue, between Seventh and Ninth Streets NW. Metro: Archives–Navy Memorial. Main exhibit hall daily 10 A.M.–5:30 P.M. in off-season; summer hours are 10 A.M.–9 P.M. Free. (202) 501-5000.

All things great and infamous are stored here, from the Declaration of Independence, to the U.S. Constitution and the Bill of Rights, to some of Richard Nixon's expletive-undeleted Watergate tapes and his letter of resignation.

Other important documents include the Emancipation Proclamation, the Japanese surrender papers from World War II, the Louisiana Purchase Treaty (signed by Napoleon Bonaparte), more than seven million still pictures such as a large collection of Civil War photographs by Mathew Brady, reels of motion-picture film dating back to the 1897 inauguration of President William McKinley, and more than eleven million maps, charts, and aerial photographs.

The National Archives is America's filing cabinet, the repository of treaties, official papers, and historical documents of all sort. Although items on display date back to the birth of the nation—and even before then—the nation did not have a formal storage place for its treasured keepsakes until 1935, when John Russell Pope's building opened.

At one entrance is a statue whose base bears a quote from Shakespeare's *The Tempest* that has become identified with the Archives itself: "What is past is prologue."

The building, with twenty-one windowless and temperature-controlled stack areas, was nearly filled even before it was completed, forcing the use of the planned central court area for stacks. And by the 1960s, the building was crammed to the rafters, requiring construction of a new facility in College Park, Maryland. Both the Washington and Maryland facilities are open to researchers.

For the public, though, the most important part of the National Archives lies beneath the Rotunda on the Constitution Avenue side of the building where America's most famous documents are offered for viewing. Don't expect to lay hands on the Declaration of Independence, though: that document, plus the U.S. Constitution and the Bill of Rights are sealed within bronze and glass cases in which the air has been replaced with inert helium gas. The cases, themselves behind dark filters, allow only a dim—but thrilling—glimpse of the papers.

At closing time, or in the event of a fire or other emergency, the huge cases automatically retract into a vault deep beneath the building.

Two murals adorn the side walls of the Rotunda: Thomas Jefferson presenting the Declaration of Independence to John Hancock, president of the Continental Congress; and James Madison presenting the Constitution to George Washington, president of the Constitutional Convention.

The outer ring of the Rotunda area houses an exhibition space known as the Circular Gallery. Special shows in that area have commemorated the documents and mementos of World War II and other subjects.

United States Department of State

2201 C Street NW. Tours by reservation only of diplomatic reception rooms weekdays 9:30 A.M., 10:30 A.M., and 2:45 P.M. Closed during official functions. Free. (202) 647-3241.

While the structure on this site was originally designed for the War Department, as World War II approached that rapidly expanding agency (now known as the Department of Defense) instead went across the river to build the Pentagon, leaving this incomplete building to the State Department.

WOW United States Capitol

Capitol Hill. Metro: Capitol South. Daily 9 A.M.–4:30 P.M., and later in summer. Closed Thanksgiving, Christmas, and New Year's Day. Tours begin at the Rotunda 9 A.M.–3:45 P.M. Visitor passes to the House and Senate galleries may be obtained from your representative or senator. The building is also open on Sunday, but no tours are offered that day. Free. (202) 225-6827.

George Washington himself laid the cornerstone of the original portion of this building in 1793; it has undergone numerous reconstructions and additions since.

The design for the Capitol was drawn by physician and amateur architect William Thornton; the first construction included only what is now the central portion of the building.

The Capitol was partially destroyed by fire after British troops set it ablaze in August of 1814; the House chamber and the Library of Congress room were ruined and the Senate chamber was damaged. The Supreme Court room was untouched. The rebuilt House chamber was modeled on the surgery theater at the Medical School in Paris, a 1775 adaptation of an ancient auditorium.

In 1851, construction was begun on wings to extend the building; included in the structures were new chambers for the House and Senate. And in 1855, Congress voted to replace the original simple copper-sheathed dome with an unusual cast-iron cap weighing 1.3 million pounds. In this town of superlatives, the interior of the dome of the U.S. Capitol has to be the most super of all.

The statuary around the base of the dome includes Washington, Jackson, and Lincoln; the most recent addition to the pantheon is Dr. Martin Luther King Jr.

At the top of the dome is a statue, *Freedom*, facing east toward Union Station, which was the direction it was thought Washington would expand. When the statue was removed for refurbishing in 1993, there was some discussion about whether it should be turned around to face the Mall when it was replaced, but it was decided for historical purposes to leave it as it was.

The interior is decorated by Constantino Brumidi's fresco, *Apotheosis of Washington*. The frieze at the bottom depicts more than 400 years of American history from Columbus to the birth of aviation; it is actually a trompe l'oeil ("fool the eye") painting and not a sculpture as it appears to be.

Getting centered. Jones Point near the White House is the geographic center of the District of Columbia. However, the dot on the floor in the middle of the Capitol Rotunda is considered the spiritual center of the capital. At that circle nine American presidents and eighteen other honorees have lain in state in final tribute.

The walls are covered with large murals depicting moments in American history. The painting of the signing of the Declaration of Independence by John Trumbull includes what may be a political inside joke: Thomas Jefferson is pictured with his foot planted on John Adams's shoe.

One painting that suddenly seemed less obscure with the release of a Disney movie in 1995 is *The Baptism of Pocahontas*; the young Native American princess is shown kneeling to receive the baptism rites while members of her family are shown looking on with curiosity and mixed feelings. John Rolfe, who later married Pocahontas, stands behind her.

Tours leave from the massive bronze doors on the east side and include the Rotunda, Statuary Hall, the Old Senate Chamber, and the House of Representatives. The standard tour, which may require you to wait in line for departures, lasts about forty-five minutes; a longer, scheduled, VIP tour is available through the offices of your congressional representatives.

Shell game. The Rotunda is actually a double dome with an inner and outer shell. Visitors can arrange through their members of Congress to take a special tour, which includes entrance to the inner dome. It's not for the faint of heart; you'll take an obscure elevator to some stairs that wind around inside the interior of the double dome.

The Old Senate Chamber is a small, ornate room. Originally a much larger room, it was divided in half at the floor level when the House of Representatives moved to its new second-floor chambers. The Senate didn't want to be one-upped by the "lower chamber," and therefore it moved to the upper half of its room. The lower level of the room was adapted for use as the Supreme Court chamber.

The Statuary Hall, also known as the "whisper chamber," was at one time the old House chamber. According to legend, John Quincy Adams used to put his head down on his desk during deliberations of the House; some thought he was sleeping, but it is now believed he was eavesdropping on conversations all the way across the room. Therein lies the origin of the nickname for the room: a strange acoustical architectural defect funnels sounds from several points in the hall to other places as clearly as through a microphone and speaker. You can try the effect yourself, or have it demonstrated for you by one of the Capitol guides.

The hall itself was intended to hold two statues representing important citizens from each of the states of the union; at the end of 1995, there were only ninety-five in place because five states had not sent their second statues. Behind a pillar is one of the more interesting statues, that of King Kamehameha I, who became ruler of the island of Hawaii after 1790 and through conquest became ruler of all the Hawaiian islands in 1810. The Statuary Hall has been restored to its 1857 glory.

The old Supreme Court chamber in the basement is a very impressive room redolent with history. Outside the dark chambers is a plaque commemorating Samuel F. B. Morse; on May 24, 1844, in what was then the Law Library of the Capitol, Morse sent the message "What hath God wrought?" to Baltimore using the first electromagnetic telegraph instrument.

Beneath the Rotunda is the Capitol Crypt, a formal chamber intended to hold the body of George Washington; his family, however, took him home to Mount Vernon for burial.

To visit the House or Senate chambers, you will need to obtain passes from your representative or senator respectively; the passes are easily obtained by calling or writing a few weeks ahead of your visit or by dropping by their offices in the Capitol. The requirement for the tickets is intended to expose visitors (and voters) to the offices of their representatives. (Foreign visitors

Current events.
Check the *Washington Post* on the morning of your visit to see if there are any special events, committee or subcommittee hearings, or important votes at the Capitol on that day.

are admitted to the House and Senate chambers by showing a passport or other identification.) You can expect to pass through several strict security checkpoints before being admitted to the seats in the galleries, and rules prohibit the use of cameras and note-taking.

Once you are admitted to one or the other gallery, you most likely will be surprised by how little is going on at most times. Except for the most critical of votes or special occasions (when you are not likely to be able to get in without special arrangements), the chambers are usually populated by only a few congressional representatives or senators. Most of the speechmaking and procedural issues are for the benefit of the Congressional Record or the video cameras that are in place in both chambers (only the House is routinely broadcast live on the C-Span cable network).

The Senate floor is simple but elegant and much smaller than most first-time visitors would imagine. The rules of the chamber permit the 100 senators to make their speeches from their seats; a clerk with a stenography machine suspended from his or her shoulders like a hot dog vendor at a ballpark approaches the desk of the speaker to record the pearls of wisdom.

The House side often has more going on simply because there are 435 voting members. Speeches are given from a lectern down in front of the tiered podium; there is an elaborate procedure to limit the amount of time given to each side of a debate, with much ceding back and forth of time among speakers. There is also a period during which members can speak on any subject, often on subjects as important to the national interest as announcing the names of the local 4H Beauty Queen.

Visitors to the Capitol are permitted to ride the underground subway system beneath the Capitol that connects to six different House and Senate buildings; entrance is off the lower level. The short rail system is the quickest way for you to get to visit the office of your representative or to go to an outlying committee room.

WOW United States Supreme Court

First Street and Maryland Avenue NE. Metro: Capitol South or Union Station. Weekdays 9 A.M.–4:30 P.M. Lectures presented on the half hour 9:30 A.M.–3:30 P.M. when court is not in session. Seating for oral arguments is on a first-come, first-served basis, with sessions beginning at 10 A.M. when scheduled. Free. (202) 479-3211, extension 4.

Fittingly, the Supreme Court, designed by Cass Gilbert and completed in 1935, is one of the most majestic of public structures in Washington. Its ceremonial front is like a Roman temple, with sixteen great Corinthian-style columns. At the top of the white marble stairs are a pair of seated sculptures, the *Authority of Law* to the left, and the *Contemplation of Justice* on the right. All around the building are friezes and sculptures that glorify the rule of law as well as some of the leading lights of the court.

Above a frieze that proclaims "Equal Justice Under Law" are sculpted figures representing *Liberty Enthroned Guarded by Order and Authority*. The figures are attended by characters garbed in Roman clothing. The faces on the young and muscled bodies are actually those of William Howard Taft (president of the United States, 1909–13, and chief justice of the U.S. Supreme Court, 1921–30), John Marshall (fourth chief justice, 1801–35), Charles Evans Hughes (an associate justice, 1910–1916, and chief justice, 1930–1941), the architect Cass Gilbert, Elihu Root (secretary of state, 1905–09 under Theodore Roosevelt and winner of the 1912 Nobel Peace Prize), and sculptor Robert Aitken.

The 13-ton bronze doors are ornamented with scenes from history, literature, and law including the Magna Carta, the Shield of Achilles representing Greek law, the Praetor's Edict for Roman law, and the Justinian code for religious law. And that's just the outside. The main hall within is lined with busts of former chief justices and more columns.

The court did not have a place of its own before 1935, meeting in various locations—including some Washington taverns and eventually two different rooms within the U.S. Capitol—during its first 146 years of existence. In 1929, William Howard Taft, the chief justice, convinced Congress to build a home for the court.

With the opening of the court's term on the first Monday in October, the members of the court hear as many as four one-hour oral arguments on Monday, Tuesday, and Wednesday of every other week. Sessions begin at 10 A.M. and may continue until 2 or 3 P.M., with a one-hour recess at noon.

Seating at the bench is determined by seniority, with the chief justice at the center and the most senior justice on his right and the next most senior justice to his left. The seating arrangement continues in this alternating manner, with the most junior justice at the far right as you face the bench.

The marshal opens each session with the phrase "Oyez, oyez, oyez," which means, "Here ye, hear ye, hear ye." The marshal is also responsible for seeing that attorneys do not exceed their allotted time by signaling to them through lights on the lectern. A white light means there is five minutes remaining, and a red light means time has expired.

The benches at the left front are reserved for the press. Use of cameras and recording devices is not permitted when the court is in session, and thus sketch artists are given seats in the press section.

Typically, each side is allowed thirty minutes to make its argument; although most lawyers are prepared to present their case as an argument, the justices often interrupt the presentations with questions.

When the court is hearing arguments, members of the public are admitted to the small courtroom. Two lines form on the plaza outside the court; one line is for those who want to listen to an entire one-hour argument, and the other, faster-moving line is for those who are willing to settle for a three-minute glimpse of the proceedings. The length of the lines usually depends on the significance of the case being argued; on slow days, you may be able to walk in early and stay. The *Washington Post* often covers upcoming cases in its Monday-morning edition during the Supreme Court term.

The oral argument portion of the term ends by mid-May, and from that time on the members of the court take the bench on Monday at 10 A.M. for short sessions of about half an hour to release orders and opinions; this continues until all cases heard during the term are decided, a process that usually takes until the end of June.

Wednesday afternoons and Fridays are usually scheduled as conference days, as is the entire week before the term begins in October. (Before each deliberation, the justices begin with the Judicial Handshake, a traditional greeting to each other that originated near the turn of the twentieth century with Melville Fuller, eighth chief justice of the court who served during 1888–1910; he was the first chief justice to have academic legal training, having attended Harvard law school.)

The outcome of cases brought before the Supreme Court is determined in the justices' conference room. Here the justices meet privately without staff to discuss argued cases, motions, and some mandatory appeals and petitions for certiorari—these are requests of the Supreme Court to hear a case that was originally decided in a lower court. More than 6,000 petitions are filed annually, but the court agrees to hear only about 120 to 150 each year. If any justice indicates an interest in a particular petition, that case is researched and then discussed; in order of seniority, beginning with the chief justice, views are stated and a vote is taken. If four justices—one short of a majority—vote to accept the case for argument, the clerk of the court will place the case on the calendar. After oral arguments by attorneys for each side, the justices again discuss the case and vote on it, with five votes required for a majority decision. An opinion of the Supreme Court must be followed by all other courts in the country.

Informal tours are given by court employees when the justices are not in session. On the lower level is a gift shop that has a broad variety of books and souvenirs about the Supreme Court and its justices. Among the items on sale are very official-looking clipboards and binders emblazoned with the words Supreme Court, enough to impress any lawyer in the nation.

The Supreme Court offers a reasonably priced snack bar and cafeteria on the lower level. Don't expect to rub elbows with a justice, though; they have their own private dining rooms.

Hanging judges. The unusual spiral staircases that climb up to the left and right sides of the Supreme Court building are self-supporting elliptical structures constructed from Alabama marble. Each staircase spirals from the basement up to the third floor with 136 steps. The design is based upon the theory of a cantilever arch and has been used in other notable buildings, including the Vatican, the Paris Opera, and the Minnesota State Capitol.

Each step extends into the wall about seventeen inches at one end, with the step above it having been cut to conform to the step beneath. In theory, if one of the steps were removed the entire spiral staircase would collapse.

You can get a glimpse of the stairs from the lower level of the court.

White House

1600 Pennsylvania Avenue NW. Metro: McPherson Square or Federal Triangle. Open for tours Tuesday to Saturday 10 A.M.–noon; closed during official functions and on some holidays. Free. (202) 456-7041 or 208-1631. Call (202) 456-2200 for the 24-hour special events recording.

Tickets are distributed at the White House Visitor Center, 1450 Pennsylvania Avenue NW on tour days beginning at 7:30 A.M.

The White House is the oldest public building in the District of Columbia and has been the seat of office for every U.S. president except George Washington.

Washington chose the location for the nation's capital, and after French engineer Pierre L'Enfant drew up the plans for the city, a nationwide competition was held for the design of what was called the "President's House." In July of 1792, James Hoban, a 30-year-old Irish-born architect, won the competition with a design based on an English country home.

Construction began on October 13, 1792, with the creation of a brickyard on the grounds; several million bricks were made for the White House and other nearby federal buildings. Some of the stonemasons were brought in from Scotland, and some of the laborers were slaves hired from their owners.

Washington was gone from office, and John Adams, the second president, moved into the still unfinished house a few months before his term ended in 1800.

The east and west terraces were built during the administration of Thomas Jefferson. James Madison and his wife Dolley decorated the house in a fine style after their arrival in 1809.

On August 24, 1814, though, British troops captured Washington and burned the White House in retaliation for the destruction of some public buildings in Canada by American forces. The fire left only the sandstone walls and interior brickwork standing.

Reconstruction began in 1815 under the supervision of Hoban again, and the White House received President James Monroe in September 1817. The north and south porticoes were added in 1824 and 1829, once again under the supervision of architect Hoban. Running water and an indoor bathroom were installed for the first time in 1833.

In the 1850s, an extensive set of greenhouse-like conservatories was built alongside the west terrace, connected to the White House through the State Dining Room. The conservatories were removed as part of the construction of the West Wing executive office building in 1902. Just seven years later, the West Wing offices were enlarged and the Oval Office built.

President Truman added a balcony to the south portico in 1948, but during the construction it was discovered that the White House was in very poor condition and actually in danger of collapse. The Truman family moved across the street to the Blair House and lived there for four years while the White House was reconstructed. All of the interior appointments were removed and the inside of the building was gutted; a new basement and foundation was dug and a steel framework was installed to take the weight off the walls.

THE WHITE HOUSE AND THE ELLIPSE

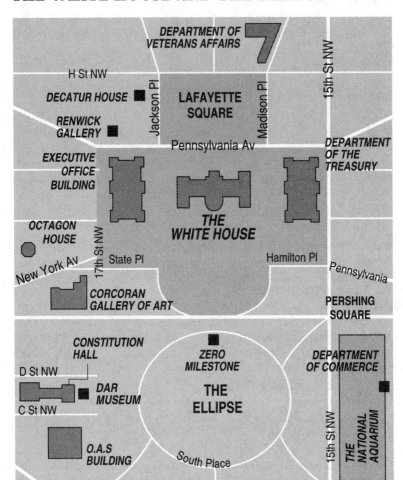

The tour of the White House includes several of the formal rooms on the first floor, including the Red, Blue, East, and the State Dining Room. Don't expect to drop in on the President in the Oval Office or visit the family quarters upstairs, though.

The White House Tour begins in the ground-floor **Library**, which is stocked with books on many subjects by American authors. The chandelier once belonged to the family of early-American author James Fenimore Cooper, whose most famous novels were part of The Leatherstocking Tales, which included *The Deerslayer* (1841), *The Last of the Mohicans* (1826), and *The Pathfinder* (1840).

The paneling of the Library, as well as that in the Vermeil Room and the China Room, was salvaged during the rebuilding of the White House in 1948–52 from timbers used in the 1817 reconstruction of the building.

The White House Visitor Center is located a block away at the corner of

Fifteenth Street and Pennsylvania Avenue. The room was originally the Great Hall of the Patent Research Library, part of the Commerce Building; it is now formally known as Baldrige Hall, in honor of former Secretary of Commerce Malcolm Baldrige. The building is constructed over where the Tiber Creek tributary of the Potomac River once flowed. The basement and sub-basement were built as waterproof as possible; the structure floats on the marshy sub-soils beneath the footings.

Right bank. The U.S. Treasury Annex at the corner of Pennsylvania and Vermont avenues, kitty-corner to the White House, was once the site of the Freed Man's Savings and Trust Company, founded March 3, 1865, to receive deposits from former slaves. Frederick Douglass served as its last president until the institution closed in June 1874.

The Vermeil Room, once used as a presidential billiard room, is decorated with portraits of recent First Ladies, and includes a collection of vermeil (gilded silver).

The China Room was assigned by Edith Wilson in 1917 for the display of china and glass pieces.

You will pass nearby **The Diplomatic Reception Room** as you head upstairs, but the room is not ordinarily open for visitors. The reception room, one of three oval rooms in the residence, is a formal room used by new ambassadors coming to the White House to present their credentials to the president, and for other diplomatic functions. President Franklin D. Roosevelt used the room to broadcast his fireside chats.

At the top of the stairs on the State Floor is **The East Room**, the largest space in the White House. It is used for press conferences, receptions, and ceremonies. The bodies of seven presidents have lain in state here; in happier times, it was the wedding site for Nellie Grant, Alice Roosevelt, and Lynda Bird Johnson. The glass chandeliers in the room date from 1902.

The Green Room was once Thomas Jefferson's dining room and is now used for receptions. Much of the furniture was crafted in New York about 1810 by famed furniture maker Duncan Phyfe. The walls are covered with watered green silk. A coffee urn on display was owned by John Adams, and the French candlesticks belonged to James Madison.

The Blue Room is a formal room used by the president to receive guests. The room is furnished in the style of the presidency of James Monroe, who after the fire of 1814, purchased pieces that include a number of chairs for the room. Portraits on the walls include those of John Adams, Thomas Jefferson, James Monroe, and John Tyler. At Christmastime, the White House tree is placed here.

Next on the tour is **The Red Room**, which is used for small receptions. Rutherford B. Hayes took the oath of office in this room in 1877 after his disputed election.

The State Dining Room can accommodate more than 100 guests for formal dinners and luncheons. The fireplace mantel includes a quotation from John Adams: "I pray heaven to bestow the best of blessings on this house and all that shall hereafter inhabit it. May none but honest and wise men ever rule under this roof."

The White House is open for garden tours on selected weekends in April and October and for candlelight tours during the Christmas season. The traditional Easter Egg Roll on the South Lawn takes place on Easter Monday.

White House Tour Schedules

Be sure to call ahead to check on ticket availability. And remember that tours are canceled if there are any official events or unusual situations; call to confirm tour schedules the night before and on the morning of a planned visit.

The busiest month is July, followed by June and August, then May, April, March, and September. The quiet season runs from October through February, with the exception of busy times around Christmas.

You can also attempt to obtain scheduled "Congressional Tours" through your representatives in Congress; these tours are given at 8:15, 8:30, and 8:45 A.M.

On a typical day, there are 5,000 tickets available for the general public and about 1,500 congressional tickets.

WOW Library of Congress

10 First Street SE. Metro: Capitol South. (202) 707-5000. Tours begin in the Jefferson Building at 10 First Street. Hours are Monday, Wednesday, and Thursday 8 A.M.–9:30 P.M.; Tuesday, Friday, and Saturday 8 A.M.–5 P.M. Free. For information, call (202) 707-8000. www.loc.gov.

The world's largest library, with nearly 110 million items in nearly every language, from ancient Chinese woodblock prints to comic books to rare first editions to compact discs.

The Library of Congress was at first exactly that, a reference library for the Congress only; President John Adams signed the bill that established the library—with an appropriation of $5,000—in 1800. The initial collection was kept in the new Capitol until August of 1814 when it was destroyed by fire set by invading British troops. Soon after, former President Thomas Jefferson offered his personal library of 6,487 books—considered one of the best in the nation—to the Congress.

The collections include the papers of twenty-three presidents, as well as manuscripts from many other important Americans, including Booker T. Washington, Walt Whitman, Alexander Graham Bell, Frederick Douglass, Irving Berlin, and Charles Mingus. Treasures include the first printed book in the Western world, and millions of maps, photographs, posters, pieces of microfilm, movies, rare books, music manuscripts, and tapes of radio and television broadcasts.

The library is also the chief copyright depository of the United States, receiving about one million new items each year; about half of them are selected for the permanent collection for research purposes. Other items come through gifts and purchases.

In recent years, the library has moved into the electronic age, opening up

Main reading room in Thomas Jefferson Building of the Library of Congress
Photo by Cameron Davidson

its catalog and some of its collections to on-line access. By the year 2000, the intent was to have five million items available in this form.

The Library of Congress complex on Capitol Hill includes three buildings:

The restored **Thomas Jefferson Building** is a soaring cathedral of the mind, with some of the grandest architecture in the capital. The Great Hall rises seventy-five feet from its marble floor to a stained glass ceiling. The Italian Renaissance–style building was constructed in 1897 and is spectacularly decorated with sculpture, murals, and mosaics of the time. Within is the most famous of the library's rooms, the Great Hall, with towering marble columns. The Main Reading Room has been restored and updated; each of the 236 desks is wired so that laptop computers can be used for note-taking, and indexes can be searched from CD-ROM readers.

The library includes two-level colonnades for Asian, European, African, and Middle Eastern reading rooms. The historic Coolidge Auditorium reopened in late 1997 as home to musical concerts, films, and lectures. For information on the concerts, call (202) 707-5502 or consult a web page at www.loc.gov/rr/perform/concert.

The Jefferson Building is also home to a changing exhibit of treasures from the collection. In 1997, the American Treasures gallery included such eclectic items as an 1886 fire insurance company's map of Tombstone, Arizona, including the OK Corral; the paperwork for Frank Sinatra's 1935 audition for Major Bowe's Amateur Hour; and an original Edison gramophone.

The art deco-design **John Adams Building** opened in 1939. The modern white marble **James Madison Memorial Building**, completed in 1980, has reading rooms for special-format collections.

UNITED STATES CAPITOL AREA

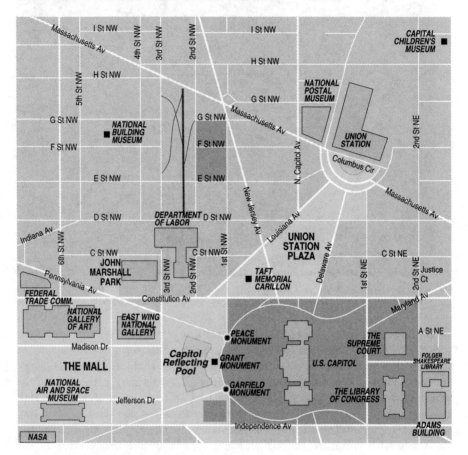

Government Behind-the-Scenes

If you took away the White House, the FBI, and the United States Capitol, the federal government would be a lot simpler . . . and Washington would still have many interesting government agencies to visit.

Many of the less celebrated institutions of Washington offer tours and exhibits. Some are intended for organized groups only. You may have to make reservations to visit those facilities open to the public, and security requirements have become increasingly intrusive in recent years.

Department of Defense (The Pentagon)

Pentagon, Arlington, Virginia. Metro: Pentagon.

One of the world's most famous buildings in the eyes of both friends and foes. As befits our civilian-led democracy, it is also one of the few military headquarters in the world that is open for public tours.

Don't expect to visit the Situation Room or peruse the files of military secrets; the ninety-minute walking tour gives you a glimpse of the cobweb of hallways, art collections of the various armed services, and displays of more medals, flags, and insignia than you'll see at ten Boy Scout jamborees.

One of the world's largest office buildings, the Pentagon has three times the floor space of the Empire State Building in New York; the U.S. Capitol could fit into any one of its five wedge-shaped sections.

The free tour is not one of the most scintillating excursions in Washington unless you are a serious military history buff. But it's interesting on another level: the Pentagon is a city unto itself, home to about 23,000 military and civilian employees with nearly eighteen miles of corridors, its own shopping mall, doctors' offices, barber shops, beauty parlors, and a motor vehicle bureau.

The Pentagon was begun in late 1941 as war clouds gathered in Europe and Asia. Plans were drawn up over a weekend and construction began within a month's time; the first occupants arrived in April of 1942 and the job was completed the following January.

There are 6.6 million square feet of floor area, with five floors plus a mezzanine and basement. The pentagonal design includes connecting corridors that make it possible to walk between any two points in the building in no more than seven minutes.

Visitors will appreciate the art collections, including a new section honoring the recently rediscovered Tuskegee Airmen, an all-black corps from World War II. You'll also see Gen. Douglas MacArthur's corncob pipe and father-and-son Congressional Medals of Honor for World War II hero Douglas and Civil War honoree Arthur MacArthur. In the Marine gallery you'll learn why they're called leathernecks (the original Marines wore leather straps around their necks to keep their heads up and to guard against sword slashes).

Tours depart every hour on the hour weekdays from 9 A.M.–3 P.M., except for holidays. In peak tourist season, tickets for an entire day's tours are often distributed by early in the day. The registration desk, which opens at 9 A.M., is at the Pentagon Metro exit. Visitors older than the age of 16 must provide a photo ID. Tours are conducted in English only, and translation into foreign language is strictly prohibited. You'll have to pass through a metal detector; use the restroom before the tour and have a drink—there's no stopping, and the water fountains are for some reason off-limits. There are several staircases along the one-mile walk, which is led by an enlisted officer who marches backward, facing visitors, for nearly the entire tour. Free. For information, call (703) 695-1776.

Department of the Interior

Eighteenth and C Streets NW. Metro: Farragut West or North. The Department of the Interior houses a museum portraying the history, goals, and programs of the department. Part of the display is the original exhibition of intricately crafted models, dioramas, and metal silhouettes prepared for the opening of the museum in 1935. Agencies within the department, represented by displays at the museum, include the Bureau of Land Management, the Bureau of

Indian Affairs, the National Park Service, the U.S. Geological Survey, the Bureau of Reclamation, and the U.S. Fish and Wildlife Service. Tours of the building include murals and sculptures depicting events and elements of our nation.

The museum is open weekdays 8:30 A.M.–4:30 P.M., except for federal holidays; all adult visitors must show photo IDs. Free. For information and reservations, call (202) 208-4743.

Department of Labor

200 Constitution Avenue NW. Metro: Judiciary Square. The department offers its Hall of Fame. On display are portraits and short biographies of Americans, such as Samuel Gompers and Eugene V. Debs, who have made important contributions to the field of labor.

Department of State

2201 C Street NW. Visitors can tour the ornate Diplomatic Reception Rooms. The suites, adorned with eighteenth-century-American furniture and decorative art, are presently used by the secretary of state and cabinet members for formal entertaining. The forty-five-minute visit explains the historical and diplomatic significance of the rooms and their furnishings; the tour is not recommended for children younger than 12.

The free tours, offered weekdays at 9:30 A.M., 10:30 A.M., and 2:45 P.M., are very limited in size and must usually be reserved several weeks in advance. Call (202) 647-3241, or send a fax to (202) 736-4232 stating your name, phone number, number of people in your party, and the date and time you would like to visit. For security reasons, you will have to provide names of all visitors and Social Security numbers for individuals in groups of five or more; you will also have to show a photo ID upon arrival.

Department of the Treasury

1500 Pennsylvania Avenue NW. Metro: McPherson Square. The Treasury Department building, alongside the White House, is a national historic landmark. Free ninety-minute tours of the Treasury Building are conducted on Saturday by volunteers; some of the offices on the tour are in use during the week by Treasury employees.

The Treasury Building was begun in 1836 and has a layout similar to that of the Old Executive Office Building on the other side of the White House. When the Greek Revival structure was completed, it was one of the largest office buildings in the world; part of it was used as a barracks for soldiers during the Civil War.

The Treasury Department building is a treasure trove of hidden delights. There are $50,000 bonds decorating some of the walls, a set of hanging staircases, and intricate gold leaf decorations at every corner.

There were originally four vaults in the building for the Treasurer of the United States and the Comptroller of the Currency; they were used to hold cash and government bonds disbursed to banks and individuals.

In 1985, while the offices and three connecting vaults of the Securities

Transactions Branch of the Bureau of Public Debt were being renovated for the U.S. Treasurer, a vault that had been hidden from view for nearly eighty years was uncovered.

Crib note. If you want a quick reminder of what the Treasury Building looks like, pull out a $10 bill and study the engraving on its reverse.

The burglarproof vault lining was installed in 1864; it included two layers of cast iron balls between alternating plates of wrought iron and hardened steel. The balls were designed to rotate freely when contacted by a drill or saw, preventing a break-in. The ornamental grill for the vault and a cross-section of the lining are on display.

The Treasury Building served as the temporary White House for a period in 1865 when Andrew Johnson assumed the presidency after the assassination of Abraham Lincoln; Johnson delayed moving across the street for six weeks as a courtesy to Lincoln's widow, Mary Todd Lincoln.

During his stay, Johnson met with state delegations and foreign ambassadors and issued a $100,000 warrant for the arrest of Confederate President Jefferson Davis, who at the time was suspected of conspiring in the assassination of Lincoln. Exhibited in the suite is a reproduction of the Treasury Guard Flag; when assassin John Wilkes Booth jumped to the stage he caught his spur on the Treasury Guard Flag hung on the presidential box, causing him to break his leg upon landing. After Lincoln's death the original flag was brought back to the Treasury Department and displayed in the corridor outside the Secretary's suite as a symbol of the nation's mourning. Today the Andrew Johnson Suite affords a spectacular view directly into the Oval Office in the White House.

Treasury Building, looking south toward the Washington Monument
Photo courtesy of Department of the Treasury

Outer reception room of Salmon Chase Suite, with portrait of Civil War financier Jay Cooke
Photo courtesy of Department of the Treasury

The restored office of Treasury Secretary Salmon Chase includes a pair of delicate allegorical ceiling murals representing Treasury and Justice, discovered under fifteen layers of paint during a restoration project.

One of the most spectacular rooms in the building is the marble Cash Room, which opened in 1869 as the government's bank; prior to its opening it was used for President Grant's Inaugural Ball, and in recent years it has been displayed as it appeared for that party.

Designed as a roofed version of an Italian palazzo, it was proclaimed at the time as the most expensive room in the world. Seven varieties of imported and domestic marble decorate the walls: gray Badiglio Italian, yellow Sienna Italian, white Italian Carrara, pink Tennessee, black Vermont, and dove-colored Vermont on the walls, and Vermont red Lisbon and white Italian Carrara on the floor. Spectacular gaslit bronze chandeliers were hung from 1869 to 1890 until they were replaced by less-pleasing improvements; the restoration of the room included replicas of the original design. The clock on the wall was one of the first such electric devices in the city.

The Cash Room was severely damaged by tons of water poured on the Trea-

sury Building to fight the fire that occurred in June 1996. Restoration of the
Cash Room and much of the rest of the building was still underway in mid-
2000. Some rooms may not be open for tours until the spring of 2001.

Free tours are conducted on Saturday mornings at 10, 10:20, 10:40, and 11
A.M. Each tour lasts approximately ninety minutes. Advance reservations are
required and can be made by calling (202) 622-0896. For security reasons, visitors must provide their name and date of birth when making reservations.
In addition, a photo ID is necessary to gain admittance to the building on
the day of the scheduled tour.

Visitors must enter the building through the Appointment Center doors,
located on Fifteenth Street between F and G Streets.

Congressional Tours (The Insider's Guide)

Nothing makes a member of Congress happier than to do something that
makes a voter in his or her district personally grateful, especially if the gift
is valuable but free. That's the reason why "Congressional Tours" are available for a number of important government facilities in Washington.

Congressional tours usually permit access to areas not included on the regular excursions and will allow you to skip waiting lines. The number of spaces
on the tours is very limited, though, and you will probably have to request
the tickets several weeks or months ahead of your visit.

Note that you can also visit all of these agencies via the general public
tours. The Congressional tours include:

White House. Guided tours offered Tuesday through Saturday 8:15, 8:30, and 8:45
A.M. You won't see any rooms that aren't on the self-guided public tour, but you'll
have a U.S. Secret Service guide and an appointment.

U.S. Supreme Court. Guided tours of the building, led by a staff member of the
court, are available with advance request through a congressional representative's
office.

U.S. Capitol. Contact the offices of your member of Congress or the Senate for
passes to see each of the houses of Congress in action; tickets can be obtained
in advance or on the day of your visit. In addition, some special tours of parts
of the Capitol, including occasional visits to the top of the dome, are available
with advance request.

Bureau of Engraving and Printing. Special forty-five-minute guided tours are
offered once daily, at 8 A.M.

Federal Bureau of Investigation. Appointments for tours of the FBI building are
available through advance request. These are the same tours offered to the public, but they avoid the need to stand in line during busy days.

Chapter 8
A Monumental City

For most of us, the concept of civic monuments conjures up a vision of the Washington Monument, the Lincoln Memorial, or (recently) the quietly moving Vietnam Memorial. And yet these are only a few of the hundreds of monuments and statues scattered through the capital city. We'll visit the most notable of them here.

The National Parks Service maintains a website of information about major Washington memorials, at www.nps.gov.

In This Chapter

The Great Monuments

 Jefferson Memorial

Korean War Veterans Memorial

 Lincoln Memorial

National Law Enforcement Officers Memorial

 FDR Memorial

 Vietnam Veterans Memorial

 Washington Monument

Heroic Statuary

Banneker Circle and Fountain

Mary McLeod Bethune Memorial

Sir Winston Churchill

Christopher Columbus

Justice William O. Douglas

Albert Einstein

Benjamin Franklin

President John F. Kennedy

Marquis de Lafayette

Abraham Lincoln

A. Philip Randolph

Theodore Roosevelt

George Washington

Daniel Webster

Statuary of War Heroes

Jane A. Delano

General Ulysses S. Grant Memorial

General Andrew Jackson

Commodore John Paul Jones

Major General James B. McPherson

General John J. Pershing Memorial

Brigadier General Count Casimir Pulaski

General Philip H. Sheridan

Memorials and Art Works

Arlington Memorial Bridge Equestrian Statues

The Awakening

The China Friendship Archway

Civil War Memorial

Congressional Cemetery

Emancipation Statue

Freedom Plaza

The Lone Sailor

The *Titanic* Memorial

Women in Military Service Memorial

Worlds Apart

MEMORIALS ON THE MALL

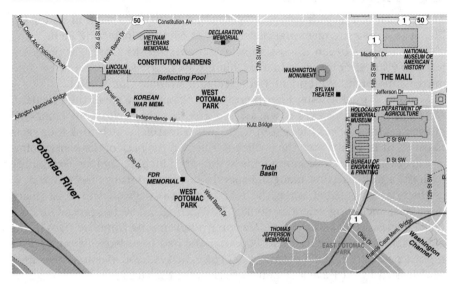

<img_wow> Jefferson Memorial

Thomas Jefferson stands upright—all nineteen feet of him—within the colon-naded temple in his honor. The memorial, created by John Russell Pope, was dedicated during World War II by President Franklin Delano Roosevelt. Pope's design echoes the domes designed by Jefferson for his own home at Monti-cello as well as the Roman Pantheon, a design concept Pope also used in his design for the National Gallery of Art.

The walls of the elegant memorial include excerpts from two documents for which Jefferson is remembered: The Declaration of Independence and the Virginia Statute for Religious Freedom. Another quote is Jefferson's own state-ment on the purpose of his life: "I have sworn on the altar of God eternal hostility against every form of tyranny over the mind of man."

The statue of Jefferson is by Rudolph Evans and depicts Jefferson as a 78-year-old man. Jefferson gazes out across the peaceful Tidal Basin.

The memorial is located on the South Bank of the Tidal Basin at Raoul Wallenberg Place (formerly Fifteenth Street SW). (202) 426-6841.

Located nearby are hundreds of cherry trees, a 1912 gift from the people of Japan; each year in late March or early April, they herald the arrival of spring.

Korean War Veterans Memorial

One of Washington's newer memorials honors an old war with a touching dis-play of nineteen ground troops moving toward a common goal. The memo-rial also recognizes the Republic of Korea and the twenty other nations that participated in the United Nations forces.

The memorial is located across the Reflecting Pool from the Vietnam Vet-erans Memorial on the Mall. (202) 426-6841.

Lincoln Memorial

Abraham Lincoln's spirit enjoys the peace that mostly escaped him during his life, at this majestic memorial that looks out over the Reflecting Pool.

The Congress began discussion of a memorial to the Civil War president just two years after his assassination, but it took nearly fifty years until a committee appointed by President Taft selected a swampy site in 1911.

Sculptor Daniel Chester French created the famous image of the president, seated in a chair, his eyes downcast and grasping the arms of the chair—all of the heaviness of his life is seen in the white marble, which took four years to carve. (It is, by the way, the image inscribed on the back of the penny coin.)

Carved into the wall around the statue are Lincoln's famous Gettysburg Address, and his second inaugural speech, delivered during the Civil War.

Historians note that when the monument was dedicated in 1922, black observers, including scientist Booker T. Washington, were segregated from white guests. In 1939, opera star Marion Anderson sang from the steps of the memorial for an audience of 75,000 after she had been barred from appearing at Constitution Hall because of her color. In 1963, Dr. Martin Luther King Jr. delivered his "I Have a Dream" speech from the steps.

The Lincoln Memorial is located at the west end of the Mall near Twenty-third Street. (202) 426-6841.

National Law Enforcement Officers Memorial

The nation remembers the more than 13,500 officers who have been killed in the line of duty at the National Law Enforcement Officers Memorial, an outdoor plaza dedicated in 1991 in Judiciary Square. The message carved into the wall explains, "It is not how these officers died that made them heroes, it is how they lived."

Names are displayed in random order on the memorial's walls; a directory is available to pinpoint particular names. New names are added each year in May in a candlelight vigil. The lushly landscaped grounds feature tens of thousands of plants, including some 14,000 orange and yellow daffodils that bloom each April. Nearby the simple memorial is a visitors center.

New York City holds the unhappy record for most losses among cities, with more than 500 deaths; California has the highest number of police deaths among the states, with more than 1,100 officers killed. U.S. Marshal Robert Forsyth was the first officer known to have been killed in the line of duty.

The memorial is at E Street between Fourth and Fifth Streets NW. Metro: Judiciary Square. The Memorial Visitors Center is located two blocks away, at 605 E Street NW. The center is open weekdays 9 A.M.–5 P.M., Saturday 10 A.M.–5 P.M., and Sunday noon–5 P.M. (202) 737-3400.

FDR Memorial

In May of 1997, official Washington dedicated a new memorial to President Franklin Delano Roosevelt, whose twelve years in office spanned the Great Depression and most of World War II.

Situated on a seven-acre site near the Jefferson Memorial, the memorial includes four outdoor "gallery" rooms with ten bronze sculptures depicting President Roosevelt, Eleanor Roosevelt, and events of their times. The park-like setting includes waterfalls and quiet pools and a wall of reddish stone inscribed with some of Roosevelt's best-known speeches.

For information, call (202) 426-6841.

🌟 Vietnam Veterans Memorial

Two starkly simple black granite walls seem to descend into the earth, taking with them the names of more than 58,000 American men and women who died in the Vietnam War. The design, at first controversial like most everything else about the war, has since been accepted and revered by nearly all. It is a very powerful abstract statement about patriotism and sacrifice.

The memorial was designed by Maya Ying Lin, at the time a 21-year-old Yale University senior; she won a national competition. The 492-foot-long memorial has the names of the dead etched on it in chronological order from the start of U.S. involvement in 1957 until 1975.

Many visitors bring flowers, letters, or other items to place near the name of a loved one; others make rubbings of the names.

Nearby are two more traditional statues added later—a statue of three soldiers by Frederick Hart, added in 1982, and Glenna Goodacre's *Women in Vietnam* memorial of 1993. (202) 426-6841.

🌟 Washington Monument

The nation's grand monument to the Father of the Country dominates the landscape of Washington, D.C.

The 555-foot-tall shaft is the tallest masonry structure in the world; when it was completed in 1884 it was the tallest structure of any type.

The original concept for the monument called for a pantheon at the base honoring heroes of the Revolution, including Washington driving a chariot. That even grander plan did not come to pass because of financial concerns.

Construction of the monument was not easily accomplished. The cornerstone was laid in 1848 by the Washington National Monument Society, a private group. Volunteers were used to haul stones, and some

The rising sun catches a face of the Washington Monument on a clear November morning.

Photo by Corey Sandler

Junior achievement. Five years after the Washington Monument was completed, it was surpassed in height by the Eiffel Tower in Paris.

of the interior blocks were gifts from states, nations, organizations, and others; a stone from Rome's Temple of Concord, sent as a gift by Pope Pius IX, was stolen by anti-Catholic groups in 1854. Incompetent management and construction brought the project to a halt in 1855, and the memorial stood unfinished at 150 feet for twenty years.

In 1876, the nation's centennial, the Congress appropriated funds to complete the job. Before funds could be raised, though, engineers had to deal with the fact that Washington had a leaning tower; the shaft had tilted because of a poor foundation. A new underpinning was put in place and some of the shoddy stones removed before new work could begin. Today the on-again, off-again construction work can be seen by careful observers—the first courses of stone are marble from Maryland, the next twenty-six feet are of a slightly different stone from Massachusetts, and the remainder switches back to the Maryland stone.

The monument is capped with a small pyramid of aluminum, which was a rare metal in 1884.

An elevator takes visitors to a small observation platform at the top; visitors can also climb or descend the 898 steps, pausing along the way to look at the 189 tribute blocks donated to help the construction.

The monument is located on the Mall between Fifteenth and Seventeenth Streets. Daily 8 A.M.–midnight in spring and summer, 9 A.M.–5 P.M. other times of the year.

Tickets to enter are distributed at a kiosk on Fifteenth Street below the monument. You can request up to six tickets per person for appointments spaced 30 minutes apart throughout the day. A limited number of advance tickets can be requested by calling (301) 350-8830. The kiosk is open in summer from 7:30 A.M.–4:30 P.M., and in winter from 8:30 A.M.–2:30 P.M. During the summer and holiday periods a day's supply of tickets can go very quickly; arrive early to stake your claim. For information, call (202) 426-6841.

Heroic Statuary

Banneker Circle and Fountain. L'Enfant Plaza near Maine Avenue and Water Street SW. A tribute to Benjamin Banneker, an African-American mathematician and astronomer, who assisted Pierre Charles L'Enfant in the original design for the capital city in 1791.

Mary McLeod Bethune Memorial. Erected in 1974 in Lincoln Park, East Capitol Street, between Eleventh and Thirteenth Streets NE. The statue honors the founder of the National Council of Negro Women. The cane she holds is the one presented to her by President Franklin D. Roosevelt.

Sir Winston Churchill. The British statesman was made an honorary citizen of the United States by President John F. Kennedy, and thus it is fitting that his statue's left foot stands on British soil at the British Embassy at 3100

Massachusetts Avenue NW, and his right foot is planted firmly in America. Metrobus: Friendship Heights or Wesley Heights.

Christopher Columbus. In front of Union Station NW. Dedicated in 1912, Columbus stands on the bow of a ship with a winged figurehead below, symbolizing Discovery. Metro: Union Station.

Justice William O. Douglas. U.S. Supreme Court Justice Douglas was a renowned outdoorsman and environmentalist, and his statue is fittingly placed along the Georgetown towpath of the C & O Canal, at Thirtieth Street NW.

Albert Einstein. Located at the National Academy of Sciences, 2101 Constitution Avenue, the large bronze memorial commemorates the centennial of the scientist's birth. A map of the known universe is laid out at his feet.

Benjamin Franklin. Statesman, writer, inventor, and postmaster, Franklin is immortalized in the courtyard of the renovated Old Post Office Pavillion on Pennsylvania Avenue at Tenth Street NW. Dedicated in 1889, the statue was a gift from Stilson Hutchins, founder of the *Washington Post*. Metro: Metro Center or Federal Triangle.

President John F. Kennedy. A mammoth bust of the martyred president is within the hall of the John F. Kennedy Center for the Performing Arts, 2700 F Street NW. Metro: Foggy Bottom/GWU.

Marquis de Lafayette. The Revolutionary War's *Soldier's Friend* looks south toward the White House from Lafayette Square on Pennsylvania Avenue, between Jackson and Madison Places NW. A naked beauty symbolizing America hands Lafayette a sword. Metro: McPherson Square.

Abraham Lincoln. Less well known than the Lincoln Memorial, this outdoor life-sized statue of Lincoln can be found at Judiciary Square, at D and Fifth Streets NW.

A. Philip Randolph. Union Station, 50 Massachusetts Avenue NE. A bronze memorial to the founder of the Sleeping Car Porters Union and the civil rights activist who was one of the organizers of the 1963 March on Washington. Located within Union Station near Gate C.

Theodore Roosevelt. This 17-foot bronze statue stands as a memorial on Theodore Roosevelt Island (an 88-acre National Park) along the Virginia side of the Potomac River. The feisty president is shown in character, making a speech with his right hand raised for emphasis.

George Washington. In a city named in his honor, there are many statues of big George, as well as a gigantic monument. Two of the lesser known can be found at the Washington Cathedral at Massachusetts and Wisconsin Avenues NW. A bronze exterior sculpture has Washington astride a horse. An interior stone work depicts Washington walking down the aisle at Christ Church in Alexandria, Virginia. Metrobus: Friendship Heights or Wesley Heights, or any bus going north on Wisconsin Avenue.

Daniel Webster. A 30-foot bronze shows Webster in a characteristic pose with a reference book in hand, on Massachusetts Avenue between Sixteenth and Seventeenth Streets. Metro: Dupont Circle.

Statuary of War Heroes

Jane A. Delano. The founder of the Red Cross nursing program is honored at Red Cross Square between Seventeenth and Eighteenth Streets, and E and D Streets NW. Also memorialized are the 296 nurses who died during World War I. The bronze work represents the Spirit of Nursing coming forward with compassion. Metro: Farragut West.

General Ulysses S. Grant Memorial. A massive bronze and marble memorial at Union Square, the east end of the Mall. Grant, leader of the Union armies during the Civil War, is mounted on a horse. Metro: Judiciary Square or Smithsonian.

General Andrew Jackson. An equestrian statue at Lafayette Park, Pennsylvania Avenue, between Jackson Place and Madison Place NW, depicts the general as he reviewed his troops at the Battle of New Orleans, the last battle of the War of 1812. Metro: McPherson Square.

Commodore John Paul Jones. A bronze and marble monument to the Revolutionary War naval hero in West Potomac Park, Seventeenth Street and Independence Avenue SW, includes fountains and a pedestal inscribed with his famous cry: "Surrender? I have not yet begun to fight!"

Major General James B. McPherson. Cast from the bronze of a captured cannon, this equestrian statue honors one of the heroes of the Civil War Battle of Atlanta. Located at McPherson Square, Vermont Avenue and Fifteenth and K Streets NW, the work depicts the general surveying the battlefield. Metro: McPherson Square.

General John J. Pershing Memorial. Maps etched in polished rose granite show how the World War I General of the Armies whipped the American Expeditionary Forces into shape. Located at Pershing Square, at Fourteenth and Pennsylvania Avenue NW. Metro: Metro Center.

Brigadier General Count Casimir Pulaski. An equestrian statue of the Revolutionary War hero stands at Pennsylvania Avenue and Thirteenth Street. Pulaski left his native Poland to join in the American Revolution; he helped win several important battles. Metro: Federal Triangle.

General Philip H. Sheridan. The dashing leader of the Union cavalry during the Civil War stands guard over a downtown traffic island at Sheridan Circle, Massachusetts Avenue and Twenty-third Street NW. Sheridan, a New York native, is shown rallying his retreating men into battle. Metro: Metro Center.

Memorials and Art Works

Arlington Memorial Bridge Equestrian Statues. Large bronze statues of horses and figures are located on both sides of the bridge, at Memorial Bridge Plaza and Rock Creek Parkway SW. Cast in Italy and surfaced in pure gold, the sculptures were given in 1951 as gifts from the Italian people to the citizens of the United States.

The Awakening. A half-buried body of a giant man emerges from the ground in this sculpture by contemporary artist Seward Johnson, at Hains Point in East Potomac Park SW.

The China Friendship Archway. Marking the entrance to Chinatown at Seventh and H Streets NW. The archway was handcrafted and decorated in the classical Chinese art of the Quing and Ming dynasties and is lit at night; it becomes the focal point of the Chinese New Year's celebrations in the area. Metro: Gallery Place–Chinatown.

Civil War Memorial. A memorial to some 185,000 African-American soldiers who fought for the Union in the Civil War, expected to be dedicated in late 1997 in the historic Shaw neighborhood of D.C. For information, call (202) 939-8719.

Congressional Cemetery. 1801 E Street SE. (202) 543-0539. The nation's first national cemetery, established in 1807, includes some ornate Victorian statuary. Among the notables buried here are composer John Philip Sousa, photographer Mathew Brady, and former FBI director J. Edgar Hoover. Open daily 9 A.M.–5 P.M. Contributions accepted. Guided tours by appointment. Metro: Stadium–Armory.

Emancipation Statue. Lincoln Park, East Capitol Street between Eleventh and Thirteenth Streets NE. (202) 690-5155. Built with funds contributed by former slaves, the statue shows Archer Alexander, the last slave captured under the Fugitive Slave Law, breaking the chains of slavery while Abraham Lincoln reads the Emancipation Proclamation.

Freedom Plaza. A modern downtown park featuring a paving design based on L'Enfant's 1791 plan for the Capital City. The large letters carved into the granite surface on the map refer to L'Enfant's notes. Located along Pennsylvania Avenue, between Thirteenth and Fourteenth Streets NW.

The Lone Sailor. One of the newest memorials in Washington, at the U.S. Navy Memorial on Pennsylvania Avenue, between Seventh and Eighth Streets NW. Honoring all who have served in the nation's navy, the bronze depicts a lone sailor with a duffle bag at his feet and the sea wind blowing in his face; he looks out over a map of all the world's oceans, cast in stone and bronze, on the plaza below. Metro: Archives.

The *Titanic* Memorial. A haunting memorial to the men who died in the sinking of the *Titanic* in April of 1912. Located next to the Washington Channel and across from East Potomac Park, it shows a partially clad male facing east with arms outstretched, representing "Self Sacrifice and the last inspiration of a departing soul." Cast in 1915, it is dedicated to the "brave men who gave their lives so that women and children could live."

Women in Military Service Memorial. A new memorial to servicewomen from all eras and services, dedicated in the fall of 1997 at Arlington National Cemetery. For information, call (703) 533-1155. www.wimsa.org

Worlds Apart. A modern sculpture shaped from 10,000 electrical appliances and concrete, along the Whitehurst Freeway near Twenty-ninth and K Streets NW. Metro: Foggy Bottom/GWU.

Chapter 9
D.C. Attractions, Churches, and Shopping Malls

Washington is a company town, but that doesn't mean there aren't other industries and other attractions. Here we'll look at some great churches, along with shopping malls (are they the same thing?), the African-American heritage of Washington, and special attractions for children.

In This Chapter

D.C. Attractions

Chesapeake & Ohio Canal

 Union Station

African-American Heritage in Washington

Historic and Notable Churches

Franciscan Monastery

Islamic Center

Metropolitan African Methodist Episcopal Church

National Shrine of the Immaculate Conception

Lillian and Albert Small Jewish Museum

St. John's Episcopal Church

Scottish Rite Supreme Council

Washington National Cathedral

Places for Children

Capital Children's Museum

Discovery Theatre at the Smithsonian

National Theatre's "Saturday Morning at the National"

Washington Dolls' House and Toy Museum

Washington Shopping Malls

Chevy Chase Pavilion

Georgetown Park

The Pavillion at the Old Post Office

The Shops at National Place and National Press Building

A Selection of Favorite Shops in D.C.

Affrica

Burberrys

Coach

Hard Rock Cafe & Merchandise Store

Planet Hollywood

Political Americana

Politics & Prose Bookstore–Coffeehouse

Rand McNally Map & Travel Store

Chesapeake & Ohio Canal

The C & O Canal was built in the mid-1800s to transport coal, lumber, and grain from rural Maryland and Pennsylvania down through the Potomac Valley to Georgetown. The canal, with its mule-drawn boats and seventy-four locks, opened the region to commerce and provided raw materials and finished goods to Washington, the canal towns, and western Maryland.

Since the region's primary inhabitants were farmers, indentured laborers skilled in carpentry, masonry, and stonecutting were brought from Europe to construct the canal.

However, the canal's success was doomed from the start. On the same day President John Quincy Adams attended the canal's groundbreaking ceremony in 1828, construction began on the Baltimore & Ohio Railroad. Due to the speed and price advantages of the railroad, the C & O was never extended to Pittsburgh as originally planned. The canal operated continually up until 1924, when a flood damaged the waterways beyond repair.

Today, the 184-mile canal is a National Historical Park that has jogging paths and walkways along most of its length from Washington to Cumberland, Maryland. The canal can also be experienced aboard the decks of authentic canal boats run by park rangers dressed in period costume. Canal boats are operated in Georgetown and in Great Falls, Maryland, a park located nine miles north of Georgetown.

Boat trips of about ninety minutes depart several times a day from mid-April through late October. Tickets are about adult $5; senior and child $3.50.

For information on tickets, call the C & O Canal at (202) 653-5190 or (301) 767-3714.

WOW Union Station

50 Massachusetts Avenue NE. Metro: Union Station. Monday to Friday 9 A.M.–9 P.M., Saturday 10 A.M.–9 P.M., and Sunday 10 A.M.–5 P.M. (202) 371-9441.

Once a great tribute to the importance of the railroad in America, and now a temple to shopping, Union Station is a spectacular Beaux-Arts structure that evokes the Arch of Constantine and other Roman gateways.

Union Station is a world unto its own just beyond the U.S. Capitol. It is one of the most breathtaking indoor spaces in a town filled with stunning public buildings.

The station—large enough to hold the Washington Monument on its side—opened in 1907 and at its peak was handling more than 100 trains a day. Today, Amtrak uses a portion of the building and the Metro has a station deep below; the sprawling remainder has been given over to an urban mall and food court.

The station was the beneficiary of a $160 million renovation in 1988, with the money spent bringing the gold leaf, marble, brass, and skylights back to architect Daniel Burnham's original vision. More than seventy pounds of gold leaf were used throughout the building in the restoration, at a cost of a half million dollars for the gold alone.

The head house, modeled after the ancient public baths of Diocletian, has a coffered 96-foot-high ceiling adorned with gold leaf. The area includes the main hall, east hall, and west hall; when first built it featured separate men's and women's waiting areas, ticketing windows, the presidential suite, and a lavish 1,000-seat dining room. The west and east halls now contain specialty shops.

On the lower level is the Union Station Food Court, one of the most eclectic collections of eateries you are likely to find anywhere, from Caribbean to Indian to Chinese to Japanese to Italian to American; from hot wings to cold noodles and most everything in between. Here are a few specifics: Bagel Works, Calypso Kitchen, Everything Yogurt, Georgetown Seafood Grill, The Great Steak and Fry Company, Ichiban Teriyaki and Tempura Kabuki Sushi Bar, Mama Ilardo's Pizzeria, Mexican Delights, Panda's Rice Bowl, Pika Pita, and Totally Turkey. The only real problem is how to make a decision; we'd suggest you bring a bunch of friends and mix and match.

Upstairs are sit-down eateries including Amer-

Safe sex. Perched along the balcony surrounding the main and west halls are thirty-six Roman legionnaires sculpted by Louis Saint-Gaudens. As designed in the early 1900s, the soldiers were originally cast as nudes. However the terminal's management ordered that shields be strategically placed in front of each statue when Union Station was opened to the public.

ica, Pizzeria Uno, Sfuzzi, and the Station Grill. B. Smith's, an upscale American eatery, is ensconced in the former Presidential Suite at the station.

Statues in the ceremonial plaza outside, created by noted sculptor Louis Saint-Gaudens, represent Fire, Electricity, Freedom, Imagination, Agriculture, and Mechanics; the inscriptions were written by Charles Eliot, president of Harvard.

African-American Heritage in Washington

In 1791, mathematician and astronomer Benjamin Banneker assisted Pierre L'Enfant with the original design of the city. When L'Enfant was relieved of his duties and took all copies of the plan back to Paris, Secretary of State Thomas Jefferson relied on Banneker, who had memorized the city plans, to reconstruct them.

Starting with Benjamin Banneker, Washington boasts a 200-year history of achievements by African Americans.

Banneker is memorialized at **Banneker Circle and Fountain**, in southwest Washington, near Maine Avenue and Water Street.

Other historical sites of African-American influence include:

Anacostia Museum and Center for African-American History and Culture. Reopens in 2001. See the listing in Chapter 5, *The Smithsonian Institution.*

Mary McLeod Bethune Council House, National Historic Site. 1318 Vermont Avenue NW. Metro: McPherson Square. Open weekdays 10 A.M.–4 P.M. Donations accepted. (202) 673-2402. Mary McLeod Bethune was the fifteenth of seventeen children, born to slaves on the McLeod Plantation in Mayesville, South Carolina. Born after the Emancipation, she was a free woman; she became an important force in the struggle for civil rights, serving as an advisor to four presidents. She moved to Washington in 1935, and her home, a nineteenth-century townhouse on Vermont Avenue, served as headquarters for the National Council of Negro Women from 1943 to 1966. It is now a museum and library.

Carter G. Woodson Home. 1538 Ninth Street NW. Now a private home and not open to the public, it was once the residence of a famed historian and founder of the Association for the Study of Negro (now Afro-American) Life and History in 1915. He was instrumental in establishing Negro History Week in 1926.

Ebenezer Methodist Church. Fourth and D Streets SE. (202) 544-1415. Metro: Capital South. The first public school for Washington blacks was opened in 1863 on this site.

Evans-Tibbs Collection. 1910 Vermont Avenue NW. (202) 234-8164. A collection of paintings and sculptures by eighteenth-, nineteenth-, and twentieth-century African-American artists, in the former home of Lillian Evans-Tibbs, the first black professional opera singer. By reservation. Metro: U Street.

Frederick Douglass Memorial Home. See the write-up in Chapter 6.

Gallery of Fine Arts at Howard University. Room 1010, 2455 Sixth Street NW. (202) 806-7070. College of Fine Arts and Alan Locke African collection.

Howard University. 2400 Sixth Street NW. (202) 806-6100. Named for

General Oliver Otis Howard, the university was founded in 1867 when the Missionary Society for the First Congregational Church of Washington recognized the need for higher education for freed blacks after the Civil War. General Howard was at the time commissioner of the Freedmen's Bureau and a strong supporter of the proposed school. Of the original campus, only the Oliver Howard House remains, a National Historic Landmark. Today, Howard is one of the most prestigious black universities in the nation, with 12,600 students.

Lincoln Park. Along East Capitol Street, between Eleventh and Thirteenth Streets NE. This park celebrates the abolition of slavery in Washington and the nation. During the Civil War, fugitive slaves sought refuge in the District, and in April 1862, Congress passed an emancipation law, which freed D.C. slaves. The park's statue of Abraham Lincoln was dedicated in 1876 and paid for with funds donated by freed slaves. In 1974, a statue of Mary McLeod Bethune was erected by the National Council of Negro Women.

Lincoln Theatre. 1215 U Street NW. (202) 328-6000. Metro: U Street–Cardozo. Between 1920 and the 1950s, U Street was known as Washington's "Black Broadway," alive with clubs, theaters, restaurants, and businesses. At the heart of the district was the Lincoln Theatre, built in 1921 in the style of the grand movie houses of the day. Most of the great black stars, including Duke Ellington, Pearl Bailey, Count Basie, Jelly Roll Morton, Redd Foxx, Billie Holiday, Ella Fitzgerald, and Cab Calloway performed there. The theater has been restored and now serves as a performing arts center.

Martin Luther King, Jr., Memorial Library. 901 G Street NW. (202) 727-1221, or 727-1111 for recorded information. The main branch of the city's public library system is a memorial to the slain civil rights leader. Of special interest are the Washingtonia Division, with a large collection of clippings and photos telling the story of the history of the nation's capital; the Black Studies Division; the Oral History Research Center; and other holdings. Metro: Gallery Place or Metro Center.

Metropolitan African Methodist Episcopal Church. 1518 M Street NW. (202) 331-1426. Open weekdays 10 A.M. to 6 P.M.; Sunday services at 8 and 11 A.M., Wednesday at noon. Metro: Farragut North or McPherson Square.

The Metropolitan's roots date back to 1822 when a group of dissatisfied blacks broke away from a predominately white church to form the first African Methodist Episcopal church in 1886. The building is now a downtown architectural landmark.

Mt. Zion Cemetery/Female Union Band Cemetery. Behind 2515–2531 Q Street NW. Two neighboring cemeteries recall the African Americans who helped develop a prosperous Georgetown and later the city of Washington. Today, these cemeteries form the oldest predominately black burial grounds in Washington.

National Museum of African Art. See the listing in the chapter about the Smithsonian Institution.

Shaw Neighborhood. See Chapter 12, "Washington's Neighborhoods."

Historic and Notable Churches

Franciscan Monastery. 1400 Quincy Street at Fourteenth Street NE. Metro: Brookland–CUA. Tours hourly Monday to Saturday 9–11 A.M. and 1–4 P.M.; Sunday 1–4 P.M. (202) 526-6800. A little bit of old California and the Holy Land, with a monastery designed in the style of old Franciscan missions and featuring reproductions of some ancient altars, including the Grotto of Bethlehem.

Islamic Center. 2551 Massachusetts Avenue at Belmont Road NW. Daily 10 A.M.–5 P.M. (202) 332-8343. The largest mosque in America, featuring a 160-foot-tall minaret facing toward Mecca. The mosque is decorated with Islamic art.

Metropolitan African Methodist Episcopal Church. 1518 M Street, between Fifteenth and Sixteenth Streets NW. Metro: Farragut North or McPherson Square. Monday to Friday 10 A.M.–6 P.M. Sunday services 8 A.M. and 11 A.M. (202) 331-1426. A one-time stop on the Underground Railroad for slaves escaping from the South, it is now an important black church. Abolitionist Frederick Douglass was a parishioner.

National Shrine of the Immaculate Conception. 400 Michigan Avenue, at Fourth Street NE. Metro: Brookland–CUA. Daily 7 A.M.–6 P.M., until 7 P.M. in summer. (202) 526-8300. The largest Roman Catholic church in America, with a 331-foot-tall bell tower and a 459-foot-long nave. The Romanesque-Byzantine church includes a collection of modern and classic mosaics, sculpture, stained glass, and paintings that would make a museum proud. Organ and carillon concerts are regularly scheduled.

Lillian and Albert Small Jewish Museum. 701 Third Street at G Street NW. Metro: Judiciary Square. Sunday through Thursday noon–4 P.M., closed Friday and Saturday. (202) 789-0900. Washington's oldest synagogue, dating back to 1876. The Albert and Lillian Small Jewish Museum presents exhibits on Jewish history in Washington. The red brick Federal Revival Old Adas Israel Synagogue was moved in 1969 from a few blocks away when the headquarters for the Metro system was built.

St. John's Episcopal Church. 1525 H Street, between Sixteenth Street and Vermont Avenue NW, at Lafayette Square. Metro: McPherson Square or Farragut North. Monday to Thursday 9 A.M.–5 P.M.; Friday 9 A.M.–4 P.M. Sunday services at 8:30 and 10:30 A.M. in the summer, and 8, 9, and 11 A.M. from Labor Day to Memorial Day; tours on Sunday by appointment. (202) 347-8766.

Every president since James Madison has sat in Pew 54 of the "Church of the Presidents," across the street from the White House. The imposing structure was designed by Benjamin H. Latrobe.

Scottish Rite Supreme Council. 1733 Sixteenth Street, between R and S Streets NW. Metro: Dupont Circle. Monday to Friday 8 A.M.–4 P.M. Free. (202) 232-3579. A somewhat secret gem, the Masonic Order's home is modeled after the Mausoleum of Halicarnassus, with black marble doors and columns. (Halicarnassus was an ancient city in Turkey; in the fourth century B.C., the widow of King Mausolus built a tomb for her husband—now called a mausoleum—that was one of the Seven Wonders of the World.) Two-hour tours are offered daily.

Washington National Cathedral. Wisconsin Avenue at Massachusetts Avenue NW. Metro: Tenleytown-AU. Daily 10 A.M.–4:30 P.M. Donations accepted. (202) 537-6200. Tours are offered Monday through Saturday from 10 A.M.–3:15 P.M., and on Sunday from 12:30 P.M.–2:45 P.M. A soaring masterpiece of a cathedral, the sixth-largest in the world was finally completed in 1991, just eighty-three years after it was begun.

The church includes some spectacular stained-glass windows, barrel vaults, and your basic English Gothic-style gargoyles. An observation gallery at the tallest point in the District offers views of the District, the Maryland suburbs, and Virginia.

For a truly elevating tour, the Washington National Cathedral Tour and Tea is offered every Tuesday and Wednesday at 1:30 P.M. The guided tour visits areas of the cathedral not on the regular tour, ending up with the ultimate in high tea, served atop Saint Paul Tower with breathtaking views of downtown Washington and surrounding states. The tea and tour costs $18 per visitor; call (202) 537-8993 for reservations.

Places for Children

In addition to Washington's most famous attractions, including the Smithsonian Institution museums, the National Zoo, the U.S. Capitol, the Bureau of Engraving and Printing, the Federal Bureau of Investigation, the White House, and the many monuments of the nation's capital, there are quite a few places intended specifically for the youngest visitors.

Capital Children's Museum. 800 Third Street NE. Metro: Union Station. (202) 675-4120. Hands-on displays exploring science, geography, and culture. www.ccm.org.

Admission: adult $6; senior $4; child younger than 2, free. Half-price admission Sunday before noon. Open 10 A.M.–6 P.M. Memorial Day to Labor Day and 10 A.M.–5 P.M. remainder of year. *Discount coupon in this book.*

Discovery Theatre at the Smithsonian. Metro: Smithsonian or L'Enfant Plaza. (202) 357-1500. www.si.edu/tsa/disctheater.

Special plays for children, held in the Arts and Industries Building, September through June. Admission $5 for all; child younger than age 1 free.

National Theatre's "Saturday Morning at the National." Metro: Metro Center. (202) 783-3372. www.nationaltheatre.org.

From puppet shows to music and dance. October through April. First-come, first-served.

Washington Dolls' House and Toy Museum. 5236 Forty-fourth Street NW. Tuesday to Saturday 10 A.M.–5 P.M.; Sunday noon–5 P.M. Metro: Friendship Heights. (202) 244-0024. Antique dollhouses, toys, and games, mostly from the Victorian era. Favorites include a turn-of-the-century block of Baltimore row houses and a 1903 New Jersey seaside hotel. Seasonal exhibits at Christmas, Easter, Halloween, and other holidays. Admission: adult $4; senior $3; child younger than 12, $2.

Washington Shopping Malls

Chevy Chase Pavilion. 5335 Wisconsin Avenue NW. More than fifty shops, boutiques, and eateries. Open Monday to Friday 10 A.M.–8 P.M., Saturday 10 A.M.–6 P.M., and Sunday noon–5 P.M. (202) 686-5335.

Women's Fashion: Blair Delmonico, Country Road Australia, Express, Joan & David, Joan Vass, Koala Blue, Laura Ashley, The Limited, Silhouette Blues, Steilmann, Talbots, Victoria's Secret.

Men's Fashion: Country Road Australia, Rock Creek, Silhouette Blues.

Georgetown Park. 3222 M Street NW. (202) 298-5577. A modern-day shopping mecca of more than 100 shops, with a Victorian flavor. Open Monday to Saturday 10 A.M.–9 P.M.; Sunday noon–6 P.M.

Women's Fashion: Abercrombie & Fitch, Ann Taylor, Cache, Casual Corner, Charter Club, Chico's, Dara Michelle, Episode, Express, Georgiou, Irresistibles, J. Crew, The Limited, Lingerie Cacique, Pavo Real Boutique, Polo/Ralph Lauren, Talbots, Victoria's Secret.

Men's Fashion: Abercrombie & Fitch, Attivo, The Custom Shop, J. Crew, J. Riggings, Niccolo, Papillon, Pavo, Polo/Ralph Lauren.

Restaurants: (Canal Walk Cafes Food Court) Clyde's of Georgetown, Dean & DeLuca, Dill Pickle Deli, Georgetown Deli, Hunan Express, Samurai Japanese, Sbarro, and Vie de France.

The Pavillion at the Old Post Office. 1100 Pennsylvania Avenue NW. (202) 289-4224. March 1–Labor Day: Monday to Saturday 10 A.M.–9 P.M.; Sunday noon–7 P.M. Remainder of year: Monday to Saturday 10 A.M.–7 P.M.; Sunday noon–6 P.M.

Completed in 1899 as the first public building in what has become known as the Federal Triangle, the area bounded by Pennsylvania Avenue and Constitution Avenue between Fifth and Fifteenth Streets.

The building, a Romanesque Revival structure that has a clock tower at its center, is one of the oldest structures in downtown Washington; architects note it is similar to the Allegheny County Courthouse in Pittsburgh. It was considered out of style almost as soon as it was completed, and there were several attempts to demolish it over the years, but—like many federal programs—it somehow held on. In the 1970s, it was renovated and its central court was opened up to create a shopping arcade and food court; offices still occupy the upper floors. There is also a small National Park Service bookstore.

Free tours of the clock tower include a ride up the glass elevator, a view of the city from the twelfth floor, and an observation deck; free-admission tours begin every five minutes. Tours run from about 10 A.M. to 5:45 P.M.; for more information call (202) 606-8691.

A bandstand on the lower level, near the food court, is used for lunchtime concerts. We'd recommend the Old Post Office and Union Station as lunch stops on a tour of Washington.

Fashions: Carmas Boutique, Condor Imports, Silk Windsor.

Restaurants: Bagel Express, Blossoms, Enrico's Trattoria, Flying Fruit Fantasy, Georgetown Deli, Hampshire Farm Rotisserie, Indian Delight, Panda Cafe, Quick Pita, Sushi Shogun, Taco Don's, Temptations, Texas Grill.

The Shops at National Place and National Press Building. F Street, between Thirteenth and Fourteenth Streets near Metro Center. More than eighty shops on three levels. Open Monday to Saturday 10 A.M.–7 P.M.; Sunday noon–5 P.M. (202) 783-9090.

Women's Fashions: Accento, Alton's, August Max Woman, Banana Republic, Caren Charles, Casual Corner, Cignal, Dallas Alice, Destination, D.C., Express, Hit or Miss, The Limited, Nitsa-Nitsa Artwear, Powers & Goode, Shingar, Victoria's Secret.

Men's Fashions: Dallas Alice, Nash's Sports & Casuals, Oaktree, Papillon, Powers & Goode.

Restaurants: American Cafe, A Slice of Italy, Au Bon Pain, Bananas, Boardwalk Fries, Boston Seafood Company, Cajun Express, Flamer's Charbroiled Burgers, Frank-N-Spuds, Hunan Express, Jerry's Subs, Kabuki Sushi Bar & Tempura, Pa-Pa's Chicken, Primo's Deli, Sbarro, Stuff 'n Turkey.

A Selection of Favorite Shops in D.C.

Affrica. 2010½ R Street NW. (202) 745-7272. Fine traditional arts of Africa. Open Tuesday 2–6 P.M., Wednesday to Saturday noon–6 P.M. Metro: Dupont Circle.

Burberrys. 1155 Connecticut Avenue NW. (202) 463-3000. Clothing, outerwear, gifts, and accessories. Open Monday to Saturday 9:30 A.M.–6 P.M.; Sunday noon–5 P.M. Metro: Farragut North.

Coach. 1214 Wisconsin Avenue NW. (202) 342-1772. Fine handmade handbags, briefcases, and leather goods. Open Monday to Saturday 10 A.M.–7 P.M., and Sunday noon–6 P.M.

Hard Rock Cafe & Merchandise Store. 999 E Street NW. (202) 737-7625. Open daily.

Planet Hollywood. 1101 Pennsylvania Avenue NW. (202) 783-7827. Open Monday to Friday 11 A.M.–1 A.M. Metro: Federal Triangle, Metro Center.

Political Americana. 1331 Pennsylvania Avenue NW. (202) 547-1685 or (800) 333-4555. Political books, buttons, bumper stickers, and more. Open Monday to Friday 9 A.M.–9 P.M.; Saturday 10 A.M.–9 P.M.; Sunday 10 A.M.–6 P.M. Abbreviated hours in winter. Also at Union Station. Open Monday to Saturday 8:30 A.M.–9 P.M., Sunday 10 A.M.–7 P.M.

Politics & Prose Bookstore–Coffeehouse. 5015 Connecticut Avenue NW. (202) 364-1919. Open Sunday to Thursday 9 A.M.–10:30 P.M., Friday to Saturday 9 A.M.–midnight.

Rand McNally Map & Travel Store. 1201 Connecticut Avenue NW. (202) 223-6751. Open Monday to Saturday 10 A.M.–9:30 P.M.; Sunday 11 A.M.–6 P.M.

Chapter 10
Power Trips: Eleven Tours of Washington

We have spent months prowling the streets of Washington and driving the roads of Virginia, and we're nowhere near done exploring. We're looking forward to spending even more time as we update this book each year.

How much time should you spend on a visit to Washington? How much time can you spare?

You can hit most of the highlights and a few special interests in a week's time. To include Williamsburg and other destinations in the countryside of Virginia, add a few days to your trip.

We offer here eleven tours; ten of them cover a day's activities, and one includes attractions in Williamsburg and Central Virginia.

We've grouped attractions by location, taking into account operating hours. Remember that these are just suggestions—this book previews dozens of other places to visit in and around Washington, and there are thousands of combinations you can create.

Be sure to check the operating days and hours listed in this book, and call ahead if you have any questions.

Tour 1: Breakfast at the President's House
White House
Ford's Theatre
The House Where Lincoln Died
Smithsonian American Art Museum*(Reopens in 2003)*
National Portrait Gallery *(Reopens in 2003)*
National Building Museum
Union Station
National Postal Museum

Here's a busy walking day tour; you can also use the Metro for the final leg.

To visit the President's house, you're going to have to get up early, especially in the busy summer and school-vacation seasons. Tickets are available at the White House Visitors Center after 8 A.M., and the house is open from 10 A.M. to noon. Be sure to call the Visitors Center the day before and the morning of your visit to check on the schedule, because the White House can be closed when there are special events.

The White House tour takes about thirty minutes; we suggest you try to get in at 10 A.M.

Our busy day continues with a visit about six blocks away to Ford's Theatre and the Petersen House across the street on Tenth Street. Allow about an hour to tour both.

You can catch lunch in downtown D.C. My favorite place to eat around here, though, is at one of the many small restaurants in Chinatown.

For the next few years, the Old Patent Building on F at Eighth Streets, home to two impressive art museums, will be closed for reconstruction. In 2003, the Smithsonian American Art Museum (formerly the National Museum of American Art) and the National Portrait Gallery will reopen in the historic building.

As you pass the Old Patent Building, continue on F Street three more blocks east to the National Building Museum, one of the lesser-known places to visit in Washington, but high on our "Wow" list. Allow about an hour to tour the building, its exhibits, and the bookstore.

The last two stops on this day's tour are at Union Station. This is the longest hike on the tour; you may want to jump onto the Metro at the Judiciary Square station and ride it one stop to Union Station.

Go first to the National Postal Museum, next door to Union Station. The museum is open until 5:30 P.M. Allow about an hour; more if you are a serious philatelist.

End your day walking through the spectacular Union Station. You might want to eat dinner at one of the restaurants or the globetrotting food court. Use the Metro to zoom back to your hotel.

Tour 2 (Weekday): A Thoughtful Day

Bureau of Engraving and Printing
U.S. Holocaust Museum
Freer Gallery of Art
Arthur M. Sackler Gallery
National Museum of African Art
Smithsonian Castle
Arts and Industries Building

We'll begin our day at the Bureau of Engraving and Printing. You might want to splurge on a taxi; otherwise take the Metro to the Smithsonian exit and walk about six long blocks to Fourteenth and C Streets. After that you can complete the tour on foot.

Visit the nation's money factory soon after it opens at 9 A.M. Allow about forty-five minutes for the tour.

(At busy times of the year, before you go to the Bureau of Engraving, I'd suggest you stop in at the U.S. Holocaust Museum on Fourteenth Street to pick up a free ticket for an 11 A.M. scheduled visit to the permanent exhibition.)

Next, walk up Fourteenth Street to the Holocaust Museum, one of the most moving places in Washington. Allow as much as two hours to go through the permanent main exhibit (timed tickets are required during busy times) and to see the other galleries. Note that some young children may find the museum disturbing; no one leaves the place without thinking about the peaks and valleys of the human spirit.

There are few places to eat lunch in this part of Washington; we'd suggest you take a lunch with you or grab a snack from one of the food trucks near the museums.

Go back to Independence Avenue and head east to visit five of the Smithsonian's smaller jewels: the Freer Gallery, the Sackler Gallery, the National Museum of African Art, the Smithsonian Castle, and the Arts and Industries Building. Allow about an hour for each museum and your day will end about dinner time.

Tour 3: Space and Time

National Air and Space Museum
National Museum of American History
National Museum of Natural History

Start your day on a high note by touring one of Washington's most spectacular museums, the National Air and Space Museum. Every visitor will find a few hours worth of amazement here; special fans of airplanes and space travel can spend much more time. There's a decent cafeteria and a large bookstore, too.

Leave Air and Space at the Mall exit and cross over to the American History or Natural History museum. We've listed American History first because it has the better restaurants if you want to catch lunch there. Both museums have impressive bookstores.

Though there are only three stops on this day's tour, some visitors may not even have their fill of riches.

Tour 4 (Weekday): The Legislative and Judicial Branches

The U.S. Supreme Court
The U.S. Capitol
Library of Congress
Folger Shakespeare Library/Capital Children's Museum

A visit to the quietly spectacular Supreme Court is in order at any time, but your visit will be even more special if you can manage to see the "Supremes" in action. The justices generally hear oral arguments in the morning on Monday, Tuesday, and Wednesday of every other week from early October until late winter or early spring. They may also be on the bench to issue rulings or conduct other business.

Consult *The Washington Post* or call the court for a schedule at the time of your visit.

Arrive at the Court at First Street and Maryland Avenue (the nearest Metro stations are Capitol South and Union Station) about 9 A.M. Lectures are presented on the half hour from 9:30 A.M. until 3:30 P.M. when the court is not in session; seating for oral arguments is on a first-come, first-served basis, with sessions beginning at 10 A.M.

There's a decent small cafeteria in the basement of the Supreme Court, and this is a good place for an early lunch.

Leave the court and cross the green park to the U.S. Capitol. Tours depart regularly from the Rotunda.

Stop by the offices of your congressional representative and one of your U.S. senators to obtain a pass to the visitors' galleries of the Congress and Senate. (If you're not particularly interested in seeing the office of your member of Congress, you can save yourself an hour or so by requesting tickets by mail a few weeks ahead of time. While you're at it, see if you can obtain one of the VIP tickets.)

After you're through at the Capitol, head back toward the Supreme Court again to tour the spectacular Jefferson Building of the Library of Congress. If you have a special interest in one of the collections, you can extend your visit there.

The next stop can be the Folger Shakespeare Library, next door to the Jefferson Building. If you are traveling with children, you may want to let them burn off their energy at the end of the day at the Capital Children's Museum, at 800 Third Street, just north of Union Station; it's open until 5 P.M.

Tour 5 (Weekday): Art and the Feds

Federal Bureau of Investigation
National Archives
National Gallery of Art
Hirshhorn Museum

The tour of the J. Edgar Hoover Federal Bureau of Investigation building is one of the hottest tickets in town, especially in the summer and during school vacations. (We're not all that sure why, because we found the visit only mildly interesting.) There are two ways to minimize your wait at the FBI: one is to get there early, and the other is to arrange for a tour by appointment through your member of Congress.

We'll assume you make it into one of the first tours of the day; arrive between 8:30 and 9 A.M. and you should be out by 10 or 10:30 A.M.

Head toward the Mall on Ninth Street and then circle the National Archives to the Constitution Avenue entrance to view the Declaration of Independence, the U.S. Constitution, and a copy of the Magna Carta. Serious scholars may want to look at other collections at the Archives.

Continue one block farther south to the National Gallery of Art on the Mall. The museum is worth ninety minutes or more; there is also a mostly modern art annex next door in the National Gallery of Art East. There's a café in the East building.

Finish up by crossing the Mall to the Hirshhorn, a temple to modern art.

Tour 6: A Green Day

National Zoological Park
Dumbarton Oaks Garden & Museum
United States National Arboretum
United States Botanic Garden

Choose a nice day to explore the great outdoors. We'd suggest you get an early start at the National Zoo; use the Cleveland Park Metro stop when you arrive and the Woodley Park–National Zoo Metro station when you leave to avoid climbing the hill on Connecticut Avenue. The zoo is worth a few hours; catch lunch there.

Serious gardening fans should walk through Rock Creek Park or catch a taxi from the zoo to Dumbarton Oaks Garden & Museum. The gardens open in the afternoon.

An alternate afternoon would be to visit the sprawling United States National Arboretum in the eastern corner of the District. There is no nearby Metro stop; we'd suggest catching a cab from Union Station.

A minipark can also be found at the United States Botanic Garden on Independence Avenue in the shadow of the U.S. Capitol.

Tour 7: The Dupont Circle Museums

Woodrow Wilson House Museum
Textile Museum
Phillips Collection
Mary McLeod Bethune Council House
B'nai B'rith Klutznick National Jewish Museum
Christian Heurich Mansion
Octagon Museum

The Dupont Circle area of Washington is chock-a-block with interesting private museums, embassies, shops, and restaurants of all descriptions. The Dupont Circle Metro stop is at the heart of it all.

Read the descriptions of the various museums in and around Dupont Circle and be sure to call to check on operating hours.

Tour 8: Arlington Cemetery and the Pentagon

Arlington National Cemetery
The Pentagon

Tour 9: A Monumental Tour

Washington Monument
Lincoln Memorial
Vietnam Veterans Memorial
Korean War Veterans Memorial

Tour 10: Out of Town

Mount Vernon	(Half day)
Civil War Sites	(Day)
Richmond	(Day)
Williamsburg	(Day)
Busch Gardens Williamsburg	(Day)
Jamestown	(Half day)
Yorktown	(Half day)

Tour 11: Monuments to Stupidity

Only in Washington would tourists gather on street corners to gawk at the site of a "third-rate burglary"; the sites of various sexual encounters that brought down congressmen, senators, presidential aides, and presidential candidates; and even the location of notorious spy capers. Wanna see them for yourself?

The Watergate. 2600 Virginia Avenue NW. Here the henchmen of President Richard Nixon broke into the headquarters of the Democratic National Committee in the months leading up to the 1972 presidential campaign. The "third-rate burglary" became messier and messier and eventually led to prison terms for members of Nixon's staff and the eventual resignation of the president himself. Today, the Watergate is still one of the better-regarded hotel and office complexes and is home to a number of Members of Congress and the presidential administration.

The Jefferson Hotel. Sixteenth and M Streets NW. Here in Suite 205 presidential advisor Dick Morris spent some of his consulting fees on a $200-per-hour hooker, sharing some of his phone conversations with President Clinton with her. The story broke in 1996 on the day Clinton was due to accept renomination as the Democratic nominee.

The Vista Hotel. 1400 M Street NW on Scott Circle. In room 727 Washington Mayor Marion Barry was videotaped lighting up a crack pipe in January of 1990; convicted on one count of cocaine possession, he sat out one term but was returned to office in 1994.

Gary Hart's house at 517 Sixth Street SE. A front-runner in the presidential campaign in 1987, Senator Gary Hart told reporters that if they really believed all the rumors about his womanizing they should follow him around; the *Miami Herald* took him up on the offer and found Donna Rice checking into his apartment one Friday night and not emerging until late the next day. Soon afterward, Hart pulled out of the race.

The Aldrich Ames Mailbox. CIA officer Aldrich Ames would mark a mailbox at Thirty-seventh and R Streets with chalk to tell his Russian handlers that he had something to share with them. The mailbox is still there, but Ames is not.

Ames and his wife were arrested in February of 1994. Subsequent investigation established that they had been paid more than $1.5 million since 1985; they apparently made no effort to hide their extra cash, buying an expensive house in Arlington, a Jaguar car, and a farm and condominiums in Colombia.

Guided Tours to Washington and Nearby

There are a number of options available to those who want a guided tour of Washington, including scheduled tours by bus, boat, or car, and custom trips by chauffeured limousine.

All About Town, Inc. Narrated tours by bus, including inside visits to the White House, Capitol, Ford's Theatre, and Supreme Court and drive-bys of most of Washington's other famous sights. Other tours visit Arlington and Mount Vernon. Free pickup from most major hotels. (202) 393-3696.

America Limousine Services, Inc. Limousine, sedans, and vans. (703) 280-8123.

Capitol River Cruises. Hour-long cruises on a riverboat with views of the monuments and Capitol. Departs hourly from 11 A.M.–8 P.M. daily with longer hours on weekends, from Washington Harbour at Thirty-first and K Streets NW. Tickets are adult $10; child ages 3–12, $5. (301) 460-7447.

D.C. Ducks. Wonderfully strange tours on former Army transport vehicles that are—depending on your point of view—boats with wheels, or trucks with propellers. Either way, the tour includes an hour-long visit to downtown and a thirty-minute cruise on the Potomac past the monuments. Vehicles depart from Union Station. Tickets are adult $24; childer older than 12, $12; child younger than 12 ride for free. Call for schedule. (202) 966-3825.

Gray Line Sightseeing Tours. The Gray Line and its sister Gold Line offer a variety of tours in Washington and surrounding areas. The company also operates Trolley Tours with unlimited reboarding. Gray Line has bus tours that leave Washington for day trips or overnight trips to Williamsburg, and day trips to Monticello, Harper's Ferry, and Gettysburg. Tours leave from many hotels and from Union Station. (202) 289-1995. www.dctourism.com/dc.

Old Town Trolley Tours of Washington. Two-hour loops of downtown and neighborhoods with unlimited reboarding privileges. Trolleys leave every thirty minutes daily. Tickets are adult $24; and child $12. (202) 966-3825.

Scandal Tours. A by-product of the comedy group Gross National Product, these tours visit the sites of some of Washington's best-known downfalls, from Watergate to Gary Hart's townhouse to various congressional and presidential low points. Costumed players from the comedy group travel with guests on the bus and reenact some of the juiciest stuff. Tours are conducted from April through Labor Day on Saturdays at 1 P.M.; reservations are required. Buses depart from the Old Post Office Pavillion at 1100 Pennsylvania Avenue. Tickets are about $30. (202) 783-7212.

Smithsonian Resident Associate Program. Guided tours of Washington neighborhoods with discussions of history, art, architecture, and industry. Reservations required. (202) 357-3030.

Tourmobile. Climb aboard a chauffeured double-length tram, more-or-less at your beck and call to visit most locations in and around the Mall. The Tourmobile vehicles loop around the Mall and extend out to Arlington Cemetery. The trip includes a narration with commentary on the museums, monuments, and buildings along the route.

The Tourmobile stops at the White House, Washington Monument, Arts and Industries Building, National Air and Space Museum, Union Station, U.S. Capitol, National Gallery of Art, Natural History Museum, American History Museum, Bureau of Engraving and Printing, U.S. Holocaust Memorial Museum, Jefferson Memorial, West Potomac Park, Lincoln Memorial, Vietnam Veterans Memorial, Kennedy Center, FDR Memorial, and Arlington National Cemetery.

Tickets can be purchased from booths along the Mall or from drivers; each ticket allows unlimited reboarding on the day of purchase. The trams run

9 A.M. to 6:30 P.M. June 15 through Labor Day, and 9:30 A.M. to 4:30 P.M. the rest of the year. Final reboarding is one hour before closing time.

Adult $16; child 3–11, $7. You can also purchase an advance ticket (adult $18 and child $8) after 4 P.M. in summer or after 2 P.M. the rest of the year; advance tickets are good for the rest of the afternoon on the day of purchase and again for all of the next day. For more information, call (888) 868-7707. www.tourmobile.com

Other offerings include the Arlington National Cemetery Tour (adult $4.75; child $2.25), the Mount Vernon Tours (adult $22; child $11), and the Frederick Douglass Tour (adults $7; children $3.50). Various combinations of tours are also offered.

Cruises and Boat Tours

C & O Canal Barge Rides. Mule-drawn barges along the C & O Canal, departing from Georgetown from mid-April through mid-October. (301) 739-4200.

Capital River Cruises. Narrated tours of Washington, from Georgetown Harbour. (301) 460-7447.

Dandy Restaurant Cruise Ship. Luncheon and dinner and dancing cruises on the Potomac River. Operates year-round with special cruises on holidays. Boats leave Old Town Alexandria waterfront. (703) 683-6090. Ticket prices about $45 for lunch or brunch cruises, about $70 to $90 for dinner cruises. Four-hour cruises with six-course meals on New Year's Eve and Fourth of July for $180.

Odyssey. Lunch and dinner cruises, Sunday Jazz Brunch on a low-slung glass-covered river barge specially designed to pass beneath the bridges on the Potomac. Departs from Gangplank Marina, Seventh and Water Streets SW. Metro: Waterfront. (202) 488-6000.

Potomac Riverboat Co. Narrated cruises of Washington and Alexandria mid-March to mid-October. (703) 548-9000.

Spirit Cruises. Luncheon and dinner cruises, and excursions to Mount Vernon, from Pier 4 at Sixth and Water Streets SW. Metro: Waterfront. (202) 554-8000.

Ballooning

How about escaping Washington, the city of hot air, for a cruise in a hot air balloon? There are tours over Maryland and Virginia from spring through fall. Rides cost about $150 to $200 per person and usually take off at sunrise or sunset.

Adventures Aloft. Float over the Sugarloaf Mountains and the valleys of western Maryland. 26809 Haines Road, Rockville, Maryland. (301) 881-6262.

Balloons Unlimited. Float through horse country near the Blue Ridge Mountains of Virginia. (703) 281-2300.

Chapter 11
Annual Events in Washington and Northern Virginia

(All events are free unless noted.)

January

Winter Season: Ice Skating. Outdoors at the National Sculpture Garden Rink, Ninth Street and Constitution Avenue NW. (202) 619-7222. Admission charged. The rink reopened in 2000 after renovations.

Reflecting Pool and the C & O Canal when conditions permit. (202) 619-7222.

Pershing Park at Fourteenth Street and Pennsylvania Avenue NW. (202) 737-6938.

Artful Evenings. Phillips Collection, 1600 Twenty-first Street NW. (202) 387-2151. Evening hours and special events on Thursdays at the Phillips Collection, including gallery talks, video screenings, and live music performances. Year-round.

Martin Luther King Jr. Birthday Observance. Lincoln Memorial. (202) 619-7222. Wreath-laying ceremonies, speeches, choirs, and color guard salute. Mid-January.

U.S. Army Band Concert Series. Bruckner Hall at Fort Myer in Arlington, Virginia. (703) 696-3399. Tuesday and Thursday evenings. Year-round.

February

Black History Month. Smithsonian Institution, (202) 357-2700. Martin Luther King, Jr., Memorial Library, (202) 727-0321. National Mall, (202) 619-7222.

Frederick Douglass Birthday Salute. Frederick Douglass National Historic Site. (202) 426-5961. Mid-February.

Abraham Lincoln Birthday Celebration. Lincoln Memorial. (202) 619-7222. Wreath-laying ceremony and reading of Gettysburg Address. Mid-February.

Chinese New Year Parade. Chinatown. (202) 789-7000. Parade with lions, dragons, and drums. January or February. www.washington.org.

Mount Vernon Open House. Mount Vernon. (703) 780-2000. Free admission and special activities to celebrate George Washington's birthday. Mid-February. www.mountvernon.org.

George Washington's Birthday Parade. Alexandria. (703) 838-4200. Parade through Old Town historic district. Mid-February. www.funside.com.

Washington Flower & Garden Show. Washington Convention Center. (202) 626-1100. Admission. Late February.

March

D.C. Armory Antiques Show. (202) 547-9077 ext. 190. Admission. Early March.

St. Patrick's Day Parade. Constitution Avenue NW. Hundreds of thousands gather to watch dancers, bands, and floats. Mid-March.

Smithsonian Kite Festival. National Mall. (202) 357-3030. Late March or early April.

Imagination Celebration. Festival of performing arts for children. Kennedy Center.

April

National Cherry Blossom Festival. Various locations. (202) 619-7222 or (202) 789-7000. Celebration culminates with Cherry Blossom Festival Parade in mid-April.

Easter Sunrise Service. Arlington National Cemetery's Memorial Amphitheatre. (703) 607-8052. Late March or early April.

White House Easter Egg Roll. South Lawn of the White House. (202) 456-2200. Late March or early April.

White House Spring Garden Tours. Jacqueline Kennedy Rose Gardens and West Lawn Gardens of the White House. (202) 456-2200. Mid-April.

Thomas Jefferson Birthday. Jefferson Memorial. (202) 619-7222. Military drills and wreath-laying ceremony. Mid-April.

Duke Ellington Birthday Celebration. Freedom Plaza. Celebration of this Washington native's contribution to American music. Mid-April.

William Shakespeare's Birthday Celebration. Folger Shakespeare Library. Music, theater, food, and exhibits. (202) 544-7077. Mid-April.

Earth Day. National Mall. (202) 619-7222.

May

National Law Enforcement Officers Memorial Candlelight Vigil. Fourth and F Streets. (202) 737-3400. Mid-May.

Memorial Day Weekend Concert. U.S. Capitol. (202) 619-7222. National Symphony Orchestra.

Memorial Day Ceremonies. Arlington National Cemetery. Wreath-laying at the Tomb of the Unknown Soldier. (703) 607-8052. Also at Vietnam Veterans Memorial, (703) 607-8052, and U.S. Navy Memorial, (202) 737-2300.

Summer Events

C & O Canal Barge Rides. Thirtieth and Thomas Jefferson Streets NW, and Great Falls Tavern, Maryland. (202) 653-5190. 90-minute tours with storytelling and song. Admission. April to October.

U.S. Botanic Garden Summer Terrace Show. (202) 225-7099. Mid-May to Mid-October.

Concerts on the Avenue. (202) 433-2525. Memorial Day to Labor Day. Tuesday evenings at the U.S. Navy Memorial.

Military Band Summer Concert Series. June to September. National Mall.

June

Alexandria Waterfront Festival. (703) 549-8300. Tall ships, ethnic foods, entertainment, and other events. Admission. Mid-June.

Festival of American Folklife. (202) 357-2700. Annual festival with

Festival of American Folklife
Photo courtesy of Washington, D.C.,
Convention and Visitors Association

entertainment, art, music, and food, sponsored by the Smithsonian Institution; draws more than a million visitors. Late June to early July.

July

National Independence Day Celebration. (202) 619-7222. Parade down Constitution Avenue, entertainment at the Sylvan Theatre at the Washington Monument, National Symphony Orchestra concert, and fireworks display over the Washington Monument.

    Mary McLeod Bethune Celebration. Lincoln Park. (202) 619-7222. Wreath-laying ceremony, gospel choirs, speeches. Mid-July.

    Virginia Scottish Games. Alexandria. (703) 838-5005. Highland dancing, bagpipes, fiddling, and heptathlon competition. Admission. Late July.

    Children's Festival. (202) 619-7222. Music, arts, and general fun at the Carter Barron Amphitheatre, Sixteenth Street and Colorado Avenue NW, sponsored by the Capital Children's Museum and the National Park Service. July or August.

August

Arlington County Fair. (703) 228-6400. Rides, entertainment, arts and crafts, food, and exhibits. Mid-August.

    U.S. Army Band's *1812 Overture* Concert. (703) 696-3718. Sylvan Theatre on the Washington Monument grounds. Mid-August.

    U.S. Navy Band Lollipop Concert. The U.S. Navy Band in a special program for children at the Jefferson Memorial.

September

Labor Day Weekend Concert. U.S. Capitol. (202) 619-7222 or (202) 416-8100. National Symphony Orchestra outdoor concert.

    D.C. Blues Festival. (202) 828-3028. Carter Barron Amphitheatre. Early September.

    Black Family Reunion. National Mall. (202) 659-0006. Weekend celebration of the African-American family with headline performers, food, and exhibits. Early September.

    Adams–Morgan Day. Music, dance, art, and food from this culturally diverse neighborhood. Early September. www.dcnet.com/am-day.

    Constitution Day Commemoration. National Archives. (202) 501-5000. Naturalization ceremony and musical concert. Mid-September.

    International Children's Festival. Vienna, Virginia. (703) 642-0862. Outdoor arts celebration for families at Wolf Trap Farm Park for the Performing Arts. Admission. Mid-September.

October

State Fair of Virginia. (804) 228-3200. Rides, headline performers, animal exhibits, parades, and farming competitions. Fairgrounds on Strawberry Hill, Richmond. Late September to early October.

    Taste of D.C. (202) 724-5430 or (202) 724-4091. Sample the offerings of several dozen of the city's best restaurants, watch entertainment, and shop at an arts and crafts festival. Admission is free, but tickets are sold for food stalls. Early October. Pennsylvania Avenue, between Ninth and Fourteenth Streets NW.

    German-American Day Festival. Union Station. (202) 554-2664. Music, food, entertainment, and arts. Early October.

    AIDS Quilt. A moving addition to the fall ceremonies on the Mall.

    U.S. Navy Birthday. U.S. Navy Memorial. (202) 737-2300. Wreath-laying ceremony. Mid-October.

    White House Fall Garden Tours. (202) 456-2200 or (202) 619-7222. Mid-October.

    Fall D.C. Antiques Show. D.C. Armory. (202) 547-9077 ext. 190. Admission. Mid-October.

November

Annual Seafaring Celebration. Navy Museum. (202) 433-4882. A family event celebrating maritime lore and history with food, arts and crafts, and entertainment. Early November.

Veterans Day Ceremonies. Arlington National Cemetery. (703) 607-8052. Also at the Vietnam Veterans Memorial, (202) 619-7222, and at U.S. Navy Memorial, (202) 737-2300.

Storytelling Festival. Martin Luther King, Jr., Library. For children.

National Christmas Show. D.C. Armory. (202) 547-9077. Early November. Vendors, crafts, entertainment, visit from Santa.

December

Christmas on S Street. Woodrow Wilson House & Museum. (202) 387-4062. Admission. Early December to early January.

Scottish Christmas Walk. Alexandria's Old Town throws a party with bagpipes, parades, and Santa Claus. (703) 548-0111. Early December. Old Town Alexandria.

People's Christmas Tree Lighting. West side of U.S. Capitol. (202) 224-3069. Early December.

Washington Crafts Show. (202) 328-2000. Ceramics, glasswork, woodwork, fiber art, paper art, and metal creations for sale. Early December.

Pearl Harbor Day. U.S. Navy Memorial. (202) 737-2300. Wreath-laying ceremony. December 7.

Old Town Christmas Candlelight Tours. Alexandria's Old Town. Music, Colonial dancing, period decorations. Admission. Mid-December. (703) 838-5005.

White House Christmas Tree Lighting and White House Tours. (202) 456-2200. The President's House is decked out for Christmas inside and outside throughout the month of December. The President traditionally lights the National Christmas Tree near the start of the month, kicking off a month of nightly musical concerts on the Ellipse. Tree lighting in early December; Pageant of Peace throughout the month; and special Christmas Candlelight Tours of the White House around Christmas Day.

Pageant of Peace. Holiday celebration for children featuring the National Christmas Tree, nightly choral performances on the Ellipse and the Mall grounds, and a display of Christmas trees representing each state and territory in the nation.

Kwanzaa Holiday Expo. The African holiday celebrating the "first fruits of the harvest" includes traditional music and dance, a children's village, fashion shows, educational workshops, and an African Marketplace. Late December. D.C. Convention Center. Consult newspapers for schedule.

Chapter 12
Washington's Neighborhoods

Overlooked in the concentration on better-known areas such as Capitol Hill and the White House are a dozen or more interesting residential, shopping, and business neighborhoods worth exploring.

In This Chapter

Adams-Morgan

Anacostia

Brookland

Capitol Hill

Chinatown

Dupont Circle

Embassy Row

F Street/Downtown

Foggy Bottom

Gallery Place

Georgetown

Howard University

K Street/Downtown

Kalorama

Pennsylvania Avenue

Potomac Park

Rock Creek Park

Shaw

Southwest

Woodley Park

Adams-Morgan

Along Columbia Road, between Eighteenth Street and Kalorama Park NW, Adams-Morgan offers a United Nations of restaurants, galleries, shops, and street vendors with an emphasis on Hispanic and Latin sources but also including European, Mexican, and other cultures. The neighborhood's clubs are open late into the night.

The name of the district is an interesting expression of multiculturalism all by itself. In the 1950s, a neighborhood organization was formed to increase cooperation among the racially segregated residents of the area; they chose to name the area after the all-white Adams school and the all-black Morgan school in the area. The annual "Adams-Morgan Day" is a much-anticipated neighborhood fair. Take a taxi; parking is difficult, and the nearest Metro station (Woodley Park/Zoo) is a 15-minute walk away.

Anacostia

East from the Anacostia River to Pennsylvania Avenue on the north, and Southern Avenue on the south and east. Named for its original Indian inhabitants, the area dates back to the arrival of Captain John Smith in 1607. The original Washington settlement area for freed blacks after the Civil War, it became a center of African-American culture. Sites of interest include the Frederick Douglass National Historic Site and the Smithsonian Institution's Anacostia Museum.

Brookland

In far upper northeast Washington, this residential neighborhood includes the Catholic University of America, the National Shrine of the Immaculate Conception, and the Franciscan Monastery. All offer tours.

Capitol Hill

Certainly one of the most exclusive "neighborhoods" in the world, Capitol Hill obviously includes the U.S. Capitol; also nearby are the Supreme Court, Library of Congress, and Senate and House Office Buildings, as well as the Folger Shakespeare Library, one of the finest collections in the world. A few blocks away is the magnificent Union Station, and behind the station is the Capital Children's Museum.

The tree-shaded residential streets in the area also offer intimate (and pricey) restaurants, galleries, and boutiques. Eastern Market, an old-style farmer's market, is held here every Saturday morning in season.

Chinatown

The Chinatown Friendship Archway, a symphony of red and gold dragons, at Seventh and H Streets NW, is the commercial center of Washington's small Chinatown, which is located at G and H Streets between Sixth and Eighth Streets. The area is easily reached through the Gallery Place–Chinatown Metro station; use the exit at H and Seventh Streets.

Come to Chinatown for an inexpensive meal (restaurants include Chinese, Mongolian, Thai, and Vietnamese menus) or to shop at the Asian grocery and gift shops. A lively Chinese New Year's Celebration fills the streets each February.

Dupont Circle

In the late 1800s and well into the twentieth century, Dupont Circle was Washington's most fashionable residential area. Today, it marches to the beat of a different drummer—it is the Greenwich Village of D.C., alive at almost all hours of the day with restaurants, shops, galleries, and unusual people. Some of the District's better ethnic restaurants and coffee shops are in the area, and there are all sorts of unusual clubs, including the District's gay-bar center.

Circular logic. Washington's Dupont Circle, originally named Pacific Circle, was renamed in 1884 to memorialize Civil War hero Rear Admiral Samuel Francis Du Pont. The admiral was a grandson of French economist Pierre Samuel Du Pont de Nemours, head of the family that became an important American industrial and banking power. In 1861, Admiral Du Pont lead the Union to victory at Port Royal, South Carolina.

The Dupont Circle area extends along Connecticut Avenue from N through T Streets NW and in the surrounding blocks east and west of the park-like circle itself. The Metro will take you directly to Dupont Circle station; the gigantic escalator that leads from the bowels of the subway to the circle is a tourist attraction all by itself.

If you can't find an interesting place to eat around here, especially along Connecticut Avenue or Seventeenth Street, you aren't hungry. There are all manner of ethnic, health food, and just plain quirky places all around.

The neighborhood also includes a number of important museums, such as the Textile Museum, the Phillips Collection, the Woodrow Wilson House, the Anderson House Museum, and the Christian Heurich Mansion. The Islamic Center on Massachusetts Avenue is open for tours by appointment.

Embassy Row

Most of the District's 150 foreign embassies and chanceries are located in this neighborhood, extending along Massachusetts Avenue NW, between Sheridan and Observatory Circle, and west of Dupont Circle. Many are housed within former mansions that were once homes to Washington's social elite; many of the homes were sold during the Depression. The Vice President's Mansion is located at Observatory Circle.

F Street/Downtown

The heart of "old downtown" is on F Street between Tenth and Fifteenth streets. Nearby to many of Washington's museums and a few blocks above the National Mall and the FBI building, the area includes the National Theatre, Ford's Theatre, the Warner Theatre, the Hard Rock Cafe, and Planet Hollywood. The Shops at National Place and the National Press Building offer an unusual collection of boutiques.

FOGGY BOTTOM TO THE WHITE HOUSE

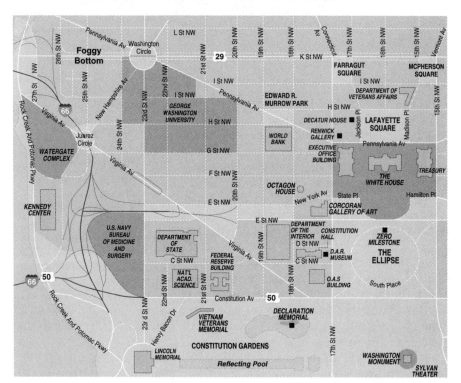

Foggy Bottom

This neighborhood earned its name because of its location: a marshy, lowland area where trader clipper ships once docked. Today, Foggy Bottom includes the area between Pennsylvania and Virginia Avenues, and from Twenty-second to Twenty-fifth Streets NW. The area includes rowhouses dating back to the early 1800s, the State Department, George Washington University, Pan American Union, and the John F. Kennedy Center for the Performing Arts. Also in the area is the Watergate Hotel complex, which includes some of the District's most exclusive restaurants.

Gallery Place

An arts district undergoing a healthy revival, the neighborhood encompasses the blocks between E and H Streets and Fourth and Ninth Streets NW. Bordering the Washington Convention Center and the new MCI Arena, the area includes the Smithsonian Institution's National Portrait Gallery and the National Museum of American Art, the magnificent National Building Museum at Judiciary Square, and many art galleries and boutiques. The Metro will deliver you to the Gallery Place Station.

Georgetown

Predating the city of Washington, Georgetown was once a thriving Colonial port where goods from western Maryland farmlands were shipped to Europe. Georgetown is the westernmost section of the city, bounded by the Potomac River on the south and by Rock Creek Park on the east.

Today, Georgetown is one of the best places in Washington in which to walk around, shop, and dine. The historic area includes restored Colonial-era homes (some of which were slave quarters before Emancipation), and a wide variety of nightclubs, ethnic restaurants, and shops.

The spectacular Dumbarton Oaks museum and formal gardens is in the area, as is Tudor Place. Georgetown is also the starting point for the C & O Canal, which extends north along the Potomac River for 185 miles.

And Georgetown University, the oldest Catholic university in the country—dating back to 1789—is a lovely place to stroll. The main entrance is at Thirty-seventh and O Streets. For information on tours, call (202) 687-5055.

Howard University

One of the most prestigious black universities in the country, it was founded in 1867 and named for its first president, Union Army General Oliver Otis Howard. Centered at 2400 Sixth Street.

K Street/Downtown

Washington's downtown business district, including K Street and surrounding blocks from Twelfth to Twenty-first Streets NW. Much of the nongovernmental business of Washington, as well as the offices of the legions of lawyers and lobbyists of the District, are located here. They are served by expense-account restaurants, fashionable shops, fancy hotels, and street vendors.

Kalorama

Kalorama draws its name from poet Joel Barlow's former estate in the area; the word means "beautiful view" in Greek. Barlow was a well-respected writer and diplomat born in 1754; among his best-known works is *The Vision of Columbus*. He served as U.S. Consul to Algiers, where he negotiated several treaties. He was killed in 1812 during Napoleon I's retreat from Moscow.

Pennsylvania Avenue

One of Pierre L'Enfant's original grand avenues, this was once the business and social center when Washington was still a small town. Market Square, at the intersection with Seventh Street, was a thriving farmer's market.

Today, of course, Pennsylvania Avenue is best known for the modest home at number 1600, better known as the White House.

The area has gone through a major renewal during the past decade, rebuilding and upgrading the avenue block-by-block and adding several new hotels, plazas, shopping areas, and office complexes.

Major visitor centers include Freedom Plaza, the Pavillion at the Old Post Office, the Willard Hotel, the National Theatre, the Treasury Department, and the White House.

Potomac Park

Washington's outdoor playground along the Potomac River. Facilities include golf, ice-skating, swimming, boating, tennis, and hiking. 900 Ohio Drive SW. (202) 485-9880.

Rock Creek Park

A sprawling urban park that has a zoo, a planetarium, a nature center, 15 miles of hiking and jogging trails, two nine-hole golf courses, picnic areas, and horseback riding. Open dawn to dusk. 5200 Glover Road NW. (202) 282-1063.

Shaw

A residential neighborhood in northwest Washington and centered near Twelfth and T Streets, Shaw was the cultural center for the District's African Americans. Duke Ellington grew up here, and the Lincoln Theatre was the heart of Washington's "Black Broadway."

Southwest

For several blocks along Maine Avenue in Southwest Washington, the waterfront has developed among sailboats, yachts, old steamboats, fishing boats, seafood markets, and restaurants. Locals gather to purchase fresh Chesapeake Bay crabs, oysters, clams, and other seafood brought upriver daily to the markets. Restaurants in the area provide views of the Washington Channel and Washington National Airport across the Potomac River.

Southwest is also the home to the Arena Stage, and the L'Enfant Plaza hotel and shopping complex. At the end of the channel walkway is the somber *Titanic* Memorial.

Woodley Park

A residential area stretching north along Connecticut Avenue, upward from Calvery Street NW. Once the "summer home" to many Washingtonians who relocated uptown to escape the summer heat, it is an area of shaded streets and rolling hills, and the setting for the Smithsonian Institution's National Zoological Park.

Several major hotels are located here, along with the Washington National Cathedral atop Mt. Saint Albans. Many of the restaurants in the area feature outdoor terraces or sidewalk cafes.

Chapter 13
Professional and Participant Sports

Professional Sports

Big-city teams with big-city arenas . . . everything except baseball, although Baltimore is less than an hour away.

Washington's two newest showplaces of sports opened in 1997. The MCI Center, at F and Seventh Streets near the Convention Center and the National Portrait Gallery, is the new home of D.C.'s NBA and NHL teams, as well as the site of concerts and special events.

Jack Kent Cooke Stadium, across the river in suburban Maryland, is the home stadium for the Washington Redskins.

Washington, D.C.

Washington Wizards. The National Basketball Association team formerly known politically incorrectly as the Bullets plays at the MCI Center in downtown near the Convention Center. The regular season runs from November through April. (202) 628-3200. www.nba.com/wizards.

Washington Mystics. The Women's National Basketball Association team plays games at the MCI Center from June through the end of August. (202) 628-3200. www.wnba.com/mystics.

Washington Capitals. The National Hockey League team, with a regular season that runs from October through April, also plays at the MCI Center. (202) 628-3200. www.washingtoncaps.com.

Washington Redskins. The National Football League team season runs from September through December. (703) 478-8900; ticket information (301) 276-6060. www.nfl.com/redskins/.

Jack Kent Cooke Stadium, is located on Raljon Road in Raljon, Maryland. The 80,116-seat stadium, with a real grass playing surface, replaced RFK Stadium, the Redskins' home for thirty-five years. RFK was the smallest stadium in the league and one of its least comfortable; the new structure makes up for most of its shortcomings. The huge stadium sells out for most events; you may have to deal with a ticket broker selling at premium rates.

Maryland

Baltimore Orioles. The Birds flock to the beautiful Oriole Park at Camden Yards in Baltimore. (410) 685-9800. The Orioles maintain a store and ticket outlet in Washington at 914 Seventeenth Street NW. (202) 296-2473. Tickets can also be purchased through Ticketmaster.

Baltimore Ravens. The Ravens roost at the 69,000-seat PSI Net Stadium at 1101 Russell Street near Camden Yards. (410) 547-8100 or (800) 551-7328. In a move that engendered great controversy, the Cleveland Browns uprooted themselves at the end of the 1995–96 NFL season and swooped down for a landing in Baltimore, where they were reborn as the Baltimore Ravens. Ravens, as in local notable Edgar Allan Poe's famous poem.

Laurel Race Track. Route 198, Laurel. (301) 725-0400. The historic track opened in 1911. The thoroughbred racing calendar runs from January through March and again in July and August. Grandstand admission to the 12,000-seat structure is $3, and clubhouse admission is $5. To drive, take exit 33A off the Baltimore-Washington Parkway to Maryland Highway 198.

Pimlico. Winner and Hayward Avenues, Baltimore, about forty-five miles north of Washington. (410) 542-9400. The second-oldest thoroughbred track in the country (after the historic track in Saratoga, New York) and the home of the Preakness, the second jewel in racing's Triple Crown. The race is held the third Saturday in May. The racing season runs from March to June and again from July to September. Grandstand admission is $3, clubhouse seats $5, and the somewhat posh sports palace costs $6.

Rosecroft Raceway. 6336 Rosecroft Drive, at Brinkley Road, Fort Washington. (301) 567-4000. Year-round harness racing, about ten miles southeast of Washington. Admission $3.

The Best Seats in the House

MCI Center. Between Sixth and Seventh and F and G Streets, NW. The current sports star in Washington is its arena, with about 20,600 seats for Washington Wizards NBA basketball, Washington Mystics WNBA hoops, Washington Capitals NHL hockey, and a wide variety of concerts, family shows, and other cultural and entertainment events.

The center has its own entrance to the Metro at Gallery Place/Chinatown. Other nearby Metro stops are Archives, Judiciary Square, and Metro Center. There are also about 10,000 parking spaces scattered within a 10-block radius.

In addition to events, the center offers its own attractions:

- **The MCI National Sports Gallery.** An interactive museum of sports memorabilia. Galleries showcase basketball, baseball, hockey, and football, along with a regular rotation of special-interest sports.
- **American Sportscasters Association Hall of Fame.** In addition to remembrances of the great voices of sport, visitors will have the opportunity to emulate broadcasting greats in a special fantasy play-by-play booth as the announcer, director, or statistician at historic sports moments.

- **Discovery Channel Destination: D.C.** A three-story superstore that takes visitors on an imaginary journey around the world.
- **Velocity Grill.** An upscale sports-themed restaurant overlooking the Wizards' practice court.

RFK Stadium. (202) 547-9077. Host to a variety of sporting events and concerts, including the D.C. United soccer team.

Oriole Park at Camden Yards. (410) 685-9800. Home of the Baltimore Orioles. There are four tiers of seats. The closest seats—probably almost impossible to obtain—are sections with even numbers from 6 (right field) to 36 (home plate) to 72 (left field). Grandstand seats, the most likely to be available on short notice, are in sections numbered from 306 (right field) to 336 (home plate) to 372 (left field). There are also some bleacher seats in right center (sections 92–98) and outfield stadium seats in left field.

Sporting and Entertainment Ticket Agencies

Baltimore Orioles Baseball Store & Ticket Outlet. 914 Seventeenth Street NW. (202) 296-2473.

Ticketmaster/Ticketron. (202) 432-7328.

Top Centre Tickets. (202) 452-9040.

Participation Sports
Jogging and Biking

Jogging in Washington. From secretaries to Secretaries, from lobbyists to the lobbied, from members of Congress to the president, early-morning and late-afternoon Washington sometimes looks like an urban road race.

The favored jogging route is a trip around the National Mall, about four-and-a-half miles for a round-trip that loops behind the Washington Monument and in front of the U.S. Capitol. Other popular routes include the following:

C & O National Historic Park. Sharpsburg, Maryland. (301) 739-4200. The towpath stretches 184 miles along the Chesapeake & Ohio Canal, from Georgetown to Cumberland, Maryland. Mule-drawn boat trips April to October. Visitor center at Great Falls, Maryland. Entrance fee: $5 per car.

George Washington Carver Nature Trail. Anacostia Museum, 1901 Fort Place SE. (202) 357-2700.

Great Falls Park. 9200 Old Dominion Drive, Great Falls, Virginia. (703) 285-2965. Park open dawn to dusk. Visitor center open daily 10 A.M.–5 P.M. Admission: $4 per vehicle.

Mount Vernon Trail. Turkey Run Park, McLean, Virginia. (703) 285-2598. A scenic 19-mile trail along the Virginia side of the Potomac River between Theodore Roosevelt Island and George Washington's home at Mount Vernon.

This trail is a favorite with Washington runners. The northern section, about four miles one-way, begins near the pedestrian crossover to Theodore Roosevelt Island across the river from the Kennedy Center and goes past National Airport through wetlands to Old Town Alexandria. The southern section, about nine miles, goes along the shores of the Potomac from Alexandria to George Washington's home at Mount Vernon.

Rock Creek Park. 3545 Williamsburg Lane NW. (202) 282-1063. Riding stables, tennis courts, thirty picnic areas, golf course, art gallery, nature center, and a network of trails. The most popular trail runs about four miles along the creek from Georgetown to the National Zoo.

Theodore Roosevelt Island. Potomac Park. (703) 285-2598. A wildlife refuge with trails, reached by a footbridge from the parking lot off of the northbound lane of the George Washington Parkway. Open daily 8 A.M.–dusk. Free.

Biking in Washington. The trails and jogging paths of Washington are just as popular with visitors on two wheels as those in sneakers, especially the National Mall, C & O Canal towpath, Rock Creek Park in and near the District, and Mount Vernon Trail in Virginia.

The Washington Area Bicyclist Association, 818 Connecticut Avenue NW, Suite 800, Washington, D.C. 20006, (202) 872-9830, publishes a guide to biking in the Washington area. www.waba.org.

The National Park Service maintains the C & O Canal, and favorite paths include a loop from near Key Bridge in Georgetown to Fletcher's Boat House. (301) 739-4200, (301) 299-3613, or (800) 252-8776.

Bicycles are available for rent from a number of companies.

Big Wheel Bikes. 1034 Thirty-third Street NW, at M Street, Georgetown, near the C & O Canal Towpath: (202) 337-0254.

Fletcher's Boat House. 4940 Canal Road NW, at Reservoir Road, along the C & O Canal: (202) 244-0461.

Thompson's Boat Center. Georgetown Channel, 2900 Virginia Avenue NW, at Rock Creek Parkway: (202) 333-9543. *Discount coupon in this book.*

Washington Sailing Marina. George Washington Parkway, 1 Marina Drive, Alexandria: (703) 548-9027. *Discount coupon in this book.*

Ice Skating

National Sculpture Garden Outdoor Rink. Ninth and Madison Drive NW: (202) 371-5340. Outdoor, winter only. Due to reopen in 2000.

Pershing Park Ice Rink. Pennsylvania Avenue, between Fourteenth and Fifteenth Streets NW: (202) 737-6938. Outdoor, winter only.

Fort Dupont Ice Arena. Thirty-seventh Street at Ely Place SE: (202) 584-5007. Indoor, year-round.

Skiing

Winter sports are available—but a bit chancy—to residents and visitors in Washington. Be sure to call ahead before driving in search of snow for skiing.

Blue Knob. About 150 miles northwest of Washington in Claysburg, Pennsylvania. The season runs from about mid-December to late March. Vertical drop of 1,072 feet, eighty acres of terrain with twenty-one trails. Day and night skiing. (814) 239-5111.

Canaan Valley Resort. About 180 miles west of Washington in North

Canaan Valley, West Virginia. The season runs from late November to late March. Vertical drop of 850 feet, seventy skiable acres. Day and night skiing. (304) 866-4121; for conditions, call (800) 622-4121. *Discount coupon in this book.*

Massanutten. About 125 miles southwest of Washington in Harrisonburg, Virginia. The season runs from mid-December to mid-March. Vertical drop of 1,150 feet. Day and night skiing. (540) 289-9441.

Ski Liberty. About sixty-five miles northwest of Washington in Carroll Valley, Pennsylvania. The season runs from mid-November to late March. Fourteen trails, day and night skiing. (717) 642-8282.

Ski Roundtop. About 120 miles north of Washington in Lewisberry, Pennsylvania. The season is early December to late March. Vertical drop of 600 feet with thirteen trails. Day and night skiing. (717) 432-9631; for conditions, call (703) 432-7000.

Wintergreen. About 170 miles southwest of Washington in Charlottesville, Virginia. The season is mid-December to mid-March. Seventeen trails. Day and night skiing. (804) 325-2200; for conditions, call (804) 325-2100.

Sailboats, Canoes, and Paddleboats

District of Columbia

Fletcher's Boat House. 4940 Canal Road NW at Reservoir Road: (202) 244-0461. Rowboat and canoe rentals on the C & O Canal, from late March to November.

Thompson's Boat Center. 2900 Virginia Avenue NW at Rock Creek Parkway: (202) 333-9543. Canoe, rowboat, and sailboard rentals, from April to October. *Discount coupon in this book.*

Tidal Basin Pedal Boats. 1501 Maine Avenue SW at Fourteenth Street. Mid-March to October 15, weekdays 10 A.M.–5 P.M.; weekends 10 A.M.–6 P.M. (202) 479-2426. *Discount coupon in this book.*

Maryland

Annapolis Sailing School. 601 Sixth Street at East Port, Annapolis: (410) 267-7205. Rent a sailboat or take a sailing course in the Chesapeake Bay, about an hour's drive from Washington.

Virginia

Belle Haven Marina. Belle Haven Park; George Washington Parkway, just south of Old Town Alexandria: (703) 768-0018. Sailboats and sailboards available for rent.

Washington Sailing Marina. George Washington Parkway, 1 Marina Drive, Alexandria: (703) 548-9027. Sunfish, Windsurfers, and Daysailers for rent April to October.

Fishing

The five-mile stretch of the Potomac River from near the Wilson Memorial Bridge in Alexandria south to Fort Washington National Park is considered one of the best fishing spots for largemouth bass in the country. Call Life Outdoors, (301) 937-0010, for information on freshwater fishing guides.

Another local fishing hole, this time for perch, is near Fletcher's Boat House on the C & O Canal.

Golf in Washington, D.C.

There are a handful of golf courses in the densely populated District of Columbia itself, and many more in the surrounding suburbs. Following is a listing of public and semiprivate courses in Washington. See Chapter 17 for a listing of courses in Northern Virginia.

East Potomac Golf Course. Haines Point SW: (202) 554-7660. Public, 18-hole course and two 9-hole executive courses. Economy.

Greens fees.	
Economy:	Less than $20
Moderate:	$20 to $39
Expensive:	$40 and more

Langston Golf Course. Twenty-fifth Street and Benning Road NE: (202) 397-8638. Public, 18-hole course. Economy.

Rock Creek Public Golf Course. Rock Creek Park; Sixteenth Street NW, near Rittenhouse Road: (202) 882-7332. Public, 18-hole course. Cart rentals available. Economy.

Horseback Riding

Rock Creek Park Horse Center. 5100 Glover Road NW at Military Road: (202) 362-0117. Riders must be 12 years or older; reservations required.

Tennis

In addition to private clubs and facilities offered by some hotels, the District has about 150 public courts available on a first-come, first-served basis. Most are run by the D.C. Department of Recreation. (202) 673-7646.

Other facilities include:

East Potomac Tennis. Haines Point Park, between Park Service headquarters and the Fourteenth Street Bridge SW: (202) 554-5962. Open 6 A.M.–11 P.M. *Discount coupon in this book.*

Anacostia Park. Between Eleventh Street and Pennsylvania Avenue Bridge SE: (202) 561-5388.

Rock Creek Tennis Center. Sixteenth and Kennedy Streets NW: (202) 722-5949. *Discount coupon in this book.*

Chapter 14
Theaters and Clubs

Washington has a rich collection of theater groups, from small community and dinner theaters to national opera, drama, and dance groups. The heart of the District's culture is the Kennedy Center for the Performing Arts, with six stages. The independent theaters have their own off-off-Broadway in a five-block section of Fourteentth Street NW. Another group can be found near Dupont Circle.

To find out what's playing at Washington-area theaters, request a copy of the Calendar of Events brochure published quarterly by the Washington, D.C., Convention & Visitors Association.

Write or call the association at: Calendar of Events brochure, Washington, D.C., Convention & Visitors Association, 1212 New York Avenue NW, Washington, D.C. 20005. (202) 789-7000.

Legitimate Theater

Arena Stage. Sixth Street and Maine Avenue SW: (202) 488-3300. The Fichandler Stage, The Kreeger Theatre, The Old Vat Room. Arena Stage productions are presented from September to June at its three theaters. A limited number of half-price tickets are available ninety minutes before each subscription performance.

To order tickets at full-price, you can contact Ticketmaster at (202) 432-7328 or Tickets.com at (703) 218-6500. www.arenastage.org.

Capitol Steps. 210 N. Washington Street, Alexandria: (703) 683-8330, www.capsteps.com. Musical political humor performed by former or current congressional staffers.

Church Street Theater. 1742 Church Street NW: (202) 265-3748.

The Dance Place. 3225 Eighth Street NE: (202) 269-1600.

Discovery Theatre. 900 Jefferson Drive SW: (202) 357-1500.

Ford's Theatre. 511 Tenth Street NW: (202) 347-4833. The actual theater (restored to historical accuracy) where President Lincoln was assassinated still

Capitol Steps performers

operates as a legitimate stage with concerts, plays, and special events throughout the year. www.fordstheatre.org.

Gala Hispanic Theater. 1625 Park Road NW: (202) 234-7174. Well-regarded theater company, with performances in Spanish and English.

Gross National Product. Bayou Nightclub, 3135 K Street NW. (202) 783-7212. Another Washington staple, their (intentional) political humor is on display every Saturday night at 7:30 P.M. Productions in recent years have included "All the President's Women" and "Sex, Lies and Zippergate." Admission: $18.

John F. Kennedy Center for the Performing Arts. New Hampshire Avenue and Rock Creek Parkway NW: (202) 467-4600. Concert Hall, Eisenhower Theater, Opera House, Terrace Theater, Theater Lab, American Film Institute Theater. You can consult www.kennedy-center.org.

Lisner Auditorium. (202) 994-1500. The stage at George Washington University, 730 Twenty-first Street NW, is home to lectures, musical performances, and stage productions.

Metrostage. 1816 Duke Street, Alexandria, VA: (703) 548-9044.

National Theatre. 1321 Pennsylvania Avenue NW: (202) 628-6161. www.nationaltheatre.org.

Olney Theatre. 2001 Sandy Spring Road, Olney, MD: (301) 924-3400.

The Shakespeare Theatre. 450 Seventh Street NW: (202) 547-1122.

Signature Theatre. 3806 South Four Mile Run Drive, Arlington, VA: (703) 820-9771.

Source Theatre Company. 1835 Fourteenth Street NW: (202) 462-1073.

Studio Theatre. 1333 P Street NW: (202) 332-3300.

Warner Theatre. Thirteenth Street between E and F Streets: (202) 783-4000. www.warnertheatre.com.

Washington Opera. Performances at the Kennedy Center, New Hampshire Avenue and Rock Creek Parkway NW: (202) 295-2400. www.dc-opera.org.

Woolly Mammoth Theatre Company. 1401 Church Street NW: (202) 393-3939. Avant-garde, challenging theater.

Buying Tickets

TICKETplace. Half-price tickets to same-day performances to many Washington and area theaters are available at the Old Post Office Pavilion, 1100

Pennsylvania Avenue NW. (202) 842-5387. (Tickets for Sunday and Monday events are sold on Saturday.) A service charge is added; cash only for tickets.

The Best Seats in the House

The Kennedy Center. (202) 467-4600. www.kennedy-center.org.

The Concert Hall was rebuilt in 1997, adding some premium seats and removing some less-than-perfect chairs. The result is a slight reduction to 2,518 seats.

Ringing the orchestra seats are twenty-one Orchestra Level Boxes. The Orchestra itself was reconfigured with additional aisles and 350 fewer seats. The premium Box Tier is one of the most popular sections of the concert hall. Also available are First and Second Tier seats which have improved sight lines.

New onstage boxes with premium views of the stage and Chorister Seating, which offers unusual performer's views at discount, were also added.

Opera House. There are three sections on the Orchestra level in center, even, and odd sections. Rows are numbered from A (front) to Z, and AA to GG.

Just above the Orchestra is the two-row Box Tier, with seats 1 and 2 at the center. The center section of the 1st and 2nd Tiers is numbered 201 to 216, and there are even and odd sections extending from them.

Eisenhower Theater. This small theater has an Orchestra level with center, even, and odd sections; rows run from A to Y. The center section has seats from 101 to 118.

A small, two-row Box Tier has section 1 at its center and extends to even and odd sections 14 and 15. The balcony seats run from A to G, with the center section numbered from 101 to 114; the even section runs from 2 to 28, and the odd section from 1 to 27.

Ford's Theatre. (202) 347-4833. www.fordstheatre.org.

The small theater has Orchestra, Dress Circle, and Balcony seating.

The Orchestra has center, right (even), and left (odd) sections, with rows running from A (front) to O. The center section is numbered from 101 to 108, the even from 2 to 20, and odd from 1 to 19.

The theater is relatively small, and no seat is very far from the stage. The best seats are in the central Orchestra and central Dress Circle and Balcony; these sections are numbered from 101 to 111. Less desirable are seats in the left and right section of the Balcony, seats numbered from 12 to 34 are on the right, and 11 to 33 on the left.

The National Theatre. (202) 628-6161 or Tellacharge at (800) 447-7400. You can also consult www.nationaltheatre.org.

The Orchestra runs from A (front) to X with center, even, and odd sections. The center section has seats from 101 to 114, even from 2 to 24, and odd from 1 to 23.

The next level up is the Mezzanine, with rows from A to M in center (101 to 113), even (2 to 24), and odd (1 to 23) sections.

The uppermost level is the Balcony, with rows from A to J in center (101 to 112), even (2 to 26), and odd (1 to 25). There are also ten small boxes on the sides of the theater. The closest boxes to the stage are A to K; boxes L and M are at the Balcony level.

Jazz Clubs in Washington

Blues Alley. 1073 Wisconsin Avenue NW: (202) 337-4141.
  Evening Star Jazz Bar. 1200 Nineteenth Street NW: (202) 785-7827.
  Market Inn. 200 E Street SW: (202) 554-2100.
  Marley's Lounge. Henley Park Hotel, 926 Massachusetts Avenue NW: (202) 638-5200.
  Takoma Station Tavern. 6914 Fourth Street NW: (202) 829-1999.
  The Vegas Lounge. 1415 P Street NW: (202) 483-3971.

Comedy Clubs in Washington

Comedy Cafe. 1520 K Street NW: (202) 638-5653.
  The Improv. 1140 Connecticut Avenue NW: (202) 296-7008.

Nightclubs and Bars in Washington

Cafe Atlantico. 405 Eighth St. NW: (202) 393-0812.
  Cafe Milano. 3251 Prospect Street NW: (202) 333-6183.
  Capitol City Brewing Company. 1100 New York Avenue NW: (202) 628-2222. Fresh-brewed beer and more.
  Club Zei. 1415 Zei Alley NW: (202) 842-2445. A Greek high-life (*zei*) club.
  Deja Vu. 2119 M Street NW: (202) 452-1966.
  15 Minutes. 1030 Fifteenth Street NW: (202) 408-1855.
  The Fifth Column. 915 F Street NW: (202) 393-3632.
  Hard Rock Cafe. 999 E Street NW: (202) 737-7625.
  The Insect Club. 625 E Street NW: (202) 347-8884.
  Kilimanjaro. 1724 California Street NW: (202) 328-3838.
  Marquis De Rochambeau. 3108 M Street NW: (202) 333-0393.
  9:30 Club. 930 F Street NW: (202) 265-0930.
  Paper Moon. 1069 Thirty-first Street NW: (202) 965-6666.
  Planet Hollywood. 1101 Pennsylvania Avenue NW: (202) 783-7827.
  The Ritz. 919 E Street NW: (202) 638-2582.
  The River Club. 3223 K Street NW: (202) 333-8118.
  The Spy Club. 805 Fifteenth Street NW: (202) 289-1779.
  The Third Edition. 1218 Wisconsin Avenue NW: (202) 333-3700.

Chapter 15
Eating Your Way
Through Washington, D.C.

If you like to eat, you're sure to find something interesting in and around Washington, D.C., which has one of the world's broadest ranges of international and ethnic restaurants. We'd be hard-pressed to come up with many cultures or parts of the world not represented.

Fine restaurants are spread throughout the District, with concentrations in and around the "Gucci Gulch," where high-paid lobbyists and lawyers meet around the main government buildings downtown near K Street NW; at Washington's premier hotels; and in Georgetown.

There are half a dozen fine Asian eateries in the District's small Chinatown, and others can be found elsewhere in the District. Some of the most eclectic offerings are located in the Dupont Circle and Adams-Morgan areas.

A Selection of the Best Restaurants and the Best Deals in Washington

Be sure to call to confirm operating hours and determine if reservations are necessary. Price categories are for mid-range dinner entrees. Budget: $10 or less for entree; Moderate: $20 or less for entree; and Expensive: $20 or more for entree.

American

Billy Martin's Tavern. Moderate. 1264 Winsconsin Avenue NW: (202) 333-7370. A Georgetown favorite since 1933; steaks, seafood, and pasta.

Capitol City Brewing Company. Budget. Two locations for tangy snacks, light meals, and fresh brews.

2 Massachusetts Avenue NE, next to Union Station on Capitol Hill: (202) 842-2337. Sunday to Tuesday 11 A.M.–12:30 A.M.; Wednesday to Saturday 11 A.M.–2 A.M.

Corner of Eleventh and H Streets NW, next to the Convention Center: (202) 628-2222. Sunday to Thursday 11 A.M.–11 P.M., bar closes 12:30 A.M.; Friday and Saturday 11 A.M.–midnight, bar closes 1:30 A.M.

Chadwicks. Budget. Two locations. Burgers, sandwiches, and salads.

5247 Wisconsin Avenue NW at Jenifer Street: (202) 362-8040. Monday to Thursday 11:30 A.M.–1:30 A.M.; Friday and Saturday 11:30 A.M.–2:30 A.M.; Sunday 10 A.M.–1:30 A.M.

3205 K Street NW at Wisconsin Avenue, Georgetown: (202) 333-2565. Monday to Thursday 11:30 A.M.–1:30 A.M.; Friday and Saturday 11:30 A.M.–2:30 A.M.; Sunday 11 A.M.–1:30 A.M.

Cheesecake Factory. Moderate. Chevy Chase Pavilion, 5345 Wisconsin Avenue NW at Military Road: (202) 364-0500. Monday to Thursday 11:30 A.M.–11:30 P.M.; Friday and Saturday 11:30 A.M.–12:30 A.M.; Sunday 10:30 A.M.–11 P.M. Sandwiches, pasta, salads . . . and cheesecake.

Daily Grill. Moderate. 1200 Eighteenth Street NW: (202) 822-5282. Monday to Thursday 11:30 A.M.–11 P.M.; Friday 11:30 A.M.–midnight; Saturday 11:30 A.M.–3 P.M., 5 P.M.–midnight; Sunday brunch 10 A.M.–3 P.M., dinner 5 P.M.–11 P.M. Two blocks from Dupont Circle, this place lays claim to classic American food from meatloaf to steak and Cobb to Caesar salads, all served in oversized portions.

Food for Thought. Budget. 1738 Connecticut Avenue NW at Florida Avenue: (202) 797-1095. Monday 11:30 A.M.–3 P.M., 5 P.M.–12:30 A.M.; Tuesday to Thursday 11:30 A.M.–12:30 A.M.; Friday 11:30 A.M.–2 A.M.; Saturday noon–2 A.M.; Sunday 4 P.M.–12:30 A.M. A mostly vegetarian, politically correct café with salads, tofu, soups, and stir-fry dishes. Live entertainment from time to time.

Georgia Brown. Moderate. 950 Fifteenth Street NW, between I and K Streets, McPherson Square: (202) 393-4499. Monday to Thursday 11:30 A.M.–11 P.M.; Friday 11:30 A.M.–midnight; Saturday 5:30 P.M.–midnight; Sunday 11 A.M.–3 P.M., 5:30–11 P.M. South Carolina recipes, including pork chops in gravy, gumbo, and grilled fish. A jazz band plays Sunday brunch.

Kramerbooks & Afterwords, A Cafe. Budget. 1517 Connecticut Avenue NW, near Nineteenth Street, Dupont Circle: (202) 387-1462. Monday to Thursday 7:30 A.M.–1 A.M.; Friday to Saturday open 24 hours; Sunday until 1 A.M. Live music Wednesday through Saturday nights. A bookstore with a café, or the other way around; soups, pastas, and grilled dishes.

Le Bon Cafe. Budget–Moderate. 210 Second Street SE at Pennsylvania Avenue, Capitol Hill: (202) 547-7200. Monday to Friday 7:30 A.M.–6:30 P.M.; Saturday and Sunday 8:30 A.M.–3 P.M. Reduced hours in fall and winter. Espresso and pastries in the morning and Pacific Rim dishes in the afternoon.

Occidental Grill. Expensive. Willard Hotel; 1475 Pennsylvania Avenue NW, near Fourteenth Street: (202) 783-1475. Monday to Saturday 11:30 A.M.–10 P.M.; Sunday noon–9:30 P.M. The Grill Room on the ground floor offers steak and seafood; upstairs "nouvelle" American fare. All around are political mementos and photos, with an eye toward the White House up the road.

Old Ebbitt Grill. 675 Fifteenth St. NW: (202) 347-4800. Seasonal American fare, a favorite of the political crowd.

Palais du Chocolat. Budget–Moderate. Quiches, croissants, tarts, espresso, cappuccino . . . and chocolate. 3309 Connecticut Avenue NW: (202) 363-2462. Sunday, Monday, and Tuesday 8 A.M.–8 P.M.; Wednesday and Thursday 8 A.M.–10 P.M.; Friday and Saturday 8 A.M.–midnight. 6925 Willow Street NW at Eastern Avenue: (202) 291-2462. Monday to Saturday 9 A.M.–6 P.M.

The Palm. 1225 Nineteenth St. NW: (202) 293-9091. A classic American steakhouse.

Planet Hollywood. Moderate. 1101 Pennsylvania Avenue NW: (202) 783-7827. Sunday to Thursday 11 A.M.–midnight; Friday and Saturday 11 A.M. to 1 A.M. It's not the food (burgers, pizza, salads), but the high-glitter atmosphere, including a Cyborg from *Terminator 2*. There is, of course, a gift shop.

Prime Rib. Expensive. 2020 K Street NW, between Twentieth and Twenty-first streets: (202) 466-8811. Monday to Thursday 11:30 A.M.–3 P.M., 5–11 P.M.; Friday 11:30 A.M.–3 P.M., 5–11:30 P.M.; Saturday 5–11:30 P.M. Changing times, changing menus: seafood now shares the billing with beef at this classic eatery. Reservations recommended.

Restaurant Nora. Moderate. 2132 Florida Avenue NW at R Street, Dupont Circle: (202) 462-5143. Monday to Thursday 6–10 P.M.; Friday to Saturday 5:45–10:30 P.M. Fresh, healthful, and American.

1789 Restaurant. Expensive. 1226 Thirty-sixth Street NW at Prospect Street, Georgetown: (202) 965-1789. Open nightly 6–10 P.M.; Saturday 5–11 P.M. Old-style American fare including rack of lamb, Maryland crab cakes, and Long Island duckling in a building that reaches back almost to the birth of the nation. Reservations and jackets required.

Tabard Inn. Moderate. 1739 N Street NW: (202) 331-8528. Monday to Thursday 7 A.M.–10 A.M., 11:30 A.M.–2:30 P.M., 6 P.M.–10 P.M.; Friday 7 A.M.–10 A.M., 11:30 A.M.–2:30 P.M., 6 P.M.–10:30 P.M.; Saturday and Sunday breakfast 8 A.M.–10 A.M., brunch 10:30 A.M.–2:30 P.M.; Saturday dinner 6 P.M.–10:30 P.M.; Sunday dinner 6 P.M.–10 P.M. Romantic dining by the fireplace or on the patio at Washington's oldest hotel.

Willard Room. Expensive. 1401 Pennsylvania Avenue NW, between Fourteenth and F Streets: (202) 628-9100. Weekdays 7:30–10 A.M., 11:30 A.M.–2 P.M., 6–10 P.M.; Saturday and Sunday 6–10 P.M. Dinner only in August. A turn-of-the-century reproduction of the splendid dining room of the historic Willard Hotel. Veal, steak, seafood, and pasta. Reservations required.

Asian (Burmese, Chinese, Japanese, Malaysian, Mongolian, Thai, Vietnamese)

Burma Restaurant. Budget. 740 Sixth Street NW, Chinatown: (202) 638-1280. Dinner nightly 6–10 P.M.; lunch Monday to Friday 11 A.M.–3 P.M. A rare introduction to an unusual Asian cuisine, offered in a casual eatery run by a retired United Nations diplomat. Burmese specialties include fish cakes with chili sauce and various noodle dishes. Reservations recommended on weekends.

Busara. Moderate. 2340 Wisconsin Avenue NW, near Calvert Street, Glover Park: (202) 337-2340. Monday to Thursday 11:30 A.M.–3 P.M., 5–11 P.M.; Friday 11:30 A.M.–3 P.M., 5 P.M.–midnight; Saturday 11:30 A.M.–4 P.M., 5 P.M.–midnight; Sunday 11:30 A.M.–4 P.M., 5–11 P.M. A very modern setting for classic Thai cuisine.

China Inn. Budget–Moderate. 631 H Street NW, Chinatown: (202) 842-0909. Sunday to Thursday 11 A.M.–1 A.M.; Friday and Saturday 11 A.M.–2 A.M. Dim sum daily 11 A.M.–3 P.M. One of the pillars of Chinatown, considered one of the best Chinese eateries in town. Order from the chef's specials for unusual and outstanding dishes.

City Lights of China. Budget. 1731 Connecticut Avenue NW at R Street: (202) 265-6688. Monday to Thursday 11:30 A.M.–10:30 P.M.; Friday 11:30 A.M.–11 P.M.; Saturday noon–11 P.M.; Sunday noon–10:30 P.M. A small eatery with large ambitions; pan-fried noodles and pot stickers are specialties.

Full Kee Restaurant. Budget. 509 H Street NW, Chinatown: (202) 371-2233. Sunday to Thursday 11 A.M.–1 A.M., Friday and Saturday 11 A.M.–3 A.M. Fabulous Chinese soups and conjee (rice porridge), and unusual pork and seafood offerings.

Himalayan Grill. Moderate. 1805 Eighteenth Street NW: (202) 986-5124. Dishes from Tibet, Nepal, and India.

Hunan Chinatown. Moderate. 624 H Street NW, Chinatown: (202) 783-5858. Sunday to Thursday 11 A.M.–10 P.M., Friday and Saturday 11 A.M.–11 P.M. House favorites include the tea-smoked duck, dumplings in spicy peanut sauce, and Szechuan beef in an unusual sweet-and-sour sauce.

Li Ho Food Restaurant. Budget. 501 H Street NW, Chinatown: (202) 289-2059. Daily 10:30 A.M.–11 P.M. Unusual fare includes Singapore rice noodles, Cantonese roast meats, and duck soup.

Miss Saigon. Budget–Moderate. 3057 M Street NW: (202) 333-5545. Weekdays 11:30 A.M.–11 P.M.; Saturday and Sunday noon–11 P.M. Gourmet Vietnamese with some unusual offerings including quail soup, grilled pork with ginger sauce, and papaya salad with beef jerky.

Mr. K's. Expensive. 2121 K Street NW at Twenty-first Street: (202) 331-8868. Monday to Friday 11:30 A.M.–11:30 P.M.; Saturday and Sunday 12:30–11 P.M. Moderate–An elegant Chinese eatery with some unusual offerings and a great deal of showmanship. Reservations recommended.

Oodles Noodles. Budget. 1120 Nineteenth Street NW: (202) 293-3138. Noodles, oodles of them.

Saigon Gourmet. Budget. 2635 Connecticut Avenue NW: (202) 265-1360. Daily 11:30 A.M.–3 P.M. and 5–10 P.M. Vietnamese specialties include grilled pork with caramelized onions and crispy noodles with chicken, vegetables, and black bean sauce.

Salsa Thai. 2016 P Street NW: (202) 872-1144. Thai seafood and other specialties.

Sichuan Pavilion. Expensive. 1820 K Street NW at Eighteenth Street: (202) 466-7790. Monday to Friday 11 A.M.–10 P.M.; Saturday and Sunday noon–10 P.M. Moderate–High-tone Chinese.

Spices. 3333-A Connecticut Avenue NW: (202) 686-3833. Moderate. Upscale Asian from Hong Kong, Malaysia, and Vietnam.

Star of Siam. Budget. Two locations. A highly regarded Thai menu including curries, seafood specialties, and stir-fry noodle dishes.

1136 Nineteenth Street NW, between L and M Streets: (202) 785-2839. Monday to Saturday 11:30 A.M.–11 P.M.; Sunday 5–10 P.M.

2446 Eighteenth Street NW at Columbia Road: (202) 986-4133. Monday to Thursday 5–11 P.M.; Friday 5 P.M.–midnight; Saturday noon–midnight; Sunday noon–11 P.M.

Straits of Malaya. Budget. 1836 Eighteenth Street NW: (202) 483-1483. Monday to Thursday noon–2 P.M. and 5:30–10 P.M., Friday noon–2 P.M. and 5:30–11 P.M., Saturday 5:30–11 P.M., Sunday 5:30–10 P.M. From Malaya to Indonesia, Thailand, China, and most points in between, comes a menu rich with unusual mixes of chilies, coconut milk, curry, and spices.

Sushi-Ko. Moderate. 2309 Wisconsin Avenue NW at Calvert Street, Glover Park: (202) 333-4187. Monday 6–10:30 P.M.; Tuesday to Friday noon–2:30 P.M., 6–10:30 P.M.; Saturday 5–10:30 P.M.; Sunday 5–10 P.M. It's not the atmosphere, it's the sushi that makes this place so popular.

Tai Shan. Budget. 622 H Street NW, Chinatown: (202) 639-0266. Sunday to Thursday 11 A.M.–11 P.M., Friday and Saturday 11 A.M.–midnight. Specialties include Cantonese roasted meats, Hong Kong soups, noodles, and smoked seafood.

Tony Cheng's Mongolian Restaurant. Moderate. 619 H Street NW, Chinatown: (202) 842-8669. Sunday to Thursday 11 A.M.–11 P.M.; Friday and Saturday 11 A.M.–midnight. A Mongolian grill is the ultimate all-you-can-eat down-home barbecue, with an Oriental twist. For about $15, diners select their own platefuls of raw meats and vegetables and assorted oils and spices and then hand them to a cook who quickly stir-fries the ingredients on a cast-iron grill. The other house offering is a Mongolian hot pot, with noodles, vegetables, and other ingredients cooked at the table in a hot stock.

Vietnam-Georgetown. Budget. 2934 M Street NW at Thirtieth Street, Georgetown: (202) 337-4536. Monday to Thursday and Sunday 11 A.M.–11 P.M.; Friday and Saturday 11:30 A.M.–midnight. Nothing much to look at; the beauty comes on the plates of this highly rated Vietnamese eatery, famed for its spring rolls and garden rolls. There's a weekday luncheon buffet.

Yanyu. Moderate. 3435 Connecticut Ave. NW: (202) 686-6968. A neighborhood eatery for Asian cuisine and sushi.

Zuki Moon Noodles. Moderate. 824 New Hampshire Avenue NW: (202) 333-3312. Monday to Friday 11:30 A.M.–2:30 P.M.; Monday to Saturday 5–11 P.M.; Sunday 5–10 P.M. Occasionally opens at 3 P.M. on Saturdays and Sundays for matinee shows. An unusual and fun fusion of Japanese and Western tastes featuring sushi, gyoza, tempura, and lots of noodle dishes. Nearby to the Kennedy Center, you can eat in or take out, with moderate impact on your wallet.

Barbecue

Rocklands Washington BBQ. Budget. 2418 Wisconsin Avenue NW, Glover Park: (202) 333-2558. Monday to Friday 11:30 A.M.–10 P.M.; Saturday 11 A.M.–10 P.M.; Sunday 11 A.M.–9 P.M. Ribs, chicken, chopped pork, and some of the spiciest bottled hot sauce this side of the River Styx.

Caribbean

Cafe Atlantico. Budget. 405 8 Street NW: (202) 393-0812. Sunday to Thursday 5 P.M.–10 P.M.; Friday and Saturday 5 P.M.–11 P.M.; Monday to Friday 11:30 A.M.–2:30 P.M.; Saturday 11:30 A.M.–1:30 P.M. for Latino Dim Sum.

Negril Eatery. Budget. 2301 Georgia Avenue NW: (202) 332-3737. Monday to Thursday 10:30 A.M.–10 P.M., Friday and Saturday 10:30 A.M.–11 P.M. A very basic setting for very interesting foods, including goat curry, jerk chicken, and various Jamaican stews.

Continental

Cafe Mozart. Budget–Moderate. 1331 H Street NW at Thirteenth Street: (202) 347-5732. Weekdays 7:30 A.M.–10 P.M.; Saturday 10 A.M.–10 P.M.; Sunday 11 A.M.–10 P.M. Stews, schnitzels, and wurst.

Iron Gate Restaurant. Budget–Moderate. 1734 N Street NW, near Seventeenth Street, Dupont Circle: (202) 737-1370. Weekdays 11:30 A.M.–10 P.M.; Saturday 5–10 P.M.; Sunday 10:30 A.M.–2:30 P.M. Mediterranean cuisine in a restored turn-of-the-century horse stable.

Seasons. Expensive. Four Seasons Hotel; 2800 Pennsylvania Avenue NW at Twenty-eighth Street: (202) 944-2000. Monday to Friday 7–11 A.M., noon–2:30 P.M., 6–10:30 P.M.; Saturday to Sunday 8 A.M.–noon, 6–10:30 P.M. A very tony place, popular with visiting celebrities.

Delicatessens

Lawsons Gourmet Provisions. Budget. Four locations. Gourmet take-out sandwiches and salad bar.

1350 I Street NW at Fourteenth Street: (202) 789-0800. Weekdays 7:30 A.M.–6:30 P.M.; Saturday 10 A.M.–4 P.M.

1350 Connecticut Avenue NW: (202) 775-0400. Weekdays 7:30 A.M.–8 P.M.; Saturday 10 A.M.–6 P.M.

1776 I Street NW at Seventeenth Street: (202) 296-3200. Weekdays 7:30 A.M.–6:30 P.M.

Thirteenth Street and G Street at Metro Center: (202) 393-5500.

Sholl's Colonial Cafeteria. Budget. 1990 K Street NW at Twentieth Street: (202) 296-3065. Monday to Saturday 7–10:30 A.M., 11 A.M.–2:30 P.M., 4–8 P.M.; Sunday 8:30 A.M.–6 P.M. Your basic cafeteria, a longtime landmark.

Toojays Restaurant. Budget. 4620 Wisconsin Avenue NW: (202) 686-1989. Daily 8 A.M.–10 P.M. You can only wish home cooking were like this; matzoball soup, overstuffed deli sandwiches, and smoked fish and pastrami shipped from New York.

Eclectic

Cities. Moderate. 2424 Eighteenth Street NW, between Columbia and Belmont: (202) 328-7194. Monday to Thursday 6–11 P.M.; Friday and Saturday 6–11:30 P.M.; Sunday 11 A.M.–3 P.M., 6–9:30 P.M. Once or twice a year they throw out the old menu and bring in a new one, focusing on a new city somewhere in the world. Diners have visited Havana, Hong Kong, Rio, Istanbul, and Mexico City. Reservations recommended.

Ethiopian

Fasikas. Moderate. 2446 Eighteenth Street NW: (202) 797-7673. Daily 5 P.M.–1 A.M.; Friday to Sunday noon–2:45 P.M. Seafood, lamb, and vegetarian specialties with a live Ethiopian band on the weekends.

Meskerem. Budget. 2434 Eighteenth Street NW, south of Columbia Road, Adams–Morgan: (202) 462-4100. Monday to Thursday and Sunday noon–midnight; Friday and Saturday noon–3 A.M. Spicy lentils, curry stews, and grilled meats in a room that will transport you to Africa. Reservations are recommended on weekends.

The Red Sea. 2463 Eighteenth Street NW, Adams Morgan. (202) 483-5000. Open daily.

Zed's Ethiopian Cuisine. Budget. 3318 M Street NW, Georgetown. (202) 333-4710. Sunday to Thursday 11 A.M.–11 P.M., Friday and Saturday 11 A.M.– 1 A.M. Rich stews and curries you scoop into your mouth with native breads.

French

Cafe la Ruche. Moderate. 1039 Thirty-first Street NW, between M and K Streets, Georgetown: (202) 965-2684. Monday to Thursday 10:30 A.M.–midnight; Friday 10:30 A.M.–1 A.M.; Saturday 10 A.M.–1 A.M.; Sunday 10 A.M.–11:30 P.M. A Parisien brasserie with outdoor tables.

La Colline. Moderate. 400 North Capitol Street NW, between E and Louisiana, Capitol Hill: (202) 737-0400. Weekdays 7–10 A.M., 11:30 A.M.–3 P.M., 6–10 P.M.; Saturday 6–10 P.M. High-tone haute cuisine. Reservations are recommended.

Le Rivage. Moderate. 1000 Water Street SW at Ninth Street: (202) 488-8111. Monday to Thursday 11:30 A.M.–2:30 P.M., 5:30–11 P.M.; Friday 11:30 A.M.–2:30 P.M., 5:30–11:30 P.M.; Saturday 5:30–11 P.M.; Sunday 5–9 P.M. A view of the sunset at the marina, and a short hike to Arena Stage for theater.

Les Halles. Expensive. 1201 Pennsylvania Avenue NW: (202) 347-6848. Open for lunch and dinner daily. Authentic French bistro and steakhouse.

Maison Blanche/Rive Gauche. Expensive. 1725 F Street NW, between Seventeenth and Eighteenth streets: (202) 842-0070. Weekdays noon–2:30 P.M., 6–9:30 P.M.; Saturday 6–9:30 P.M. Its name is a tip of the hat (in French) to the White House nearby, and staffers and lobbyists favor its classic and modern dishes. Reservations recommended.

Greek

Mykonos. Moderate. 1835 K Street NW: (202) 331-0370. Greek specialties in an Aegean island setting. Daily except Sunday.

Indian

Aditi. Budget. 3299 M Street NW at Thirty-third Street, Georgetown: (202) 625-6825. Monday to Thursday and Sunday 11:30 A.M.–2:30 P.M., 5:30–10 P.M.; Friday and Saturday 11:30 A.M.–2:30 P.M., 5:30–10:30 P.M. A very popular eatery with spicy tandoori meat and vegetarian dishes, a favorite of restaurant critics. One of the reasonably priced sampler dishes is a good choice. Reservations recommended.

Irish

Fado Irish Pub. Moderate. 808 Seventh Street NW: (202) 789-0066. A bit of the real thing.

Italian

Armand's Chicago Pizzeria. Budget. 226 Massachusetts Avenue NE, between Second and Third Streets: (202) 547-6600. Monday to Thursday 11:30 A.M.–10 P.M.; Friday and Saturday 11:30 A.M.–11 P.M.; Sunday 4–10 P.M. Voted best pizza in the District in a magazine poll.

A.V. Ristorante Italiano. Budget–Moderate. 607 New York Avenue NW at Sixth Street, Mt. Vernon Square: (202) 737-0550. Monday to Thursday 11:30 A.M.–11 P.M.; Friday 11:30 A.M.–midnight; Saturday 5 P.M.–midnight. Closed first two weeks of August. Casual and good, a local institution for more than forty years, serving pizza, pasta, and Italian country fare, including rabbit and tripe.

Faccia Luna. Moderate. 2400 Wisconsin Avenue NW, Glover Park: (202) 337-3132. Sunday to Thursday 11:30 A.M.–11 P.M.; Friday and Saturday 11:30 A.M.–midnight.

Galileo. Expensive. 1110 Twenty-first Street NW, between L and M Streets: (202) 293-7191. Monday to Thursday 11:30 A.M.–2 P.M., 5:30–10 P.M.; Friday 11:30 A.M.–2 P.M., 5:30–10:30 P.M.; Saturday 5:30–10:30 P.M.; Sunday 5–10 P.M. Seafood, pasta, and game specialties. Reservations recommended.

I Matti. Moderate. 2436 Eighteenth Street NW at Columbia Road, Adams–Morgan: (202) 462-8844. Monday to Thursday noon–2:30 P.M., 5:30–10:30 P.M.; Friday and Saturday noon–2:30 P.M., 5:30–11 P.M.; Sunday 5:30–10 P.M. *I Matti* means "the crazies," and there are a lot of Washingtonians who feel that way about the pizza, pasta, and seafood here.

I Ricchi. Expensive. 1220 Nineteenth Street NW, between M and N Streets: (202) 835-0459. Monday to Thursday 11:30 A.M.–2 P.M., 5:30–10 P.M.; Friday 11:30 A.M.–2 P.M., 5:30–10 P.M.; Saturday 5:30–10:15 P.M. Fine Tuscan fare.

Obelisk. Expensive. 2029 P Street NW, between Twentieth and Twenty-First Streets: (202) 872-1180. Monday to Saturday 6–10 P.M. A very small eatery with a changing prix-fixe five-course dinner. Reservations recommended.

Pizzeria Paradiso. Budget. 2029 P Street NW, between Twentieth and Twenty-first Streets, Dupont Circle: (202) 223-1245. Monday to Thursday 11 A.M.–11 P.M.; Friday and Saturday 11 A.M.–midnight; Sunday noon–10 P.M. Unusual pizza toppings cooked in a wood-fired oven and other inventive fare.

Vincenzo. Expensive. 1606 Twentieth Street NW, near Q Street, Dupont Circle: (202) 667-0047. Weekdays noon–2 P.M., 6–9:30 P.M.; Saturday 5:30–10 P.M. Seafood and pasta specialties. Reservations recommended.

Lebanese

Bacchus Restaurant. Moderate. 1827 Jefferson Place NW at M Street: (202) 785-0734. Monday to Thursday noon–2:30 P.M., 6–10 P.M.; Friday noon–2:30 P.M., 6–10:30 P.M.; Saturday 6–10:30 P.M. Lebanese specialties of stuffed eggplant with pomegranate sauce, lamb with nuts, and hummus. Reservations recommended.

Mama Ayesha's. Budget. 1967 Calvert Street NW at Twentieth Street, Adams–Morgan: (202) 232-5431. Open daily 11:30 A.M.–11 P.M. Top-rated Middle Eastern cuisine, with an emphasis on Lebanese specialties.

Mexican

Enriqueta's. Budget. 2811 M Street NW at Twenty-ninth Street, Georgetown: (202) 338-7772. Monday to Thursday 11:30 A.M.–2:30 P.M., 5–10 P.M.; Friday 11:30 A.M.–2:30 P.M., 5–11 P.M.; Saturday 5–11 P.M.; Sunday 5–10 P.M. Party on at this casual eatery with specialties including stuffed peppers, fajitas, and enchiladas.

Lauriol Plaza. Moderate. 1801 Eighteenth Street NW at S Street, near Dupont Circle: (202) 387-0035. Monday to Thursday and Sunday 11:30 A.M.–11 P.M.; Friday and Saturday noon–midnight. A mix of Mexican, South American, and Spanish dishes in a lively, casual room.

Mixtec. Budget–Moderate. 1792 Columbia Road NW, Adams–Morgan: (202) 332-1011. Sunday to Thursday noon–10 P.M.; Friday and Saturday 11 A.M.–1 A.M. An unusually wide-ranging Mexican menu.

South American

Coco Loco. Moderate. 810 Seventh Street NW: (202) 289-2626. Monday to Friday 11:30 A.M.–2:30 P.M.; Monday to Thursday 5:30–10:30 P.M.; Friday and Saturday 5:30–11 P.M., nightclub 10 P.M.–3 A.M. A Brazilian tapas and steak house in a perpetual state of Carnival.

Seafood

Legal Sea Foods. Moderate. 2020 K Street NW: (202) 496-1111. Monday to Thursday 11 A.M.–10 P.M.; Friday 11 A.M.–10:30 P.M.; Saturday 4–10:30 P.M.; Sunday 4–9 P.M. Also located in National Airport's new terminal. Boston's best-known seafood eatery gone south.

McCormick & Schmick's. Moderate. 1652 K Street NW: (202) 861-2233. Monday to Thursday 11 A.M.–11 P.M.; Friday 11 A.M.–midnight; Saturday 5 P.M.–midnight; Sunday 5–11 P.M. An outpost of the well-known Pacific Northwest eatery, featuring fresh seafood and an old-style elegance.

Sea Catch. Moderate. 1054 Thirty-first Street NW at M Street, Georgetown: (202) 337-8855. Monday to Saturday noon–3 P.M., 5:30–10:30 P.M. Crab cakes, fresh fish, and a nice view of the canal. Reservations recommended.

Spanish

El Rincon Espanol. Budget–Moderate. 1826 Columbia Road NW at Eighteenth Street, Adams–Morgan: (202) 265-4943. Monday to Thursday and Sunday 11 A.M.–midnight; Friday and Saturday 11 A.M.–1 A.M. They've got the corner on paellas, sizzling shrimp dishes, and more.

Steak

Capital Grille. Expensive. 601 Pennsylvania Avenue NW: (202) 737-6200. Upscale steakhouse, with an ultimate martini bar.

Exchange. Moderate. 1719 G Street NW: (202) 393-4690. Near the White House and popular with the West Wing crowd and reporters.

Morton's of Chicago. Expensive. 3251 Prospect Street NW at Wisconsin Avenue, Georgetown: (202) 342-6258. Monday to Saturday 5:30–11 P.M.; Sunday 5–10 P.M. An outpost of the Chicago original. Reservations recommended.

Tex-Mex

Austin Grill. Budget–Moderate. 2404 Wisconsin Avenue NW, Glover Park: (202) 337-8080. Monday 11:30 A.M.–10 P.M.; Tuesday to Thursday 11:30 A.M.–11 P.M.; Friday and Saturday 11:30 A.M.–midnight; Sunday 11 A.M.–10:30 P.M. The Texas chili is mighty hot, and the rest of the menu ain't bad, either.

Cactus Cantina. Budget. 3300 Wisconsin Avenue NW at Macomb Street: (202) 686-7222. Monday to Thursday and Sunday 11 A.M.–11 P.M.; Friday and Saturday 11:30 A.M.–midnight. Near the National Cathedral.

Restaurants by Area

Adams-Morgan

Cafe Creole. 2435 Eighteenth Street NW: (202) 234-0404. Cajun.

    Fasika's. 2447 Eighteenth Street NW: (202) 797-7673. Ethiopian.

    La Fourchette. 2429 Eighteenth Street NW: (202) 332-3077. French.

    Meskerem. 2434 Eighteenth Street NW: (202) 462-4100. Ethiopian.

    Peyote Cafe. 2319 Eighteenth Street NW: (202) 462-8330. Southwestern.

    The Red Sea. 2463 Eighteenth Street NW: (202) 483-5000. Ethiopian.

    Roxanne. 2319 Eighteenth Street NW: (202) 462-8330. Southwestern.

    Sam Marco. 2305 Eighteenth Street NW: (202) 483-9300. Italian.

Archives

Capital Grille. 601 Pennsylvania Avenue NW: (202) 737-6200. Steaks.

    Bertolini's. 801 Pennsylvania Avenue NW: (202) 638-2140. American.

Capitol Hill

B. Smith's. 50 Massachusetts Avenue NE: (202) 289-6188. Southern.

Bangkok Orchid. 301 Massachusetts Avenue NE: (202) 546-5900. Thai.

Cafe Berlin. 322 Massachusetts Avenue NW: (202) 543-7656. German.

Capitol City Brewing. 2 Massachusetts Avenue NE: (202) 842-2337. American.

La Colline. 400 North Capitol Street NW: (202) 737-0400. French.

Monocle. 107 D Street NE: (202) 546-4488. American.

Thai Roma. 313 Pennsylvania Avenue SE: (202) 544-2338. Thai.

Two Quail. 320 Massachusetts Avenue NE: (202) 543-8030. American.

Chinatown

Mr. Yung's. 740 Sixth Street NW: (202) 628-1098. Chinese.

Tony Cheng's. 619 H Street NW: (202) 842-8669. Chinese.

Cleveland Park

Spices. 3333-A Connecticut Avenue NW: (202) 686-3833. Asian.

Yanyu. 3435 Connecticut Avenue NW: (202) 686-6968. Asian.

Convention Center

A.V. Ristorante Italiano. 607 New York Avenue NW: (202) 737-0550. Italian.

Coeur de Lion. Henley Park Hotel; 926 Massachusetts Avenue NW: (202) 414-0500. American.

Jaleo. 480 Seventh Street NW: (202) 628-7949. Spanish.

Luigino. 1100 New York Avenue NW: (202) 371-0595. Italian.

The Morrison-Clark Restaurant. 1015 L Street NW: (202) 898-1200. American.

Downtown

Capital Grille. 601 Pennsylvania Avenue NW: (202) 737-6200.

City Lights of China. 1731 Connecticut Avenue NW at R Street: (202) 265-6688.

Fado Irish Pub. 808 Seventh Street NW: (202) 789-0066

Himalayan Grill. 1805 Eighteenth Street NW: (202) 986-5124. Tibet, Nepal, and India.

Hard Rock Cafe. 999 E Street NW: (202) 737-7625. American.

Les Halles. 1201 Pennsylvania Avenue NW: (202) 347-6848. Steaks.

Luigi's. 1132 Nineteenth Street NW: (202) 331-7574. Italian.

Maison Blanche/Rive Gauche. 1725 F Street NW: (202) 842-0070. French.

Metro Center Grille and Bar. Marriott Metro Center Hotel; Twelfth and H Streets NW: (202) 737-2200. American.

Mykonos. 1835 K Street NW: (202) 331-0370. Greek.

Occidental Grill. 1475 Pennsylvania Avenue NW: (202) 783-1475. American.

Old Ebbitt Grill. 675 Fifteenth Street NW: (202) 347-4800. American.

Oodles Noodles. Budget. 1120 Nineteenth Street NW: (202) 293-3138.

The Palm. 1225 Nineteenth Street NW: (202) 293-9091.

Planet Hollywood. 1101 Pennsylvania Avenue NW: (202) 783-7827. American.

Red Sage. 605 Fourteenth Street NW: (202) 638-4444. Southwestern.

Two Continents. Hotel Washington; 515 Fifteenth Street NW: (202) 347-4499. French.

The Willard Room. The Willard Hotel; 1401 Pennsylvania Avenue NW: (202) 637-7440. American.

Dupont Circle

Annie's Paramount Steak House. 1609 Seventeenth Street NW: (202) 232-0395. American.

Brickskeller. 1523 Twenty-second Street NW: (202) 293-1885. American.

Bua. 1635 P Street NW: (202) 265-0828. Thai.

The Burro. 1621 Connecticut Avenue NW: (202) 483-6861. Mexican.

Cafe du Monde. 2412 Eighteenth Street NW: (202) 234-0420. Continental.

Cafe Japone. 2032 P Street NW: (202) 223-1573. Japanese.

Cafe Luna. 1633 P Street NW: (202) 387-4005. American.

Cafe Petitto. 1724 Connecticut Avenue NW: (202) 462-8771. Italian.

Carmella Kitty's. 1602 Seventeenth Street NW: (202) 667-5937. Cajun.

Coyote Bar & Grill. 2020 Florida Avenue NW: (202) 265-3078. Southwestern.

Donna Adele. 2100 P Street NW: (202) 296-1142. Italian.

El Bodegon. 1637 R Street NW: (202) 667-1710. Spanish.

El Caminante. 2002 P Street NW: (202) 331-8963. Spanish/Mexican.

Gabriel. Radisson Barcelo Hotel; 2121 P Street NW: (202) 822-8021. Spanish.

I Matti. 2436 Eighteenth Street NW: (202) 462-8844. Italian.

Il Radicchio. 1509 Seventeenth Street NW: (202) 986-2027. Italian.

International Market Place. Embassy Row Hotel; 2015 Massachusetts Avenue NW: (202) 939-4250. American.

Iron Gate Restaurant. 1734 N Street NW: (202) 737-1373. Mediterranean.

Italian Kitchen. 1637 Seventeenth Street NW: (202) 328-3222. Italian.

Jolt 'N Bolt. 1918 Eighteenth Street NW: (202) 232-0077. Coffeehouse.

Kramerbooks & Afterwords, A Cafe. 1517 Connecticut Avenue NW: (202) 387-3825. American.

La Fonda. 1639 R Street NW: (202) 232-6965. Mexican.

La Frontera Cantina. 1633 Seventeenth Street NW: (202) 232-0437. Mexican/ Spanish.

La Tomate. 1701 Connecticut Avenue NW: (202) 667-5505. Italian.

Las Cruces. 1524 U Street NW: (202) 328-3153. Mexican.

Lauriol Plaza. 1801 Eighteenth Street NW: (202) 387-0035. Mexican.

Lulu's New Orleans Cafe. Twenty-second and M Streets NW: (202) 861-5858. Cajun.

Peppers. 1527 Seventeenth Street NW: (202) 328-8193. American.

Pesce. 2016 P Street NW: (202) 466-3474. Seafood.
Polo Indian Club. 1736 Connecticut Avenue NW: (202) 483-8705. Indian.
Ruth's Chris Steak House. 1801 Connecticut Avenue NW: (202) 797-0033.
Steaks.
    Salsa Thai. 2016 P Street NW: (202) 872-1144. Thai.
    Sam and Harry's. 1200 Nineteenth Street NW: (202) 296-4333. Steaks.
    Skewers. 1633 P Street NW: (202) 387-7400. Middle Eastern.
    Soho Tea and Coffee. 2150 P Street, NW: (202) 463-7646. Coffeehouse.
    Taj Mahal. 1327 Connecticut Avenue NW: (202) 659-1544. Indian.
    Trumpets. 1603 Seveneenth Street NW: (202) 232-4141. American.
    Vidalia. 1900 M Street NW: (202) 659-1990. American/French.
    Zorba's Cafe. 1612 Twentieth Street NW: (202) 387-8555. Greek.

Farragut North

Bombay Palace. 2020 K Street NW: (202) 331-4200. Indian.
    China Joy Restaurant. 1827 M Street NW: (202) 296-6082. Chinese.
    Muer's Seafood. 1101 Connecticut Avenue NW: (202) 785-4505. Seafood.

Farragut West

Dominique's. 1900 Pennsylvania Avenue NW: (202) 452-1126. French.
    Ginza. 1009 Twenty-first Street NW: (202) 833-1244. Japanese.
    Marrocco's. 1120 Twentieth Street NW: (202) 331-9664. Italian.
    The Prime Rib. 2020 K Street NW: (202) 466-8811. Steaks.
    Sushi Kappo Kawasaki. 1140 Nineteenth Street NW: (202) 466-3798.
Japanese.
    Thai Kingdom. 2021 K Street NW: (202) 835-1700. Thai.

Foggy Bottom

Aquarelle. The Watergate Hotel; 2650 Virginia Avenue NW: (202) 298-4455.
French.
    Blackie's House of Beef. 1217 Twenty-second Street NW: (202) 333-1100.
    Colonnade. ANA Hotel; 2401 M Street NW: (202) 457-5000. American.
    Encore Cafe. The Kennedy Center: (202) 416-8555. American.
    Galileo. 1110 Twenty-first Street NW: (202) 293-7191. Italian.
    Garden Cafe. State Plaza Hotel; 2116 F Street NW: (202) 861-8200.
American.
    Kinkead's. 2000 Pennsylvania Avenue NW: (202) 296-7700. Seafood/
American.
    Roof Terrace Restaurant. The Kennedy Center: (202) 416-8555. American.
    Washington Grill. Sheraton City Centre Hotel; 1143 New Hampshire
Avenue NW: (202) 775-0800. American.

Georgetown

Aditi. 3299 M Street NW: (202) 625-6825. Indian.
    Billy Martin's. 1264 Winsconsin Avenue NW: (202) 333-7370.

Bistro Francais. 3128 M Street NW: (202) 338-3830. French.

Cafe Babalu. 3235 M Street NW: (202) 965-4141. Southwestern.

Cantina Romana. 3251 Prospect Street NW: (202) 337-5133. Italian.

Citronelle. The Latham Hotel; 3000 M Street NW: (202) 625-2150. French.

Clyde's of Georgetown. 3236 M Street NW: (202) 638-5200. American.

Donatello. 2514 L Street NW: (202) 333-1485. Italian.

Geppetto Restaurant. 2917 M Street NW: (202) 333-2602. Italian.

Japan Restaurant. 1715 Wisconsin Avenue NW: (202) 337-3400. Japanese.

Pad Thai. 1608 Wisconsin Avenue NW: (202) 342-3394. Thai.

The River Club. 3223 K Street NW: (202) 965-3229. American.

Sarinah Satay House. 1338 Wisconsin Avenue NW: (202) 337-2955. Indonesian.

Sea Catch. 1054 Thirty-first Street NW: (202) 337-8855. Seafood.

1789 Restaurant. 1226 Thirty-sixth Street NW: (202) 965-1789. American.

Tony and Joe's. 3000 K Street NW: (202) 944-4545. Seafood.

Zed's Ethiopian Cuisine. 3318 M Street NW: (202) 333-4710. Ethiopian.

L'Enfant Plaza/Waterfront

The Gangplank. 600 Water Street SW: (202) 554-5000. Seafood.

Hogate's. 800 Water Street SW: (202) 484-6300. Seafood.

Le Rivage. 1000 Water Street SW: (202) 488-8111. French/Seafood.

Pier 7. 650 Water Street SW: (202) 554-2500. Seafood.

McPherson Square

Cafe Amadeus. 1300 I Street NW: (202) 962-8686. German.

Cafe Mozart. 1331 H Street NW: (202) 347-5732. German.

Exchange. Moderate. 1719 G St. NW: (202) 393-4690.

Gerard's Place. 915 Fifteenth Street NW: (202) 737-4445. French.

Tenleytown

Armand's Chicago Pizzeria. 4231 Wisconsin Avenue NW: (202) 686-9450. American/Italian.

Woodley Park

Lavandou. 3321 Connecticut Avenue NW: (202) 966-3003. French.

Mrs. Simpson's. 2915 Connecticut Avenue NW: (202) 332-8300. American.

New Heights. 2317 Calvert Street NW: (202) 234-4110. American.

Chapter 16
Hotels in Washington, D.C.

A Place to Lay Your Head

If you want to stay in the thick of things, Washington has a wide variety of hotels, guest houses, and a handful of motels. Prices range from a rather pricey "budget" level of about $75 into the lower stratosphere. Parking in the District is difficult to find and expensive, too. Most visitors find it easier to leave the car in the garage and use the Metro or taxis.

You should also consider staying outside the District in one of the Virginia or Maryland suburbs. Room rates are generally lower, and Washington is still easily reached by Metrorail.

Rates at District hotels are typical for a large city but can spike upward when there is a major event in town—the Inauguration, the Fourth of July celebration, a major parade or gathering, or just about anything else can result in a "No Vacancy" sign or a doubling of prices.

We suggest you use a discount hotel service or listings such as the AAA guide. Reservation services sometimes have good deals on rooms, although they, too, are subject to blackouts or high prices during special events. Here are a few services to call; most do not charge for their efforts but may impose stiff cancellation fees if your plans change.

1-800-USA-Hotels. *(Coupon in this book.)* (800) USA-HOTELS. www.1-800-USA-HOTELS.com.

Capitol Reservations, Inc. (800) 847-4832. www.hotelsdc.com.

Hotel Reservations Network. *(Coupon in this book.)* (800) 964-6835. www.hoteldiscount.com.

Travel Store. *(Coupon in this book.)* (800) 826-3119. www.travel-store.com.

Washington, D.C. Accommodations. (800) 554-2220. You can also consult www.wdcahotels.com.

Washington, D.C., Hotels

The following are standard rates at a selection of hotels in Washington. Rates may increase on holidays and for special events, and they may be lower at off-peak times. Be sure to call hotels and ask for their lowest rates.

Price ratings are relative. Budget prices in Washington and other big cities may be equal to those called moderate or even deluxe elsewhere.

Budget: About $50 to $125
Moderate: About $100 to $200
Luxury: About $200 and higher

Budget

Best Western Capitol Skyline Hotel. 10 I Street SW: (202) 488-7500 or (800) 458-7500.

Best Western Downtown Capitol Hill. 724 Third Street NW: (202) 842-4466 or (800) 242-4831.

Capitol Hill Suites. 200 C Street SE: (202) 543-6000 or (800) 424-9165.

Carlyle Suites Hotel. 1731 New Hampshire Avenue NW: (202) 234-3200 or (800) 964-5377. An art-deco all-suite hotel on a residential street near Dupont Circle.

Center City Travelodge Hotel. 1201 13th Street NW: (202) 682-5300 or (800) 578-7878.

Channel Inn Hotel. 650 Water Street SW: (202) 554-2400 or (800) 368-5668. On the waterfront at Washington Channel.

Days Inn Connecticut Avenue. 4400 Connecticut Avenue NW: (202) 244-5600 or (800) 952-3060.

Days Inn–Gateway. 2700 New York Avenue NE: (202) 832-5800 or (800) 329-7466.

Embassy Inn. 1627 Sixteenth Street NW: (202) 234-7800 or (800) 423-9111.

Governors House. 1615 Rhode Island Avenue NW: (202) 296-2100 or (800) 821-4367.

Hampshire Clarion Hotel. 1310 New Hampshire Avenue NW: (202) 296-7600 or (800) 368-5691.

The Henley Park Hotel. 926 Massachusetts Avenue NW: (202) 638-5200 or (800) 222-8474. A small English-style hotel in a converted 1918 Tudor-style apartment house.

Holiday Inn Capitol at Smithsonian. 550 C Street SW: (202) 479-4000 or (800) 465-4329

Holiday Inn Central. 1501 Rhode Island Avenue NW: (202) 483-2000 or (800) 465-4329.

Holiday Inn Downtown. 1155 Fourteenth Street NW: (202) 737-1200 or (800) 465-4329.

Holiday Inn Georgetown. 2101 Wisconsin Avenue NW: (202) 338-4600 or (800) 465-4329.

Hotel Harrington. Eleventh and E Streets NW: (202) 628-8140 or (800) 424-8532.

Howard Johnson Hotel & Suites. 1430 Rhode Island Avenue NW: (202) 462-7777 or (800) 368-5690.

Kalorama Guest House. 1854 Mintwood Place NW: (202) 667-6369. Four turn-of-the-century townhouses with period decorations.

Lincoln Suites. 1823 L Street NW: (202) 223-4320 or (800) 424-2970.

Normandy Inn. 2118 Wyoming Avenue NW: (202) 483-1350.

Quality Hotel Downtown. 1315 Sixteenth Street NW: (202) 232-8000 or (800) 368-5689.

Radisson Barcelo Hotel. 2121 P Street NW: (202) 293-3100 or (800) 333-3333. The former Omni Georgetown, now owned by a Spanish company, has 208 rooms and 92 suites, and claims European-style service for its converted apartments. The hotel's restaurant, Gabriel, features Spanish dishes.

Red Roof Inn. 500 H Street NW: (202) 289-5959 or (800) 843-7663.

Savoy Suites Georgetown. 2505 Wisconsin Avenue NW: (202) 337-9700 or (800) 944-5377.

State Plaza Hotel. 2117 E Street NW: (202) 861-8200 or (800) 424-2859.

Tabard Inn. 1739 N Street NW: (202) 785-1277. Rooms are in three connected Victorian townhouses.

Washington Hilton and Towers. 1919 Connecticut Avenue NW: (202) 483-3000 or (800) 445-8667.

Windham Centre Hotel. 1143 New Hampshire Avenue NW: (202) 775-0800 or (800) 996-3426.

The Windsor Inn. 1842 Sixteenth Street NW: (202) 667-0300 or (800) 423-9111.

The best deal in town, albeit also one of the most spartan, is the **Washington International Youth Hostel** at 1009 11th Street NW. (202) 737-2333 or (800) 909-4776. The hostel offers 250 beds in male and female dormitories. For information on hostelling consult www.hiayh.org.

Another great deal can be had at the **Hotel Harrington**, a restored 1914 hotel located downtown a few blocks from the White House, near the FBI building. It's not fancy, but it's clean, secure, and a good deal, with rates below $100 per night; there are also family rooms and suites for not much more. The Harrington is at Eleventh and E Streets NW. (202) 628-8140 or (800) 424-8532.

Moderate

Best Western New Hampshire Suites Hotel. 1121 New Hampshire Avenue NW: (202) 457-0565 or (800) 528-1234.

Canterbury Hotel. 1733 N Street NW: (202) 393-3000 or (800) 424-2950. A small residential-style suites hotel.

Doubletree Guest Suites. 801 New Hampshire Avenue NW: (202) 785-2000 or (800) 222-8733.

Doubletree Hotel Park Terrace. 1515 Rhode Island Avenue NW: (202) 232-7000 or (800) 222-8733.

Embassy Square Summerfield Suites. 2000 N Street NW: (202) 659-9000 or (800) 424-2999 or (800) 833-4353.

Embassy Suites Hotel. 1250 Twenty-second Street NW: (202) 857-3388 or (800) 362-2779.

George Washington University Inn. 824 New Hampshire Avenue NW: (202) 337-6620 or (800) 426-4455.

The Georgetown Inn. 1310 Wisconsin Avenue NW: (202) 333-8900 or (800) 368-5922.

Georgetown Suites. 1111 Thirtieth Street NW: (202) 298-1600 or (800) 348-7203.

Georgetown Suites–Harbour Building. 1000 Twenty-ninth Street NW: (202) 298-1600 or (800) 348-7203.

Hilton Washington Embassy Row. 2015 Massachusetts Avenue NW: (202) 265-1600 or (800) 445-8667.

Hotel Washington. 515 Fifteenth Street NW: (202) 638-5900 or (800) 424-9540.

Hyatt Regency Washington. 400 New Jersey Avenue NW: (202) 737-1234 or (800) 223-1234.

J W Marriott Hotel. 1331 Pennsylvania Avenue NW: (202) 393-2000 or (800) 228-9290. A modern landmark with nearly 800 rooms.

Lincoln Suites–Downtown. 1823 L Street NW: (202) 223-4320 or (800) 424-2970.

Morrison Clark Inn. 1015 L Street NW: (202) 898-1200 or (800) 332-7898.

One Washington Circle. 1 Washington Circle NW: (202) 872-1680 or (800) 424-9671.

Phoenix Park Hotel. 520 North Capitol Street NW: (202) 638-6900 or (800) 824-5419.

The River Inn. 924 Twenty-fifth Street NW: (202) 337-7600 or (800) 424-2741.

Washington Courtyard by Marriott. 1900 Connecticut Avenue NW: (202) 332-9300 or (800) 842-4211.

Washington Marriott. 1221 Twenty-second Street NW: (202) 872-1500 or (800) 228-9290.

Washington Monarch Hotel. 2401 M Street NW: (202) 222-2266.

Washington Suites. 2500 Pennsylvania Avenue NW: (202) 333-8060 or (877) 736-2500.

Wyndham Bristol Hotel. 2430 Pennsylvania Avenue NW: (202) 955-6400 or (800) 996-3426.

Luxury

The Capitol Hilton. 1001 Sixteenth Street NW: (202) 393-1000 or (800) 445-8667. An old (and renovated) grande dame of Washington that has hosted every president since FDR; the hotel has more than 500 rooms.

Four Seasons Hotel. 2800 Pennsylvania Avenue NW: (202) 342-0444 or

(800) 332-3442. A luxurious haunt of the rich and famous. Some rooms overlook Rock Creek Park or the C & O Canal.

Grand Hyatt. 1000 H Street NW: (202) 582-1234 or (800) 223-1234.

Hay-Adams. Sixteenth and H Streets NW: (202) 638-6600 or (800) 424-5054. A 1927 landmark on Lafayette Square, built on the former site of the homes of John Hay (Theodore Roosevelt's secretary of state) and historian Henry Adams.

Hotel Sofitel. 1914 Connecticut Avenue NW: (202) 797-2000 or (800) 424-2464.

Jefferson Hotel. 1200 Sixteenth Street NW: (202) 347-2200 or (800) 368-5966. A small luxury hotel built in 1923 near the White House and featuring period decorations and a high level of service.

Latham Hotel Georgetown. 3000 M Street NW: (202) 726-5000 or (800) 528-4261.

Loews L'Enfant Plaza Hotel. 480 L'Enfant Plaza East SW: (202) 484-1000 or (800) 635-5065.

The Madison. 1177 Fifteenth Street NW: (202) 862-1600 or (800) 424-8577.

Marriott Metro Center. 775 12th Street NW: (202) 737-2200 or (800) 228-9290.

Marriott Wardman Park Hotel. 2660 Woodley Road NW: (202) 328-2000 or (800) 228-9290.

Omni Shoreham Hotel. 2500 Calvert Street NW: (202) 234-0700 or (800) 843-6664. A 1930s resort hotel, restored to its former glory, with 800 rooms.

Park Hyatt. Twenty-fourth and M Streets NW: (202) 789-1234 or (800) 233-1234.

Renaissance Mayflower Hotel. 1127 Connecticut Avenue NW: (202) 347-3000 or (800) 468-3571. Another of the grande dames of Washington, it opened in 1925 and is still drawing appreciative eyes. Many presidential inaugural balls have been held here, and J. Edgar Hoover had lunch here every day for twenty years.

St. Regis. Sixteenth and K Streets NW: (202) 638-2626 or (800) 325-3535.

Swissotel Watergate Hotel. 2650 Virginia Avenue NW: (202) 965-2300 or (800) 424-2736.

Washington Court Hotel. 525 New Jersey Avenue NW: (202) 628-2100 or (800) 321-3010.

Washington, D.C. Renaissance Hotel. 999 Ninth Street NW: (202) 898-9000 or (800) 486-3571. A modern luxury hotel with more than 800 rooms.

Westin Fairfax. 2100 Massachusetts Avenue NW: (202) 293-2100 or (800) 325-3589. A spectacular luxury hotel, built in 1924, and well kept up.

Westin Grand Hotel. 2350 M Street NW: (202) 429-0100 or (800) 937-8461.

The Willard Inter-Continental Hotel. 1401 Pennsylvania Avenue NW: (202) 628-9100 or (800) 327-0200. A National Landmark, dating all the way back to 1901 and renovated in 1986 to restore its turn-of-the-century grandeur. An earlier hotel on the site was built before the Civil War.

Wyndham Washington, D.C., City Center. 1400 M Street NW: (202) 429-1700 or (800) 847-8232.

Part III
Northern Virginia and Maryland

Chapter 17
Virginia: History All Around

You can feel the tides of history in Virginia, from the unsuccessful first English settlement of 1584 at Roanoke to the first colony at Jamestown about a quarter-century later, from the cradles of Revolution at Williamsburg and Richmond to the battlefield at Yorktown that ended the war with Great Britain, from the suburbs of the eventual seat of the federal government in the District of Columbia to the blood-soaked fields of Civil War battle sites.

And even before the English settlers at Jamestown, of course, Virginia was populated by Algonquian-speaking tribes in villages along the rivers near Chesapeake Bay.

Virginia was one of the most prosperous of the colonies and early states because of its farm products and its ports; much of the economy was based on slavery, though, and that led to the state's secession from the Union in 1861. More major Civil War battles were fought on Virginia soil than anywhere else in the nation.

The tenth of the original thirteen states to ratify the Constitution, Virginia joined the United States on June 25, 1788. Its capital is Richmond, a location that has remained unchanged since the government relocated from the difficult-to-defend Williamsburg at the start of the Revolutionary War. Among Virginia's native sons were George Washington and Thomas Jefferson. Indeed, four of the first five U.S. presidents were born in Virginia.

In This Chapter

Alexandria

Alexandria Colonial and Civil War Sites

George Washingtonia in Alexandria

Arlington National Cemetery

 Newseum

Fredericksburg

Monticello

Charlottesville

 Mount Vernon

Wolf Trap Farm Park for the Performing Arts

Eating Your Way Through Northern Virginia

Accommodations in Virginia

Golf in Northern Virginia

Alexandria

Alexandria offers some of the best views of the District of Columbia, a stone's throw across the Potomac River. The old seaport has a charm of its own and offers some good deals to visitors willing to make a ten-minute commute by Metro or car to Washington.

First settled in the 1670s, Alexandria was a flourishing tobacco port in the early eighteenth century; by the 1790s it was one of the busiest ports in the country.

In 1748, a teenaged George Washington was among the surveyors who laid out the streets of Alexandria; in 1765, he built a townhouse of his own there.

At first Alexandria was part of the District of Columbia, a result of Virginia's grant to the federal government in 1791, but it was given back to the state in 1846. During the Civil War, much of the town was occupied by federal troops who used it as a key fortification to defend Washington.

Alexandria's historic district, Old Town, includes more than 2,000 eighteenth- and nineteenth-century buildings now used as residences, art galleries, boutiques, and restaurants.

The Metro's King Street stop leaves you a bit more than a mile to the heart of Old Town; taxis and buses await in the parking lot below the station most of the day. The DASH bus connects from the Metro to downtown. For information, call (703) 370-3274.

Visitors can purchase multi-admission discount coupons to five Alexandria museums: Gadsby's Tavern, Carlyle House, Lee-Fendall House, the Robert E. Lee House, and the Stabler-Leadbeater Apothecary Shop. Tickets are available at the participating museums and at the Alexandria Visitors Center at 221 King Street. (703) 838-4200. You can consult the Internet for more details at www.funside.com.

Visitors center. Alexandria maintains a visitors center at Ramsay House, 221 King Street, a reconstructed eighteenth-century home. For information, call (703) 838-4200. www.funside.com.

Alexandria Colonial and Civil War Sites

Boyhood Home of Robert E. Lee

Lee lived at 607 Oronoco St. from 1811 to 1816 and again from 1820 to 1825 until he left to study at West Point. The home is now a private residence and not open to the public.

You can, though, cross the street to 614 Oronoco, the **Lee-Fendall House**, also home to a branch of the Lee family and restored to its mid-nineteenth-century appearance inside and outside. Open 10 A.M.–4 P.M. Tuesday to Saturday; 1–4 P.M. Sunday. (Closed mid-December to early February.) Admission: adult, $4; student $2; child younger than 11, free. (703) 548-1789.

Carlyle House Historic Park

121 North Fairfax Street. (703) 549-2997. Tuesday to Saturday 10 A.M.–4:30 P.M. and Sunday noon–4:30 P.M. Tobacco merchant John Carlyle built his stone mansion in 1753 in a style that was evocative of his native Scotland. Two years after its completion it was used for an important conference between British General Edward Braddock and five colonial governors during the French and Indian War; turned down in his request for funding for the war, Braddock asked England for new taxes, contributing to the growing revolutionary fervor. The home was restored in the 1970s and is open for tours on the half hour beginning at 10 A.M.; from January to March the last tour is at 4 P.M. Admission: adult, $4; child ages 11–17, $2.

Fort Ward Museum and Historic Site

4301 West Braddock Road. (703) 838-4848. Earthworks and gun emplacements from the Civil War, part of the fortifications of Washington. Open Tuesday to Saturday 9 A.M.–5 P.M.; Sunday noon–5 P.M. Admission: free.

Old Presbyterian Meeting House

321 South Fairfax Street. (703) 549-6670. Open by appointment, the building dates to 1744 and includes the Tomb of the Unknown Soldier of the Revolutionary War. It was also used for funeral services for George Washington. Admission: free.

Stabler-Leadbeater Apothecary Shop

105–107 S. Fairfax Street. (703) 836-3713. Opened for business in 1792, today it is a museum of old-time medicine. Admission: adult $2.50; student 11–17, $2; child younger than 11, free. Open Monday through Saturday 10 A.M.–4 P.M. and Sunday 1–5 P.M.

George Washingtonia in Alexandria

Christ Church

118 North Washington Street. (703) 549-1450. Older than the nation itself, the church was completed in 1773. George Washington owned a pew here; in the next century, the church was attended by Robert E. Lee. Open for tours Monday through Friday 9 A.M.–4 P.M.; Saturday 10 A.M to 4 P.M. Sunday services 8, 9, 11:15 A.M., and 5 P.M. Sunday tours from 2 to 4 P.M.

Gadsby's Tavern Museum

134 North Royal Street. (703) 838-4242. George Washington partied here. The original ballroom was removed from the tavern in 1917 and installed in the Metropolitan Museum of Art in New York; a reproduction of the room and restored eighteenth-century bedrooms are on display. Open Tuesday to Saturday 10 A.M.–5 P.M., Sunday 1–5 P.M. (Reduced hours October to March. Special events are offered around Christmas.) Admission: adult $4; child 11–17, $2.

George Washington Grist Mill

Mount Vernon Memorial Highway. (703) 780-3383. A reconstructed eighteenth-century mill like the one built by Washington on the site in 1770. Closed for restoration through mid-2000.

George Washington Masonic National Memorial

101 Callahan Drive. (703) 683-2007. Washington was master of a local Masonic Lodge and is memorialized with a 333-foot-tall tower and museum completed in 1932. Items on display include the Washington family Bible and the clock from his bedroom at Mount Vernon, stopped at the moment of his death. Free admission for tours and tower.

The memorial in Alexandria was patterned after an ancient lighthouse in Alexandria, Egypt.

Arlington National Cemetery

The nation's most famous resting place, Arlington National Cemetery, is the final home to several hundred thousand veterans, the Tomb of the Unknowns, and the gravesites of many fallen heroes, including President John F. Kennedy and his brother Senator Robert F. Kennedy.

President Kennedy lies beneath an eternal flame and alongside his wife Jacqueline Kennedy Onassis and two of their children. Senator Kennedy was granted his wish to rest beneath a tree not far away.

The cemetery was championed by Army Quartermaster General Montgomery Meigs who led the efforts to bury Washington's Civil War dead on the grounds of Confederate general Robert E. Lee's family estate. The property that included Arlington House, Lee's home, was seized in 1864 on the pretext that taxes had not been paid in person by the owner. Although the U.S. Supreme Court eventually ruled that the government had improperly taken the land, Lee's son gave the property to the federal government in 1882.

More than two thousand Union soldiers as well as a number of Confederate troops are buried at Arlington. A second president, William Howard Taft, is buried there as well. Also in the cemetery are memorials to the crew of the space shuttle *Challenger*; the Rough Riders who died at San Juan Hill; and the crew of the *Maine*, which blew up in Havana harbor and led to the Spanish–American War.

The cemetery is open every day 8 A.M.–5 P.M., and until 7 P.M. from April to September. There is a parking lot at the site, or visitors can take the Metro's Blue line to the stop at the cemetery.

Nearby to the cemetery is **Arlington House,** a memorial to Robert E. Lee. The spectacular Greek-style house was built in the 1800s by George Washington Parke Custis, President Washington's step-grandson; Robert E. Lee married Custis's daughter in 1831, and the estate became their home until the outbreak of the Civil War in 1861. After Lee resigned his commission to join the Confederate Army, the home was occupied by federal troops.

Tours of Arlington House are offered by the National Park Service. The estate is open 9:30 A.M.–4:30 P.M. daily, and until 6 P.M. (703) 289-2500 or (703) 557-0614.

⬛ Newseum

1101 Wilson Boulevard in Arlington. (888) 639-7386 or (703) 284-3700. A celebration of journalism and journalists; you'll have a chance to be a television anchor or radio sportscaster and take home a tape of your broadcast, put your face on a magazine cover, and work with some of the latest high-tech devices for broadcast and print journalism.

In the Interactive Newsroom, you'll use touch-screen computer programs to test your skills as an investigative reporter, or play editor in selecting front-page stories. In the Ethics Center, you'll get to wrestle with some of the knotty problems faced by reporters and editors.

At the entrance, a large globe is made of the metal nameplates from nearly 2,000 newspapers; an Associated Press news ticker circles with the latest news. The sprawling museum is worth a visit of several hours.

Artifacts on display include a bronze bell sent from China from about 475–221 B.C. used to summon people for meetings or worship; drums from Asian countries, including Burma, Thailand, the Philippines, India, and Tibet, used to inform people a distance away about ceremonies, danger, and council meetings; an ancient Egyptian court report on papyrus, dated to 1100 B.C. and reporting the trials of tomb robbers who were tortured until they confessed to plundering the mummies of the sons of the pharaoh Ramses the Great; a letter from Italy of about 1400 showing how medieval scribes and monks spread handwritten news in letters and books; a 1455 Gutenberg Bible from Germany; and a woodcut of about 1493 showing the burning of books in Nuremberg, Germany.

The Newseum is funded by the Freedom Forum, which is itself endowed by the Gannett Company.

You can get there by taking the Blue or Orange line to the Rosslyn Station, a two-block walk. Admission: free. Open Tuesday through Sunday 10 A.M.–5 P.M. www.newseum.org.

Fredericksburg

Fredericksburg is a very real place in American history and also the site of at least two George Washington legends of somewhat uncertain veracity.

It was here that young George is supposed to have chopped down the cherry tree, at least that is the story told by Mason Locke Weems, an Anglican preacher and traveling bookseller who wrote a biography of President Washington about 1800 that contained the story, a parable about honesty.

It was also here that the adult General Washington is supposed to have thrown a silver coin across the Rappahannock River—not the Potomac River or the Delaware River as some believe. The Rappahannock is about 300 feet wide at this point, by the way, which would have made George a promising Major League prospect.

You can read about some of the Civil War battle sites in and around Fredericksburg in the next chapter.

Interesting Washingtonia places to visit in the area include:

Rising Sun Tavern. 1306 Caroline Street. (540) 371-1494. Daily 9 A.M.–5 P.M. Built about 1760 as a home by Charles Washington, it was visited a number of times by brother George and was a hotbed of revolutionary activity. The house was converted to a tavern in 1792 and has been restored. Reduced hours December to February. Admission: adult $3; child 11–17, $1.

Hugh Mercer Apothecary. 1020 Caroline Street. (540) 373-3362. Daily 9 A.M.–5 P.M. The restored store of a Scottish doctor who fought in the French and Indian War and was a close friend of George Washington. He served as a commander in the Revolutionary War at the Battle of Trenton in New Jersey; he was killed at Princeton. World War II general George S. Patton was a descendant. Reduced hours December to February. Admission: adult $3; child 6–17, $1.50.

Kenmore. 1201 Washington Avenue. (540) 373-3381. Daily March to December 10 A.M.–5 P.M.; Sunday noon–5 P.M.; January and February open Saturday 10 A.M.–4 P.M.; Sunday noon–4 P.M.; and weekdays by reservation. Built by Fielding Lewis, who was married to George Washington's sister Betty, the home features ornately decorated interiors, including plaster reliefs and period furnishings, and it is surrounded by formal gardens. Admission: adult $6; child 6–17, $3.

Mary Washington House. 1200 Charles Street. (540) 373-1569. Daily 10 A.M.–4 P.M. March to November; reduced hours remainder of the year. A boy's gotta take care of his mom, even when the relationship is famously strained, so George bought this home near Kenmore for his mother in 1772. The restored home includes some family heirlooms. Admission: adult $4; student $1.50.

Fredericksburg Area Museum and Cultural Center. Old Town Hall and Market House; 907 Princess Anne Street, Fredericksburg. (540) 371-3037. Open March 1 through November 30, Monday to Saturday 10 A.M.–5 P.M. and Sunday 1–5 P.M.; remainder of the year the museum closes an hour earlier. www.famcc.org.

Galleries tell the story of the area from prehistoric times through Indian and Colonial settlement, the Revolutionary and Federal eras, the Civil War and Reconstruction, and modern days. Admission: adult $4; child 6–18, $1.

Belmont. The Gari Melchers Estate and Memorial Gallery; 224 Washington Street, Falmouth. (540) 654-1015. The former home of the renowned artist at the turn of the century includes works and possessions. March to November, Monday to Saturday 10 A.M.–5 P.M.; Sunday 1–5 P.M. Reduced hours remainder of the year. Admission: adult $4; child 6–18, $1 .

Chatham. 120 Chatham Lane, Stafford. (540) 371-0802. Daily 9 A.M.–5 P.M., except Christmas Day and New Year's Day. An eighteenth-century Georgian-style mansion that served as Union headquarters during the Battle of Fredericksburg. Here Clara Barton and Walt Whitman were among those who treated wounded soldiers. Admission: adult older than 16, $3; child free.

Masonic Lodge No. 4 A.F. and A.M. 803 Princess Anne Street, Fredericksburg. (540) 373-5885. Daily 9 A.M.–4 P.M.; Sunday 1–4 P.M. George Washington's home Masonic lodge; a museum at the site includes relics of his membership. Admission: adult $2; child 13–18, $1.

Fredericksburg Historic Tour

A discount ticket package will save money on admission to Fredericksburg-area historic sites. For information, call (540) 373-1776 or consult the web at www.fredericksburgva.com.

The Hospitality Pass offers reduced admission to Kenmore, the Mary Washington House, Fredericksburg Area Museum, Hugh Mercer Apothecary, Rising Sun Tavern, Belmont, and the James Monroe Museum. Tickets are priced: adult $19.75; student $7, 6–18.

The Pick Four allows admission to four of the seven participating sites and is priced at $13.75 for adults and $5.50 for students. The discount tickets are available at the area visitors center or the individual sites.

【WOW】 Monticello

Monticello is a masterpiece of eighteenth-century architecture and landscaping. Visitors see the stunning building and tour the gardens and groves. The Thomas Jefferson Memorial Foundation displays the house and gardens on nearly 2,000 of the original 5,000 acres. More than 500,000 people visit each year.

Located on Route 53, three miles southeast of Charlottesville, Virginia. (804) 984-9822 or (804) 984-9800. From Washington, take Route 66 west to Route 29 south. Open 8 A.M.–5 P.M. March to October, and 9 A.M.–4:30 P.M. at other times of the year.

Thomas Jefferson inherited a large estate from his father at the age of fourteenand began construction of his grand home in 1769, when he was twenty-six years old. For most of the following forty years Jefferson was involved in new construction and enlargement of the house.

Jefferson sketched the drawings for the house himself, based in part on English books on architecture. There are thirty-three rooms in the house itself, plus ten others in outbuildings.

Bricks and nails were made at Monticello; and stone, brick, and carpentry work were done by local craftsmen and slaves.

Rooms available on the public tours of the house include the spectacular Entrance Hall, crowded with pictures and artifacts. Jefferson's intellectual curiosity is represented by the busts he chose to exhibit, which include the French economist Turgot and the writer Voltaire, as well as one of Alexander Hamilton, his political rival. Also shown in the hall are some of the Native-American artifacts brought back by explorers Meriwether Lewis and William Clark, on an expedition undertaken during Jefferson's term as president.

The Book Room contains much of Jefferson's library of some 7,000 books; Jefferson was said to be able to read seven languages. Jefferson's Bedroom, where he died, includes a clock he designed.

The formal dining room includes copies of Old Master paintings and scenes of America's natural wonders. James Hemings, one of Jefferson's slaves, studied cooking in France while Jefferson was there.

Visitors can also marvel in the little "neat" ideas of Jefferson. Amazing for his day, they include a seven-day calendar clock, semiautomatic glass doors, and a bed that can be entered from two rooms.

Admission: adult $11; child 6–11, $6. www.monticello.org.

About Thomas Jefferson

Thomas Jefferson, author of the Declaration of Independence and the third president of the United States, spent nearly his entire adult life in public service. He was born in 1743 at Shadwell, Virginia. His father Peter was a successful planter and surveyor, and his mother Jane Randolph came from a distinguished local family.

In 1772, he married Martha Wayles Skelton; they had six children during their 10-year marriage, but Martha and four of the children died at a young age.

Jefferson inherited slaves from his father and father-in-law, and held as many as 200, about half of them children younger than sixteen. About eighty slaves lived at Monticello, while the others lived on nearby plantations and at an estate he owned in Bedford County. Jefferson freed only two slaves during his life, and five more in his will, and he chose not to pursue two others who ran away; all were members of the Hemings family.

Early in his life, Jefferson practiced law and served in local government as a magistrate and a member of the Virginia House of Burgesses. As a member of the Continental Congress, he was chosen in 1776 to draft the Declaration of Independence. He later returned to Virginia and served in the legislature, and then as governor from 1779 to 1781.

He returned to public service in 1784 with a posting to France as trade commissioner and

Brain trust. President John F. Kennedy, speaking at a White House dinner in 1962 honoring Nobel Prize winners, said, "I think this is the most extraordinary collection of talent, of human knowledge, that has ever been gathered together at the White House, with the possible exception of when Thomas Jefferson dined alone."

Monticello
Photo courtesy of the Monticello/Thomas Jefferson Memorial Foundation, Inc.

then as Benjamin Franklin's successor as minister. Out of the country at the time, he had no direct role in the framing of the U.S. Constitution, although he expressed some reservations that the document did not adequately safeguard individual freedoms.

In 1790, Jefferson was named secretary of state in President George Washington's cabinet; six years later he became vice president after losing the top job to John Adams by three electoral votes. In 1800, he defeated Adams and became president. Among his achievements was the purchase of the Louisiana Territory in 1803 and his support of the Lewis and Clark expedition west.

He retired to Monticello in 1809 and spent the last seventeen years of his life there. During that time he sold his vast collection of books to the government to help create the Library of Congress. At the age of seventy-six, he was involved in the founding of the University of Virginia.

Jefferson died, fittingly, on July 4 in the year 1826, the fiftieth anniversary of the signing of the Declaration of Independence.

Charlottesville

Nearby to Monticello is the University of Virginia, which embodied Jefferson's ideas on academics as well as his sensibilities; the campus was designed as an "academical village" with rows of neoclassical-design buildings facing a long lawn, with the main building—a pantheon-like rotunda—at one end.

Some of the student housing remains little changed from the founding of the university, including the West Range where famous residents have included Edgar Allan Poe and Woodrow Wilson.

WOW Mount Vernon

George Washington slept here regularly, in his own house, from 1747 until his death in 1799. The fabled Georgian-style mansion at Mount Vernon, overlooking the Potomac River near Alexandria, was built in 1743 by Washington's half brother Lawrence; George moved there in 1754 and acquired the property in 1761.

Washington expanded the 2,300-acre tobacco plantation during the years until he held some 8,000 acres, making Mount Vernon one of the largest plantations in Virginia. He expanded the home when he married Martha Dandridge Custis, a widow with two children, and again a few years later. With each remodeling the house became more and more ornate, including an eight-column portico on the river facade, 126 feet above the Potomac.

Many of the rooms feature original furnishings, including Martha Washington's tea service, some original volumes from George Washington's library, and pictures imported from England before the Revolution. An interesting historical item is a key to the Bastille, sent from Paris by Lafayette after the French Revolution.

The home and more than thirty acres of the beautiful gardens and woodlands have been restored. Outside the house are outbuildings that were used for food preparation and other tasks; nearby is the tomb where George Washington, his wife Martha, and other family members are buried. Also on the grounds is a slave cemetery for many of those who worked the plantation.

Mount Vernon can be reached by car, bus tour, or boat cruise. The home is located at the end of the George Washington Parkway in Virginia, sixteen miles from downtown Washington, D.C. Open every day of the year, including Christmas, Mount Vernon admits visitors from April through August 8 A.M.–5 P.M.; from November through February 9 A.M.–4 P.M.; and March, September, and October 9 A.M.–5 P.M. Admission: adult $9; senior ages 62 and older, $8.50; child 6–11, $4.50. *Discount coupon in this book.* (703) 780-2000. www.mountvernon.org.

Wolf Trap Farm Park for the Performing Arts

A national park celebrating the performing arts, Wolf Trap is located on 117 acres of woodlands near Vienna, Virginia, about midway between Washington, D.C., and Dulles International Airport.

Wolf Trap is off the Airport Toll Road, about eighteen miles west of Washington. (703) 255-1860 for a recording, or (703) 255-1900.

Catering to a wide range of musical tastes, the outdoor stages present classical, jazz, pop, and rock. Regular performers include the Metropolitan Opera and the Alvin Ailey Dance Theatre. Visitors can purchase box suppers or take along their own picnic dinner to enjoy on the lawn.

The park is open year-round, with outdoor performances scheduled from late May through September.

You can consult a web page at www.wolf-trap.org.

Tickets are also available through ProTix, at (703) 218-6500.

Eating Your Way Through Northern Virginia

Here's a selection of the best restaurants and deals in the Virginia suburbs of Washington. Be sure to call ahead to confirm hours and make reservations.

Barbecue

Red Hot & Blue Memphis Pit Barbecue. 1600 Wilson Boulevard, Arlington. (703) 276-7427. Sunday to Thursday 11 A.M.–10 P.M.; Friday 11 A.M.–11 P.M.; Saturday 11 A.M.–11 P.M. Ribs—wet (with barbecue sauce) or dry (coated with spices)—are the specialty at the original location of this local institution that is now widespread throughout the region and elsewhere. Other good things to eat include pulled pig and above-average nachos as an appetizer. A good bargain.

    Southside 815. 815 South Washington Street, Alexandria. (703) 836-6222. Sunday to Thursday 11:30 A.M.–10:30 P.M.; Friday and Saturday 11:30 A.M.– 11 P.M. Budget prices for good-ole-Southern specialties from grits, fried tomatoes, and collard greens to chicken, shrimp, and sausage casseroles and catfish po' boys.

Cajun-Thai

Cajun Bangkok. 907 King Street, Alexandria (Old Town). (703) 836-0038. Sunday to Thursday 5–10 P.M.; Friday and Saturday 5–11 P.M. What do Cajun and Thai menus have in common? The answer is hot pepper, found in large proportion in dishes at this unusual eatery. Specialties include Crying Tiger (grilled steak with a fiery pepper sauce) and catfish with crushed pecans.

Chinese

Fortune Chinese Seafood Restaurant. 5900 Leesburg Pike, Falls Church (Baileys Crossroads). (703) 998-8888. Sunday to Thursday 11 A.M.–10:30 P.M.; Friday and Saturday 11 A.M.–midnight. A wide array of dim sum served from rolling carts every day, including fried and steamed dumplings and more exotic offerings such as chicken feet with black bean sauce.

    Hunan Number One Restaurant. 3033 Wilson Boulevard, Arlington. (703) 528-1177. Daily 11 A.M.–2 A.M. Despite its name, this well-rated eatery specializes in Hong Kong-style Cantonese recipes. Seafood specialties include fried flounder, Sea Treasure in Nest, and shark's fin dumplings; also worth sampling are spareribs with black bean sauce. Dim sum is available every day, with a larger selection weekends.

Continental

Tivoli. 1700 North Moore Street at Wilson Boulevard, Arlington. (703) 524-8900. Weekdays 11:30 A.M.–2:30 P.M., 5:30–10 P.M.; Saturday 5:30–10 P.M. An elegant, traditional Italian and Continental restaurant, moderately priced.

French

Cafe Parisian Express. 4520 Lee Highway, Arlington. (703) 525-3332. Monday to Saturday 8 A.M.–9:30 P.M. At last: a fast-food and take-out eatery for fine French fare, from croissants to boeuf bourguignon.

L'Auberge Chez Francois. 332 Springvale Road, near Georgetown Pike, Great Falls. (703) 759-3800. Dinner every night, with lunch on Sunday only. Closed Monday. Tuesday to Saturday 5:30–9:30 P.M.; Sunday 1:30–8 P.M. High-tone, high-priced cuisine.

Indian

Aarathi Indian Cuisine. 409 Maple Avenue, East Vienna. (703) 938-0100. Sunday to Thursday 11:30 A.M.–2:30 P.M. and 5:30–10 P.M.; Friday and Saturday 11:30 A.M.–2:30 P.M. and 5:30–10:30 P.M. Tandoori oven specialties, vegetarian curries, and sampler plates.

Cafe Taj. 1379 Beverly Road, McLean. (703) 827-0444. Daily 11:30 A.M.–2:30 P.M. and 5:30–10 P.M. A high-tone Indian restaurant with traditional offerings, including chicken and lamb cooked in a tandoori oven, spicy lamb vindaloo, and more.

Food Factory. 4221 North Fairfax Drive at North Stuart Street, Arlington. (703) 527-2279. Weekdays 11 A.M.–10 P.M.; weekends noon–10 P.M. Budget goodies, including grilled kabobs.

Haandi Indian Restaurant. 1222 West Broad Street, Falls Church. (703) 533-3501. Sunday to Thursday 11:30 A.M.–2:30 P.M. and 5–10 P.M.; Friday and Saturday 5–10:30 P.M. More tandoori specialties, including murg tandoori, a marinated chicken dish.

Italian

Faccia Luna Pizzaria. 2909 Wilson Boulevard, Arlington (Clarendon). (703) 276-3099. Monday to Thursday 11 A.M.–11 P.M.; Friday and Saturday 11 A.M.–midnight; Sunday 4–11 P.M. Pizza, pasta, calzones, and sandwiches in an informal setting.

Generous George's Positive Pizza. 3006 Duke Street, Alexandria. (703) 370-4303. Sunday to Thursday 11 A.M.–11 P.M.; Friday and Saturday 11 A.M.–midnight. As the sign says: big, positively fresh pizza with all sorts of toppings. A local specialty is "Positive Pasta Pie," which is exactly what it sounds like: pasta on top of pizza crust.

Japanese

Atami Restaurant. 3155 Wilson Boulevard, Arlington. (703) 522-4787. Lunch and dinner daily; Sunday dinner only. A Japanese-Vietnamese hybrid in the Clarendon area, including sushi (with an all-you-can-eat special), sukiyaki, tempura, and more.

Matuba Japanese Restaurant. 2915 Columbia Pike, Arlington. (703) 521-2811. Monday to Thursday 11:30 A.M.–2 P.M. and 5:30–10 P.M.; Friday 11:30 A.M.–2 P.M. and 5:30–10:30 P.M.; Saturday 5:30–10:30 P.M.; and Sunday 5:30–10 P.M. A Japanese eatery with a broad menu. Start with moderately priced sushi and go on to kushi yaki skewered meats and vegetables, and specialties that include deep-fried pork cutlets.

Tachibana Japanese Restaurant. 4050 Lee Highway, Arlington. (703) 528-1122. Monday to Thursday 11:30 A.M.–2 P.M. and 5–10:30 P.M.; Friday 11:30 A.M.–2 P.M. and 5–10:30 P.M.; Saturday 5–10:30 P.M. Sushi galore, plus specialties such as nabemono clay-pot stews.

Laotian

Bangkok Vientiane. 926A West Broad Street, Falls Church. (703) 534-0095. Sunday to Thursday 11 A.M.–10 P.M.; Friday and Saturday 11 A.M.–11 P.M. Interesting dishes, including duck combined with green beans, mint, and hot peppers; chicken pate; and "waterfall" beef (rare beef with lemon juice, hot peppers, and mint leaves).

South American

El Pollo Rico. 2917 North Washington Boulevard, Arlington. (703) 522-3220. Daily 11 A.M.–10 P.M. Budget–Moderate. Extraordinary Peruvian-style charcoal-broiled chicken.

Steakhouses

P. J. Skidoos Restaurant. 9908 Lee Highway, Fairfax: (703) 591-4515. Monday to Saturday 11:30 A.M.–2 A.M.; Sunday 10 A.M.–9 P.M. Well-regarded budget-priced steaks and chicken.

Tom Sarris Orleans House. 1213 Wilson Boulevard, Rosslyn. (703) 524-2929. Monday to Friday 11 A.M.–11 P.M.; Saturday 4–11 P.M.; Sunday 4–10 P.M. A local favorite for beef of all varieties.

Taverns

Union Street Public House. 121 South Union Street, Alexandria. (703) 548-1785. Monday to Thursday 11:30 A.M.–10:30 P.M.; Friday and Saturday 11:30 A.M.–11:30 P.M.; Sunday 11 A.M.–10:30 P.M. A wide selection of exotic and local beers and burgers, seafood, gumbo, and sandwiches.

Tex-Mex

Hard Times Cafe. Four locations. Chili of all sorts, including Texas style, Cincinnati, and vegetarian.

3028 Wilson Boulevard at North Highland Street, Arlington. (703) 528-2233. Monday to Thursday 11:30 A.M.–10:30 P.M.; Friday and Saturday 11:30 A.M.–11 P.M.; Sunday noon–10:30 P.M.

1404 King Street, Alexandria. (703) 683-5340. Monday to Thursday 11 A.M.–10 P.M.; Friday and Saturday 11 A.M.–11 P.M.; Sunday 4–10 P.M.

3028 Wilson Boulevard, Clarendon. (703) 528-2233. Open Monday to Thursday 11 A.M.–10 P.M.; Friday and Saturday 11 A.M.–11 P.M.; Sunday 4–10 P.M.

394 Elden Street, Herndon. (703) 318-8941. Monday to Thursday 11 A.M.–11 P.M.; Friday and Saturday 11 A.M.–midnight; Sunday noon–10 P.M.

Rio Grande Cafe. Two locations. Go beyond the basics to unusual offerings, including grilled quail, frog legs, and barbecued goat.

4301 North Fairfax Drive, Arlington. (703) 528-3131. Monday to Thursday 11 A.M.–10:30 P.M.; Friday and Saturday 11 A.M.–11:30 P.M.; Sunday 11:30 A.M.–10:30 P.M.

Reston Town Center; 1827 Library Street, Reston. (703) 904-0703. Monday to Thursday 11 A.M.–10:30 P.M.; Friday 11:30 A.M.–11:30 P.M.; Sunday 11:30 A.M.–10:30 P.M.

South Austin Grill. 801 King Street, Alexandria. (703) 684-8969. Monday 11:30 A.M.–10 P.M.; Tuesday to Thursday 11:30 A.M.–11 P.M.; Friday and Saturday 11:30 A.M.–midnight; Sunday 11 A.M.–10 P.M. Hot, hot, hot chili; if it's not hot enough, you can add one of the industrial-strength sauces from the table.

Thai

Crystal Thai Restaurant. 4819 Arlington Boulevard, Arlington. (703) 522-1311. Monday to Thursday 11:30 A.M.–10:30 P.M.; Friday and Saturday 11:30 A.M.–11 P.M.; Sunday noon–10 P.M.

Duangrat's. 5878 Leesburg Pike at Columbia Pike, Falls Church. (703) 820-5775. Monday to Thursday 11:30 A.M.–2:30 P.M. and 5–10:30 P.M.; Friday to Saturday 11:30 A.M.–11 P.M.; Sunday 11:30 A.M.–10:30 P.M.

Pho 75. 3103 Graham Road, Falls Church. (703) 204-1490. Daily 9 A.M.–8 P.M.

Pilin Thai Restaurant. 116 West Broad Street, Falls Church. (703) 241-5850. Monday to Thursday 11:30 A.M.–10 P.M.; Friday and Saturday 11:30 A.M.–11 P.M.; Sunday 5–9 P.M.

Rabieng Thai Restaurant. 5892 Leesburg Pike, Falls Church. (703) 671-4222. Sunday to Thursday 4–10 P.M.; Friday and Saturday 4–10:30 P.M.

Star of Siam. 1735 North Lynn Street, Arlington. (703) 524-1208. Monday to Friday 11:30 A.M.–11 P.M.; Saturday 4–11 P.M.; Sunday 4–10 P.M.

Tara Thai. 226 Maple Avenue, Vienna. (703) 255-2467. Monday to Thursday 11:30 A.M.–3 P.M. and 5–10 P.M.; Friday 11:30 A.M.–3 P.M. and 5–11 P.M.; Saturday noon–3:30 P.M. and 5–11 P.M.; Sunday noon–3:30 P.M. and 5–10 P.M.

Vietnamese

Chesapeake Seafood and Crab House. 3607 Wilson Boulevard, Arlington. (703) 528-8888. Daily 11 A.M.–10 P.M. Don't let the name or the all-American appearance fool you; a wide range of Vietnamese specialties lies within.

Little Viet Garden. 3012 Wilson Boulevard, Arlington. (703) 522-9686. Monday to Friday 11 A.M.–2:30 P.M., 5–10 P.M.; Weekends 11 A.M.–10 P.M.

Pho 75. 1711 Wilson Boulevard, Arlington. (703) 525-7355. Daily 9 A.M.–8 P.M.

Queen Bee. 3181 Wilson Boulevard, Arlington (Clarendon). (703) 527-3444. Daily 11:15 A.M.–10 P.M.

Xinh Xinh Restaurant. 6621 Wilson Boulevard, Falls Church. (703) 534-5730. Daily 11 A.M.–10 P.M.

Accommodations in Virginia

Budget: $70 or less
Moderate: $70–$200
Luxury: $200 and more

Alexandria

For information about lodging in Alexandria, just across the river in Virginia, call Alexandria Hotel Accommodations at (800) 296-1000, or the Alexandria Convention & Visitors Bureau at (800) 388-9119. You can also consult web pages for the Alexandreia CVB at http://ci.alexandria.va.us\alexandria.html.

Hotels in Alexandria include:

Best Western Old Colony Inn. 615 First Street. (703) 739-2222 or (800) 528-1234. Airport, Metro shuttles. Moderate.

Courtyard by Marriott. 2700 Eisenhower Avenue. (703) 329-2323 or (800) 321-2211. Moderate.

Embassy Suites Old Town. 1900 Diagonal Road. (703) 684-5900 or (800) 362-2779. Moderate.

Executive Club Suites. 610 Bashford Lane. (703) 739-2582. Moderate.

Hampton Inn. 5821 Richmond Highway. (703) 329-1400 or (800) 426-7866. Airport, Metro shuttles. Moderate.

Holiday Inn–Eisenhower. 2460 Eisenhower Avenue. (703) 960-3400 or (800) 465-4329. Walk to Metro. Moderate.

Holiday Inn Historic Hotel and Suites. 625 First Street. (703) 548-6300 or (800) 465-4329. Moderate.

Holiday Inn–Old Town. 480 King Street. (703) 549-6080. Moderate.

Morrison House. 116 South Alfred Street. (703) 838-8000 or (800) 367-0800. Country inn. Moderate.

Ramada Alexandria. 4641 Kenmore Avenue. (703) 751-4510 or (800) 272-6232. Airport, Metro shuttles. Moderate.

Ramada Plaza–Old Town. 901 North Fairfax. (703) 683-6000. Moderate.

Sheraton Suites. 801 North Saint Asaph Street. (703) 836-4700 or (800) 325-3535. Airport, Metro shuttles. Moderate.

Washington Suites. 100 South Reynolds Street. (703) 370-9600 or (800) 222-3333. Metro shuttle. Moderate.

Arlington

For information on lodging in Arlington, call the Arlington Convention and Visitors Service at (800) 677-6267.

Americana Hotel. 1400 Jefferson Davis Highway. (703) 979-3772 or (800) 548-6261. Airport shuttle. Budget.

Arlington/Rosslyn Courtyard by Marriott. 1533 Clarendon Boulevard. (703) 528-2222 or (800) 321-2211. Shuttle to Metro. Moderate.

Best Western Key Bridge. 1850 North Fort Myer Drive. (703) 522-0400 or (800) 528-1234. Moderate.

Best Western Pentagon. 2480 South Glebe Road. (703) 979-4400 or (800) 528-1234. Airport, Metro shuttle. Moderate.

Cherry Blossom Travelodge. 3030 Columbia Pike. (703) 521-5570 or (800) 578-7878. Budget.

Comfort Inn Ballston. 1211 North Glebe Road. (703) 247-3399 or (800) 228-5150. Moderate.

Crowne Plaza National Airport. 1489 Jefferson Davis Highway. (703) 416-1600 or (800) 227-6963. Airport shuttle. Moderate.

Crystal City Courtyard by Marriott. 2899 Jefferson Davis Highway. (703) 549-3434 or (800) 321-2211. Airport shuttle. Moderate.

Crystal City Marriott. 1999 Jefferson Davis Highway. (703) 413-5500 or (800) 228-9290. Airport shuttle. Moderate.

Crystal City Motel. 901 South Clark Street. (703) 416-1900. Budget.

Crystal Gateway Marriott. 1700 Jefferson Davis Highway. (703) 920-3230 or (800) 228-9290. Airport shuttle. Moderate.

Days Inn Arlington. 2201 Arlington Boulevard. (703) 525-0300 or (800) 329-7466. Metro shuttle. Moderate.

Days Inn Crystal City. 2000 Jefferson Davis Highway. (703) 920-8600 or (800) 329-7466. Airport shuttle. Moderate.

Doubletree Hotel National Airport. 300 Army Navy Drive. (703) 416-4100 or (800) 222-8733. Airport shuttle. Moderate.

Econo-Lodge Arlington. 6800 Lee Highway. (703) 538-5300 or (800) 553-2666. Budget.

Econo-Lodge Iwo Jima. 3335 Lee Highway. (703) 524-9800. Budget.

Econo-Lodge Pentagon. 566 Columbia Pike. (703) 820-5600 or (800) 553-2666. Budget.

Embassy Suites. 1300 Jefferson Davis Highway. (703) 979-9799 or (800) 362-2779. Metro, Airport shuttles. Moderate.

Highlander Motor Inn. 3336 Wilson Boulevard. (703) 524-4300 or (800) 786-4301. Budget.

Holiday Inn Arlington at Ballston. 4610 North Fairfax Drive. (703) 243-9800 or (800) 465-4329. Moderate.

Holiday Inn Rosslyn Westpark. 1900 North Fort Myer Drive. (703) 807-2000 or (800) 465-4329. Moderate.

Hyatt Arlington. 1325 Wilson Boulevard. (703) 525-1234 or (800) 233-1234. Moderate.

Hyatt Regency Crystal City. 2799 Jefferson Davis Highway. (703) 418-1234 or (800) 233-1234. Airport, Metro shuttles. Moderate.

Marriott Key Bridge. 1401 Lee Highway. (703) 524-6400 or (800) 228-9290. Moderate.

Motel Fifty. 1601 Arlington Boulevard. (703) 524-3400. Airport shuttle. Budget.

Quality Hotel Courthouse Plaza. 1200 North Courthouse Road. (703) 524-4000 or (800) 228-5151. Metro shuttle. Moderate.

Quality Inn Iwo Jima. 1501 Arlington Boulevard. (703) 524-5000 or (800) 228-5151. Moderate.

The **Ritz-Carlton Pentagon City.** 1250 South Hayes Street. (703) 415-5000. Airport shuttle. Luxury.

Sheraton Crystal City. 1800 Jefferson Davis Highway. (703) 486-1111 or (800) 325-2525. Airport shuttle. Moderate–Luxury.

Sheraton National. Columbia Pike and Washington Boulevard. (703) 521-1900 or (800) 325-2525. Airport, Metro shuttles. Moderate.

Virginian Suites. 1500 Arlington Boulevard. (703) 522-9600 or (800) 275-2866. Metro shuttle. Budget.

Golf in Northern Virginia

Here is a listing of public and semiprivate courses in Northern Virginia. See also Chapter 13 for a listing of courses in Washington, D.C., and Chapter 19 for courses in Williamsburg, VA.

Algonkian Regional Park Golf Course. 47001 Fairway Drive, Sterling. (703) 450-4655. Public 18-hole course. Moderate.

Bowling Green Country Club. Route 2, Box 1340, Front Royal. (540) 635-2024. Two public 18-hole courses. Economy–Moderate.

Brambleton Regional Park Golf Course. 42180 Ryan Road, Ashburn. (703) 327-3403. Public 18-hole course. Moderate.

Bristow Manor Golf Club. 11507 Valley View Drive, Bristow. (703) 368-3558. Semiprivate 18-hole course. Expensive.

Browning's Golf Course. Route 4, Unionville. (540) 854-4454. Public 18-hole course. Economy.

Bryce Resort. Route 263 West, Basye. (540) 856-2124. Resort 18-hole course. Moderate.

Burke Lake Course. 7315 Ox Road, Fairfax. (703) 323-1641. Public 18-hole course. Economy.

Carper's Valley Golf Club. 1400 Millwood Pike, Winchester. (540) 662-4319. Semiprivate 18-hole course. Economy.

Caverns Country Club. Luray. (540) 743-7111. Semiprivate 18-hole course. Economy.

Fair Oaks Golf Park. 12908 Lee Jackson Memorial Highway, Fairfax. (703) 222-6600. Public 9-hole course. Economy.

Front Royal Country Club. Route 522, Front Royal. (540) 636-9061. Public 9-hole course. Economy.

The Gauntlet at Curtis Park. 58 Jesse Curtis Lane, Fredericksburg. (540) 752-0963. Public 18-hole course designed in 1994 by P. B. Dye. Expensive.

Goose Creek Golf Course. 43001 Golf Club Road, Leesburg. (703) 729-2500. Semiprivate 18-hole course. Moderate.

Greendale Golf Club. 6700 Telegraph Road, Alexandria. (703) 971-3788. Public 18-hole course. Economy.

Herndon Centennial Golf Course. 909 Ferndale Avenue, Herndon. (703) 471-5769. Public 18-hole course. Moderate.

Greens fees.	
Economy:	Less than $20
Moderate:	$20 to $39
Expensive:	$40 and more

Jefferson Golf Course. 7900 Lee Highway, Falls Church. (703) 573-0443. Public 9-hole course. Economy.

Lakeview Golf Course. Route 11, Harrisonburg. (540) 434-8937. Three semiprivate 9-hole courses (Lake, Peak, and Spring) with water hazards that can be played as three 18-hole combinations. Moderate.

Lansdowne Golf Club. 44050 Woodridge Parkway, Lansdowne. (703) 729-8400. Resort 18-hole course designed by Robert Trent Jones, Jr. Expensive.

Lee's Hill Golfers Club Of Virginia. 10200 Old Dominion Parkway, Fredericksburg. (540) 891-0111. Public 18-hole course. Moderate.

Manassas Hills Golf Club. 7804 Davis Ford Road, Manassas. (703) 368-2028. Public 9-hole course. Economy.

Massanutten Golf Course. Route 644, McGaheysville. (540) 854-9890. Semiprivate 18-hole course designed by Arnold Palmer. Economy.

Meadows Farm Golf Course. 4300 Flat Run Road, Locust Grove. (703) 854-9890. Public 18-hole course. Moderate.

Penderbrook Golf Club. 3700 Golf Trail Lane, Fairfax. (703) 385-3700. Semiprivate 18-hole course. Moderate.

Pinecrest Golf Course. 6600 Little River Turnpike, Alexandria. (703) 941-1061. Public 9-hole course. Economy.

Pohick Bay Golf Course. 10301 Gunston Road, Lorton. (703) 339-8585. Public 18-hole course. Economy–Moderate.

Prince William Golf Course. 14631 Vint Hill Road, Nokesville. (703) 754-7111. Public 18-hole course. Moderate.

Reston Golf Course. 11875 Sunrise Valley Drive, Reston. (703) 620-9333. Public 18-hole course. Expensive.

Shenandoah Valley Golf Club. Route 2, Front Royal. (540) 636-4653. Semiprivate 18-hole course. Economy–Moderate.

The Shenvalee. 9660 Fairway Drive, New Market. (540) 740-3181. Public 18-hole course. Moderate.

South Wales Golf Club. 18363 Golf Lane, Jeffersonton. (540) 937-3250. Public 18-hole course. Economy.

Stoneleigh Golf Club. 35271 Prestwick Court, Round Hill. (540) 338-4653. Semiprivate 18-hole course. Moderate.

Twin Lakes Golf Course. 6100 Clifton Road, Clifton. (703) 631-9099. Public 18-hole course. Economy–Moderate.

Virginia Oaks Golf Course. 950 Virginia Oaks Drive, Gainesville. (703) 551-2103. Semiprivate 18-hole course. Moderate–Expensive.

West Park Golf Club. 59 Clubhouse Drive SW, Leesburg. (703) 777-7023. Public 18-hole course. Moderate.

Chapter 18
Civil War Sites

The Civil War began and ended not far from Washington. The armies of the Union and the Confederacy met in their first major battle near a small creek named Bull Run. The war ended at McLean House, a remote Virginia home in the town of Appomattox Court House.

Abraham Lincoln was elected president in 1860, and within a month South Carolina seceded from the Union. Just before he took office in 1861, six more states—Mississippi, Florida, Alabama, Georgia, Louisiana, and Texas—quit the United States. They were joined later by Virginia, Arkansas, Tennessee, and North Carolina to form the Confederate States of America. On April 12, 1861, war broke out when Confederate cannons shelled Fort Sumter in Charleston Harbor, South Carolina. The Rebel forces were victorious, and it wasn't until 1865 that the Union regained the fort.

Lincoln, revered for setting free the slaves and saving the Union, came slowly to his position. He had not called for the abolishment of slavery before the outbreak of the Civil War. And the Emancipation Proclamation of January 1, 1863—nearly two years into the war—set free only the slaves of those states still in rebellion against the Union.

Much blood was shed by both sides in Virginia; the Rebel forces were never able to break through to capture or destroy Washington, D.C., and Union troops were repeatedly foiled—until near the end of the war—in their attempts to plunge deep into the Confederacy and take its capital at Richmond.

In this section, we'll explore some of the Civil War battlegrounds and historic sites in and around Washington and down to Richmond.

Civil War Discovery Trail

A link to more than 300 sites in sixteen states and the District of Columbia, the trail includes battlefields, historic homes, railroad stations, cemeteries, and parks. A Civil War Discovery Trail guidebook that includes more than 400 sites in twenty-four states is available from the group. For more information on the trail and the Civil War Trust, call (800) 298-7878, www.civilwar.org.

Washington During the Civil War

Washington, D.C.'s population of about 60,000 doubled in size soon after the Civil War broke out in 1861. Federal troops guarded the seat of government, and many soldiers passed through the capital en route to their fighting assignments. Union troops were quartered in buildings including the Capitol, where some camped beneath the Rotunda; the Capitol was later used as a hospital.

The present site of the U.S. Supreme Court once held the Old Brick Capitol that was used by the Congress in the aftermath of the British destruction in the War of 1812; the building served as a prison during the Civil War.

Although Confederate troops drew close to Washington several times, there was only one major assault during the war, when rebel forces briefly occupied Fort Stephens in 1864.

Arlington, Virginia

Arlington National Cemetery holds the graves of 5,000 African Americans, including some freed slaves, who fought in the Union Army during the Civil War.

Also within the boundaries of the cemetery is the former site of Freedman's Village, a town that once housed 10,000 freed slaves; it was built in 1863 on land that had been part of Robert E. Lee's estate, Arlington House.

The village was first intended to be a home for thousands of former slaves who had lived in the District of Columbia; the slaves in the federal city were set free a year before Lincoln issued the Emancipation Proclamation that released slaves in the Confederate states. Little remains today of the once-thriving community.

Fredericksburg, Virginia, and Surrounding Area

Fredericksburg. General Ambrose E. Burnside and his Union army arrived at Stafford Heights overlooking Fredericksburg in mid-November of 1862; on December 11, his troops crossed the Rappahannock River. The Battle of Fredericksburg, fought on December 13, 1862, was another in a series of unsuccessful attempts by Union forces to move south and take the Confederate capital at Richmond. Along the Sunken Road, General Robert E. Lee won an overwhelming victory. The visitors center is the starting point for a thirty-minute walking tour. The bookstore there has an excellent collection of titles on local history and the Civil War in general.

Behind the center is a hill known as Marye's Heights; behind a stone wall at the base of the hill is a road. When the Union Army occupied Fredericksburg on December 11 and 12, the Confederate forces waited behind the wall and atop the heights. There is a tintype-style photograph on the wall that shows the carnage at the spot along the wall where you stand.

The Sunken Road, also known as Telegraph Road, connected Fredericksburg to Richmond, some fifty-five miles to the south. Generations of wagon travelers wore the section of the road into the ground in the area; the stone wall was built to keep the hillside from collapsing.

The assault to the left was lead by General George Meade of the Union army at Prospect Hill; the Union forces were successful for a while before Confederate reserves drove them back to their original position. A second assault at Marye's Heights was a disaster for the Union soldiers, who were mowed down by fire from artillery on the heights and infantry behind the stone wall. Union General Burnside sent wave after wave against the Rebel positions to no avail; some 13,000 Union troops were killed or wounded on that day.

Fredericksburg and Spotsylvania National Military Park. Four significant Civil War battle sites lie in and around Fredericksburg and Chancellorsville. Park headquarters and a visitors center are located in Fredericksburg. www.nps.gov /frsp.

Fredericksburg National Cemetery. More than 15,000 soldiers lie buried in the cemetery here—only 2,473 of them in named graves. Historians say that most of those buried here were non-officers; officers were mostly brought home for burial by family members. A thirty-minute walking tour through the cemetery includes stops at several monuments. Among them are **Moesch Monument**, honoring Joseph Anton Moesch, an immigrant from Switzerland who was part of the Eighty-Third New York Volunteers, also known as the "Swiss Rifles." Colonel Moesch was killed at the **Wilderness**. Also in the cemetery is the **Parker's Battery Memorial**. Two guns of Parker's Virginia Battery were in position on May 3, 1863, when Union troops broke through the Confederate lines as part of the larger Chancellorsville campaign ten miles away.

The cemetery is part of the Fredericksburg and Spotsylvania National Military Park.

See also listings for Fredericksburg in Chapter 17.

Chancellorsville. After the disaster at Fredericksburg, President Lincoln replaced General Burnside with General Joseph Hooker. On April 27, 1863, Hooker marched the bulk of his army upstream and crossed over to arrive at Chancellorsville three days later. General Lee moved quickly westward toward Hooker, forcing the Union troops to abandon their position and establish a vulnerable defensive line; "Stonewall" Jackson attacked the line on May 2 in a successful surprise assault. (In the fighting, Jackson was accidentally shot and mortally wounded by his own troops.) General Lee eventually drove the Union forces back across the Rappahannock River.

Stonewall Jackson Shrine. The seriously wounded General Jackson was

Fredericksburg Battlefield Visitor Center. Lafayette Boulevard, US 1 Business, Fredericksburg: (540) 373-6122. www.fredericksburgva.com.

Fredericksburg Visitor Center. 706 Caroline Street, Fredericksburg: (540) 373-1776 or (800) 678-4748.

James Monroe Museum. 908 Charles Street, Fredericksburg: (540) 654-1043. A collection of some of the possessions and papers of the fifth president, who began his career practicing law here. Some of the pieces were purchased while Monroe served as emissary to France and were later used in the White House. Open daily from March 1 to November 30 9 A.M.–5 P.M.; remainder of the year 10 A.M.–4 P.M. Closed at end-of-year holidays. Adult $4; student younger than 18, $1.

taken on May 2, 1863, to the site of this shrine, a field hospital near Wilderness Tavern where his left arm was amputated. Two days later he was taken twenty-seven miles away to a point behind Confederate lines at Guiney's Station south of Fredericksburg; on May 10 he died of pneumonia.

Wilderness. The Wilderness battlefield, west of Chancellorsville, was the site of the first of several battles between Generals Lee and Grant. On May 5 and 6 of 1864, the two armies fought to a draw until General Grant moved his army south toward Spotsylvania Court House.

Spotsylvania Court House. On May 7, 1864, both armies converged on an intersection that controlled a direct route to Richmond. Lee's troops arrived first and dug trenches from which they withstood a series of Union attacks. One of the battles in the area was at a place known as "Bloody Angle," considered one of the most intense hand-to-hand combat battles of the war. Grant abandoned the field on May 21.

Richmond, Virginia

Richmond was the capital of the Confederacy for most of the Civil War; the government moved there in the spring of 1861 from Montgomery, Alabama. The state seceded from the Union in 1861 with a vote in the Virginia State Capitol, and General Robert E. Lee accepted command of the army of Virginia there.

Hundreds of Civil War–era buildings still exist in Richmond. See the section on Richmond in this book for details about the Museum of the Confederacy and the White House of the Confederacy; both are located at 1201 East Clay Street. (804) 649-1861. Open Monday to Saturday 10 A.M.–5 P.M.; Sunday noon–5 P.M. Admission: adult $9; senior $8.50; student 7–18, $5. www.moc.org.

Richmond National Battlefield Park Visitor Center. The National Park Service facility is located on the site of the Confederation's Chimborazo General Hospital, at 3215 East Broad Street, in Richmond. (804) 226-1981. Open daily 9 A.M.–5 P.M. Admission: free. www.nps.gov/rich.

When the Chimborazo Hospital was built in 1862 it was the largest in the world; more than 75,000 Confederate soldiers passed through its doors during the Civil War.

Fort Harrison. (804) 226-1981. Among many war sites around Richmond is Fort Harrison, distinguished by the fact that fourteen African-American soldiers in the Union Army earned Medals of Honor in the battle to capture the fort in September of 1864. Open May through September. Admission: free.

Appomattox Court House National Historical Park

The bloody Civil War formally came to an end at the McLean House in Appomattox Court House on April 9, 1865, when Confederate General Robert E. Lee surrendered to Union General Ulysses S. Grant. Three days later, the Confederate troops paraded past Union ranks at Surrender Triangle, giving up their arms and battle flags; Grant permitted the former enemies to keep their horses and sidearms and return to their homes.

In 1893, a would-be entrepreneur bought the McLean House and dismantled it for eventual reconstruction as a commercial exhibit in Washington; the
plan never came to fruition, and the house was reconstructed, as were two
dozen other buildings of the era, including a few shops, a tavern, and homes.
Open daily 8:30 A.M.–5 P.M. Admission: adult $2; child 16 and younger, free.
(804) 352-8987.

The Appomattox Visitor Information Center is located a few miles away in
the town's old train depot. It includes information on a number of historic
sites in the area. (804) 352-2621.

You can obtain a map for a driving tour between Appomattox and Petersburg, which traces twenty stops along Lee's retreat at the end of the war.

Appomattox is located on Route 24, eighty-five miles west of Richmond.

Hampton Roads

The famed battle of the ironclads, the *Monitor* vs. the *Merrimack*, was fought
on March 9, 1862, in Hampton Roads. The USS *Monitor* and the CSS *Virginia*
(renamed from *Merrimack* when its iron armor was added by Confederate
forces) fought a fierce but inconclusive battle. The skirmish, though,
essentially marked the beginning of the end of the wooden battleship in
warfare.

An exhibit about the ironclads is included at the Mariners' Museum;
100 Museum Drive, Newport News, Virginia. Admission: adult $5; student $3;
child 5 and younger, free. (800) 581-7245 or (757) 596-2222. www.mariner.org.

Virginia Historical Parks and Battlefields

The general web address for Virginia parks and battlefields is www.nps.gov.

Appomattox Court House National Historical Park. (804) 352-8987.

Fredericksburg and Spotsylvania National Military Park. (540) 371-
0802. Admission: adult $3; child 17 and younger, free.

Manassas National Battlefield Park. (703) 361-1339. Admission: adult $2.

Petersburg National Battlefield. Admission: adult $3. (804) 732-3531.

Richmond National Battlefield Park. (804) 226-1981.

Frederick, Maryland

Maryland was a border state during the Civil War, with factions supporting
both sides in the conflict.

To reach Frederick, Maryland, forty-five miles north of Washington, take
Route 355 north 10 miles toward Bethesda, picking up I-495 north for a short
jog onto I-270. Proceed thirty-three miles north toward Frederick.

Frederick Visitor Center. 19 East Church Street, Frederick. (301) 663-8687
or (800) 999-3613.www.visitfrederick.org.

Monocacy National Battlefield. The battle along the Monocacy River on
July 9, 1864, may have saved Washington, D.C., from falling to the Confederacy. Confederate General Jubal Anderson Early and his troops were headed
east to raid Washington when they were met by the forces of Union General

Another civil war.
General Lewis Wallace
went on to make a
career as an author;
his most famous book
was *Ben Hur.*

Lewis Wallace. The Confederate troops were delayed just enough to allow the District of Columbia to be reinforced.

Wallace and his mostly untested troops were in place at Frederick Junction, three miles southeast of Frederick, where the Georgetown Pike to Washington and the National Road to Baltimore both crossed the Monocacy River. Wallace spread his troops to cover the bridges of both turnpikes.

The Confederate forces outnumbered the Union troops by about 18,000 to 5,800, and after a day of bloody battle, the Union troops were forced to retreat toward Baltimore; they left behind more than 1,600 dead and wounded.

General Early took his troops into the District of Columbia the next morning, advancing as far as Fort Stevens. But his bloodied and exhausted men were unable to counter the arrival of fresh Union troops, and by the end of the day they withdrew.

A visitors center can be found at 4801 Urbana Pike, Frederick. (301) 662-3515. www.nps.gov/mono/mo_visit.htm.

Barbara Fritchie House. According to legend, Barbara Fritchie of Frederick waved her American flag in defiance of the Confederate troops of "Stonewall" Jackson during the Battle of Antietam. She was immortalized in John Greenleaf Whittier's poem set where "The clustered spires of Frederick stand, Green-walled by the hills of Maryland." According to Whittier's 1864 poem, Fritchie told Jackson's soldiers, "Shoot, if you must, this old gray head, But spare your country's flag."

In Frederick, the Barbara Fritchie Replica House and Museum memorializes the event with a reconstructed home at 154 West Patrick Street. For information and hours, call (301) 698-0630.

Interestingly, it is possible that Fritchie became famous because of an error. Some historians say that it was a woman by the name of Mary Quantrill who waved her flag at the Confederate soldiers; Mrs. Fritchie, they say, mistakenly was given credit and waved her flag at the Union soldiers who came later.

Chapter 19
Colonial Williamsburg and Carter's Grove

Colonial Williamsburg

From about 1699 until 1780—the days that led up to the Revolution and the adoption of the U.S. Constitution—Williamsburg was the political, social, and cultural center of America. Here the debates of the patriots set the concept for American democracy.

Today, Williamsburg lives again, faithfully restored to the eighteenth century as it appeared on the eve of the American Revolution. Some three million visitors come to the area each year.

Colonial Williamsburg covers 173 acres of the 200-acre town laid out in 1699 by Royal Governor Francis Nicholson. The Historic Area is modeled on a map of the area from 1781, when the town was used to billet French troops during the siege of Yorktown.

The Historic Area includes eighty-eight original structures and hundreds of reconstructions. All of the structures in the area were restored or rebuilt; none were moved into the area. Within the buildings, 225 rooms are furnished with appropriate American and English items from a collection of 50,000 pieces of furniture, paintings, china, glass, silver, pewter, textiles, tools, and carpeting.

There are ninety acres of gardens and greens, sixteen exhibition sites, ten retail shops, and seventeen historic trade presentations.

Historic interpreters, costumed as colonial workers and professionals, are stationed within the Historic Area to tell the stories of eighteenth-century Virginia society. In some cases, the interpreters portray real citizens of two centuries ago.

The grand avenue of Williamsburg is Duke of Gloucester Street, which runs one mile from the Wren Building at the College of William and Mary to the Capitol, bisecting the old town. The road is flanked on each side by Francis and Nicholson Streets, named after Francis Nicholson, the royal governor who laid out Williamsburg as Virginia's second capital.

Colonial Williamsburg is a theme park without a fence and ticket gates.

You can walk in and among the restored buildings and visit the shops and restaurants without buying an admission pass. You do, though, have to display a general admission ticket to enter any of the exhibition sites and trade shops. Tickets are also required to visit the museums run by the Colonial Williamsburg Foundation.

It is very difficult to find long-term parking in and around the Historic District, which butts up against the College of William and Mary campus. There are, though, acres of spaces at the Visitor Center; shuttle buses run from the center to the Historic District. The Visitor Center includes a gift shop and bookstore and also presents regular showings of *Williamsburg—The Story of a Patriot*, a thirty-five-minute film about the area. (The film, produced in 1956, stars Jack "Book-em, Dano" Lord.)

Tickets and Hours

For information call (800) 447-8679. www.colonialwilliamsburg.org.

Hours: January to end of November the park opens 9:30 A.M.

Closing hours from 4:30–5:30 P.M. at various times of the year.

Evening programs scheduled throughout the year. Prices listed here were in effect in mid-2000.

Colonial Williamsburg Ticket plans

Annual Pass

Adult	$65
Child (6–17)	$22.50

Good for unlimited admission to all ticketed sites, museums and daytime programs throughout the year, history walks, free parking at the Visitor Center, preferred reservations, special communications, discounts on carriage rides, discounts on selected Williamsburg Institute programs. There is a 25 percent discount on all evening programs (except during the Christmas Season) and a 15 percent discount on regularly priced merchandise purchases of $50 or greater.

General Admission Ticket

Adult	$30 (valid for 1 day; each additional day within 7 day-period, $5)
Child (6–17)	$18 (valid for 1 to 7 days)

Governor's Palace (purchased separately)

Adult	$18
Child	$11

Carter's Grove (purchased separately)

Adult	$18
Child	$11

Carter's Grove is open Tuesday to Sunday, 9 A.M.–5 P.M. In recent years, Carter's Grove has been closed from January 1 until early March.

Carriage rides: $15, $10 with admission.

Wagon rides: $10, $5 with admission.

Birth of a Restoration

During the Revolution, Thomas Jefferson moved Virginia's seat of government from the difficult-to-defend Williamsburg to Richmond in 1780. Williamsburg descended into relative obscurity, little changed for the next century-and-a-half, with the exception of some damage suffered during the Peninsula Campaign of the Civil War.

In 1926, the Reverend W. A. R. Goodwin, rector of Bruton Parish Church— then and now an active Episcopal church in use since 1715—approached philanthropist John D. Rockefeller Jr., in hopes of restoring Williamsburg to its Colonial past.

Rockefeller and his wife, Abby Aldrich Rockefeller, agreed to the plan and oversaw the restoration project from **Bassett Hall**, the eighteenth-century farmhouse that was their Williamsburg home. They contributed $68 million for the preservation of eighty-eight original structures and the reconstruction of many smaller buildings on their original sites.

John D. Rockefeller Jr., authorized the first purchase for restoration—the Ludwell-Paradise House—in December of 1926, and restoration began two years later. The first restored building opened was the **Wren Building** at the College of William and Mary in September of 1931. The **Raleigh Tavern**, the first exhibition building, opened in 1932, and the **Capitol** and **Governor's Palace** opened in 1934.

He continued his involvement with Williamsburg's restoration until his death in 1960.

Today, the Historic Area is operated by a nonprofit organization, with about 3,500 employees.

Colonial Williamsburg receives 900,000 to one million visitors per year, out of a total of about three million tourists to Williamsburg and the surrounding areas.

The busiest times at Colonial Williamsburg are holiday weekends, including the Fourth of July, Labor Day, Easter, homecoming at William and Mary at the end of October, Thanksgiving, and the Grand Illumination in early December.

In the summer months, from June to August, visitors are mostly families. The spring and fall are popular with seniors and school groups. The winter is an especially good time for visitors who enjoy a slower pace and want to spend extra time in the museums, exhibition buildings, and trade shops.

Driving Advice

Williamsburg is about 160 miles southeast of Washington. In addition to Washington's National Airport, visitors can fly into Richmond International Airport, about fifty miles away; Norfolk International Airport, about forty miles away; and Newport News/Williamsburg International Airport in Newport News, about fifteen miles distant.

To drive from Ronald Reagan Washington National Airport to Williamsburg, pick up I-395 southbound for about nine miles to I-95 at Springfield.

Puttin' on the DOG.
If you hear locals referring to events on "DOG Street," don't show off the fact that you're from out of town by trying to find it on your street map. DOG Street is the nickname for Duke of Gloucester Street, Williamsburg's main drag.

Take I-95 south about eighty-four miles to near Richmond; pick up I-295 eastbound and proceed fifteen miles toward Highland Springs. Switch to I-64 eastbound and drive forty-one miles to the Colonial Parkway exit in Williamsburg.

If you are driving to Colonial Williamsburg, the best place to purchase tickets is at the visitors center, where you can pick up the shuttle bus to the Historic District. Tickets are also available at the Greenhow Lumber House, Merchants Square Information Station, Williamsburg Inn, and Williamsburg Lodge.

Note that at certain times of the year the visitors center will open at 8:30 A.M. and remain open until 8 P.M. However, many exhibits will not open until 9:30 A.M. It is worth visiting the bookstore within the visitors center, which has a nice collection of local history books as well as maps, Civil War books, Revolutionary War books, and information about gardening and other crafts.

If you arrive a little bit early, it is interesting to watch the workers strolling across the pastures and down the paths to their jobs, fully dressed in Colonial garb and carrying implements appropriate to their jobs. Most do a great job of staying in character. On one of my visits, a Marine Corps helicopter flew by overhead; most of the tourists looked up to watch it go by, but the workers treated it as if it were a particularly noisome but insignificant bird.

Leave your car in one of the 2,000 spaces at the visitors center parking lots; there is no long-term parking in the Historic Area. With your ticket you will receive a copy of the *Visitor's Companion,* a weekly events newspaper that includes hours of operation, special programs and events, and a map. Locate the bus route that makes a circuit from the visitors center around the Historic Area. Major stops include the Governor's Palace, Francis Street shops, the Abby Aldrich Rockefeller Folk Art Center, the Public Hospital, and Merchants Square.

The Historic Area is about one mile long by a half-mile wide and encompasses 88 original buildings. There is no parking in the Historic Area; short-term parking is available on some of the outlying sections, including Merchants Square.

Duke of Gloucester and several adjacent streets are closed to traffic from 8 A.M. to 10 P.M.

The Governor's Palace and the Capitol are the most popular destinations; head for one or the other first on a busy day. The *Visitor's Companion* includes a map; study it carefully and select your must-sees before you begin your tour to reduce the amount of walking.

The shuttle bus from the visitors center follows a five-mile loop, with nine stops. It makes its first stop near the Governor's Palace, and that is our favorite place to start the day; if you're feeling frisky, Stop One is only a few blocks' walk from the parking lots. When you exit the bus, you'll walk through a dewy horse pasture with a hand-split rail fence on your left; on the right is a brick wall compound for the Governor's Palace. It's an instant transport back to the 1700s with little to take away the illusion.

The sights of Williamsburg and environs are close enough together for visitors to go from one to another easily. You can zip from Colonial Williamsburg down to Busch Gardens in less than fifteen minutes. Busch Gardens is about three miles from Carter's Grove, and about six miles from Jamestown. The Yorktown Victory Center is about a twenty-minute drive from Williamsburg.

Williamsburg Exhibits and Museums

Check the daily schedule for closings; tickets are required for entrance.

Abby Aldrich Rockefeller Folk Art Center. The nation's leading collection of American folk art, established in 1930. Nearly 3,000 objects on display include paintings, drawings, and wood and metal sculptures. The core of the collection is made up of 424 objects donated in 1939 by Mrs. Rockefeller. The museum, first opened in 1957, was expanded in 1992.

The Folk Art Museum has a very interesting and eclectic collection, from an Indian maiden figurehead that had once adorned a sailing vessel, to locomotive ornamentation, to tobacconist shop figures, to figureheads of American icons such as Abe Lincoln and Santa Claus.

Among interesting exhibits is the collection of tea canisters and teapots. After Bostonians destroyed hundreds of chests of tea in 1773 to protest Britain's tax on imports to the colonies, the very drinking of tea was considered a political act; the budding Revolutionists urged a switch to coffee. After independence, though, many of the former colonists happily went back to tea as their drink of choice.

Introductory tours lasting thirty minutes are offered throughout the day; check the *Visitor's Companion* or the museum front desk for times.

Bassett Hall. Bassett Hall, south of Francis Street in the Williamsburg Historic Area, dates to the mid-eighteenth century; a two-story extension was added in the nineteenth century. Mr. and Mrs. John D. Rockefeller Jr., acquired the house in 1927 for use as a private home, and they

Originality. To be called *original* at Colonial Williamsburg, a house must have some element of the original structure remaining. Some "original" structures contain 90 percent of their old timbers, while others have as little as a single colonial 2 × 4 in a stairway.

Restoration is work done on original structures, including preservation of their parts. Where necessary, craftspeople create duplicates of missing or damaged pieces.

Reconstruction is the reproduction of a lost building based on research. At Colonial Williamsburg, reconstructed buildings are raised on the foundations of the original, or on their site.

Children ahead. Try to avoid getting trapped behind large school groups. They'll slow you down and are likely to be boisterous. If they head into a building to take a tour, skip that building and come back to it later.

More great events of Williamsburg. The House of Burgesses adopted Virginia's Resolution for Independence on May 15, 1776, an act that led to the adoption of the Declaration of Independence in July of that year in Philadelphia.

George Mason produced the Virginia Declaration of Rights, a precursor to the federal Bill of Rights, on June 12, 1776.

The Williamsburg area was included in the so-called Peninsular campaign during the American Civil War. The campaign was an ultimately unsuccessful attempt by the Union army, under the command of General George McClellan, to capture Richmond by invading the Virginia peninsula between the York and James rivers. Confederate forces evacuated Yorktown and Norfolk, but General Robert E. Lee withdrew the Confederate army to Richmond and eventually forced McClellan to retreat from the peninsula with a counteroffensive in the Seven Days Battles.

usually spent four to six weeks there each spring and fall; their last joint visit took place in 1947.

Abby Aldrich Rockefeller used the home as the setting for her collection of American folk art.

Mr. and Mrs. John D. Rockefeller III were married in Bassett Hall in 1960 and decided to maintain the interiors. When the house, its contents, and the surrounding 585-acre tract were given to the Colonial Williamsburg Foundation in 1979, the rooms were little changed from the way they had appeared when they were occupied by the elder Rockefellers.

Outbuildings include a teahouse, smokehouse, kitchen, and dairy. Reservations are necessary for visits to Bassett Hall at some times of the year; they can be made at the Special Programs desk at the visitors center. Tours are offered 9 A.M.–5 P.M. every day except Wednesday. For more information, call (757) 220-7642.

Brush-Everard House. John Brush, gunsmith and first keeper of the Magazine on Market Square, built his home in 1718. It was later owned by William Dering, a dancing master who taught the gentry of Williamsburg how to perform the minuet at governor's functions. Another owner, about 1755, was Thomas Everard, the clerk of the York County Court and later mayor of Williamsburg. The house is available for tours at various times of the year and is used for special educational programs.

Capitol. The Capitol was the seat of Virginia's Colonial government for seventy-five years. Here in 1765, Patrick Henry denounced the Stamp Act, and on May 15, 1776, the Virginia Convention unanimously proposed that the Continental Congress "Declare the United Colonies free and independent states." On June 12, 1776, a Virginia convention approved George Mason's declaration of rights and on June 29 adopted the first constitution for the new commonwealth of Virginia.

About fifty to seventy-five visitors are admitted at a time to the Capitol building. You'll enter into the House of Burgesses on the lower level; the Governor's Council is the upper house, literally and figuratively.

The first of two Capitol buildings was completed on this site in 1705; as an unusual precaution against fire, the building was constructed without chimneys, and the use of candles and tobacco was prohibited. But the wheels of bureaucracy intervened, and two chimneys were added in 1723 after complaints about records being "exposed by the Damps." The building burned to the ground in 1747.

A second Capitol on the same site was completed in 1753 and was used through pre-Revolutionary times. After Virginia's government was moved to Richmond in 1780, the building was all but abandoned, and in 1832 it, too, was destroyed by fire.

During the reconstruction of Colonial Williamsburg, there was debate about whether to reconstruct the first or second Capitol. Although the second Capitol was the one used for some of the major events leading up to the Revolution, there were few records about its design. Thus, the Capitol as rebuilt represents the original building.

Under Colonial rule, the legislative process was heavily weighted in favor of the Crown, and it followed a very slow course. The burgesses were the only elected representatives of the colony; the Governor's Council was appointed by the king. All bills had to pass two houses, then be signed by the royal governor, and finally sent on to London to be allowed or disallowed by the king.

The twelve members of the Governor's Council often kept their appointment within the family. There was no separation of powers in the Colonial government; five of the members of the Governor's Council also served as the Supreme Court, with the governor as chief justice.

On display at the House of Burgesses is the original 1730s chair of Speaker of the House John Robinson.

Colonial Williamsburg scene
Colonial Williamsburg Foundation, Williamsburg, Virginia

Patrick Henry delivered his famous "Caesar-Brutus" speech in Williamsburg on May 30, 1765, offering to the House of Burgesses his resolutions in defiance of the Stamp Act. Said Henry, "Caesar had his Brutus; Charles the First his Cromwell; and George the Third may profit by their example. If *this* be treason, make the most of it."

George Washington introduced the Virginia Resolves against the Townshend Acts on May 16, 1769, in Williamsburg. The Townshend Acts were revenue acts passed by the English Parliament to replace the repealed Stamp Acts. The duties they placed on various imports led to the Boston Tea Party and the Boston Massacre.

The "Vinegar Bible" on the table in the Governor's Council dates to 1711; it received its unusual name because of a typo where "vineyard" is written as "vinegar."

The colony's courts above the county level also met in the Capitol building. The county court handled local matters, misdemeanors, disputes over items worth less than ten pounds, and slave matters. The General Court, the high court of Virginia, met twice a year to handle disputes of higher value and criminal charges against white males and females, including murder, theft (the third instance of hog stealing being a particularly serious offense), and treason.

The jury was sequestered without food, water, or "comfort" until a verdict was reached, which probably resulted in fairly quick decisions. Burning or branding on the hand was the most common punishment. Serious crimes were punished by lashes: thirty-nine for a male, thirteen for a female. When jail time was ordered, sentences were usually fairly short because of the expense of housing prisoners. The most serious offenses were dealt with by hanging. Sentences had to be carried out within ten days.

Courthouse. The restored original county court building was the home of the James City County Court and the Hustings Court (municipal court) for the city of Williamsburg. Modern-day visitors can sit in the jury box or the dock and participate in re-creations of cases from the Colonial era.

DeWitt Wallace Gallery. Special exhibits on arts and crafts of Colonial Williamsburg, as well as the Foundation's permanent collection of English and American decorative arts, are found here. The ten galleries include 8,000 objects from the seventeenth through nineteenth centuries. DeWitt Wallace was the founder of *The Reader's Digest*, and the endowment by the DeWitt Wallace Fund for Colonial Williamsburg is the largest single gift to the area after that of the Rockefeller family.

Items on display include textiles, furniture, ceramics, glass, metals, tools, instruments, prints, and paintings. The concept of decorative arts is very broadly interpreted in this unusual collection. You'll find ornate seventeenth- and eighteenth-century weapons, including some fearsome-looking long rifles, a matchlock musket from 1620, and flintlock weapons. You'll find a hurdy-gurdy from about 1758, old English guitars, a spinet from about 1750, and pedal harps. Another corner displays a collection of pipe tampers that have fanciful heads, and a large selection of pewter tankards dating from as early as 1675.

My favorite decorative item is a beautifully crafted orrery, a mechanical model of the solar system demonstrating the motion of the planets around the sun. It was invented in the early eighteenth century and named after Charles Boyle, the fourth Earl of Orrery, for whom the first apparatus was made.

You can catch a light, reasonably priced meal at **The Gallery Café** at the back of the main hall; offerings include soup, sandwiches, and pasta.

Governor's Palace. The Palace was the official residence of seven royal governors of the colony of Virginia, and of the first two governors of the commonwealth, Patrick Henry and Thomas Jefferson.

The building is furnished as it was about 1770 during the occupancy of Norborne Berkeley, the Baron de Botetourt.

Yes, ma'am. On one of my visits, I entered the house of Mary Stith and listened to a presentation by a woman who said she was named Ann Wager, the mistress of the Bray School for teaching the catechism to Negro and Indian children in 1774. She was asked by a young child how much time the kids spent in school. "Every day," she said. "Why?" she continued, "Is there a reason why you should not be in school?"

The Governor's Palace is fronted by the Palace Green, a long, open grassy common that stretches a few blocks to Duke of Gloucester Street, the heart of Colonial Williamsburg that stretches from Bruton Parish Church all the way to the Capitol half a mile away.

The Palace was long gone when the development of Colonial Williamsburg was begun—it had been destroyed by fire in 1781. The property had been used by the town for a school building. Rockefeller bought property from the town and built a new school across the road. After the old school was removed, archaeological digs uncovered the foundation location for the original Palace.

The Palace was reconstructed primarily on the basis of a copper engraving of the town found at the University of Oxford, the only known picture. Thomas Jefferson also had some drawings in his possessions.

The Palace accepts thirty-four visitors at a time, in tours that are spaced about ten minutes apart. You can expect lines of up to an hour at busy times and on some early mornings when busloads of visitors arrive all at once.

Norborne Berkeley was the first Colonial governor to actually live in Virginia; other governors had stayed behind in England and sent lieutenant governors to serve in their stead.

The place was a bit of a comedown for someone such as Botetourt. There were twenty-two rooms in the small palace; being a nobleman, Botetourt might have had a castle of 100 rooms at home in Wales.

The Front Hall is stunning, decorated with hundreds of swords, rifles, and pistols. The ceiling of the entrance hall is a rosette of rifles with bayonets fixed, like an NRA dream. The display of arms was meant as a message of the

Into the night. Formal dinner parties in the Governor's Palace were late-night affairs. Dinner was served about 10 P.M., and entertainment went on until 2 A.M. In the heat of summer the entertainment would spill outside to the gardens, which were extensions of the house.

Upward. There is a lot of climbing on the tour of the Governor's Palace and the Capitol. Visitors who have disabilities may have difficulty reaching the upper floors.

Wrong question. Some of the characters are very good at staying in their roles. I was in the post office when a visitor entered and asked the elegant woman who was sitting there and quietly reading whether there was a good meal to eat in one of the taverns. "I'm not in the habit of frequenting taverns," she sniffed, although she did allow that she had heard a bit about some of the places from others.

might of the Colonial powers; the weapons, though, were also ready for use if needed.

The Palace tour includes the governor's bed chamber, which was also used for small gatherings. Visitors will note the small bed for the shorter people of the time, as well as the discreetly positioned chamber pots and privies.

Through much of the Palace, the floors were left bare in deference to the unpaved streets, muddy paths, and animal droppings.

The wall covering of the governor's office is gold-tooled Spanish leather. The walls were taken from a home in London that was partially destroyed in World War II.

There are touches of Oriental style in the guest quarters, including chairs with bamboo-like finishing.

The high ceilings and cross-ventilation of the Palace were designed to dissipate the heat of the Virginia summer. Note, too, the Venetian blinds on most of the windows; these devices, remarkably similar to modern-day blinds, were popular in the homes of the wealthy. Fabric was rarely used for drapes because of the expense.

As you face the Governor's Palace, to the right is the wheelwright and nearby is the windmill, and copper and rural trades. The Governor's Palace Kitchen is in an outbuilding to the left of the Palace alongside a small pond.

Magazine. The octagonal Magazine, erected in 1715, was Colonial Virginia's storehouse for guns, ammunition, and military supplies. The action of British Governor Dunmore on the night of April 20, 1775, in removing gunpowder belonging to the colony touched off the revolution in Virginia before news of the battle of Lexington even reached Williamsburg.

The Magazine, one of the original buildings, was completely gutted at one point; its interior has been rebuilt. All of the firearms in the exhibit are original, mostly British military weapons that date from 1740 to 1790.

The reconstructed guardhouse was originally built during the French and Indian War.

Play Booth Theater. Between the Capitol and Campbell's Tavern, nearby to the Brush-Everard House, this open-air theater is located on the site of an eighteenth-century theater that was frequented by George Washington, Thomas Jefferson, and other prominent Virginians; scenes from period plays are presented regularly. Open seasonally.

Public Gaol. North of the Capitol on Nicholson Street, this unpleasant place held accused persons until their cases came to trial in the Capitol. Prisoners, or their families, could buy food and drink from the local taverns to supplement the poor official menu. Part of the brickwork of the walls of the Gaol is original.

Private property. A handful of private residences are scattered in and among the restored and reconstructed buildings of Colonial Williamsburg. Visitors are asked to respect the privacy of the owners.

Public Hospital of 1773. A reconstruction of the first institution in America devoted solely to the treatment of the mentally ill, the building today serves as the entrance to the DeWitt Wallace Decorative Arts Gallery.

In the early years of its existence the public hospital was part jail and part infirmary. The belief that mentally disturbed persons could be cured or helped in some way was a relatively new concept, and some of the devices you will see on display at the hospital are unsettling, including a "tranquilizer chair," which featured a head restraint and leg manacles. To calm or to cure patients the staff prescribed potent drugs, employed a "ducking chair" or plunge bath, and used bleeding instruments. Doctors also believed occasional intimidation could have beneficial results.

The Public Hospital, with twenty-four cell-like rooms, admitted its first patients on October 12, 1773. Among the exhibits today is one of the barren cells with barred windows and chains fixed to the walls to make sure the patients would not escape.

Raleigh Tavern. Virginia's leaders often met at the Raleigh Tavern, Williamsburg's most popular inn. Here, in 1769, a group of Burgesses adopted the proposal of George Mason for a boycott of British goods. Five years later, the Burgesses again met in the Apollo Room to issue the call for the first Continental Congress. The reconstructed building is decorated with English and American furnishings based on the inventories of the early keepers. (After the death of a person of substance—mostly white landowners and business owners—a complete inventory of possessions was drawn. Many of these inventories survive and were used in the reconstruction at Williamsburg.)

Alongside the Raleigh Tavern is the Raleigh Tavern Bakery, offering some interesting and inexpensive snacks, including sweet potato muffins, Sally Lund bread, ham biscuits, oatmeal cakes, and gingerbread cakes.

Randolph House. The home of Peyton Randolph, Speaker of the House of Burgesses. The first of three sections of the house was built about 1715. The interior includes some of the best examples of paneled rooms in Williamsburg. Open seasonally.

Shield's Tavern. See the section "Dining in the Williamsburg Historic Area" later in this chapter.

Wetherburn's Tavern. Wetherburn's Tavern, an original eighteenth-century

Catching up. In 1995, Colonial Williamsburg relocated the Cary Peyton Armistead House from its former position directly in front of the Capitol building. The Victorian home was built in 1894, and the daughter of the owner lived there until her death in 1984. It was replaced by a restored eighteenth-century coffeehouse, which had earlier stood on the site.

VIPs. Among the more than 100 million visitors to Colonial Williamsburg have been Presidents Franklin Roosevelt, Harry Truman, Dwight Eisenhower, Lyndon Johnson, Richard Nixon, Gerald Ford, Jimmy Carter, Ronald Reagan, and Bill Clinton.

In addition, more than 100 heads of state and government officials from around the world have toured the site as part of a visit to Washington. The ninth Summit of Industrialized Nations brought leaders of Great Britain, Canada, France, Germany, Japan, Italy, the European Economic Community, and the United States to Williamsburg in 1983.

building expanded to its present size after 1751, was one of the best-known taverns in Williamsburg. It has been restored to its appearance of about 1760. A visit includes a tour of the tavern and the work and living area of Henry Wetherburn's twenty-nine slaves.

Wythe House. Wythe House, one of the existing buildings restored by Colonial Williamsburg, was little changed during the years; all that had to be done to restore it to its pre-Colonial appearance was to remove a porch added in the eighteenth century.

George Wythe was a lawyer who taught Thomas Jefferson, and he was a signer of the Declaration of Independence. He also dabbled in scientific experiments, and there are some preserved specimens and devices on display. The house actually belonged to the family of his wife Elizabeth; at age sixteen she was overseer of the house, including seventeen slaves.

The fire in the kitchen at Wythe House is usually burning, and you can learn about the foods of the time. On one of my visits, chickens roasted in the fireplace; an intricate mechanical rotisserie was turned by gears moved by a weight across the room. Chickens were cooked to medium rare in Colonial times; they were killed and cooked immediately, so there was less threat from salmonella and other health problems.

Historic Trade Sites and Special Attractions at Williamsburg

Check the daily schedule for closings.

Blacksmith. Smithies forge nails, tools, and iron hardware used throughout the town.

Cabinetmaker. A workshop where artisans produce fine Virginia furniture and musical instruments.

Carpenter's Yard. A workshop for framing and finish work for buildings in Williamsburg.

Carriage and Wagon Rides. Daily 10 A.M. to 4 P.M., weather permitting.

Geddy House and Foundry. James Geddy and his sons were gunsmiths and founders at this location from about 1737 to 1777. The original house is now used for brass, bronze, silver, and pewter casting.

Gunsmith. Smiths build rifles, fowling pieces, and pistols from wood, brass, iron, and steel.

Harness and Saddlemaker. An original building, used to create harnesses, saddles, military equipment, and other leather products.

Milliner. The latest eighteenth-century styles for gowns, shifts, and other items of clothing are created in this original building.

Pasteur & Galt Apothecary Shop. Operated by physician-surgeon-druggist Drs. William Pasteur and John Galt from 1775 to 1778. On display are medical and dental equipment, surgical tools, and medicines.

Printing Office. The home of the Virginia colony's first newspaper. The printing press down below the post office is worth a visit. The printer presses the pages of individual pieces of type (known as "forms") with an ink ball. Rag paper is put on top, and a lever is pulled to apply great pressure from above. The room is filled with drying pages from whatever book is currently under way.

Shoemaker. Plain and fancy shoes and boots for gentlemen.

Wheelwright. Construction and repair of vehicles used in the town.

Wigmaker. The perukemaker creates the finest wigs, curls, and queues for the gentry.

Windmill, Cooper, and Rural Trades. At Robertson's mill, wind-driven sails power grinding stones. Other artisans create casks and barrels.

Other Places of Interest

Bruton Parish Church. An active Episcopal church in use since 1715. Open for tours Monday to Saturday 9 A.M.–5 P.M.; and Sunday noon–5 P.M.

Bruton Parish was formed in 1674 when several existing groups of Virginia Anglicans (now known as Episcopalians) were merged. It took its name from a parish on the River Brue in Somerset, England; it was the home of several distinguished members, including a royal governor, Sir William Berkeley, and Thomas Ludwell, a secretary of Virginia.

The church was designed by Governor Alexander Spotswood and completed in 1715. The east end of the church was extended twenty-two feet in 1752, and the church tower added in 1769.

The high box pews include seats dedicated to U.S. Presidents Washington, Jefferson, Monroe, and Tyler, all of whom worshipped at the church. The Governor's Pew was reserved for royal governors and members of the Governor's Council. In Colonial times, the canopied chair was also curtained for privacy and warmth in the unheated church.

The West Gallery was usually occupied by students from the College of William and Mary; some of their 200-year-old initials are carved in the railing.

During Colonial times in Virginia, there was little distinction between church and state; in fact all officeholders were required by law to attend church regularly. The Virginia Anglicans, though, were leaders in the "disestablishment" of the church, a movement that took hold in Williamsburg. George Mason and James Madison drafted the sections on religious toleration

Sounds of liberty. The bell in the tower at Bruton Parish was presented to the church in 1761. In 1766, it celebrated the repeal of the Stamp Act. On May 15, 1776, it celebrated the passing of a resolution by the House of Burgesses in Williamsburg to establish a state constitution and to instruct the Virginia delegates in Congress to offer a resolution to declare the united colonies free and independent states. In 1783, it celebrated the ratification of the treaty of peace between the United States and Great Britain.

Spotted. Governor Alexander Spotswood led an expedition in 1716 to the wilderness western portion of the Virginia colony; they visited the Blue Ridge Mountains and the Shenandoah Valley. At the end of the journey, the voyagers were given golden horseshoe pins by Spotswood. In addition to a pair of golf courses, Spotswood is memorialized by Spotsylvania County in Virginia, the site of several bloody Civil War battles.

in the Declaration of Rights of 1776; Thomas Jefferson's Statute for Religious Freedom was introduced in 1779.

The parish—and Williamsburg itself—went into a continuing decline after the Revolution.

Dr. W. A. R. Goodwin became rector of Bruton Parish Church in 1903 and set his priorities to include preservation of Williamsburg's landmarks, beginning with a partial rework of the church itself from 1905 to 1907. Goodwin recruited John D. Rockefeller into his dream, leading to Colonial Williamsburg as we know it today. A bust of Goodwin is shown near the doorway.

The church itself was one of the restoration projects initiated by Rockefeller in 1937; work included restoring the interior to its Colonial appearance.

Today, Bruton Parish has the largest congregation in its history, with 1,700 members. The church's bell, presented to the parish in 1761, still calls parishioners and visitors to worship.

Wren Building. The oldest academic building in America, in continuous use since 1695, is located at the College of William and Mary.

Days in History

History buffs may want to make their visits to Williamsburg during one of the "day in history" events, which trace the decline of British influence in North America, culminating in Virginia's independence. During a four-day period, visitors become part of the events that helped ignite the revolution, including dramatic reenactments, encounters with "people of the past," and walking tours. In recent years, programs have included The Gathering Storm—April 1775, The Sword is Drawn!—November 1775, and Virginia Declares Independence—May 1776. Contact Colonial Williamsburg for schedules and prices.

Special Evening Programs at Williamsburg

Throughout the year, Colonial Williamsburg offers special evening programs that expand on the experience of the Historic Area. Check the *Visitor's Companion* newspaper on the day of your visit for the schedule.

Examples of programs include:

The Subject is Murder: Williamsburg's Most Wanted, in which visitors meet, question, and deliberate over the guilt or innocence of some of the most notorious accused murderers of colonial Virginia.

Lanthorn Tour of Selected Trade Shops. An evening walk through the streets of Williamsburg and into four candlelit trade shops.

Legends of the Past Tour. A walking tour that includes reenactments of some of the stories and legends of the times.

Cry Witch. Visitors at the Capitol will participate in the re-creation of the trial of Grace Sherwood, accused of witchcraft, and reach a verdict.

Affairs of the Heart. An exploration of racial relationships, at the Wythe House. The program looks at a gentry marriage and its effects on the households of the groom and his intended bride. Visitors will meet William, who has had a child by his slave Rachel, as he ponders his decision to marry and carry on his family's name. Presented in season at Carter's Grove.

The Military by Night—A Candlelight Tour. A re-creation of life for soldiers in the Virginia regiments during the American Revolution.

Cross or Crown. With Thomas Jefferson as a guide, visitors participate in a reenactment of some of the debates about individual freedom conducted by the founders of our nation.

Remember Me. An elderly slave uses music and stories to recall his past.

Colonial Williamsburg scene
Colonial Williamsburg Foundation, Williamsburg, Virginia

Jumpin' the Broom: The Re-Creation of a Slave Wedding. Esther and Manuel pledge their love at Carter's Grove slave quarters.

Science, Conjuration, and Humbug Amusements at the Courthouse. Stories, puppetry, and magic from old Williamsburg.

Annual Events at Williamsburg

Check with the visitors center for information on these special annual events.

Independence Day. The Colonial Williamsburg Fife and Drum Corps begin the day with a march to Bruton Parish Church. There, a military field altar is constructed, and prayers for peace and the nation are offered. The ceremony concludes with the tolling of Virginia's Liberty Bell. An evening garden party at the Governor's Palace celebrates the occasion with period entertainment and Virginia delicacies. The day ends with an evening salute on Palace Green by the Fife and Drum Corps, followed by fireworks.

Grand Illumination. The month-long Christmas holiday season at Colonial Williamsburg begins with the Grand Illumination, a traditional celebration that attracts thousands of visitors. A late-afternoon cannon blast signals the time for lighting of candles in the windows of homes, shops, and public buildings throughout the Historical Area. The illumination is followed by eighteenth-century fireworks, singing, dancing, and music at outdoor stages illuminated by lanterns and candles.

Carter's Grove

Eight miles east of Williamsburg, Carter's Grove on the James River includes the Winthrop Rockefeller Archaeology Museum; the partially reconstructed 1619 Wolstenholme Towne; eighteenth-century slave quarters; and the 1754 Mansion.

The entrance to Carter's Grove lies off Route 60 East, past the entrance to Busch Gardens.

The slave quarters are part of Colonial Williamsburg's growing acknowledgment of the role of African Americans in the area; half the population of eighteenth-century Williamsburg was black.

As you approach Carter's Grove, you will come to a marker for Martin's Hundred, a large plantation founded by the Virginia Company of London in 1617 and later assigned 21,500 acres. It was settled in 1619, but most of the early residents were killed or captured in the Indian Massacre of March 22, 1622. The site of its administrative center, Wolstenholme Towne, was discovered by archaeologists in 1977.

Robert "King" Carter purchased 1,400 acres of the land early in the eighteenth century and gave his name to the area. After the death of Carter, the estate passed to his eldest daughter, Elizabeth, and later to her second son, Carter Burwell, who built the grand mansion. A total of five generations of Burwells owned the land before it was sold in 1838. More than a dozen other families held title to the land until Archibald McCrea and his wife bought the property in 1928; they were the last to live there. It was purchased for the Colonial Williamsburg Foundation in 1969.

You'll walk from the visitors center at Carter's Grove across an elevated footpath over a deep forest gully; it's a very different, more primeval feeling than at Williamsburg just a few miles away.

The rough, low-ceilinged slave quarters seem just barely adequate; a small sustenance garden surrounds the shacks. Although they look very primitive, they are actually representative of most of the pre-Colonial-era residences in rural areas for free families and slaves. According to historians at Carter's Grove, only about 15 percent of the population were living in urban centers like Williamsburg and few had grand houses like Burwell's on the river.

There is very little at all to interfere with the feeling of being transported back in time. There are no cars or other modern devices to be seen from anywhere within Carter's Grove.

Some of the walkways are paved with crushed shells, a paving technique still in use in parts of New England.

The mansion at Carter's Grove was expanded and enhanced in the 1930s by its new owners, Archibald and Molly McCrea. Although the work was going on at about the same time as the early work at Williamsburg, there was no real attempt to restore in the same historically correct manner used at Williamsburg because the house was being built for the McCreas as a showplace for their social world.

The roof was raised and a third floor was installed in what had been the attic. Two wings were created to attach to existing outbuildings, and modern amenities including bathrooms and kitchens were added.

The Winthrop Rockefeller Archaeology Museum, on the site, portrays the history and archaeology of the settlement. The mansion on the site, which dates to 1754, has been restored to the Colonial Revival style of the 1930s.

The Country Road

Cars can return to the Historic Area via the Country Road, an eight-mile path through woodlands, meadows, and ravines that arrives on South England Street near the Williamsburg Lodge and the Abby Aldrich Rockefeller Folk Art Center. The road runs one-way only, from Carter's Grove to Williamsburg.

The paved concrete road is barely one lane wide. Soon after you leave Carter's Grove you are into the woods, driving through a green tunnel of trees and bushes, across a narrow wooden bridge over a marsh, and back into the woods. I came along several groups of deer standing alongside the road.

It is an experience not many modern drivers have anymore. At most times of the day (the road is closed at dark), you won't see another driver for much of the trip. There is no sign, except for your own vehicle, that you haven't gone back to the mid-eighteenth century. A trip along the country road at its 15-mile-per-hour speed limit takes about thirty minutes.

Hotels, Dining, Shopping, and Recreation in Williamsburg

Hotels

More than 10,000 hotel and motel rooms are available in the Williamsburg area. Lodging arrangements can be made by calling the Williamsburg Hotel/Motel Association at (800) 446-9244. In the height of the summer season, hotel rates are at their highest and rooms may be difficult to obtain. At off-peak times, call around to a few places to find better rates.

Dining in the Williamsburg Historic Area

Chowning's Tavern. An informal tavern. Daily for lunch 11 A.M.–3:30 P.M.; dinner from 4:30 P.M. Specialties include Brunswick stew, Welsh rabbit, bubble and squeak, and bangers and mash. Dinner from $6 to $13.

Christiana Campbell's Tavern. George Washington ate here. Specializes in seafood and local offerings. Dinner only from 5 P.M.; closed Sunday. Here you can sup on oyster fritters, sweet potato muffins, and peanut butter pie. Entrees from about $19 to $23.

King's Arms Tavern. One of the high-tone establishments of its day, its name became unpopular after the Revolution and it became known as "Mrs. Vobe's." One of the house specialties is Virginia peanut soup. Daily for lunch 11:30 A.M.–2:30 P.M.; dinner from 5 P.M. Garden food service noon to 8 P.M., weather permitting. Specialties include filet stuffed with oysters, game pie, and sour cherry trifle. Dinner entrees are priced from about $20 to $25.

Shields Tavern. The first tavern at this site opened shortly after the Capitol was completed in the early 1700s. By the time James Shields became keeper in the 1740s it was a popular meeting place for burgesses, travelers, and townspeople. The tavern survived two difficult events in 1747: first a fire destroyed the Capitol and took away some of its business, and later that year the town suffered from an epidemic of smallpox that spread to Shields's family and his town slaves.

Shields died in 1750, and his widow operated the tavern for a few months before she remarried and moved up the street to help run the tavern belonging to her new husband and former competitor, Henry Wetherburn.

The original tavern disappeared before the Civil War, and it was reconstructed in 1954 on the same site. The tavern interior was reconstructed in 1988 based on buildings of the time.

There are eating places in the main building and in the rough-hewn log basement, where you'll eat by candlelight. There is little to distract from the illusion of being in the 1700s except for the occasional flash of a credit card.

The menu includes modern-day versions of Colonial favorites, including an eighteenth-century sampler that at the time of one of my visits featured cream of crayfish soup or black bean soup, chicken fricassee, salt-cured ham, spoon bread, and syllabub—an old-fashioned dessert of whipped cream, lemon, wine, and sherry that could keep as long as nine days without refrigeration.

Refreshments from the bar include bumbo (a mixture of rum, sugar, and water), and sangaree (a drink made from an eighteenth-century recipe using Madeira wine, lemon, and orange), a variation on modern sangria drinks.

Open daily for breakfast 8:30 A.M.–10 A.M.; lunch 11:30 A.M.–3 P.M.; garden food service noon–5 P.M., weather permitting. Dinner from 5 P.M. On Sunday, brunch is served from 10 A.M. to 2:30 P.M., and dinner from 5 P.M. Dinner entrees are priced from about $16 to $24.

Dining Near the Williamsburg Inn and Williamsburg Lodge

Cascades. For hearty breakfasts, try the Hunt Breakfast. Casual family dining. Breakfast, except Saturday, 7:30–10 A.M.; Sunday brunch 8 A.M.–2 P.M. Daily lunch service 11:30 A.M.–2 P.M.; dinner 5:30–9 P.M. Dinner entrees from about $12 to $24.

Williamsburg Inn Regency Dining Room. A luxurious, formal eatery with specialties that include Atlantic salmon and rack of lamb. Jacket and tie required for dinner and Sunday brunch. Daily for breakfast 7:30–10 A.M.; lunch noon–2 P.M.; and dinner 6–9 P.M. Sunday brunch noon–2 P.M. Dinner entrees from about $22 to $32.

Williamsburg Inn Regency Lounge. Breakfast and lunch buffet, with casual dinner service. Breakfast daily 7–10 A.M.; lunch 11:30 A.M.–3 P.M.; and dinner 6–10 P.M.

Williamsburg Lodge Dining Room. Daily breakfast 7–10:30 A.M.; lunch 11:30 A.M.–2:30 P.M.; and dinner 6–10 P.M. Friday and Saturday seafood buffet 6–9 P.M.; Sunday brunch 9 A.M.–2 P.M. Dinner entrees from about $15 to $22; seafood feast adult $23.25; child $9.95.

Williamsburg Lodge Cafe. Family dining, including southern fried chicken and crab cakes. Monday to Saturday 2:30–10 P.M.; Sunday breakfast 7–11 A.M., lunch and supper noon–10 P.M.

Dining Near Merchants Square and Visitor Center

Seasons Restaurant. Main courses run from about $11 to $20 and include blackened chicken, Hawaiian chicken, hickory grilled shrimp, New York strip steak, and prime rib. Appetizers feature a Charleston seafood chowder and a salad buffet. Sunday buffet brunch is also offered.

Wallace Gallery Cafe. Light lunch and snacks at the gallery, near Merchants Square. Open daily 10 A.M.–5 P.M.

Shopping in Williamsburg

Williamsburg has developed two very different but equally attractive types of shopping. For those who enjoy antiques and reproductions from the Colonial era, there is a significant collection of shops selling this type of item, primarily in and around Colonial Williamsburg itself.

The other shopping draws are the dozens of factory-outlet shops along Richmond Road, selling everything from clothing to candles to candy.

Shopping in the Merchants Square in the Historic Area

Colonial Post Office. Reproductions of eighteenth-century prints and maps for sale. Postcards mailed here are hand-canceled using the original Williamsburg postmark.

Golden Ball. Fine gold and sterling-silver jewelry and hollowware.

Greenhow Store. Candy, tricorner hats, and other souvenirs.

Mary Dickinson Store. Accoutrements for the eighteenth-century lady of fashion.

McKenzie Apothecary. Herbs, spices, and apothecary items.

M. Dubois Grocer. Tavern foods, including Virginia ham, peanuts, preserves, and wine.

Prentis Store. Williamsburg's oldest retail store, selling leather goods, ironwares, pottery, and other items.

Raleigh Tavern Bakery. Gingerbread, apple cider, cakes, and breads.

Tarpley's Store. Home furnishings that include baskets, pottery, soaps, and candles.

In and Around Colonial Williamsburg

The Bookstore. College of William and Mary bookstore; 106 Jamestown Road: (757) 221-2480.

Quilts Unlimited. Merchants Square; 440 Duke of Gloucester Street: (757) 253-8700.

Toymaker of Williamsburg. Merchants Square; Duke of Gloucester Street: (757) 229-5660.

Richmond Road

Williamsburg's shopping district is mostly found in and around the Colonial Williamsburg area, and on Richmond Road/Route 60 West.

It is on Richmond Road that you will find representatives of the nation's fast-food eateries and local restaurants, dozens of motels, and an impressive collection of discount and outlet shops.

The first group of outlet stores is closer to Colonial Williamsburg on Route 60; you'll find several modern shopping centers filled with shops. But don't stop there; keep driving westward about five miles—the stores will drop away for a while and give way to farmland—and then you will come to the old Williamsburg Pottery Center, a ramshackle collection of old potting sheds that is filled with all sorts of outlet shops.

A Touch of Earth. 6580 Richmond Road: (757) 565-0425. American crafts gallery.

Boyer's Diamond & Gold Outlet. 6564 Richmond Road: (757) 565-0747.

Candle Factory Outlet. 7521 Richmond Road, at Williamsburg Soap & Candle Co., seven miles west of Williamsburg: (757) 564-3354. Shops include the Candle Shop, Needlecraft Shop, Candy Shop, Christmas Shop, Country Store, and Emporium.

Lamplighter Shoppe. 6502 Richmond Road: (757) 565-4676. Period specialty lighting.

Pfaltzgraff Factory Store. Pottery complex, Lightfoot: (757) 564-3064.

Prime Outlets at Williamsburg. 5715-62A Richmond Road: (757) 565-0702. Designer outlet center with shops that include Brooks Brothers, Cole Haan, Eddie Bauer, Ann Klein, and more.

Williamsburg Doll Factory. 7441 Richmond Road: (757) 564-9703.

Williamsburg Outlet Mall. I-64, Exit 234, Route 60: (757) 565-3378. More than sixty stores, including outlets from Arrow, Bass, Bugle Boy, Dress Barn, Jockey, L'Eggs, Levi's, London Fog, Swank, Totes, and many others.

Williamsburg Pottery Factory. Route 60 West, Lightfoot: (757) 564-3326. Four million people a year visit this 200-acre complex founded in 1938. Shops include pottery, glass, crystal, fine china, plants, carpets, kitchenware, candles, brass, toys, wicker, linens, furniture, and more. This place has to be seen to be believed—it is the exact opposite of the picture-perfect modern mall and a whole lot more fun. We especially enjoy the food section, where you can purchase spices and sauces from places you may not have known existed. Good for a few hours of shopping entertainment; call for hours, which vary seasonally.

Recreation at Williamsburg

There is a wide range of outdoor recreational opportunities in and around Williamsburg. Many of the golf courses are affiliated with resorts, but most are open to visitors.

Golf

Colonial Williamsburg's Golden Horseshoe Golf Courses at the Williamsburg Inn. The signature hotel at Colonial Williamsburg offers two championship courses and an executive course.

The Gold Course, designed by Robert Trent Jones in 1964, winds 6,750 yards through woodlands and over water. It stands alongside the Williamsburg Inn.

The Gold Course is a fairly traditional but difficult challenge with narrow fairways and small greens. In championship play, Jack Nicklaus holds the course record with a four-under-par 67.

The Green Course was designed in 1991 by Robert's son, Rees Jones. The course, a few miles south of the Williamsburg Inn, was cut out of 250 acres of dense woodlands that had been the private vacation playland of the Rockefeller family until the property was given to the Colonial Williamsburg Foundation in 1979.

The Green Course is wider and longer, playing to 7,120 yards from the championship tees. The links' design includes mounding and tall pines along the fairways and is generally more forgiving than the older course.

Additionally, there is the nine-hole 1,865-yard Spotswood course, also designed by Robert Trent Jones.

Greens fees for the championship courses in mid-2000 for the Gold course were $115 for visitors and $105 for guests of Colonial Williamsburg hotels;

at the Green course, fees were $95 for visitors and $90 for hotel guests. The Spotswood greens fee was $29 plus $15 for a cart. Call (757) 220-7696.

Ford's Colony Country Club. Located four miles west of Williamsburg, the club has two 18-hole wooded and wet courses. The four nines—red, white, blue, and gold—can be played in any order, with lengths from 5,500 to 6,700 yards.

The greens fee in mid-200 was $40 to $80 Monday through Thursday and $50 to $90 Friday through Sunday depending on time of day, including cart fee. *Discount coupon in this book.*

For information and reservations, call (757) 258-4130.

Kingsmill Golf Club. Home of three highly rated courses, the club sits alongside Busch Gardens Williamsburg, about ten miles southeast of Colonial Williamsburg. The club lies along the James River and near a large Anheuser-Busch plant; with the right wind conditions, the fairways are redolent with the sweet tang of brewing beer.

The River Course, designed by Pete Dye and playing 6,776 yards from the championship tees, has hosted the PGA Anheuser-Busch Golf Classic in recent years. It includes a range of elevated greens and deep ravines. The most famous hole is the 177-yard par-3 17th, which runs parallel to the river.

The Plantation Course was designed by Arnold Palmer and Ed Seay. The fairways weave through tall pines to greens that are considered an especially difficult putting challenge. The Woods Course was designed by Tom Clark with Curtis Strange (who has a home at Kingsmill).

Greens fees for the River Course seven days a week are $150; resort guests receive a discount. At the Woods and Plantation courses, green fees every day are $100.

Also at Kingsmill is the Bray Links par three, nine-hole course on the banks of the James River. The course includes glow-in-the-dark markers, and some lighting allows golfing into the dark. There's also a driving range.

For information and reservations at Kingsmill Golf, call (757) 253-3906 or (800) 832-5665. www.virginiagolf.com/kingsmill.html.

Tennis at Williamsburg

Kingsmill Tennis Club. Fifteen clay courts. $12 per hour for resort guests, and $36 per hour for visitors. Hard courts free to guests and $18 per hour for hard courts. For reservations, call (757) 253-3945.

Williamsburg Inn. Eight courts near Providence Hall. For reservations, call (757) 229-1000.

Boating

Waller Mill Park. Route 645, just off Route 60 West. A free city park, with canoes, rowboats, and paddleboats available for rent. Open from April to October.

Chapter 20
Jamestown and Yorktown

Jamestown Settlement

The Jamestown-Yorktown Foundation is an agency of the Commonwealth of Virginia, administering Jamestown Settlement and the Yorktown Victory Center. A combination ticket with Yorktown Victory Center is available: adult $14; child 6–12, $6.75. Seniors 62 and older receive a 10 percent discount. Ticket prices for Jamestown alone are adult $10.25; child 6–12, $5.

The museum, located on Route 31 South, is open daily 9 A.M.–5 P.M., except Christmas and New Year's Day. (757) 253-4838. www.historyisfun.org.

Directions from Colonial Williamsburg to Jamestown

Take Colonial Parkway west and south to its end, about ten miles.

The Loneliness of Jamestown

Spain and Portugal were global powers in the sixteenth century, with major trading posts in Asia, Africa, and the Americas. English traders and military sought to counter Spain's growing influence, and by the end of the century they had moved into the Mediterranean and the Far East; the initial moves to the Americas included unsuccessful colonies near Jamestown in the 1570s and at Roanoke, Virginia, in the 1580s.

On December 20, 1606, fourteen years before the Pilgrims landed in Plymouth, Massachusetts, 104 men and boys set sail from England in three tiny merchant ships.

The *Susan Constant*, *Godspeed*, and *Discovery* arrived at what is now Jamestown Island in the spring of 1607, and on May 14 of that year the passengers began building the first permanent English colony in America. It was intended as a profitmaking venture of the Virginia Company of London.

The story of the settlement is told at two sites in Jamestown: The Jamestown Settlement, run by the Jamestown-Yorktown Foundation, an agency of the Commonwealth of Massachusetts, and the Colonial National Historical Park, run by the National Park Service.

And the area became instantly more attractive to millions of youngsters

The real Pocahontas.
According to the legends (and as more or less retold by Disney) Pocahontas, daughter of Chief Powhatan, saved the life of Captain John Smith from execution by Powhatan. She was captured by Captain Samuel Argall in March 1613, near Henricus Historical Park in Richmond. Argall was unable to negotiate with Chief Powhatan, and Argall passed Pocahontas along to Reverend Alexander Whitaker, minister at the Henricus church; it was there that she was converted to Christianity and baptized Rebecca. After her marriage in 1614, she and John Rolfe returned to a location in what is now Chesterfield County at a plantation known as "Varina." Rolfe took her to England in 1616, where she was received as a princess. A year later, she died as they prepared to return home and was buried at Gravesend, England. She was just twenty-two when she died.

with the release of the Disney film *Pocahontas*, which more or less retold the true story of the Native American princess at Jamestown.

The settlers at Jamestown moved to a more favorable site in Williamsburg in 1699, abandoning the first "permanent" English settlement in the New World.

Today's Two Jamestowns

There are actually two Jamestowns to visit; one is real but not very exciting, and the other is completely fabricated but very educational.

The original town site is maintained by the National Park Service and includes the foundations for the actual fort; the foundations, though, are buried below ground for preservation. Significant archaeological digs are under way in the area most of the time.

Also in the park is a reconstructed church and a mass grave for some of the 440 (out of 500) colonists who died in the winter of 1609–10.

Jamestown Settlement

The Commonwealth of Virginia's historical park is located about a mile from the original site and is completely reconstructed.

The Jamestown Settlement is open 9 A.M.– 5 P.M. daily. Admission: adult $9.75; child 6–12, $4.75. A combination ticket with Jamestown Settlement is adult $13.50; and child $6.50.

Some 500,000 visitors per year come to the Jamestown restoration, and about 100,000 visit the state's other restoration at Yorktown (see section later in this chapter). Busiest times at Jamestown are April through early fall.

The small restoration area includes some interesting re-creations of Native American villages and an English fort; the biggest draw is the three re-created ships tied up on a small pier on the James River. (The ships themselves are considered historically accurate and include some tight spaces and steep stairs that may not be easily negotiated by all visitors.)

The museum at the restoration displays an interesting collection of items, including a silver Siegburg stoneware jug, supposedly presented by King James I to Pocahontas as a New Year's gift during her visit to England. She died, at age twenty-two, before being able to return and was buried on March 21, 1617, in Gravesend, England.

There are three principal galleries at the museum, covering the Powhatan Indians, the English settlers, and the story of Jamestown. The museum also features a twenty-minute film, *Jamestown: The Beginning*, which dramatizes the difficult first twenty years of the colony.

Shortly before the English settlers arrived in 1607, the powerful leader Powhatan won control of thirty-two Algonquian-speaking tribes in coastal Virginia. The Powhatan Indian Gallery traces the story of the tribe, going back more than 10,000 years, examining their food, shelter, clothing, social structure, religion, and government.

Slow boat to Virginia. A plaque at the visitors center commemorates the voyage of the *Godspeed* in 1985. In that year, the ship now moored at the restoration successfully re-created the 1606–1607 voyage of the settlers from England to Virginia, following the original route and with no auxiliary power.

Outside the doors of the museum, the restoration is frozen in time in 1614, seven years after the first settlers arrived; that date was chosen because it marked the first arrival of women at the outpost. (That date also predates by five years the first arrival of slaves at Jamestown, and that subject is not explored in depth at the restoration.)

Interpreters at the restoration do not take on the stories of real settlers, but instead are well schooled as teachers about their areas of specialization at the village, fort, or ships.

One of the Native-American dwellings is a "yehakin," a form of tepee made of woven reeds or marsh grass. A fire was usually kept going at all times, and there was a small hole in the roof for the smoke to exit, although much of the smoke would linger just a few feet above the floor, and people within would hunch down low to stay out of it.

Seventeenth-century navigation aboard the Susan Constant *at Jamestown Settlement*
Photo by Commonwealth of Virginia
Jamestown–Yorktown Foundation

Shipping news.
Godspeed. Overall
length 68′, beam 14′8″,
mainmast height 55′.
Passengers and crew in
1607, approximately
fifty-two. The replica was
built in 1984.
   Discovery. Overall
length 49′6″, beam
11′4″, mainmast height
42′. Passengers and crew
in 1607, approximately
twenty-two. The replica
was built in 1984.
   Susan Constant.
Overall length 116′,
beam 24′10″, mainmast
height 95′. Passengers
and crew in 1607,
approximately seventy-
one. The replica was
built in 1990.

A "scarecrow hut" on stilts was used by young boys to practice hunting skills and to scare off birds or animals that might scavenge in the gardens.

The restoration does not have anybody playing the character of Pocahontas, but the interpreters at the site are able to tell what is known about her story at Jamestown, including life as a young member of the Powhatan tribe when the English came, and her brief association with people such as John Smith, her marriage to John Rolfe, and her departure for England where she lived and died. Jamestown historians are somewhat suspicious of John Smith's story because his is the only account of Pocahontas saving his life.

Soon after arriving, the English settlers built a palisaded fort for protection against attacks they feared might come from Native Americans or from Spanish explorers. In 1610, James Fort was described as a triangular wall constructed of planks and posts; within its walls was a storehouse, church, and guardhouse. Much of the construction was "wattle and daub"; wattle is woven wood held together with mud and grasses, known as daub. By 1617, the fort was in total disrepair.

There is a great deal of attention to detail at the restoration, down to color and shape of the rough posts that make up the fort. Several years ago the posts began to rot out; before they were replaced, the restoration sent an artist to England to look at some original watercolors of similar forts of that time. The result included lighter colors for the wood and split logs instead of round posts.

Modern visitors can explore the forge and blacksmith's shop, the church, and an armory; an interpreter regularly demonstrates loud and inaccurate matchlock muskets and rifles regularly; these weapons are open-pan gunpowder devices that use loose charges. Children can try on replicas of seventeenth-century English armor.

The first thing that strikes visitors when they arrive at the three ships is how small they are; stop and consider a voyage across the Atlantic within one.

The *Susan Constant, Godspeed,* and *Discovery* arrived at the mouth of Chesapeake Bay in April 1607; their trip had been delayed about six weeks when they were stuck just off the coast of England because of bad winds.

The initial voyage from England to Jamestown carried only men, because the settlers were establishing a military outpost. Freight included twenty-four cannons, which also served as ballast on the trip over; all of the heavy cannons as well as heavy barrels of supplies had to be hoisted into and out of the cramped holds below deck.

Researchers lost track of the *Susan Constant* after its first voyage; the vessel returned to England and may have been renamed or lost. The *Godspeed* also returned to England. The *Discovery* stayed at Jamestown because its small size allowed the settlers to navigate the river and other nearby areas.

The *Susan Constant* is the third such vessel to bear that name in Jamestown. The 1990 reproduction replaced one that Jamestown built as a temporary display in 1957; the wooden timbers rotted away. In any case, the first reconstruction was not believed to be historically accurate in its design.

The original *Susan Constant* disappeared from the records after its 1607 voyage to Jamestown, but researchers found documents in England, including a 1606 High Court of the Admiralty case, that included some of its specifications. Archaeological work on old shipwrecks, including that of the *Sea Venture*, wrecked in Bermuda in 1609 while en route from England to Jamestown, provided more information.

The original ship was constructed of English elm and oak, but this lumber was not available to modern carpenters; instead, researchers went to South America to obtain rot-resistant hardwoods such as greenheart, mora, purpleheart, and courbaril. Construction began in December 1989, with much of the work done by hand to maintain the appearance of the main and lower decks. Modern paints were applied to the hull to help preserve it. The new *Susan Constant* underwent sea trials in February 1991.

One modern improvement—hidden from the public—is the twin diesel engines in the hold. They were added for safety and to help ensure that the vessel could meet its appointed schedule for educational events in the area.

Driving to Jamestown

As you drive from Williamsburg toward Jamestown on the Colonial Parkway, the road suddenly opens up to a broad vista with creeks on one side and the bay on the other side.

At this location, a small group of Spanish Jesuits attempted a settlement in September of 1570. According to state historians, they were believed to have entered James River, landed along the creek, and crossed the peninsula to establish a mission near the York River. Six months later they were all massacred by Indians, except for one young boy who was rescued by a relief expedition in 1572.

On May 12, 1607, the colonists who the next day went on to establish Jamestown, landed at the mouth of what is now College Creek. One of the visitors, Captain Gabriel Archer, liked the spot and wanted to settle there but was outvoted by the others; for more than a century the creek was known as Archer's Hope.

The great Indian massacre of March 22, 1622, during which a quarter of the population of Virginia was slain, came nearest to Jamestown at the small community of Archer's Hope, where five persons were killed.

As you head toward Jamestown, the James River lies on the left side; it was known by the Native Americans as the Powhatan River. Colonists renamed it in honor of James I, their sovereign. Rising in the Appalachians, it flows eastward 340 miles to Chesapeake Bay; its mouth is the shipping port of Hampton Roads.

The Colonial National Historical Park

The Colonial National Historical Park, under the jurisdiction of the National Park Service, includes the site of the original Jamestown landing, the Yorktown battlesite, and the Colonial Parkway that connects them both.

Within the gates of the Jamestown park are ongoing archaeological excavation projects as well as exhibits including the reconstructed Glasshouse where you will see costumed craftsmen demonstrating the art of glassblowing, one of the first industries in America. Nearby are the ruins of the original glass furnaces built in 1608.

At the Jamestown Visitor Center and Museum are exhibits and a fifteen-minute orientation film. The museum contains one of the most extensive collections of seventeenth-century artifacts in the country. In season, park rangers conduct tours.

The tides of the James River have washed away part of the former town, but ruins of the early settlement are still visible, including the brick tower of a church built on the island in 1639. Statues and monuments memorialize important personalities and events in Jamestown's past, while twentieth-century bricks outline the excavated foundations of three seventeenth-century homes. The Tercentenary Monument, erected in 1907 on the 300th anniversary of Jamestown's founding, is a 103-foot-tall shaft of New Hampshire granite. There's also a statue of Pocahontas near the Visitor Center, and one of Captain John Smith.

Finally, there is the Loop Drive, a five-mile auto tour through the marshes and pine forests of the island, presenting views much like those seen by the first colonists in 1607.

Open year-round 9 A.M.–5 P.M. Admission is $5 per person 17 years and older. Visitors who have National Park Service passes, including Golden Eagle, Golden Age, and Golden Access, are allowed free entrance. (757) 898-3400. www.nps.gov/colo.

Colonial National Historical Park is located a short distance from Interstate 64 (I-64). Eastbound from the Richmond area via I-64, take route 199, exit 242A for Jamestown or exit 242B for Yorktown, to the Colonial Parkway. Follow the parkway to its end.

Other James River Plantations

The James River settlements were in many ways the cradle for the southern economic system, giving rise to plantation farming, slaveholding, and a British-tinged culture. Some plantations open for tours include:

Edgewood Plantations. A Victorian-Gothic home dating to the 1870s, it includes twelve large rooms with ten fireplaces and a ghost. (800) 296-3343.

Flowerdew Hundred. An archaeological dig has uncovered much of the history of this plantation that dates back to 1618. An escorted tour includes a museum, a reconstructed kitchen of the 1820s, and the commemorative eighteenth-century-style, wind-powered gristmill. Open Tuesday to Sunday 10 A.M.–5 P.M. from April through November. Winter visits by appointment. Admission: adult $4; child $2.50. South side of the James River, off Route 10, at 1617 Flowerdew Hundred Road, Hopwell, Virginia. (804) 541-8897.

Shirley Plantation. A working plantation, it has been occupied by the same family for hundreds of years. (804) 829-5121 or (800) 232-1613. Open daily 9 A.M.–5 P.M. Abbreviated hours in winter. Admission: adult $9; senio, $8; child 13–21, $6; child 6–12, $5.

Yorktown

Yorktown was a prosperous tobacco port in the seventeenth century, and the banks along the York River were filled with handsome brick homes of the shipowners and traders. The Revolutionary War came to Yorktown in 1781 when British general Cornwallis retreated into Virginia after his unsuccessful campaign in the Carolinas; arriving in the port of Yorktown, he and his 7,000 troops fortified their position and waited for reinforcements they expected to come from Sir Henry Clinton in New York. Clinton delayed, and the French fleet of Admiral de Grasse blockaded Chesapeake Bay. From the land side, Generals Washington and Rochambeau rushed south from positions as far away as Rhode Island while the armies under the command of Steuben and Lafayette held Cornwallis in place.

Surrounded and running out of food, the trapped British general surrendered on October 19, 1781. Soon after, Britain sued for peace, and the thirteen rebellious colonies were able to form the United States of America.

Today, visitors to Yorktown can tour the battleground and see Colonial-era homes, the historic wharf along the York River including the Watermen's Museum on Water Street, which explores the history and lore of the fishermen of the Chesapeake Bay, and a visitors center operated by the National Park Service.

Park Service signs indicate the positions of British, French, and American forces throughout the siege. At the battle site is the Victory Monument inscribed with the names of Americans known to have lost their lives in the Yorktown campaign. Nearby is another monument commemorating the French allies who died at Yorktown.

Directions from Colonial Williamsburg to Yorktown

Take the Colonial Parkway east about eleven miles. You will come to an exit to Route 238 to the Yorktown Victory Center; about a mile farther on, the road ends at the Yorktown National Park Visitor Center.

Yorktown Victory Center

Open daily 9 A.M.–5 P.M., except Christmas and New Year's Day. (757) 253-4838. www.historyisfun.com.

Admission: adult $7.25; child 6–12, $3.50. A combination ticket with James-town Settlement: adult $13.50; child $6.50.

The Yorktown Victory Center opened in 1976 as one of three state bicen-tennial centers; its impressive new exhibition galleries were added in 1995.

The Road to Revolution is an open-air exhibit that traces some of the most important events that led to the American Revolution, presented on a time line. Pavilions along the pathway explore such events and issues as the French and Indian War and its effects on the relationship between Great Britain and the colonies, the resistance of the colonists to new taxes imposed by the British to pay off war debts, the Tea Act and the Boston Tea Party, and, finally, the events that led up to armed conflict at Lexington and Concord.

The center's Exhibit Galleries hold more than 500 period artifacts, includ-ing maps, books, military equipment, personal effects, and household objects. Among the best displays is "Yorktown's Sunken Fleet," which tells the story of the British ships lost during the siege of 1781—many of which still lie on the bottom of the York River. Some of the items on display were recovered from underwater exploration sites. Although some of the ships were sunk by enemy fire, at least a dozen vessels were scuttled to prevent their capture. Sur-veys in the 1970s located nine of the ships, and one, the *Betsy*, was the object of extensive archaeological exploration. Among items on display from that ves-sel are musket balls, ceramics, military items, and personal effects.

A Time of Revolution, an eighteen-minute movie set in an encampment dur-ing the Siege of Yorktown, is presented every half-hour.

The Witnesses to Revolution gallery personalizes the War for Indepen-dence using the experiences of ten people whose lives were greatly affected by the conflict. Among them are Boston King and Jehu Grant, two slaves who cast their lots with opposing sides in the Revolution, and Little Abraham, a Mohawk chief who struggled to keep his tribe neutral in the conflict.

Outside the exhibit hall is a Continental Army Encampment. Interpreters representing soldiers and their families who accompanied them to war depict daily life during the Revolution. Demonstrations include cannon and musket firing, military drills, and a field kitchen. Another area depicts a farmsite of the 1780s, with a garden, tobacco barn, and log kitchen.

The Yorktown Victory Center and Jamestown Settlement are administered by the Jamestown–Yorktown Foundation, an educational agency of the Com-monwealth of Virginia.

Colonial National Historical Park at Yorktown

The National Park Service's site at Yorktown is free to the public and includes reconstructed earthworks and siege lines marking the pattern of British and American troops during the battle. Cannons, including many pieces dating back to the Revolution, stand ready behind some of the embattlements.

Re-created 1780s farm at Yorktown Victory Center
Photo by Commonwealth of Virginia Jamestown-Yorktown Foundation

The tour of the battlefield begins at the National Park Service Visitor Center where the battle on land and at sea is presented through a series of multimedia exhibits. Visitors can also walk through a full-sized replica of the quarterdeck of a British warship and examine artifacts that include the field tents used by General George Washington during the siege.

There is also a sixteen-minute film, and park rangers offer tours in season; auto tape tours can be rented at the Visitor Center gift shop. Nearby are the restored eighteenth-century homes of Augustine Moore and Thomas Nelson.

The **Moore House** is where the surrender terms for the battle of Yorktown were negotiated.

The home of Thomas Nelson Jr., a signer of the Declaration of Independence and commander of the Virginia militia, is considered a fine example of Georgian architecture. The walls still bear the scars of cannonballs fired in 1781. Interior woodwork reveals modifications made in 1862 when the house served as a hospital during the Civil War. The Nelson and Moore homes are open for tours for most of the year, closed in the winter.

The Yorktown site is open daily 9 A.M.–5 P.M., with extended hours from spring through fall. For information, call (757) 898-3400.

The Yorktown Visitor Center is open daily in summer months from 8:30 A.M.–5:30 P.M., in winter months from 9 A.M.–5 P.M., and in spring and fall from 8:30 A.M.–5 P.M.

Newport News

Naval fans will want to add a visit to Newport News, one of America's most important military ports and shipping centers, about thirty-two miles east of Williamsburg and not far from Yorktown.

Newport News was an important embarkation point for supplies during World War II and also played a part in nearly every major American military adventure.

To drive to Newport News, head east on Route 199 to I-64 East; travel twenty-three miles to I-664 South into the city.

Mariners' Museum. 100 Museum Drive: (757) 596-2222. For information, call (800) 581-7245, or consult the Web page at www.mariner.org.

Open daily from 10 A.M.–5 P.M. Admission: adult $5; student $3; child ages 5 and younger, free. A family ticket for four people is $13. *Discount coupon in this book.*

One of the largest international maritime museums in the world, it features more than 35,000 maritime items that include ship models, scrimshaw, maritime paintings, decorative arts, intricately carved figureheads, navigational instruments, working steam engines, and more. Also on display are artifacts from the ironclad USS *Monitor*, which engaged in a famous clash with its Confederate counterpart the CSS *Virginia* (formerly the USS *Merrimack*) in the Civil War. The remains of the *Monitor* herself lie on the ocean bottom off North Carolina's Outer Banks, where the ship sank in a storm in 1862.

Peninsula Fine Arts Center. 101 Museum Drive: (757) 596-8175. Art exhibitions.

Virginia Living Museum. 524 J. Clyde Morris Boulevard: (757) 595-1900. Native wildlife and plants. *Discount coupon in this book.*

War Memorial Museum of Virginia. 9285 Warwick Boulevard: (757) 247-8523. Artifacts from every U.S. war since the Revolution.

U.S. Army Transportation Museum. Building 300; Washington Boulevard, Fort Eustis: (757) 878-1182.

WILLIAMSBURG, YORKTOWN, AND JAMESTOWN

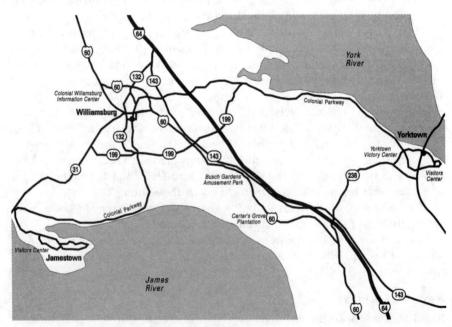

Chapter 21
Busch Gardens Williamsburg

Tucked into the lush woods of Old Virginia is a fanciful re-creation of Old World Europe merged with modern-day entertainment, by most every opinion one of the prettiest amusement parks in the world.

Busch Gardens Williamsburg, like the other Anheuser-Busch parks around the nation, is an unusually green theme park, in this case set on 360 acres of rolling countryside.

Each of the nine areas of the park is designed to evoke a particular part of Europe, with the addition of more than thirty thrill rides, live shows, restaurants, and a children's adventureland. New in 2000 was Jack Hanna's Wild Reserve, an animal adventure area set in the ruins of a seventeenth-century castle and offering closeup views of gray wolves and other creatures.

Busch Gardens Williamsburg is about fifteen minutes from Colonial Williamsburg and worth most of a full day. Nearby is Water Country USA, open for wet recreation in warm months. And Anheuser-Busch also operates a beer brewery just outside of the park; it is open for free tours most days.

Must-Sees

- **WOW** Apollo's Chariot (coaster)
- **WOW** Alpengeist (coaster)
- **WOW** Loch Ness Monster (coaster)
- **WOW** King Arthur's Challenge (simulator)
- **WOW** Land of the Dragons (adults without children excused)
- **WOW** Big Bad Wolf (coaster)
- **WOW** Drachen Fire (coaster)
- **WOW** Wild Maus (coaster)
- **WOW** Escape from Pompeii (water ride)
- **WOW** Roman Rapids (water ride)

Power Trip

Busch Gardens Williamsburg has two basic tourist conditions: crowded and lonely. It is crowded for much of the summer, holiday periods, and most weekends; it is pleasantly underpopulated in the spring and fall.

You'll know very quickly whether you'll need to put into effect a Power Trip plan if you arrive soon after opening time and are shown to a parking space that seems to be located in the next county.

On busy days, set your goal for one of the major attractions as soon as you enter any major park. The Apollo's Chariot coaster in the Festa Italia section is a major draw for thrill seekers, along with the Alpengeist coaster in Rhinefeld. If these rides seem too wild for your tastes, you might want to start your day at Escape from Pompeii, a bit lower down on the thrill scale.

If you come to the park after the first wave of visitors is already in line, head away from Alpengeist or Apollo's Chariot for one of the other attractions and finish your day where the early birds started.

Depending on the season and crowd, some parts of the park will open later than others. For example, on the slow day when I visited, the English area and Pompeii opened at 10 A.M., but Fiesta Italia didn't open until 10:30 A.M.

Busch Gardens 2000 Ticket Prices

One-day pass
General admission	$37
Child (3–6)	$30
Senior (55+)	$34

Twilight admission after 3 P.M. for 7 P.M. close;
after 5 P.M. for 10 P.M. close.
General admission	$31
Child (3–6)	$24

Two-day pass
General admission	$53
Child	$44

Three-day pass, unlimited admission to
Busch Gardens and Water Country USA
within a 14-day period
General admission/Child	$60

Season pass Busch Gardens Williamsburg
General admission	$93.95
Child	$73.95

Eurosplash Pass (Busch Gardens/Water
Country USA season pass)
General admission	$125.95
Child	$105.95

Parking

Cars $6, Oversized vehicles $9

Hours vary for twilight tickets depending on closing hours; call for information. Three-day tickets must be used within fourteen days of purchase.

Operating Schedule: The park opens at the end of March, operating weekends, certain Fridays, and Easter week through mid-May. From mid-May through Labor Day the park is open daily. From Labor Day through the end of October, the park is open daily except for Wednesday and Thursday. Operating hours begin at 10 A.M., with closing at 7 P.M. in the off-season and 10 P.M. or midnight in the summer season and holidays. In the fall, the park closes at 6 P.M. weekdays. Call (800) 772-8886 to confirm hours and operating days. Busch Gardens maintains a Web page at www.buschgardens.com.

Hamlets

England: Banbury Cross

Beneath a replica of London's Big Ben, and near Shakespeare's Globe Theatre lies a quaint English hamlet that has shops, restaurants, and entertainment.

Pirates, a rollicking 4-D adventure, sets sail from The Globe Theatre in Banbury Cross, led by comic actor Leslie Nielsen and Monty Python star Eric Idle, who also wrote the appropriately silly story.

Nielsen and his gang search for a pirate's treasure on a Caribbean island. They think they've got the booty all to themselves, but then there's Davey, a young lad played by Adam Wylie of the television series *Picket Fences*, who has survived the journey and secretly waits on the island to plot his revenge.

Davey crafts booby traps that send the buccaneers on a frenzied escapade. The pirates battle fierce bats and angry hornets and journey through a dark, mysterious cave. High-tech effects and 4-D images pull guests into the midst of the action. The fifteen-minute film is presented on a 60-foot-wide, three-story-high screen.

In 2000, Busch Gardens opened **Jack Hanna's Wild Reserve**, focusing on the elusive gray wolf. Visitors will learn about the wolf's fierce loyalty to its pack, observe its unique behavioral patterns, and most important, understand the need to protect it.

Nearby, an interactive aviary is home to a flock of lorikeets, known for their brilliant plumage and their ability to acclimate to humans. Inside the aviary, guests become perches as lorikeets alight on arms, shoulders and even heads.

England: Hastings

At the **Threadneedle Faire**, visitors can test their skills on thirteenth-century Medieval England games of crossbow, Jacob's Ladder, and slingshot.

The area is also home to **Eagle Canyon**, a natural habitat for bald eagles. The birds were brought here because of injuries suffered in the wild; though their rehabilitation from injury is complete, the effects of their injuries prevent them from being returned to their native habitat. Also nearby is **Feathered Follies Theatre**, home of the "World of Birds" show that includes free-flight demonstrations by hawks, owls, vultures, and other creatures.

WOW King Arthur's Challenge. A high-tech trip back in time for a journey of sensation and fantasy through a legendary castle.

Loch Ness Monster
Photo by Scott K. Brown © 2000 Busch Gardens Williamsburg

There are two identical simulators, each seating about sixty travelers for a four-minute ride. On busy days, we'd suggest heading for King Arthur's Challenge early or late in the day.

The attraction replaces the fanciful Questor simulator adventure.

Hastings is also the location for a pair of special shows: Totally Television, a live song and dance revue saluting the 60-year history of television, and The Enchanted Laboratory, a mystical show based on computer animation and special effects.

Scotland: Heatherdowns

The home of the fearsome Loch Ness Monster, one of the largest roller coasters in the world. Much more down to earth are the world-famous **Anheuser-Busch Clydesdales**; they can be seen in their stables here and on tour around the park.

WOW **Loch Ness Monster.** The yellow tracks of the Loch Ness Monster fly out over the river from its home in Heatherdowns. It's a bit smaller than Drachen Fire, another huge coaster; likewise, the turns and drops on Loch Ness are a bit smaller but tighter. The wheels stay beneath your car, except when the car and the track are over your head, of course. Just for thrills, the trains dive through a dark cavern about midway through the trip.

The two-minute ride travels 3,240 feet. The first drop is 114 feet, accelerating riders to a top speed of more than sixty miles per hour in 2.5 seconds down a 55-degree angle. The main elements of the ride are the 48-foot-high first loop, the Monster's Lair, with a tight 40-foot spiral that will hold you in thrall for a long eighteen seconds, the third drop of sixty-six feet, and the second loop, which interlocks with the original loop of the ride.

France: Aquitaine

A petite French village that includes **Le Grand Gourmet**, a European dessert shop offering live entertainment.

In the summer, the **Royal Palace Theatre**, a 5,200-seat amphitheater, is home to ice shows, laser shows, and other special events.

The statue in the French courtyard represents the archangel Michael thrusting a spear through an attacking Lucifer who has disguised himself as a winged demon.

La Grand Glace offers ice cream cones.

New France

A bit of Canada by way of France, with gift shops for pottery, leather crafts, and dolls. And apropos of not much is a country music show, Country 'Cross Country.

Le Scoot. A wet and slightly wild log flume.

Three Rivers Smokehouse. On the border between New France and Aquitaine is a barbecue smokehouse; in it's case, a French Canadian version of similar eateries at other Busch parks. You can order chicken, pork ribs, smoked briskets, and sampler platters for about $5 to $7. Before making your selection, check out the grill through the glass window that's around the side.

Tintype Shop. A stand offers an unusual variation on the dress-up photo studio. The instant pictures produced here are printed on sheets of metal, like an old tintype photo. Prices run from about $11 to $20.

Dizzy dizzy. Do you love roller coasters but lose your lunch when the cars go inverted? More to the point, do your young children love anything and everything on wheels or rails, and you don't? I take two Dramamine tablets (or generic travel sickness pills available in most pharmacies) in the morning, and perhaps a booster pill in the afternoon, and I'm off to the races.

The pill will also work for most children, in smaller doses.

Please, though, check with your family doctor if you have any doubts about the appropriateness of this over-the-counter medication for you or your children, especially if it will be used in combination with any other medicines. And be aware that some users find that Dramamine makes them sleepy, which could be a danger if you have to drive home from the park.

Germany: Rhinefeld

This German village is built around the **Kinder Karrussel**, an antique carousel manufactured in 1819. Visitors can take cruises on the "Rhine River" that flows through the park.

WOW Alpengeist. A terrifying avalanche crashed into Busch Gardens Williamsburg in the spring of 1997 with the arrival of Alpengeist, an attraction that claimed four world records in roller coaster history. Alpengeist—a ski lift gone wild—is the tallest and fastest inverted roller coaster ever cre-

The strolling Boogie Band

Photo by Scott K. Brown © 2000 Busch Gardens Williamsburg

ated at 195 feet and sixty-seven miles per hour, also including the largest vertical loop at 106 feet, and largest drop at 170 feet (nearly seventeen stories) to appear on any inverted roller coaster to date. Riders sit on a bench locked in by an overhead harness; feet dangle free, except when their feet are over their heads.

The three-minute, 3,828-foot ride reaches a maximum G-force of 3.7 during the Cobra Roll, a boomerang inversion over the Rhine River. There's also an "Immelman" inverse diving loop; a Flat Spin, described as similar to flipping a pancake; and a Zero-G 360-degree roll. The trains consist of eight four-passenger cars.

Alpengeist (the name means "Ghost of the Alps") is the fourth among Busch Gardens's lineup of world-class roller coasters.

WOW   **Land of the Dragons**. A children's adventureland featuring a three-story-tall tree house, a children's theater, and pint-sized rides.

Germany: Oktoberfest

The entertainment gets wild at Oktoberfest, home to two of the fiercest roller coasters in the world, the **Big Bad Wolf** and **Drachen Fire**.

WOW   **Big Bad Wolf**. Its growl is a lot worse than its bite, if you can get up the nerve to get close. The Big Bad Wolf and others of its type were once a revolution in roller coaster technology. Riders are suspended from an overhead track, swinging out to the left and right as well as following the upward climbs and downward plunges of the rail.

Riders are firmly locked into place with a harness that comes down over their head and prevents arm movement; some may find the getup somewhat confining.

The ride itself is relatively short, with two principal high-speed areas. Although it is not as high or as fast as some other coasters at the park—and it does not go upside down—it seemed to me that you do perceive a great deal of change in gravitational force and some passing lightheadedness, but little in the way of weightlessness. Perhaps it is because the side-to-side swings pull the blood from your head to your legs.

The main plunge takes you on a picturesque drop toward the river and through a puff of mist.

While you're in the neighborhood, walk over toward Drachen Fire, even if you are not going to ride it. You'll be rewarded with a close-up view of Big Bad Wolf swinging by you, and a good view of the astounding Drachen Fire ride layout.

WOW **Wild Maus.** A coaster that sends four passengers at a time around a tight-turning steel track within a stack of tracks. The ride lasts about a minute-and-a-half, and the ten trains can accept about 1,120 passengers per hour.

Low riders. How high is high enough? Visitors must be at least forty-two inches tall to ride **DaVinci's Cradle, Flying Machine, Pompeii, Big Bad Wolf, Roman Rapids,** and **Wave Slings.** The minimum height is forty-eight inches for **Drachen Fire** and the **Loch Ness Monster.** Children under fifty-six inches in height must be accompanied by an adult for the **Skyride.**

Remember that these regulations are for the safety of young visitors; don't put heel lifts in kids' shoes or try to sneak them past the rulers at the turnstiles. It's not worth it.

The Wild Maus
Photo by Lawrence Jackson ©2000 Busch Entertainment Corp.

Hot times. The Roman city of Pompeii was wiped out in the summer of A.D. 79. Mount Vesuvius, which had lain dormant for centuries, suddenly awoke and bombarded the Mediterranean coastal city—an early luxury resort—for three days. Archaeologists believe that 16,000 residents perished under 20-foot piles of pumice and ash. The volcano's eruption was so fast that many were buried where they stood, leaving shells or molds of their bodies perfectly preserved in the ash.

Also preserved were many of the buildings of Pompeii. When the town was excavated, researchers found massive stone blocks that show the tracks of ancient chariot wheels, finely furnished homes with mosaic floors, and even wall slogans from an election of nearly 2,000 years ago.

WOW **Drachen Fire.** This is one seriously twisted ride, a huge steel roller coaster that has more ups-and-downs and twists than an entire congressional delegation.

The blue track and pylons of Drachen Fire (Dragon Fire) lie just past Oktoberfest. After a long, slow climb to the highest point on the ride, the coaster cars drop sharply, twisting and turning upside-down before entering into a set of tight descending loops. And that's just the beginning. Each time you think you may be coming to the end of the ride, there's another plunge or twist or upside-down section.

The steel construction allowed the designers to put just about every conceivable squiggle onto the track, and I can't think of many they missed. Unusual elements include the Batwing, which rolls cars upside down twice in a boomerang-like motion; the Cutback, which rotates cars upside down on the inside of a loop; and the Camelback Hump, which delivers a zero-G floating effect.

The two-minute ride travels 3,550 feet, with a top speed in excess of sixty miles per hour.

For those who are not brave—or crazy—enough to ride Drachen Fire, there are several places where you and your camera can approach and watch others go through its exquisite torture.

Das Festhaus, a 2,000-seat German festival hall complete with an Oompah band and dancers. The large, barnlike restaurant opens at 11:30 A.M. for German foods, including knockwurst, bratwurst, smoked pork, and hot German potato salad. Shows start at lunch and continue through dinnertime.

Other rides in Oktoberfest include **Der Wirbelwind** wave swing and **Der Autobahn** bumper cars.

Italy: San Marco

A little slice of Italia, home to restaurants, shops, and entertainment, including the **Escape from Pompeii** water voyage.

Entertainment includes "That's Amoré," where classical Italian and Italian-American songs are presented on a regular schedule beginning around lunchtime. In the summer visitors can also enjoy the sounds of swing when the **Starlight Orchestra** takes the stage.

Next to San Marco is Da Vinci's Garden of Inventions, which features five rides dedicated to the famed fifteenth-century inventor and artist.

WOW **Escape from Pompeii.** Boarding a 20-passenger boat, visitors climb an incline to float back in time to explore the ancient Italian city of Pompeii. That's the easy part; to get out, they'll have to escape the flames of the volcanic eruption of Mount Vesuvius.

Guests are invited by the archaeological staff to tour a section of ruins that has become flooded by natural springs during the years. The journey begins as a tour boat lifts the visitors to the top of the ruined structure.

Once inside, a tremendous rumbling and booming noise is heard. The work lights flicker and then die, and all that is left are the dim emergency lamps. The boat enters a room where just minutes before archaeologists had been studying wall paintings. The rumble suddenly gives way to the sound of a huge timber cracking above; the supports crash down all around the boat.

The boat moves on to a large, majestic room with ancient mosaic floors and statues cracked and damaged by the flames of the erupting volcano. As the boat traverses the room, flames begin to spread everywhere.

The room fills with steam from the flowing lava . . . and the boat keeps

Escape from Pompeii
Photo by Scott K. Brown ©2000 Busch Entertainment Corp.

moving toward certain doom. The only way out is over a five-story drop into the lake below.

The Escape from Pompeii ride has very nice fire effects, including a neat overhead river of flame and a few crashing statues, but it is a very short ride (about four minutes) and there is only one plunge—what you see from the observation area is what you get.

Enter the glass-shielded observation area near the base of the drop where you can stand and watch the boats come over the top. You'll stay more-or-less dry within; actually, if you were to move an inch or so outside the shield you would get a lot wetter than the people on the ride do.

You will get wet in varying degrees. The very front row and the last row seem to get the wettest; if you want to get the least wet—I didn't say keep dry—you should go for the center seat in one of the two center rows. You also might want to take along a plastic bag for yourself or your camera, or leave any valuable items with another member of your party before you go on board.

There are two over-and-under rides. One is the **Battering Ram**, which is a pirate ship ride that rocks back and forth from an axis above your head—at least it's over your head when the ride begins; at some point in the ride, the axis will be beneath your upside-down head.

DaVinci's Cradle is a variation of the same ride, this time with the axis in the middle of the swing arm. Your movement is almost rectangular as you go back and forth until you go over in a complete circle.

Either way, they are surprisingly powerful, low-tech devices.

Ristorante della Piazza opens at 11:30 A.M., offering overstuffed club sandwiches, cannelloni, spaghetti, and chicken parmigiana for about $6 to $7. The attractive setting decorated in coral and green has indoor and out-door eating areas.

There is also an espresso and latté counter nearby.

Italy: Festa Italia

Across the bridge from San Marco, Festa Italia is like a permanent Italian street festival. It is also a dead-end at the Roman Rapids—if you don't want to ride the boat or take a spin on the teacup or tilt-a-whirl rides.

WOW **Apollo's Chariot.** The wild "hypercoaster" took roost in 1999, immediately becoming one of the major draws of the park. As many as three trains can simultaneously operate on the mile-long track, which sends riders through a succession of nine "camel back" humps in the track; the largest of the nine drops is an impressive 210 feet and the trains reach a top speed of more than seventy miles per hour.

Guest seats are elevated above the car frame, creating a sensation of free flight during the two-minute ride.

Apollo was the Greek and Roman god of the sun. According to myth, Apollo could be seen aboard his chariot driving the sun across the sky. When Apollo's son, Phaeton, took the reins from his father, he lost control of the powerful steeds. Phaeton drove too close to the heavens and then plunged too close to the earth, scorching both realms.

The new ride became nationally infamous at its grand opening when male model Fabio, a celebrity "god" taking the first official trip, was slightly injured in a collision with a bird. This sort of accident almost never happens, but for some reason, the gods ordained a meeting of the minds in front of dozens of cameras and reporters.

WOW **Roman Rapids.** This white-water raft adventure is attractively set among make-believe Roman ruins. The sign outside warns that riders will get "soaked"; we recommend you carry nothing on this ride you would not carry into a Roman bath.

To add insult to injury, there's a spot on the waterway where observers can shoot at the raft riders with coin-operated water guns.

Sea Dragon. A high-speed circular thrill ride.

Turkish Delight. A spinning teacup ride, nicely shielded from the sun and rain by a tent.

Trade Wind. A tilt-a-whirl, also undercover.

LeMans Raceway. Visitors ride in reproductions of old flivvers on junior and adult tracks.

Other Areas

Hospitality Center. A showcase for Anheuser-Busch enterprises, including brewery operations; adults can sample some of the beers.

Aeronaut Skyride. Gondolas connect England, France, and Germany in a 3,000-foot-long triangular path. The skyride runs in one direction only, from Zeppelin Landing to Banbury Cross to Aquitaine and back to Zeppelin Landing. You must exit the gondola at each station and get back in line there if you want to continue to another station.

The four-person gondola is a comfortable way to check out the lay of the land, giving good views of much of Busch Gardens. It also provides a way to avoid the hills and stairs that lie between Zeppelin Landing and Banbury Cross.

As you leave Heatherdowns and go across toward Aquitaine, you'll have a good view of the Clydesdale horse stables. In the fall, the view of the changing colors of the trees is worth a peek, although visitors from the Northeast will note the more limited palette available to southern trees.

Train. Balmoral Castle and Die Hochbiengen steam locomotives circle the park on a 1.5-mile course, crossing the Rhine River on a towering trestle. The trains make stops in Heatherdowns, New France, and Festa Italia.

Eagle One. A computer-operated sky bus, Eagle One, links Hastings with the Anheuser-Busch Hospitality Center.

Water Country USA

Surf's up at Water Country USA, a water park set on forty acres of beautiful woodlands, three miles west of Busch Gardens Williamsburg and less than ten minutes from Colonial Williamsburg.

Designed with a '50s and '60s beach theme, Water Country USA offers an excellent antidote to a warm summer day.

In 2000, the park introduced Bobsled, watery toboggan race.

Tickets

Prices were in effect for the 2000 season and are subject to change.

General admission:	$28.00
Child (3–6)	$20.50
Senior	$25.20
Twilight, after 3 p.m. (Adult/Child)	$19.00
Three-day pass, Water Country USA and Busch Gardens (Adult/Child)	$60.00
Season pass	
Adult	$93.95
Child	$73.95

Operating Schedule: Open early May weekends. Open daily from mid-May to Labor Day, plus two weekends in mid-September. The park is open 10 A.M.–8 P.M. in the summer months, closing one or two hours earlier at other times. Call (800) 772-8886 to confirm hours before your visit.

Slip Sliding Away

A new splish-splashin' water adventure awaits guys and gals at the mid-Atlantic's largest water play park in 2000. Guests are invited to gear up, four at a time, for a high-speed toboggan race full of twists, turns and banks.

Water Country USA's new zoom flume propels passengers at a rate of twenty-two feet per second—faster than any other ride in the park. And that, you can bank on, dude.

The **Bob Sled Ride** is a four-person surf-boggan raft through a summertime frozen landscape. The fastest and steepest of all Water Country USA slides, the 701-foot-long tube drops seventy-six feet.

At the center of the park is **Surfer's Bay**, a giant wave pool that has four-foot-high rollers.

Aquazoid. The coolest new thrill at Water Country USA, a four-person family water-raft ride that takes place within a completely enclosed darkened tunnel. Flashes of light and fiber optic lighting color the inside of the tube, and other images will appear on a water curtain within.

Big Daddy Falls. A river-raft ride on a gigantic four-person inner tube that splashes through 670 feet of twists and turns into a dark tunnel and then drops into a river that plunges over a PG-rated waterfall. The mammoth ride can take as many as 1,440 riders per hour.

Malibu Pipeline. Inspired by the awesome Bonzai and Oahu surfing pipelines, this two-person tube ride features double water flumes that are completely enclosed for most of its twisty, turny descent. The tubes break out into the open just before they plummet over a waterfall into a large splash pool.

Rambling River. A peaceful inner-tube ride on a lazy river through the scenic woods of the park.

Jet Stream. Four twisting, turning flumes send riders on a 415-foot plunge on inner tubes to a splash pool below.

Peppermint Twist. A tangle of tubes that spins riders down and around 180-degree curves to a watery splashdown.

Atomic Breakers. Whitewater rapids and whirlpools are connected by cascading waterfalls.

Wild Thang. A two-person ride around and around and over waterfalls.

The Lemon Drop, Water Country USA
© 1995 Water Country USA

Double Rampage. Thrill-seekers are propelled seventy-five feet straight down a slippery ramp on "Surf-boggans"; at the bottom they skim to a stop on a 120-foot watery skid pad.

Adventure Isle. A zany water obstacle course that has swinging ladders and inner-tube walks.

Lemon Drop. "Hydrochutes" rocket riders into a splash pool.

The children's area includes **Kids' Kingdom**, a world of pint-sized water slides, fountains, and play equipment.

Cow-A-Bunga. A new children's play area built around a 4,500-square-foot heated pool. There's a kiddie speedboat, three water slides, and lots of fountains.

Water Shows

Aquabatics. Presented daily in the **Caban-a-Rama Theatre**, the show combines breathtaking high dives from an 85-foot-high tower into an 11-foot-deep pool, and gravity-defying trampoline routines.

W. C. Duck Water Safety Show. Water Country USA's official mascot, W. C. Duck, helps teach children about water safety through song and dance and audience participation at the **Minnow Matinee Theater**.

Also presented at the Minnow Matinee Theater is the **Sea to Believe** show, which combines magical illusions and juggling routines for children of all ages.

Chapter 22
Richmond and Kings Dominion

In This Chapter

Richmond

Richmond has been the capital of the Commonwealth of Virginia since 1779, after the Founding Fathers moved out of difficult-to-defend Williamsburg during the Revolutionary War.

Then less than a century later, Richmond became the capital of the Confederacy during the Civil War from 1861 to 1865.

Richmond is one of the most important and most beautiful Revolutionary-era settlements in America; that beauty has persisted to this day in many of its restored homes and buildings and its dozens of monuments and statues.

Getting to Richmond

Richmond is about 109 miles south of Washington, D.C., via I-395 and I-95. Plan on about two hours to drive.

Richmond International Airport is just outside the city and offers more than 150 daily flights by carriers that include American, American Eagle, Continental, Delta Connection, Delta, Northwest, Northwest Airlink, United, United Express, USAir, and USAir Express.

The Greyhound/Trailways bus terminal is just outside downtown at 2910 North Boulevard. (800) 231-2222.

Amtrak connects to Washington and points beyond from a station outside of town at 7519 Staples Mill Road. Amtrak also serves Williamsburg with one or two trains a day. For information on Amtrak service, call (800) 872-7245.

The Story of Richmond

A settlement and trading post were established along the banks of the James River in 1637. William Byrd II, who inherited much of central Virginia, laid out what was to become the city of Richmond 100 years later on one of his estates.

The church in the village of Richmond, St. John's, was a center of Revolutionary rhetoric and was visited by Founding Fathers George Washington, Thomas Jefferson, and Patrick Henry, whose speeches led to the establishment of the Virginia militia.

During the war that followed, the state capital was moved from the more vulnerable Williamsburg to Richmond. The city, though, was entered by General Benedict Arnold, the turncoat whose very name now connotes treason, and was partly burned in 1781. Arnold's occupation lasted only a day, but Richmond was again invaded by Lord Charles Cornwallis and his troops on his way to the climactic battle at Yorktown.

The prosperous tobacco industry in the area and the deepwater port formed the foundation for the economy of Richmond.

In addition to its famous white Founding Fathers, Richmond was also the home of a number of notable African Americans, including Maggie Lena Walker, the nation's first black woman bank president; Wimbledon tennis champion Arthur Ashe; and the first elected black governor, Lawrence Douglas Wilder.

Museums and Government Buildings

Governor's Mansion. Ninth and Grace Streets. Call for tour times. (804) 371-8687. The oldest continuously occupied governor's house in the country, completed in 1814.

Virginia's state capitol. Jean-Antoine Houdon, a French-born neoclassical sculptor who lived from 1741 to 1828, produced pieces on some of the most notable men of his time, including Washington, Voltaire, Thomas Jefferson, Benjamin Franklin, and Prince Henry of Prussia. In his life, Washington posed for only one statue, the statue by Houdon that stands inside the Capitol Rotunda in Richmond.

State Library of Virginia. 800 East Broad Street. Monday to Friday 9 A.M.–5 P.M. Free. On Saturday, only the library shop and reading rooms are open to the public. (804) 692-3500. The collected records of Virginia and Virginians, dating back to 1823.

Virginia State Capitol. Free tours: December to March 9 A.M.–5 P.M. daily; 1–5 P.M. Sunday. April to November 9 A.M.–5 P.M. daily. (804) 698-1788. Thomas Jefferson laid out the design for the State Capitol building in 1785. Constructed of red brick, it was covered with stucco in 1800 and expanded in 1906, retaining most of its character over the years.

The tour includes details of the famous marble statue of George Washington by sculptor Jean-Antoine Houdon; Washington posed for the artist. Aaron Burr's treason trial was held here.

Richmond's Monuments

Monuments are scattered almost everywhere in Richmond, but Monument Avenue in the northwest quadrant forms an artistic and historical spine to the city. The creation of the Boulevard to celebrate heroes of the Confederacy began in 1890 when the Lee Monument was dedicated, with additional statuary installed during the next thirty-nine years. There were no further additions to Monument Avenue until 1995, when city officials elevated native son tennis star and writer Arthur Ashe to the Richmond pantheon with a monument at Roseneath Avenue.

Franklin Street becomes Monument Avenue at Lombardy Street, and the monuments extend west about one mile.

Jefferson Davis. The first and only president of the Confederate States of America. Created by Edward V. Valentine and installed in 1907, Monument Avenue at Davis Avenue in the Fan District.

General Thomas J. "Stonewall" Jackson. Confederate general Thomas J. "Stonewall" Jackson died of wounds from "friendly fire" at the battle of Chancellorsville in 1863. The monument by F. William Sievers was dedicated in 1919 at the Boulevard and Monument Avenue north of the Fan District.

General Robert E. Lee. Lee led the Army of Northern Virginia from June 1, 1862, until its surrender at Appomattox. Jean Antoine Mercie's statue was dedicated in 1890 at Allen Avenue on Monument Avenue, east of the Fan District.

Matthew Fontaine Maury. The inventor of the electrically controlled torpedo as a Confederate naval officer (supposedly with the aid of experiments with powder charges in his bathtub), Maury is also considered the father of modern oceanography. Created by F. William Sievers, the monument was dedicated in 1929 at Belmont Avenue at the western end of Monument Avenue.

General Jeb Stuart. The commander of the Confederate cavalry died a few blocks from the site of his statue at Lombardy Street and Monument Avenue as the result of wounds suffered in 1864 at Yellow Tavern, north of Richmond. The monument by Fred Moynihan was dedicated in 1907.

Other Monuments

Bell Tower. Now used as a visitors center, the brick tower on Capitol Square behind the State Capitol was built in 1824 to warn of fires and other threats.

Bojangles (Bill Robinson) Monument. The famous dancer and actor was born in Richmond's Jackson Ward, and he donated a traffic light at the intersection of Adams and Leigh Streets to help children cross the street. That intersection now includes a monument to his memory.

A. P. Hill Monument and Grave. Laburnum and Hermitage Road. Confederate General A. P. Hill, killed near Petersburg on April 1, 1865, is buried beneath a monument on a traffic island north of downtown.

McGuire Monument. During the Civil War, Hunter Holmes McGuire served as medical director of "Stonewall" Jackson's army; after the war, he was an important physician in Richmond and the state.

Poe Monument. The great author Edgar Allan Poe, born in 1809 in Boston, was raised by the Allan family of Richmond after he was orphaned at the age of two. He attended the University of Virginia and West Point briefly but was thrown out of both because of rule infractions. He died in 1849 as the result of alcoholism. The Edgar Allan Poe Museum is in the Shockoe Bottom district.

Smith Monument. William Smith was governor of Virginia 1846–49 and again 1864–65. In the best tradition of government contractors, Smith acquired the nickname "Extra Billy" because he milked incentives in a federal mail-delivery contract.

Soldiers' and Sailors' Monument. Located at the south end of Twenty-ninth Street. A monument dedicated in 1894 to Confederate soldiers and sailors, it overlooks the James River and the former Confederate Naval Yard. According to local lore, William Byrd II gave Richmond its name when he saw the view from this spot and thought it was similar to the vista in Richmond upon Thames in England.

Virginia War Memorial. U.S. Route 1, north of the Lee bridge over the James River. Open daily. A memorial to the fallen from World War II, Korea, and Vietnam; relics from battle sites around the world are incorporated into the memorial.

Washington Monument. Installed in 1858, the image of Washington on horseback was used on the seal of the Confederate States of America and continues as the symbol of the City of Richmond. Jefferson Davis was sworn in as president of the Confederacy at this statue on February 22, 1862.

Historical Sites in Richmond

Belle Isle. A 60-acre island in the James River, it was the site of a notorious Civil War prison camp and nineteenth- and twentieth-century ironworks and quarries. Open during daylight hours.

Beth Ahabah Museum and Archives. 1109 West Franklin Street. (804) 353-2668. Sunday and Monday 10 A.M.–3 P.M.; Tuesday and Wednesday 10 A.M.–4 P.M.; and Thursday 10 A.M.–2 P.M. Donations accepted. A collection of items that illustrate local Jewish life and history, as well as items from around the world. Artifacts on display include a copy of George Washington's 1791 letter to Hebrew congregations in Philadelphia, New York, Charleston, and Richmond; Confederate war bonds signed by Judah P. Benjamin, secretary of state; and a cornerstone from a German synagogue burned by Hitler's supporters during the 1938 Kristallnacht.

Black History Museum and Cultural Center of Virginia. Zero Clay Street. (804) 780-9093. Tuesday to Saturday 10 A.M.–5 P.M., Sunday from 1 P.M. Admission: adult $4; senior and student $3; and child 12 and younger, $2. A collection of artifacts about black life in Richmond and Virginia located in a restored 1832 Greek Revival building in Jackson Ward.

Bolling Haxall House. 211 East Franklin Street. (804) 643-2847. Monday to Friday 9 A.M.–4 P.M. Admission: free. A restored pre-Civil War home built for wealthy flour-mill owner Bolling Haxall.

Egyptian Building. 1223 East Marshall Street. An unusual Egyptian

Revival structure built in 1845 as part of the Medical College of Virginia. Early twentieth-century financier Bernard Baruch contributed the ornate Art Deco interior in honor of his father, who attended the school.

Federal Reserve Bank of Richmond's Money Museum. (804) 697-8108. Federal Reserve headquarters, 701 Byrd Street. Open Monday to Friday 9:30 A.M.–3:30 P.M. Admission: free. A museum of money, from stone coins of Yap Island to modern currency, with special collections of Virginia's own money and Confederate coinage and currency.

Hollywood Cemetery. Cherry and Albemarle Streets. (804) 648-8501. Open to visitors daily 8 A.M.–5 P.M. The burial site of notables such as U.S. Presidents James Monroe and John Tyler, Confederate President Jefferson Davis, Generals Jeb Stuart and George Pickett, and the graves of 18,000 Confederate soldiers, including more than 2,000 removed from the Gettysburg battlefield. Maps are available at the office.

The Jefferson Hotel. 100 West Franklin Street. Built in 1895 and rebuilt after a fire in 1901, this grand hotel is still in use. It includes a statue of Thomas Jefferson in the upper lobby near a pool that once held a collection of live alligators.

Jewish Cemetery. Twenty-first and Franklin Streets. One of the first Jewish cemeteries in America, dating from the 1790s. By the middle of the nineteenth century, many of the graves were moved to the Hebrew Cemetery at Fourth and Hospital Streets.

Lee House. 707 East Franklin Street. General Robert E. Lee returned to his family here after surrendering the Confederate Army at Appomattox Court House in April 1865; the famous Mathew Brady photograph of Lee was made on the house's back porch. Lee later moved on to Lexington, Virginia, when he was appointed president of Washington University (now known as Washington and Lee).

Libby Prison. Between Twentieth, Twenty-first, Cary, and Canal Streets. The site of another notorious Civil War prison. The building itself was moved to Chicago for exhibition at the 1892 World's Fair, and all that remains is a plaque on the flood wall at the site.

John Marshall House. Ninth and Marshall Streets. Tuesday to Saturday 10 A.M.–4:30 P.M. Admission: adult $3; senior $2.50; and student $1.25. (804) 648-7998. The oldest brick house in Richmond, dating to 1790, it was the home of

About John Marshall. John Marshall (1755–1835) was the fourth chief justice of the U.S. Supreme Court, serving from 1801 to 1835. A delegate to the Virginia assembly and a defender of the U.S. Constitution, he served as special envoy of the young nation to France during 1797–98. After he returned home, he served as a representative to Congress during the years 1799–1800 and then as secretary of state in President John Adams's cabinet.

As chief justice, Marshall was involved in many important rulings that helped establish the importance and independence of the court, including *Marbury v. Madison*, which codified the power of the court to rule on the constitutionality of legislation.

John Marshall for forty-five years. Restored as a museum, it contains artifacts from the life of the former chief justice of the United States.

Masonic Hall. Franklin Street, between Eighteenth and Nineteenth Streets. Built in 1787, it served as a hospital during the War of 1812. It is the oldest Masonic meeting hall in the United States.

Maymont House (Dooley Mansion). 1700 Hampton Street. Open 10 A.M.–7 P.M. (closes at 5 P.M. in winter). Tours Tuesday to Sunday every thirty minutes, noon–4:30 P.M. Donation: adult $4; child $2. (804) 358-7166. A formal Victorian mansion and 100-acre landscaped estate on the James River.

> **Hero remembered.**
> A plaque at the Monumental Church commemorates Gilbert Hunt, a slave blacksmith who saved many lives during the fire of 1811 at the Richmond Theater.

Monumental Church. 1224 East Broad Street. Open only for special tours. An Episcopal church built in 1814 on the site of the Richmond Theater, where a disastrous fire on December 26, 1811, killed seventy-two people, including the governor of Virginia; many of the victims are buried in a vault beneath the church.

Museum of the Confederacy and the Confederate Executive Mansion (White House of the Confederacy). 1201 East Clay Street. Open Monday to Saturday 10 A.M.–5 P.M.; Sunday noon–5 P.M. Admission: adult $6 museum only, $7 house only, $9 combination ticket; child ages 7–12, $3, $4, and $5. (804) 649-1861. One of the best collections of Civil War artifacts. Treasures include uniforms and possessions of Generals Robert E. Lee, "Stonewall" Jackson, and Jeb Stuart. Also on display is Robert E. Lee's tent, looking as if the general has just stepped out to inspect his troops.

The Confederate Executive Mansion, the wartime home of Jefferson Davis and also known as the White House of the Confederacy, is nearby to the museum and open for tours.

Old City Hall. 1001 East Broad Street. Built in 1894 as a city hall in Victorian-Gothic style, it is now a private office building. Visitors can enter the first floor during ordinary business hours and see the cast-iron interior courtyard.

Old Dominion Railroad Museum. Hull and First Streets. Open Saturday and Sunday 11 A.M.–4 P.M. Donations accepted. (804) 233-6237. A small collection of photographs and artifacts about area rail service, located within a restored Railway Express Agency car.

Edgar Allan Poe Museum (Old Stone House). 1914–16 East Main Street. Open Tuesday to Saturday 10 A.M.–4 P.M. and Sunday to Monday noon–4 P.M. Admission: adult $6; senior and student $5. (804) 648-5523. The Old Stone House, built about 1737, is the oldest structure in Richmond. It is now used to display items about author Edgar Allan Poe, who grew up in Richmond.

Pumphouse–3 Mile Lock Park. Pumphouse Road, near Boulevard Bridge. The remains of some of the locks and other structures of the James River and Kanawha Canal, including a stone arch built in 1789. Also in the area is an 1883 pumphouse.

Richmond Children's Museum. Fifth Street near Jackson Street. Open

Monday to Saturday 9 A.M.–5 P.M.; Sunday noon–5 P.M.; extended hours for school vacations in summer. Also open Mondays from June through August. (800) 474-7000. Admission: adult $5; child ages 2–12, $3; and children younger than 2 free. For kids and those who bring them around, a hands-on place with exhibits, including the WRCM TV Studio, the Children's Bank, the RCM Supermarket, and the Computer Station. A favorite spot is The Cave, a replica of a Virginia limestone cave.

Richmond National Battlefield Park Headquarters. Chimborazo Visitors Center: 3215 East Broad Street. Daily 9 A.M.–5 P.M. Admission: free. (804) 226-1981. A good place for an introduction to Richmond-area battlefields. The National Park Service center offers a short film, museum, and bookstore.

St. John's Episcopal Church. 2401 East Broad Street. Open Monday to Saturday 10 A.M.–4 P.M.; Sunday 1–4 P.M. Last tour 3:30 P.M. Admission: adult $3; senior $2; child ages 7–18, $1. (804) 648-5015. In the days leading up to the American Revolution, this was a hotbed of political debate; it was in this church on March 23, 1775, that Patrick Henry gave his famous "Give me liberty or give me death" speech to the Second Virginia Convention.

The oldest church in Richmond, St. John's was erected in 1741. George Wythe, one of the signers of the Declaration of Independence and an important figure in Williamsburg, is buried here, as is Elizabeth Arnold Poe, mother of Edgar Allan Poe.

St. Paul's Episcopal Church. 815 East Grace Street. Daily 10 A.M.–3 P.M. (804) 643-3589. The so-called Cathedral of the Confederacy was used by President Jefferson Davis and General Robert E. Lee. During services here on April 2, 1865, Davis received word that Union forces had broken through at Petersburg, and the evacuation of Richmond was begun immediately. Built in 1845 in the Greek Revival style, the church is still in use.

Science Museum of Virginia. 2500 West Broad Street. Open daily 9:30 A.M.–5 P.M. Admission: adult $5; child ages 4–12, $4; and senior 60 and older, $4.50. IMAX films $5 extra. *Discount coupon in this book.* (800) 659-1727 or (804) 367-6552. The former Richmond, Fredericksburg, and Potomac Railroad Broad Street Station, designed in 1919 by John Russell Pope (architect of the National Gallery of Art, Jefferson Memorial, and other Washington monuments), offers science exhibits, an IMAX theater, and a five-story dome multimedia planetarium. An aquarium displays freshwater fish of the James River. One planetarium show is included with admission.

Shiplock Park. Dock and Pear Streets. The James River and Kanawha Canal system connected to the Richmond docks here with a lock completed in 1854. The canal bypassed seven miles of falls and continued for nearly 200 miles into Virginia's western mountain ranges.

Shockoe Cemetery. Hospital and Fifth Streets. Chief Justice John Marshall, Revolutionary War hero Peter Francisco, and Union spy Elizabeth Van Lew are among the notables buried here. The cemetery also is the final resting place for hundreds of Union and Confederate soldiers.

Shockoe Slip. Between Twelfth and Fourteenth, Main, and Canal Streets. A shopping district located near what was once the Great Turning Basin on the James River canal system. Warehouses and tobacco factories dating from the seventeenth century were destroyed in the Great Evacuation Fire of April 2–3, 1865; the area was rebuilt in the years after the Civil War. Today, Shockoe Slip is a fashionable shopping and entertainment district.

Tredegar Iron Works. Tredegar Street at the James River. During the Civil War, the Tredegar Iron Works produced more than a thousand artillery pieces for the Confederate forces, and the iron armor for the *Merrimack* (renamed the *Virginia* for the Confederacy) was also made here. Tredegar was a major reason the Confederate capital was relocated to Richmond.

Valentine Court End. 1015 East Clay Street. (804) 649-0711. Monday to Saturday 10 A.M.–5 P.M.; Sunday noon–5 P.M.; tours every hour until 4 P.M. Admission: adult $5; senior and student $4; child ages 7–12, $3. A museum celebrating the culture and history of Richmond. It includes the restored 1812 Wickham House.

The Court End district is a treasure trove of old residences and buildings, including seven National Historic Landmarks, three museums, and eleven other buildings listed on the National Register of Historic Places.

Virginia Fire and Police Museum. 200 East Marshall Street. (804) 644-1849. Tours 10 A.M.–4 P.M. Monday through Friday, and by prior arrangement on Saturday. A small museum of old fire and police artifacts.

Virginia Historical Society/Center for Virginia History. 428 North Boulevard. (804) 358-4901. Open Monday to Saturday 10 A.M.–5 P.M.; Sunday 1–5 P.M. (galleries only). Admission: adult $4; senior $3; and child and student $2. Includes galleries and a library exhibit of the history of Virginia. Originally built in 1912 as a memorial to Confederate soldiers, Battle Abbey includes a famed mural, the *Seasons of the Confederacy*. www.vahistorical.org

Virginia Museum of Fine Arts. Boulevard at Grove Avenue. (804) 340-1400. Galleries open Tuesday to Sunday 11 A.M.–5 P.M.; Thursday until 8 P.M. Donations accepted. A wide-ranging collection of art from ancient Egyptian sculptures to modern abstracts and most everything in between.

Maggie Lena Walker National Historical Site. 110½ East Leigh Street. (804) 771-2017. Open Wednesday to Sunday 9 A.M.–5 P.M. Maggie Lena Walker established a black-owned bank, insurance company, and a newspaper in the late nineteenth century; the bank, now named Consolidated Bank & Trust, is the oldest such bank in the country today. Her 22-room home was built in 1883.

Historic Neighborhoods in Richmond

Fan District. Within Broad and Main Streets, Monroe Park, and the Boulevard. A spectacular collection of late nineteenth-century and early twentieth-century Victorian homes. The streets "fan" out from Monroe Park.

Jackson Ward. Within Belvidere, Marshall, and Fourth Streets, and I-95/64. Sometimes called the "Birthplace of Black Capitalism," the Jackson Ward area became a business and cultural center for blacks after the Civil War. Maggie Lena Walker became the first black woman bank president in 1903. Many of the homes include ornamental iron work.

Shockoe Bottom. Within Fifteenth and Twenty-first, Dock, and Broad

Streets. A former warehouse district now a popular residential, restaurant, and entertainment area. Historic sites in the area include numerous Civil War hospitals. Main Street Station was once the hub of transportation in Richmond, and future plans call for restoration of rail service to the old station.

The Seventeenth Street Farmer's Market may be the oldest in the nation, dating back to the seventeenth century. Native Americans traded produce in the area, and Colonial settlers used the land along the former bed of Shockoe Creek for fairs; it became a formal marketplace in 1779.

Until recently, regular flooding made restoration of this area difficult; a multimillion dollar flood wall has saved the neighborhood.

Visitors centers. The Metro Richmond Convention and Visitors Bureau operates three visitors centers, offering brochures, maps, and a hotel reservation service.

Bell Tower on Capitol Square. Open Monday to Friday 9 A.M.–5 P.M. (804) 786-4484.

Richmond International Airport. Open weekdays 9:30 A.M.– 4:30 P.M. Monday to Friday. (804) 236-3260.

Robin Hood Road Visitor Center. Near the Boulevard exit from I-95/64. Daily 9 A.M.– 5 P.M. Longer hours in summer. (804) 358-5511.

Richmond Averages

	Minimum Temperatures (°F)	Maximum Temperatures (°F)	Precipitation (inches)
January	28	47	3.1
February	29	50	3.0
March	36	59	3.7
April	45	70	3.0
May	54	78	3.8
June	63	85	3.6
July	68	88	5.4
August	66	87	4.9
September	60	81	3.5
October	47	71	3.3
November	38	61	3.2
December	30	50	3.2

James River Plantations

The area around Richmond was once home to sprawling working plantations; a number of them are maintained as museums and re-creations.

Belle Air Plantation. 11800 John Tyler Highway, Charles City. (804) 829-2431. A seventeenth-century gem with original heartpine timbers and a Jacobean stairway. Open 9 A.M.–8 P.M. by appointment.

Berkeley Plantation. 12602 Harrison Landing Road, Charles City. (804) 829-6018. The birthplace of Benjamin Harrison, signer of the Declaration of Independence, and William Henry Harrison, ninth president of the United States. Site of the first official Thanksgiving in 1619; "Taps" was composed here in 1862. Open daily 9 A.M.–5 P.M. Admission: adult $9; child ages 13–16, $6.50; and child ages 6–12, $4.

Evelynton Plantation. 6701 John Tyler Highway, Charles City. (800) 473-5075 and (804) 829-5075. Originally part of the Westover Plantation and named after William Byrd's daughter, the 2,500-acre working plantation has been the home of the Ruffin family since 1847; Edmund Ruffin is credited with firing the first shot of the Civil War at Fort Sumter. The area was the site of Civil War skirmishes in 1862 during the Peninsula Campaign. The grounds and home are open for tours from 9 A.M.–5 P.M. Call for Saturday hours.

Sherwood Forest Plantation. 14501 John Tyler Highway, Charles City. (804) 829-5377. A mid-eighteenth-century home that served as the residence of John Tyler after he served as president from 1841 to 1845. The home was restored and furnished with possessions of President Tyler's; it is still occupied by his descendants. Open daily 9 A.M.–5 P.M. Admission: adult $9; student $6; senior $8; and child younger than 5, free.

Shirley Plantation. Eighteen miles south of Richmond off Route 5 in Charles City. (800) 232-1613. The oldest plantation in Virginia, founded in 1613, and the home of the Carter family since 1723. The 800-acre working plantation includes a main mansion that dates from 1723 and several brick outbuildings in a Queen Anne forecourt. The main brick barn includes an ice cellar beneath. Open daily from 9 A.M.–5 P.M. Admission: adult $9; child ages 13–21, $6; child ages 6–12, $5; child ages 5 and younger, free.

Westover. 7000 Westover Road, Charles City. (804) 829-2882. Built about 1730 by William Byrd II, founder of Richmond and Petersburg, it includes spectacular grounds and gardens open for tours 9 A.M.–6 P.M. daily. The house itself is open only on special occasions.

Wilton House Museum. 215 South Wilton Road. (804) 282-5936. An ornate lower James River plantation house completed in 1753 as the centerpiece of a 2,000-acre plantation and home to the Randolph family for more than a century. The Randolphs entertained George Washington, Thomas Jefferson, and the Marquis de Lafayette at the home. The home was moved and reconstructed at its present site in 1933. Open Tuesday to Saturday from 10 A.M.–4:30 P.M., and Sunday from 1:30–4:30 P.M. Last tours leave at 3:45 P.M. Closed February. Admission: adult $4; student and senior $3; child 6 and younger free.

Four of the plantations—Berkeley, Evelynton, Sherwood Forest, and Shirley—offer a discounted block of tickets that can be purchased at any of the locations. For information call (800) 704-5423.

One other unusual home museum in the area is **Agecroft Hall** in Richmond, a sixteenth- and seventeenth-century English manor that was disassembled and brought from Lancashire, England, to Virginia in 1926. 4305 Sulgrave Road. (804) 353-4241. Inside are authentic furnishings of the period. Open Tuesday to Saturday from 10 A.M.–4 P.M., and Sunday from 12:30–5 P.M. Admission: adult $5; senior $4.50; student $3; and child 5 and younger, free.

Pamplin Historical Park/National Museum of the Civil War Soldier

Pamplin Historical Park preserves the ground where Union troops commanded by Lt. Gen. Ulysses S. Grant broke through the elaborate defenses established by Confederate General Robert E. Lee near Petersburg on April 2, 1865. The battle led to the evacuation of both Petersburg and the Confederate capital at Richmond later that day, and one week later Lee surrendered to Grant at Appomattox Court House in one of the final events of the war.

The park includes an interpretive center, battle trail, and Tudor Hall, the Boisseau family plantation. Pamplin is located in Dinwiddie County near Petersburg, about thirty miles south of Richmond off I-85.

Open daily from 9 A.M.–5 P.M. with extended summer hours. Park admission, including the museum: adult $10; child ages 6–11, $5; and senior $9. For information, call (877) 726-7546 or (804) 861-2408, or consult the Web at www.pamplinpark.org.

The National Museum of the Civil War Soldier opened in May of 1999. Visitors select a soldier guide at the entrance and then use a personal audio device to follow their experiences through the exhibits. Guests enter an early war training camp, hear a sermon from a chaplain at a camp revival, visit a sutler's tent (the crude mess hall and provisioner), and learn about the life of the wounded or imprisoned soldier. At a reconstructed military encampment, such as the one on the site in the winter of 1864–65, costumed soldiers demonstrate their camp duties. The museum's central attraction is Trial by Fire, a high-tech exploration of the sounds and sights of the Civil War.

Paramount's Kings Dominion

More than two million people a year visit the Eiffel Tower, right off of Interstate 95 in Doswell, Virginia.

Of course, it's merely a replica, but a mighty big one at 330 feet, and it is the part of the 400-acre Kings Dominion theme park that is visible from the road. There is, of course, much more, including the spectacular **Volcano, The Blast Coaster**.

Youngsters have a metropolis of their own at Nickelodeon Central, which celebrates some of the characters and shows of the Nickelodeon television network. At **Rugrats Toonpike**, very young drivers take a spin around the familiar Rugrats neighborhood.

Included within the park's fences and available for the same ticket is the Water-Works water park.

Anaconda, Paramount's Kings Dominion
© *Paramount Parks Inc.*

Kings Dominion Ticket Prices
Prices were in effect for the 2000 season.

  Single-Day Pass

General (7 and older)	$35.99
Senior (55 and older)	$30.99
Child (3–6, or under	
48 inches)	$25.99
Child (2 and younger)	Free

Two-day passes are also available; you can also purchase season passes, valid for unlimited visits to any Paramount Park.
  Parking for autos and vans is $6. For information, call (804) 876-5561. www.kingsdominion.com.

Kings Dominion is located seventy-five miles south of Washington, or twenty miles north of Richmond, at exit 98 of I-95. There are several motels and campgrounds in and around Doswell and many more in the Richmond area.

The park is usually open on weekends only, from the end of March through late May, and then daily until after Labor Day. In the fall, it reverts to weekend operation until mid-October. Opening time is 10 A.M. on Saturday and 10:30 A.M. the rest of the week. The park stays open until 7 or 8 P.M. in early and late season, and until 10 P.M. at other times.

Call to confirm operating hours before your visit. The busiest days are weekends, with Sunday usually less crowded than Saturday. Concert days usually draw the largest crowds of all.

WaterWorks opens near the end of April and operates until Labor Day weekend. Hours are noon–7 P.M. most days; the water park stays open until 8 P.M. on nights when Kings Dominion is open until 10 P.M.

Roller Coasters

Volcano, The Blast Coaster. What a blast! The big draw at the park is the world's first linear induction–suspended roller coaster.

Suspended in their seats from an overhead track with their legs dangling below, visitors are blasted from the top of a manmade volcano by an electromagnetic propulsion system at speeds of up to seventy miles per hour. The cars then travel back into the mountain before being catapulted vertically 155 feet from the center of the crater and into the first of four heart-rolling inversions, circling back around the mountain before dropping another eighty feet and returning into the mountain.

It's all over in about two minutes, if you're counting.

Volcano, the tenth coaster at King's Dominion, is located in the Congo theme area in the former Lost World area.

The Outer Limits: Flight of Fear. A spectacular roller coaster that turns the lights out on all visitors. The 2,764-foot ride takes place in total darkness, beginning with an electromagnetic launch instead of a clanking lift hill and including thirty vertical curves and more than twenty-five compound horizontal curves. Cars reach a speed of more than fifty miles per hour four seconds after beginning their journey within the indoor building in the Congo theme area.

About the Outer Limits theme: the journey into the unexplained begins at the ride's entrance, which appears to be a restricted government compound.

Riders entering within learn that the compound contains an alien spacecraft; once riders are loaded aboard their vehicles, the aliens take control for the journey to the outer limits.

Xtreme SkyFlyer. Another unusual attraction that combines the thrills of hang gliding and skydiving. Guests are strapped into a flight suit and raised to a launch height of 152 feet; suspended from twin towers, the flyer pulls on a parachute-style ripcord and then swoops forward and down at speeds of more than sixty miles per hour. Use of the SkyFlyer comes at an additional charge over the cost of admission of about $24.95 for a solo ride, $19.95 each with a friend, and $14.95 each for a triple ride.

Anaconda. A one-of-a-kind steel coaster that takes riders through a vertical loop, a sidewinder loop, a butterfly, and a corkscrew at more than fifty miles per hour. And how's this for a specialized world's-record claim: the Anaconda is the only looping roller coaster in the world that includes an underwater tunnel.

Grizzly. Nestled among the backwoods of the Old Virginia section of the park, this wooden coaster's double figure-eight track was patterned after Coney Island's famed Wildcat, which operated from 1911 through 1964.

Hurler. A wooden roller coaster in the Wayne's World section of the park, featuring towering hills and hairpin turns. The Hurler includes a lift hill of eighty-three feet and reaches speeds of up to fifty miles per hour on 3,157 feet of track.

Rebel Yell. A wooden, twin racing roller coaster sends one train traveling forward while its twin moves backward. Riders are sent over twelve hills and travel at speeds up to sixty-five miles per hour.

Scooby Doo. A small, wooden coaster designed for children of all ages. The track doubles back on itself.

Shockwave. This steel coaster sends riders through a 360-degree vertical loop and a 540-degree horizontal loop—while *standing up!*

Other Attractions

Berserker. A swinging starship that completes a 360-degree loop.

James Bond 007: Flight of Fear. A ride simulator that will shake and stir you. (Ask a Bond fan if you don't get the joke.)

Paramount Theatre. Live singing and dance productions. (The ice rink at the theater was removed in 1997.)

White Water Canyon. A wet and wild adventure in manmade river rapids.

Nickelodeon Splat City

Gak! If you don't know what that is, you don't have preteen children in your house. Gak is the green slime stuff that is the star of many Nickelodeon television shows aimed at youngsters.

At Kings Dominion, Nickelodeon Splat City is a three-acre community for kids that offers challenging games, interactive events, and the Green Slime Bowl—a 1,100-seat outdoor arena that is home to a version of the "super

White Water Canyon, Paramount's Kings Dominion
© *1995 Paramount Parks Inc.*

sloppy" game show "Mega Mess-a-Mania" which presents the best moments from hit television shows such as "Double Dare" and "What Would You Do?"

On the **Rugrats Toonpike**, mini-drivers take the wheel of their own little cars for a spin around the Rugrats neighborhood where they'll meet most of the diapered crowd, including Angelica, Tommy, Chuckie, Phil, Lil, and Dil, and even have a near-run-in with Reptar the reptile.

Meet Blue! is based on "Blue's Clues," a popular computer animated television series that stars Blue, a most energetic puppy.

On **Nickelodeon Space Surfer**, riders pilot their own vehicles, swooping and surfing ninety feet in the air.

Over the top of the area is the Slime Derrick, a 35-foot-tall pressure-release valve for the relentless force of Green Slime that moves through the area; at regular intervals, a green torrent erupts.

The Gakmeister, Ms. Darla Boogaire, presides over the Gak Kitchen. And the Green Slime Zone is an interactive pipework maze that allows visitors to watch the secret Green Slime depurification process. Explorers are encouraged to tread carefully to avoid causing an overhead pipe to burst and gush ooze.

Children's Attractions

Busytown Cafe. A dining "experience" for kids, using characters and story-lines made popular by Richard Scarry.

KidZville. A four-acre children's fantasyland that offers rides, shows, and games. Included is Taxi Jam, a kiddie-level roller coaster. You'll also find play areas where children and parents can play together; a favorite is the **Kidz Construction Company**, a hands-on construction area.

Kid's Shows. Special entertainment for children includes **The Backyard Circus**, a participatory show at the Town Square Gazebo.

WaterWorks

WaterWorks features six wet acres. Admission to the water park is included with general admission to Kings Dominion.

New in 2000 was the **Pipeline Peak** water slide complex, It includes **Night Slider**, the world's tallest enclosed dark tube slide, a 77-foot drop; **Power Plunge**, an enclosed body slide with corkscrew-like coils that twist and turn riders in total darkness; **Turbo Twister**, an enclosed two-person inner tube slide that propels surfers from a 45-foot level, and **Rip Slide**, a 495-foot-long enclosed two-person inner tube slide with pretzel-like twists.

Big Wave Bay is a 650,000-gallon wave pool, and **Surf City Splash House**, a family fun house that has more than fifty interactive features, including a swinging bridge, water slides, bucket conveyors, and a 40-foot-high bucket that tips a boatload of water onto volunteers.

Attractions include fifteen slides of various sizes and configurations, from the winding **Torrential Twist** to the high-speed **Monsoon Chutes**; **Splash Island**, a water play area designed just for young children; and **The Lazy River**, a relaxing quarter-mile river raft ride.

Kingswood Amphitheatre Concerts

During the summer, Kings Dominion offers several musical concerts at the amphitheatre within the park. There is a charge (about $6 to $10) for the concerts, in addition to admission to the park.

Tickets can be purchased at Kings Dominion, or through Ticketmaster outlets in Washington and Northern Virginia. For information about concerts, call (804) 876-5152.

SMITHSONIAN MUSEUM STORES

Receive 15% off a purchase of $35 or more **or**
Receive 20% off a purchase of $70 or more!

Show this for your discount in all stores at the Museums listed below. Offer may not be combined with other coupons or discounts. Expires 12/31/01.

5 00001 00001 1

Arts & Industries Building

This store offers "the best of the Smithsonian," a selection of our favorite products from stores across the Mall. The Museum Store also features merchandise highlighting special exhibitions, including African-American and Native American items. In addition, there is an expanded section devoted to Smithsonian Catalogue merchandise. (202) 357-1369

The Castle

The store at the Information Center is a great source for souvenirs and guidebooks. (202) 633-9216

Hirshhorn Museum & Sculpture Garden

A large selection of contemporary art books, exhibition catalogs, graphics, and innovative toys is offered in this store. Exquisitely designed and crafted gifts and jewelry have been chosen to highlight the museum's collection. (202) 357-1429

National Air and Space Museum

The main, three-level store and two "satellite" stores (Dog Tags and the Planetarium Store) celebrate the evolution of flight and space exploration through models, books, kites, science toys, posters, and freeze-dried foods. (202) 357-1387

National Museum of African Art

This Museum Store offers a fine selection of African jewelry, baskets, textiles, musical instruments, dolls and crafts, along with related graphics, books and recordings. (202) 786-2147

National Museum of American History

Stores in this museum offer beautifully detailed reproductions and contemporary American crafts, jewelry, regional foods, toys and the Smithsonian's largest selection of books and videos. We even have an exciting store featuring American Music! (202) 357-1527

National Museum of Natural History

This museum features a Gallery Store and a Family Store, in addition to a Gems and Minerals Store and other special exhibition stores, all celebrating the splendors of nature, the cultural diversities of our world...and dinosaurs! You'll find an exciting array of merchandise, including our largest jewelry selection. (202) 357-1536

National Postal Museum

Stamp lovers and collectors will enjoy this store filled with merchandise celebrating postal history, transportation and philately. (202) 633-8180

Renwick Gallery

This store features handmade American crafts and jewelry, as well as books on design, decorative arts and architecture. (202) 357-1445

Ronald Reagan National Airport

This store features a variety of merchandise from stores on the mall.

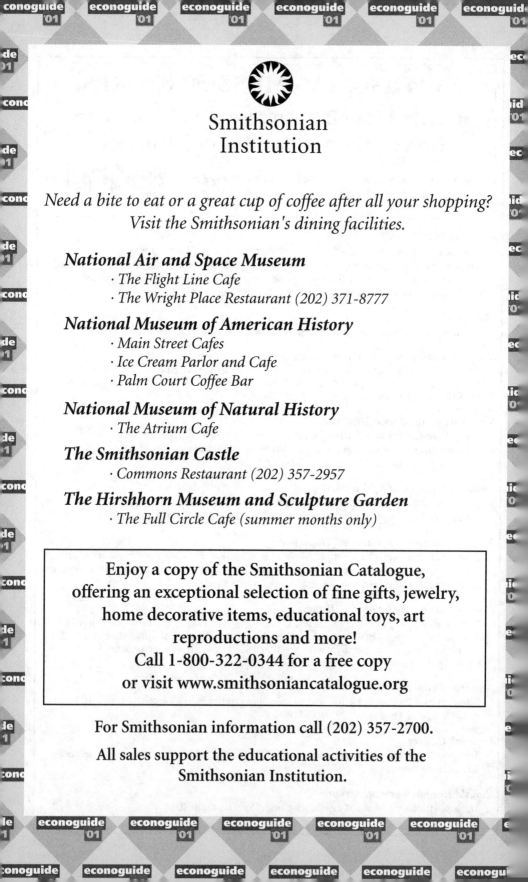

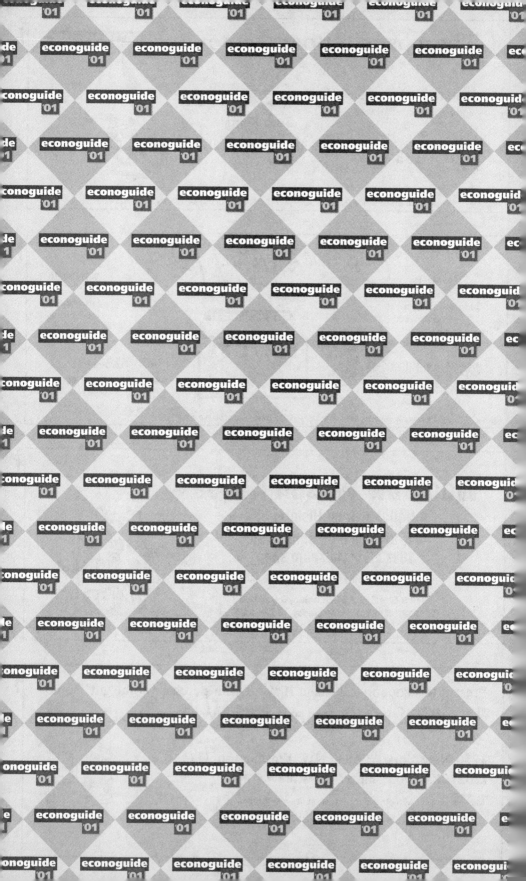

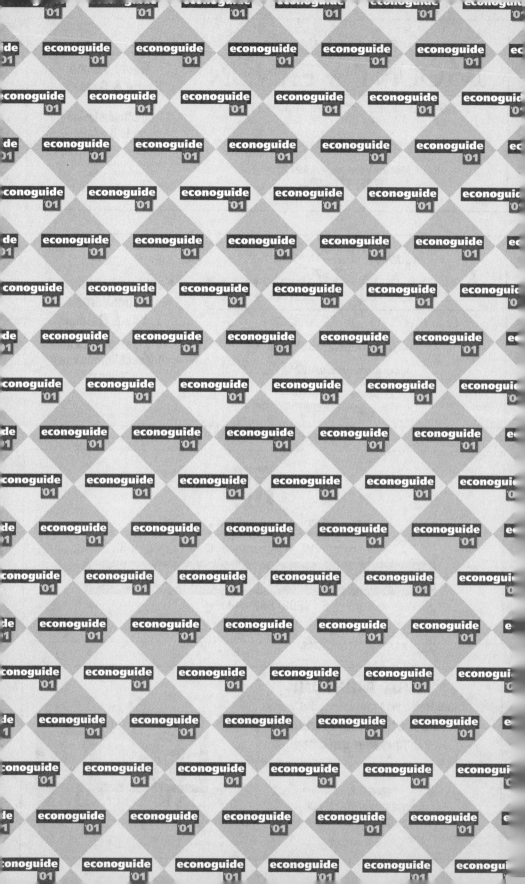

Spend quality time at *discount prices.*

Enjoy a **30%** Discount

**We make your vacations more enjoyable at Four Points
Sheraton, because we provide the things you need
to relax. Like a swimming pool, fitness center, and the
convenience of room service and a restaurant.
All for a price that's surprisingly less than you'd expect.**

In the Nations Capitol...

Four Points Hotel Washington DC Downtown

Four Points Hotel Washington DC Pentagon

Four Points Hotel Bethesda

And in Historic Williamsburg, Virginia...

**Four Points Hotel & Suites
Williamsburg Historic District**

Call **1-800-325-3535** and
ask for the ECONO rate, or go to fourpoints.com for more information.
See reverse for full location listings, terms and conditions.

Four Points®

Sheraton

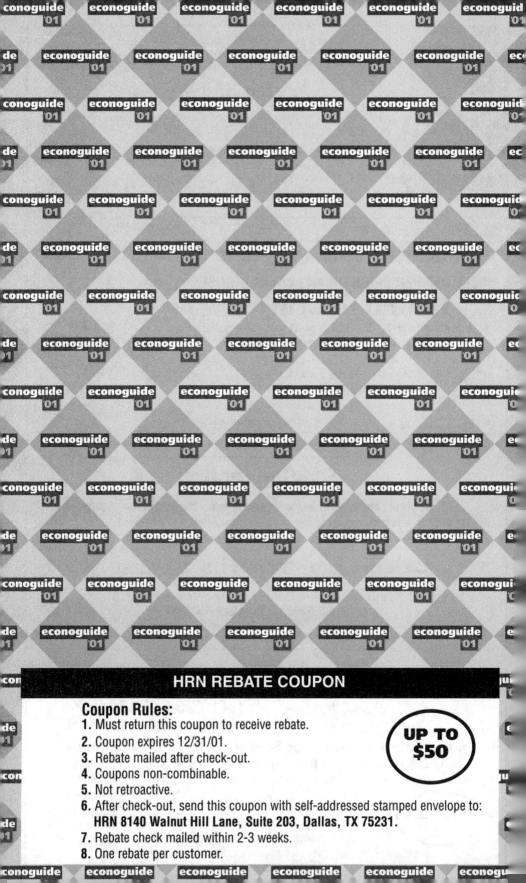

HRN REBATE COUPON

UP TO $50

Coupon Rules:

1. Must return this coupon to receive rebate.
2. Coupon expires 12/31/01.
3. Rebate mailed after check-out.
4. Coupons non-combinable.
5. Not retroactive.
6. After check-out, send this coupon with self-addressed stamped envelope to:
   HRN 8140 Walnut Hill Lane, Suite 203, Dallas, TX 75231.
7. Rebate check mailed within 2-3 weeks.
8. One rebate per customer.

Williamsburg National Golf Club

3700 Centerville Road, Williamsburg, VA 23188
(757) 258-9642

$5 off daily greens fee and cart rate

* * *Golf Digest* "Top Ten You Can Play in Virginia"
* * Three-and-a-half star rating by *Golf Digest*
* * *Washington Golf Monthly* Top 100 in the Middle Atlantic
* * Nicklaus design

Expires 12/31/01

WA01-15

Ford's Colony at Williamsburg
Save $18 when you play 18 holes

Experience Williamsburg's ONLY Global Positioning System
(Accurate yardage from tee to green via satellite)
Offer includes a cart featuring a
ProLink Satellite Global Positioning System
Call the Pro Shop at (757) 258-4130 for tee times.

240 Ford's Colony Drive, Williamsburg, Virginia 23188
Coupon not valid with any other special promotion.
Soft spikes & collared shirts required.
Expires 12/31/01

WA01-21

www.fordscolony.com

Golf Shoes Plus
Golf shoes, walking shoes, and street shoes

Mention ECONOGUIDE #1001 for a ***10% discount***
on any one pair of shoes

www.golfshoesplus.com
Expires 12/31/01

WA01-18

PRO'S EDGE

Pro's Edge
The Big $moke Golf Clubs

Mention ECONOGUIDE #1002
for a ***25% discount***
on one club *or* one complete set
of 1, 3, 5, & 7 wood, any flex available.

www.thebigsmoke.com
Expires 12/31/01

WA01-20

PRO'S EDGE

Quick-Find Index to Attractions

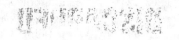